A Call To GREATNESS

(A Spiritual Journey of Self-Discovery and Self-Expression)

Dhyana Press
San Francisco, California

The Teachings of A Course in Congruence

by

IsanaMada

DHYANA PRESS
P. O. Box 470700
San Francisco, CA 94147

ORIGINAL ARTWORK: Raul Miyar, Atlanta
(Some renderings based on original illustrations by Michelle Riley)

COVER DESIGN: Rex Ray, San Francisco

AUTHOR PHOTO: Eric Slomanson, San Francisco

Printed in the United States by McNaughton & Gunn, Inc.

FIRST EDITION

Publisher's Cataloging in Publication Data
(Prepared by Quality Books, Inc.)

IsanaMada.
A call to greatness : a spiritual journey of self-discovery and self-expression / IsanaMada.
p. cm.
Includes bibliographical references and index.
Preassigned LCCN: 93-72543
ISBN 0-9635218-1-0

1. New Age movement. 2. Self-actualization (Psychology) I. Title.

BP605.N48183 1994 291
QBI93-22662

DEDICATION

With heartfelt gratitude I dedicate this book to the memory of Carl Rogers, Ph.D., the wise and devoted pioneer who formalized for us the concept of congruence and persuaded us to engage life as an ever-evolving adventure of "becoming." Dr. Rogers showed us that remarkable benefits accrue to human beings through the informed and compassionate mentoring of their caring teachers. May we all accept the challenge he offered us—to fulfill our human potential by becoming congruent expressions of our innerness and by living life as "a flowing, changing process in which nothing is fixed." I pray that Dr. Rogers would appreciate my humble attempt to bring his astute concepts to the community-at-large in this form.

With equal gratitude I also dedicate this book to my other teachers: the intelligent and well-educated men and women who have kept the concept of congruence alive in their lecture halls, classrooms, seminar rooms, and writings. To Frances Vaughan, Ph.D., I offer an especially respectful and grateful bow of my head. Her stewardship of the fascinating arena of transpersonal psychology has served to raise to the next level our understanding of ourselves as, at once, psychological and spiritual beings. Her consciousness and her efforts on our behalf are most certainly a strong influence in our world today.

To Ken Wilber I proffer the kind of respect a disciple spontaneously extends to a Master. For the years since 1985, Mr. Wilber has stirred in me a sense of awe-filled reverence in response to the remarkable teachings his fine mind and his efforts have produced. He is a clear-speaking bridge for us between the truly erudite levels of intellectual understanding and our ability to comprehend at this time. His spiritual scholarship has changed my life.

To Sri Da Avabhasa I am always on my knees. This outrageous Spiritual Master seemed to nosedive into my life in 1986, leaving the mark of his immense Spiritual Presence and his vast human intelligence all over me and everything I do. As a demonstration of "becoming" we could ask for no better model. Sri Da Avabhasa set my soul on fire and melted the margins of my resistance and my ordinary considerations about pushing the limits of Spiritual Process. Om Ma Da.

LET US REST IN THE ARMS OF THE
UNKNOWABLE MYSTERY AS WE ACT WITH
GREAT PASSION AND GREAT COMPASSION
FOR THE HIGHEST GOOD OF OUR WORLD
—AND ALL THE WORLDS.

ACKNOWLEDGEMENTS

With gratitude I acknowledge all of the superb beings who have served to feed the mind, quicken the Spirit, and expand the consciousness of the growing number of students of Higher Truth:

My "thank you" to Matthew Fox, the scholarly priest, who envisions for all of us a spiritual renaissance based in the mysticism of humankind, the intelligence of truth, the love of God, the caretaking of Mother Earth, and the compassionate fraternity of humans. This spiritual hero has risked it all to stand up for his convictions in a milieu of intolerant censorship and stringent recriminations.

My "thank you" to Brian Swimme, the reverent scientist and cosmic myth-maker, who reaches down from his star-studded height to teach us and to evoke in us the awe of the cosmos and the will to "surprise the universe."

My "thank you" to Bernadette Roberts, the epitomy of the Christian contemplative, whose personal *Path To No-Self* has touched me deeply and whose ability to stand alone in the fiery depths of the abyss has served us all in unspeakable ways.

My "thank you" to Ken Carey, a champion of things unseen and a messenger of things unheard by ordinary ears.

My (posthumous) "thank you" to Joseph Campbell, whose life work—anthologies of mythology—came just in time to help us better understand what is happening in our own times and our need for a new mythology.

My "thank you" to Jean Houston, whose keen eyes are able to see *The Possible Human* and whose sweeping *Search for the Beloved* is anchored in the practical stuff of human being and human becoming.

My "thank you" to Hannah Hurnard, whose account of the difficult climb to the High Places has made it possible for the rest of us to better endure the climb.

My "thank you" to Ram Dass, whose personal unfoldment has always translated itself to include a unique seva to all of mankind.

My (posthumous) "thank you" to Carl G. Jung, whose exhaustive works have served all of us in understanding ourselves and each other so much better.

My "thank you" to Christopher Hills, the evolved "techno-hermit who lives in the middle of the redwood forest," for his brilliant works—*Nuclear Evolution* and *Rise of the Phoenix*—two tomes which riveted my attention and stretched my mind way beyond its then-present limits. His present work on *The New Paradigm* promises further stretching for me.

My "thank you" to Barbara Marx Hubbard, whose visionary view glistens with the loving prescience of things the rest of us can only hope for.

My "thank you" to Jacquelyn Small whose naming of therapists as *Transformers*, whose intelligent therapeutic approach, and whose compassionate spiritual leadership have served to sharper our understanding and soften our perceptions.

My "thank you" to Peter Russell, whose *Global Brain* made us all more "global" in our experience of ourselves and whose *White Hole in Time* reminds us of the urgency of purpose now woven into the tapestry of our lives.

My "thank you" to Satprem, whose devoted service to The Mother marks him as a humble servant to us all, and whose communications of Sri Aurobindo's life and teachings most directly serve to stretch our minds and inspire our personal journeys.

My (posthumous) "thank you" to P. D. Ouspensky, whose brilliant, no-nonsense approach to the investigations of things human, have served to set us all on our ear and caused us to face the realities of our own lives.

My "thank you" to Loy Young, whose Tibetan Mystery School teachings have provided me with an on-going reference with which to view myself and others and with which to stretch myself still further.

My "thank you" to Virginia Burden Tower, whose *The Process of Intuition*, first validated what was occurring in my own life and gave me a way to think about and speak about it to others.

My "thank you" to Christian de la Huerta, whose loyal, loving, devoted, and selfless service to me has made it possible for me to continue along the path on which Spirit shines its steady light. Without his saintly sacrifices and tireless labor, this work would not be published at this time.

My "thank you" to all other teachers, healers, authors, spiritual leaders, and spiritual journeyers whose lives represent the search for and the stand for truth in our world. Pranam.

TABLE OF CONTENTS

PART THREE —— INTO THE ABYSS

TABLE OF ILLUSTRATIONS

FOREWORD

The past ten years of my life stand as a testimony to the relevance and timeliness of the teachings of Krishna to Arjuna in the Bhagavad Gītā, to the teachings of Lord Buddha, Jesus The Christ, Sri Aurobindo, Da Avabhasa, and so many other truly august spiritual beings who have dwelt among us at different times and who have instructed us about the ways, the means, and the extraordinary results of life lived as true spiritual process. I say this with deepest humility and an overriding sense of awe and amazement that I have been so blessed. Ten years ago, I could never have guessed that I would be saying such a thing.

In a revelatory moment, my humanity—with all that implies—was mysteriously touched by an unseen force which immediately changed me in obvious ways. That invisible something, then, began to lead, guide, and direct me along a circuitous path toward an unknown destination. I certainly have not reached that destination yet. But I have completed certain phases of the journey which I began in early 1984, and am now able to reflect intelligently on the coherent stage-specific meanings with the help of inspired, wise, and well-communicated writings by others who have wandered their own paths and who have, then, translated—or have had translated for them—their transformative journeys.

The inner excitement I have experienced since I emerged from a very dark Dark Night of the Soul springs from the realization that transformation is available to those of us who are ready and, thus able, to relinquish the hold we have on our lives. To literally give up control of our lives—our bodies, our emotions, our minds, and our spirits—we must learn to live a life based on trust: that obscure, enigmatic, and hard-to-get-a-hold-of concept, which asks of us everything and promises nothing. That thrilling realization makes possible everything which before seemed impossible. It is that thrilling realization which has bubbled up in me again and again throughout the past ten years and which bubbles up still. I imagine that the reader will be able to feel the bubbles from time to time in the pages of this book about—what else—spiritual process.

Just as most of the great spiritual beings have been true students of life, I have noticed a resurgence of the "student of life" approach in recent years at all levels of our society. So many of us seem to know, inside, that the pronouncements of dogmatic religious manuals and governmental handbooks have fallen short of answering and dealing with the profound questions of our age. More and more of our society's young people are turning away from the dictates and the common formulas which have held our house of straw together with their toothpicks-and-string stratagems, which, obviously, do not meet the challenge of these times.

Any of us who have been called forth to tramp along "the road less traveled," have found out, one way or another, that life on earth is a school, and that we are to identify ourselves as students within that school. Our individual role as student is not to be evaluated by how much we know, but rather, by how much we realize that we do not know; how well we are able to leap beyond our cynicism to a state of informed innocence; how frequently we are able to align ourselves with the high principles, the evolutionary precepts, and the reformative practices of the larger context; and how devotedly we serve the process of real learning in ourselves and in others.

Our arrogance falls away as we contemplate that the universe in which we find ourselves began, very mysteriously, some fifteen billion years ago. Our false pride suffers a blow when we realize that our own brain system still includes the reptilian brain which first appeared some three hundred million years ago. Our pomposity is deflated when we realize that over ninety-nine percent of our human brain is still a duplicate of our primate predecessors who first appeared seventy million years ago. Such realizations serve not only to keep us humble, but to support us to be natural students who are inherently curious, hungry for understanding, and capable of insightful learning. Using our keen and expandable intellect to learn and to transcend the confines of the lower mind capacity, we become brilliant beyond our wildest dreams. We become our wildest dreams—able to leap intellectual buildings in a single bound of inspiration.

This book is the symbolic consummation of my first ten years lived as spiritual process. *A Call To Greatness* is just that: a calling forth of the greatness in each of us at this time, when our impulse for greatness seems ready to emerge: a calling forth of our greatness at this time, when we really need that greatness as a primary presence in this world. So many of the teachings which are appearing at this time exude an informed hopefulness. This book, too, stands on an, at once, fierce and fragile, informed and trusting hopefulness for us all. Just as Lord Krishna taught Arjuna, in many ways we are being taught to understand ourselves as a species and as individual human beings—at the level of inspiration. May we learn our lessons well, advance along our own learning curves, and leap to the ever higher levels of learning.

From cover to cover I make statements about and references to self-discovery and Self-expression; and, by use of the lower case "s" and upper case "S" draw a distinction between the levels of self/Self. For purposes of clarification, the following is my premise for that distinction: The lower self is the presently accepted standard by which western society gauges our humanity. It includes only the first three levels of consciousness—physical, emotional, and mental—and mentality is held as the focal point of our identity and the most significant aspect of our humanity. The higher Self is the latent or not fully activated "other half" of our wholeness. It includes the three higher levels of consciousness—human potential or existential, metaphysical, and spiritual—of which the ineffable Higher Consciousness, Designing Intelligence, or God is held as the focal point of our identity and the most significant aspect of our humanity.

The process of self-discovery has to do with gaining true understanding about our lower (egoic) self in order that we may begin to intervene in its automatic responses. Understanding of the involuntary reflexes and functions as well as the conditioned reactions of our body/mind, allows us to view ourselves and others in a new way—a way which offers us a far broader range of choice as to how we think and how we behave.

Self-expression has to do with speaking and acting based on basic views, attitudes, and intentions which are superior to or transcendent to the basic views, attitudes, and intentions of the lower (egoic) self, which are all fear based. True Self-expression derives from the higher, wholistic principles which lie at the core or center of our true being. By learning to source the Self, our frontal, surface, or egoic personality loses its ability to influence our choices and to control our lives in ways which invariably block our evolvement.

I ask the forbearance of those readers who have strong feelings and thoughts against the use of the male nouns and pronouns to refer to both males and females. It is a problem that many authors are grappling with and dealing with in different ways these days. Because the English language does not accommodate such reference in other than difficult to read, intrusive, and awkward reformulations of syntax or combinations of letters and words (i.e. s/he, his/her, him/her), I have chosen to honor above all the communication of the message of this book in as smooth and readable a style as possible, which means the use of male nouns and pronouns. To me, these wordforms imply an androgynous (before gender) reality, which bespeaks our wholeness and our oneness.

*Let us declare our intention
to stand as Beacons of Hope and
Agents of Change amidst the
confusion, the pain, the fear,
and the sorrow of our world.*

INTRODUCTION

Thinking Big and Starting Small

> *We see that the world around us is not so great, and we aspire for it to change, but we have become wary of universal panaceas, of movements, parties, and theories. So we will begin at square one, with ourselves such as we are; it isn't much, but it's all we have. We will try to change this little bit of the world before setting out to save the other.*[1]

A Call To Greatness is primarily a sincere acknowledgement of the exceptional potential which lies beyond the surface consciousness of humankind. It is secondarily an educational preachment on the ways and means and limitations of a level of consciousness beyond which many humans have begun to evolve—the exclusively egoic structure of consciousness which emerged somewhere between 3,500 years ago and 200,000 years ago, according to my sources.

The acknowledgement of greatness in us modern human beings is not frivolous on my part, since I personally feel the pulsing life of that greatness within, and I have received reports from many people over the past ten years that they feel it too. I personally experience the expression of the greatness in ways which are surprising to me; and I have witnessed the greatness begin to express itself in others once they began "at square one," gaining understanding about themselves, the evolutionary process, and the remarkable possibilities for true evolvement inherent in the commingling of readiness and timing.

In the process of evolving, there has always been a small segment of the existing human population in whom the evolutionary leap mysteriously occurred sooner than in the community-at-large. And, it was to those heroes that others paid homage and to whom they turned for leadership. Because they were given "eyes to see" at a new level of consciousness, they were able to bring rebirth to what had been a dying culture. In some ways we can bridge back to earlier times and examine how things occurred—and many have done that. But, in some significant ways, the times in which we find ourselves living have no precedent. We have no one to follow. We are the pathfinders, the trail blazers, the epochal explorers of the mysteries of the unknown.

We live in times which have been prophetically proclaimed the "apocalypse." In defining "apocalyptic," the dictionary uses the words "wildly unrestrained," "climactic," and "ultimately decisive." And, to those of us who are well-informed about what is happening in the four corners of our world these days, we can observe that the multi-faceted, complex, and ungovernable milieus which our societies have become, can well be spoken of in those terms. These are the times which have been pointed to as the end of history. These are the times which have been "seen" by prophets and visionaries as times of unimaginable change. These are the times when we can expect anything but business as usual.

And as for the process which is carrying us along toward an ultimate leap in consciousness, I will use a powerful metaphor from Virginia Burden Tower's book *The Process of Intuition*. She says:

> *The biologist suggests that there is a time in the life cycle of a water creature when he makes his terrible effort to move to land, and one can imagine him stumping along on his broken fins and the distress of that first breath drawn more from prophecy than from common sense; and yet one may suppose a kind of propulsion of the spirit that yearned so joyously toward the new state that the creature hardly felt the parts and pieces of himself being dropped along the way.*[2]

So for those who are "stumping along" on the shores of the "new state," *A Call To Greatness* is a salute of acknowledgement for their "terrible effort," a manual of how to breathe more easily in the new realm, and a celebration of the "propulsion of spirit" which moves them along toward the summits of re-Creation.

Monkey See: Monkey Do

We are fascinated with each other. We watch each other with great interest. We carefully observe each other, learn from each other, and use each other as models for our own behaviors. Whatever generation we represent, our role models have been the generations which have preceded us here on earth; and we each have done our best to emulate what seems to work (one way or another) from those whom we have watched as we pieced together the puzzle of how to do life. Our observations may have led us to choose ways and means which were the exact opposite of those who were consciously or unconsciously modeling behaviors for us; but, they, too, directly influenced our attitudes and behaviors by demonstrating the *antithesis* of the identities which we had begun to create.

I suggest that for some time we have been doing little more than acting out a variety of stereotyped roles—roles which have become boilerplate molds for ourselves and our younger generations to fit into. And, although each of us may add our own particular nuances to the roles, the central character of the roles are as recognizable as that of a "valley girl." And although these stereotypical roles do provide us with a point of departure from which we may begin to experience life in our society, they should be recognized to be emulations of others' behaviors and quickly outgrown. Once we have dressed ourselves in the fashion of the role and marked our space with signs of the role, we must begin to access our deeper Self and "flesh out" our stereotypes with the stuff of archetypal living. We must bring to every aspect of our lives our true Self.

During the decades since my youth, things have changed so much. Nearly every facet of life in America has undergone an amazing metamorphosis, although during the 1950's, we thought that we were and that our life was very modern. There is one aspect of human behavior, however, that still somewhat parallels earlier periods: that of untruthful relating between and among human beings. Although we live in a real Age of Communication—with radio, telephone, and television signals permeating the space in which we live and breathe—generally, we are not adept at discovering how we really feel/think about things and communicating that simple, clear truth to each other. We are still stuck, both in attempting to tell each other what we think the other wants to hear, and in being rebellious rather than being truthful. We are still stuck in saying the things which will allow us to just get by rather than communicating the truth and allowing the consequences of our communications to shape our lives.

During the past thirty years, our attention has, again and again, been drawn to the general lack of truthful communication in our land by a variety of teachers and therapists. And, over the past few decades many people have been attending workshops, seminars, groups, and classes which raise one's consciousness as to the need for truthful communication and which help one to develop good communication skills. It is not unusual to meet graduates of such forums wherever we go today. Schools, churches, corporations, and many other organizations have embraced such curriculums in their attempts to better serve their students, congregations, employees, or members. And, although the consciousness has definitely been raised and some valuable tools have been provided us in these forums, something important is still missing in our ability to speak to and relate with each other. The point is that most people are still not in touch with their inner responses nor capable of communicating what they feel inside. I suggest that what is missing is 1) a much larger context in which to view ourselves as human beings, and 2) a basic understanding about the fundamentals of being human. I suggest that we must start with the big questions and, from that larger perspective, examine the in-the-moment relational transactions which make up our daily lives.

As large numbers of our society have realized the personal emptiness implicit in stereotypical role playing, we have achieved a readiness to take off the masks and plunge deeper into the search for the truth of ourselves. We now watch television and film "characters" divulging the deeper needs and higher aspirations which we all share. In many cases, these characters have become our evocateurs, giving us indirect permission and direct inspiration to become more truthful. The super-technology of our Age of Communication has made common knowledge of the "secrets" of our leaders. Many of us no longer gaze starry-eyed at people who have somehow gained the public's attention by way of stereotyped roles within politics and entertainment. We have become more discerning and are much more interested in the "substance" of the person who abides behind the mask.

A Course In Congruence is about that personal *substance*, which translates as pure potential. It is a body of knowledge which is not only permission-giving and evocative, but which also includes a larger (evolutionary) context for our lives and basic information about ourselves which will act to speed us along our path of self-discovery and Self-expression.

For the millions who are now ready, it is no longer "modern" to feel/think one thing and say another, creating conflict in ourselves and confusion in our relationships. It is no longer "cool" to take the easy way out by acting as though we agree with others in order to fit in. It is no longer enough to live stereotyped lives of unfulfilled potential. From SuperMom to SuperExecutive to SuperStar we simply need more of ourselves and each other now. We have "maxed-out" on the superficiality of levels of communication and being which were modeled for us by previous generations. We strongly feel the need to delve deeper and to go higher. That readiness marks us as a part of the cutting edge of awakening consciousness in these pivotal times. By becoming more fully human, we will provide outstanding role models for future generations.

A CALL RECEIVED AND A COVENANT SEALED

The story of *A Course In Congruence* is bound up in the larger story of what I call my "accelerated Spiritual Process." And, although my Process includes much more than the creation and provision of these teachings, an important part of that Process has been my relationship to these teachings. In order to clarify for the reader how I came to this relationship, I offer the following account.

In March of 1986 I had to make a decision that I did not relish making because my options were limited and all of them were inconvenient. I was teaching in an alternative school for adolescents, and as a condition of my contract, I was required to complete several hours of graduate level course work in my teaching area by June 1. I decided to earn some of those credits in a lecture/research paper course at Florida International University. The others I decided to acquire by participating in a two-weekend-long communications training in Pompano Beach, in April. Although I was very resistant to "wasting that much time sitting in a training, when I had so many other things I needed to be doing," those two weekends were so highly significant in my Process that my sense of wonderment still soars when I reflect on the sheer brilliance of it.

There were fifty participants in the training, plus one Trainer and two apprentice trainers. I realized that I was not the only one who did not want to be there soon after my arrival. The buzz in the ladies' room, in the lobby area, and in the training room itself, as we waited for the seminar to begin, was all about that. Since we were all there to earn needed college credits, nearly everyone was complaining about having to be there.

At the first break—as we stood outside in the soft Florida evening—the trainees continued to complain about being there; and they began to voice their judgments of the Trainer, the material, the room, the distances they had come, the bad coffee, etc. We all obviously thought we were there only to fulfill the contractual requirements for State Board Certification. Without knowing it, I was there for a much more important reason.

The sessions were held on Friday evenings, and all day on Saturdays and Sundays. After the Trainer opened the first session by outlining all of the value we would be receiving during the next days, we sat in a large circle and, one-by-one introduced ourselves to the group. At some point in that long process, I heard a silent voice say to me, "*Teach A Course In Congruence*." And I felt myself immediately respond with a silent, inner "*YES*!" I had never heard the word "congruence" before, but I was highly energized by the direct guidance, and I knew, without a doubt, that it was another pivot in my process.

Rather than stay overnight in Pompano, I drove back and forth to Miami between sessions. When I arrived home late that Friday night, I spent two hours referencing my psychology texts, trying to find the word "congruence." I finally found it in the works of Carl Rogers. It meant "an accurate matching of the inner experience with the outer expression." It meant "authenticity," "genuineness," "realness." I was thrilled. That is exactly what my own process had brought me to, and I was to teach it to others.

At some point during the Saturday morning session of the training, I decided that I was going to be congruent throughout the seminar, as an experiment. The process that ensued as a result of that decision was fascinating, uncomfortable, and truly enlightening.

The teaching was uninspired. The group energy was very low. And there was obviously an unspoken agreement among the participants that everyone would just endure the experience, go through the motions in the training room, and vent their frustration during breaks and meal times. It was obvious that there was a generalized agreement that it was all a waste of time and a meaningless endeavor. As the lunch hour approached, nothing of any substance or real value had been offered in the seminar, and the Trainer had, a few times, reiterated the list of specific communication skills that we could expect to gain there. I raised my hand, was called on, stood up and stated my name (which was the prescribed protocol), and, in a well-modulated voice, said, "I really do not want to be here; but since I am here, I sincerely want to receive value from the seminar. Six hours have already passed, and I have received none. When will we begin to get some of that information from the list that you have read a few times?"

The Trainer's face became a study in surprised, speechless confusion. He did not know how to react; he could think of nothing to say. I HAD BROKEN THE SILENT AGREEMENT. A hush had fallen over the room. The other participants seemed breathless, shocked, ill-at-ease. The Trainer laughed nervously, assured me that we would begin in earnest after lunch, and dismissed the group. I WAS SHUNNED. As we left the room, everyone averted their eyes and nervously distanced themselves from me, as they invited each other to lunch. "Interesting!" I thought. I contemplated the implications of my demonstration as I ate my lunch alone.

Returning after lunch to the Holiday Inn where the training was being held, I entered the ladies' room. The conversations all stopped, and a silence was maintained until I left. "Interesting!" I thought. And that is the way we continued throughout the first weekend: From time to time during the seminar, I would feel a real need for self-expression about what was happening or was not happening in the seminar, and I would communicate that with courage, self-discipline, and gracefulness. On each occasion, my congruence elicited a reaction similar to the one which followed my initial demonstration.

The Trainer became a bit paranoid. I could tell he was anticipating my comments or questions with an obvious level of dread. I was so unpopular that I had a difficult time finding a partner on the many occasions we needed one to do a process. I ate lunch and dinner alone and stood by myself at break. When they were outside the training room, I could hear the other participants still complaining about the training, the room, the distances they had come, the coffee, etc. But once they re-entered the room, they put on a "good" act—acting as though they were very interested, and fully aligned with the Trainer and everything that was going on there. I had seen this happening all of my life, and it had always been abhorrent to me. But, this time, I did not have to pretend in any way that I was a part of it. Neither did I have to feel rebellious and reactive about it. I merely maintained my own sense of self and allowed myself to be authentic and natural—just me, with none of that other nonsense added. And, although the experience was uncomfortable for me, I felt a wonderful freedom.

During the week back in Miami—between the two weekends in Pompano—I reflected on the experience a lot. I realized that I had been living congruently to a great degree since my moment of truth in 1984. And even though I was fully committed to complete the experiment I had begun, my discomfort level was high; I dreaded returning for the second weekend of the seminar. On Friday, during the long drive to Pompano, I wondered if there had been a change of heart on any of their parts regarding me during that week. When I entered the ladies' room, before the first session, silence fell over the room again. Nothing had changed. We continued the seminar. I continued my experiment.

Sometime during that second Saturday afternoon session, an interesting thing happened. The young man who sat across from me in a process we were doing said, "I want to tell you that I really admire you for what you have been doing here. I wish I could do that." After that, some others who partnered with me also made unsolicited statements which included the words "admire," "respect," "honor," etc. "Interesting," I thought. (But I was still left alone during breaks and lunch and dinner hours.)

At some point on Sunday, I began to be chosen for processes, rather than having to wait until everyone else had been chosen and being the one who was "left over." At one point, one of the apprentice trainers asked me if she could be my partner. Instead of doing the process, she spent the whole time telling me how much she admired what I was doing and asking me questions about it. "Very interesting," I thought.

After all the teaching had been done, all the processes completed, and the final test administered, we began the closing session, which was the graduation ceremony. Once again we sat in the large circle, as we had on that first Friday evening. The Trainer stood at a podium just inside the circle at one end of the room. He would call the name of a participant, the participant would rise, walk to the podium, and receive his/her certificate of completion from the Trainer, who would shake the participant's hand. Everyone else would applaud.

Since my name was Riley, most of the names had already been called before I heard mine. With apprehension I rose from my chair and began to walk the length of the large room toward the Trainer. My mind raced. My body was tense. The ordeal of the past week had obviously taken its toll. THEN A TOTALLY UNEXPECTED SERIES OF EVENTS BEGAN TO HAPPEN ALL AT ONCE. The Trainer stepped out from behind the podium and began to walk toward me, his hand outstretched; and applause broke out all around the room, with such feeling, volume, and intensity that it startled me. Then, EVERYONE STOOD UP. **I was receiving a standing ovation!**

As the grinning Trainer met me in the middle of the room and shook my hand with surprising vigor, some of the participants whistled, some let out catcalls, some laughed, and some cried. I was astonished. I was speechless. I began to laugh and cry with them.

They left their chairs and converged in the center of the room and gleefully began to retrace the course of my earlier communications and their responses to them. It was great fun for the whole group—even for the Trainer. I was not gleeful. Instead, I was flooded with feelings of humble amazement. I had become their hero, out of the very truth of myself!

MEETING THE CHALLENGE

Back in Miami, although I was still in the process of researching and writing five papers for my course at the University, teaching at the alternative school full-time, conducting a meditation group, and maintaining a small Rebirthing practice, I began to do the research for *A Course In Congruence*. With so many other things to attend to, my attention was irresistibly drawn to the subject of congruence throughout the day; and late at night—and during every other free moment—I sat at my dining room table, which was piled high with books containing fragments of information on the subject, and worked on the project. I poured over the books, lovingly excerpting the rich morsels of inspired teachings of those authors who had previously explored the concept of congruence in some way. My typed notes on the subject kept growing steadily, and I began to feel very alone and very lost in the voluminous array of references. As I persevered, I became troubled about my seeming inability to manage the material in a way that would bring it together in a coherent course of study. I had already announced that I would begin teaching the course in mid-June, and had begun accepting registrations. When the first day of June rolled around, I was getting panicky. I began to doubt whether I could accomplish what I had been called to do.

One evening, as I sat at the table, feeling lost and overwhelmed, I felt a strong urge to try and *draw* what it was that I wanted to teach my students. My weakest area of expression has, admittedly, always been drawing, to the point that I have felt handicapped in that way. Nevertheless, I took out a piece of blank paper and began to draw a model of my own spiritual process. I had never seen a drawing of spiritual process before, so I had no reference other than what had occurred in my own case. I labored over it for a couple of hours, and when I finished, I felt satisfied that it depicted what I wanted others to know. Then I took out another piece of blank paper, and I began to create a line drawing of the ego, identifying its various functions and neurotic tendencies. I labored over that drawing for a couple of hours, and when I finished, I felt satisfied about its message. Then I drew several rough sketches of puzzle pieces, and I labeled them with some of the elements of congruence. And, last, I drew a model of congruence itself. When I completed that last rough sketch, I went to bed and slept soundly, knowing that I had found the way to manage the material and present *A Course In Congruence*. Those simple models became the touchstones of the teaching.

The first meeting of the first students of *A Course In Congruence* was a very big deal for me. I was up against the wall of time right up to the last moment. In fact, my nails were still wet when the first student knocked on my door. I had worked so diligently to create the seminar, knew that it was great stuff, but still felt tremulous about my own ability to deliver the teaching fully. With my fifteen students assembled in my living room for their first class, I passed out their personal notebooks and took my place on the chair at the front of the room. As I sat down a rush of stark white terror ran through my body. I felt frozen, rigid, unable to move. I began the seminar by being congruent: I said, "I am terrified!" They all laughed. We had begun.

Those ten weeks were precious weeks for me, as I fleshed out the words on the paper and made them real for all of us. The group meeting, which was, for the most part, made up of mature professionals, became the central focus of everyone's week—and we all were changed dramatically by the teachings we had come together to explore. I felt so much empathy and love for them as sincere seekers of truth. At the last meeting of *A Course In Congruence*, I ritualized their completion with a simple graduation ceremony and presented each of them with a certificate of completion. I also read them the following letter which I had written to them that day.

September 17, 1986

Dear Students,

When I responded to the call to create *A Course In Congruence*, I had no idea what a challenge it would be for me—a challenge, a stretch, a confronting on many levels of my own intention, my own commitment, my own resistance, my own unyielding desire to know and to serve and to fulfill my own potential as a human being. It has been an on-going experience of wrestling with the material, monitoring my own feelings and emotions, pressing through resistance and surrendering, surrendering, surrendering to my greater Self, in an attempt to make this experience a valuable one for you in your process of becoming.

I salute you. I love you. I have tremendous compassion and admiration for each of you. And I humbly thank you for bringing your search for truth here to my living room—for sharing yourselves with me.

I have shared with some of you my occasional urges to choke, smack, hit, kick and scream at you—to have you get it, get it, get it—balanced with an overwhelming compassion which keeps me on my chair, and an unconditional love which allows, allows, allows you your experience.

There is not a doubt about your willingness. There is not a doubt about your desire to know. There is not a doubt about *what* you desire. There is only certainty that you will continue to be led by your higher Self, your true Self, your God Self, along the path you have chosen.

Congruence, authenticity, genuineness, realness will speed you on your way, will bring you satisfaction, will reclaim for you your personal power, your emotional strength and your mental and physical well-being.

Know who you are. Open more and more to the fascinating and fulfilling process of self-discovery. Take a stand for yourself out of *your* feelings. Stay close to *your* emotions. Detach, detach, detach from emotional energies, expectations, and judgments of others. Communicate who you are, how you feel, what you think, what works for you and what does not work for you. Define who you are in having, doing and being whatever it is that your highest good dictates.

Commit to serving your own highest good and *fear forward*—and miracles are sure to happen for you. Draw on your own sense of what is right, what is most loving, and step out a little further into participation, into life, knowing that you are never alone.

My warmest good wishes to you. Thank you for answering your call.

In the Glow of Your Greatness,
Mayda Riley

We all wept.

It Works! A Testimonial

Having taught this extraordinary body of work many times and in several different forms—ten-week courses, eight-week courses, six-week courses, three-day intensives, and in private sessions—I have never ceased to be amazed at its power, its wisdom, its love, and its effectiveness in changing perceptions, reordering priorities, clearing the past, clarifying confusion, causing breakthrough in expression, and providing a foundation of understanding which make it possible for students to "go it alone" in closest attunement with their own high Self.

Some years ago I had several private clients who had spent long years in therapy (six to nine years)—and who were still attending private and group sessions weekly—who began to clear up dramatically as a result of these teachings. Their therapists were shocked and impressed and incredibly supportive once they had perused the course material. I have had psychology professors bring their classes to lectures I have given on college campuses about these concepts and practices. I have stood before students of all ages (thirteen to seventy-something) and from all races, ethnicities, religions, and professions, with the same heartful responses and the same remarkable results.

The teachings of *A Course In Congruence* have continued to unfold themselves in me through the years. I have learned what self-discovery truly is out of my own intimate relationships with these teachings through the years. I have experienced time and time again how the substance of each concept runs deeper and deeper into the caverns of ourselves and provides us hidden aspects of our humanity which we have not seen firsthand and have not thoroughly explored before. I have been amazed again and again at the seemingly bottomless well of insights, revelations, eureka's!, and aha's! which lie within our own remarkable humanness. It is out of my own experience of congruence that the strength of my conviction comes: That we can rise to any occasion simply because, with God's Grace, we are *equal to any circumstance* and *greater than any circumstance*.

It is my heartfelt personal thesis—which has been validated by so many who have already been exposed to these teachings—that the experience of personal freedom I felt, as I stood alone in my own authenticity those weekends in Pompano Beach, Florida, is the very freedom for which many people yearn, but which they do not know how to achieve on their own yet. By way of a fascinating and enigmatic process, I was shown the particular elements and characteristics of our humanity by which we can quickly gain perspective on where we have gone wrong and how we can correct that wrongness in our own lives in order to reclaim our own precious humanity and experience a solid sense of self. From that center we are able to walk the enchanting path of self-discovery and shine forth as authentic expressions of our greatness, which has lain hidden behind the hateful masks of acculturated role playing under whose weight we have chafed.

As I suspected, I had not been the only one who felt uncomfortable when my peers felt one way and acted another—when they were two-faced and expected me to be the same. I had not been the only one who felt smothered by the excessive phoniness among my contemporaries which long ago became the standard for social behavior in our society. I had not been the only one who despised the small-minded gossip mongering which was prevalent in all groups, no matter how sophisticated or high-minded they supposedly were. I had not been the only one who silently protested the high levels of reactivity and arrogance which rose as unbreachable barriers between otherwise bright and intelligent people. I had not been the only one who noticed the denial of human emotions in some people and the overemotionality in others. I had not been the only person who knew that there was a churning confusion in most people about anger—what to think about it, how to cope with it, and how and when to express it. I had not been the only one who observed the widespread experience of separateness in people and their use of inauthentic behaviors in attempts to fit in with whatever group they were somehow associated.

I, too, had done all of those things of which I disapproved. I, too, had felt the shallowness of relationships which could have been meaningful and significant if the walls of self-protection could somehow have been dissolved. I, too, had experienced the emptiness of relationships to which I was a party simply because I wanted to or felt I ought to fit in. I, too, had felt disappointed that relational transactions were, for the most part, hollow and insincere surface encounters with little merit or weight. I, too, had needed MORE.

I had begun to experience that much needed MORE in January, 1984, as the result of a most extraordinary moment of transcendence and the resultant unfoldment of my truly accelerated spiritual process. And, the more my own experience of being filled to the brim with all that I had ever longed for has expanded and established itself as normal, the more I have wanted to assist others to attain that enviable state. The key that unlocks the door is congruence, for within our very Self lie the answers to all of our questions, the light which shines on our own path—and our path itself. Within our very Self abides all that is great. We only need a little help in accessing and expressing that greatness.

A New World Vision

All over this land and around the world there are millions of people who are now ready to move beyond the limitations that have held them in lives of unfulfilled potential—lives that do not reflect the significance of this auspicious period of our history nor their own eagerness for Self-expression. It is to those people that I enthusiastically and lovingly offer this book. These teachings have been a true labor of love for me since 1986; and I have always known that, in every sense of the word, they represent a strong, clear call to action—a call for the potential heroes of our time to become the extraordinary beings they really are, now!

These extraordinary people, who feel trapped in ordinary lives, respond to such a call with fear and doubt, with all kinds of apprehensions—the considerations with which they have been conditioned to approach life. But they do respond. They take those most important first steps, which lead them on and on to the quantum leaps which their inner calling so desires. They surrender themselves to the hero's journey—the journey of self-discovery and Self-expression.

There is an awakening happening on this planet! And there are untold millions of people who are consciously participating with that process of awakening. Our world is now a "global community"—a world community which must find ways to deal with the very serious crises that we as a species have created.

While the economists have struggled with the complex implications of a world economy; while the environmentalists have grappled with the threats to our eco-systems; and while Heads of State have searched for ways to resolve national dilemmas, nationalistic differences, and global challenges, I have reached out to individual human beings who have become aware of an inner calling—a calling that drives them to find understanding and to become more than they have been yet. For I do believe that the solution to our global problems is as fundamental—and as awesome—as changing the level of consciousness out of which the individual and the whole species functions.

There **is** a lower consciousness! There **is** a higher consciousness! And that has not been really acknowledged yet by other than the truly high thinkers of all times and today's emergent culture. I am a representative of that emergent culture. I say that we must awaken, that we must discover who we really are. We must move beyond the limitations of the lower levels of consciousness—and we must do it now!

Besides contributing to the good of all, living at the higher levels of consciousness dramatically improves the quality of life in individual human lives. Life becomes worth living—with a rich sense of purpose and meaning not available before.

We are an evolving species. And those of us who are ready can actually quicken the pace of the evolutionary process by discovering who we really are and by expressing ourselves fully in the world. That is the greatest service any of us can provide—for ourselves, for our loved ones, and for the community-at-large.

LET US SHINE FORTH AS FULLY HUMAN EXPRESSIONS OF OUR GREATER SELVES AMIDST THE TRAGEDIES AND THE MIRACLES OF OUR TIMES.

Part One

A LOOK BEFORE YOU LEAP

...The ideal that beckons us, the goal that guides our steps, is not really in front; it does not draw us, but pushes us; it is behind—as well as in front and inside. Evolution is the eternal blossoming of a flower that was always a flower. Without this seed in the depths nothing would move, because nothing would need anything. This is the world's Need—this is our ***central being****.*

...It is supremely ***within****, as it is supremely above and below and everywhere—it is a* ***giant point****. When we have found it, all is found, and all is there. The adult soul recovers its origin, the Son recovers the Father, or, rather, the Father, who became the Son, becomes Himself again...*

—*SATPREM*

Sri Aurobindo or The Adventure of Consciousness[1]

LET US REMEMBER THAT OUR
PURPOSE IS TO EXPERIENCE AN
INNER EVOLUTION—THE TRANSCENDENCE
OF SELF-CENTEREDNESS.

CHAPTER ONE

A Call to Greatness

> *Sometimes I think that the greatest achievement of modern culture is its brilliant selling of samsara [the world of illusion] and its barren distractions. Modern society seems to me a celebration of all the things that lead away from the truth, make truth hard to live for, and discourage people from even believing that it exists. And to think that all this springs from a civilization that claims to adore life, but actually starves it of any real meaning; that endlessly speaks of making people "happy," but in fact blocks their way to the source of real joy.*
>
> —*Sogyal Rinpoche*[1]

A belly full of the nonsense!

In *MoreThanMe* I wrote: "I am horrified by the world I live in. I am just as shocked, disgusted and disillusioned today by the offensive atrocities that are perpetrated by human beings upon human beings as I was as an adolescent. I cannot even imagine that there is a world like our world, and I cannot imagine my living in it. The only thing that saves it for me is that there are so many magnificent beings on Earth at the same time I am here. But, my questions remain: 'How do we stand it?' 'What must we come together and do about it?'"[2] What a thing to say! What could possibly cause a person who has been so blessed, who has been so gifted, who has mysteriously been allowed the extraordinary experience of "illumination" to think and to say such a thing? I feel sure anyone who would read *MoreThanMe* or *A Call to Greatness* knows the answer to that question. But it is important for me that I communicate that answer for myself and for others at this time.

All of my life I have somehow known that there is something very, very wrong not with the world, but with the way human beings think and behave. Our world today is really not much different than the world of several centuries ago in that then, as now, human beings lied and cheated and stole from one another. Then, as now, human beings warred against each other and perpetrated horrifying atrocities upon each other in the name of some supposed ideal having to do with family, state, nation, or religious belief—or, even, *in the name of God.* How stupid! How primitive! How unconscious! How unacceptable!

The primary difference today is that there are many more human beings living together on the planet than at any other time in the history of the world, and our communication systems make it possible for us to see and hear about the lying, the cheating, the stealing, the murdering, the warring, etc. in the comfort of our own homes—some of which are modern-day versions of ancient mini-fortresses, secured against invasion by "the enemy." Another difference is that the innocence of our children has become infected with the virus of adult corruption, cold-heartedness, and cruelty. The distortions within our children's psyches now allow them to cross freely back and forth across the line between human decency and human impropriety.

WE MUST STAND FREE OF THE HISTORICAL FABRIC AND BEGIN TO WEAVE A WHOLE NEW TAPESTRY —ONE WOVEN WITH INTELLIGENT AND HUMANE THOUGHTFORMS AND BEHAVIORS.

What—in the name of all that is holy—is wrong with us? And what—for Christ's sake—can we do about this tragic comedy of errors that we have created and still do create as a species? Haven't we had a belly full of this nonsense by now? Isn't it time that we open our droopy eyes and look directly at what is happening in our world? Isn't it time that we tell the undeniably obvious truth: This is not the way we should be thinking and behaving!? Isn't it time that we stop fooling ourselves and attempting to fool each other about the way things are? Isn't it time that we stop serving our own silly agendas and begin to live for the higher purpose of leaping ourselves and our entire species out of this quagmire of pitiful unLawfulness? Isn't it high time that we rise to the occasion and that we meet the high-minded demand on us that our very humanness represents? The increasing complexity and chaos within our societies appear to signal the end of the world as we have known it. And, during this obvious transition period between the old and the new *global consensus*, there are many obvious signals which seem to shout "It is time!"

Many really intelligent, high-minded, and self-sacrificing human beings have lived in and died in this world. They have left us pre-millennial humans an empowered legacy of heroism based in truth from which we may experience an inner empowerment, and against which the low-minded foolishness of our age cannot prevail. We must stand upon the foundation that they have built for us and know ourselves to be the torchbearers of our own age. We must feel our own destinies and our own purposes as surely as we feel our own breath entering our bodies. We must carry the torch of truth and freedom which blazes within our sometimes imperceptible, but always present, greaterness. We must wrench ourselves free from identification with our unenlightened history; we must stand as beacons of hope for the future, which presses itself upon our human consciousness; and we must authentically and unreservedly shine that greaterness in every measurable inch of this God-given world we inhabit together. We must do so with deepest humility, with unparalleled devotion to purpose, and with unspeakable gratitude for the opportunity to have Self-expression achieved in us.

What has been wrong with us? Why have we potent human creatures continued to think and act in ways which reflect such low levels of intelligence and such a lack of species-sensitive consciousness? How has the human psyche become so twisted that it can reconcile the profound levels of self-sacrificing love for one's own child with the ability to murder another's child in war? How is it able to reconcile its heartfelt applause of heroic human gestures to save one person's life at the same time that it prizes its abilities to strategize the slaughter of thousands or hundreds of thousands of other lives in war? How is the twisted human psyche able to reconcile the love and respect for certain races of human beings and, at the same time, foment hatred and engage in hate-full acts against other races of humans? How is the twisted psyche able to reconcile a parent's instinctive love and protectiveness of its child with its willful neglect or physical abuse of that same innocent and helpless child? How is the twisted psyche of a religious leader who, with great passion, preaches about a stunning conversion when he was "saved" and who calls millions of others "to be saved in the name of Jesus," able to reconcile his regular visits to prostitutes between sermons? How can the twisted psyche of a president of the United States reconcile his daily declarations about truth in government with his daily meetings about covert operations: Watergate, Iran-Contra, etc.? How can the twisted psyches of "leaders" or "experts" who are called to speak to their public about important subjects, reconcile their knowledge of the truth with their blatant and often embarrassing denial of the truth in television interviews? And on and on and on.

The statistical reports of what is actually occurring in our modern society are appalling. Even though I have been listening to such reports since I was a young woman, I have never developed a skin thick enough to keep me from being shocked at the sheer number of diseases, murders, sexual crimes, cases of child abuse, kidnappings and car-jackings, white-collar crimes, et cetera.

Here are just a few of those statistics:

A rape occurs every minute.

2,000 to 4,000 Catholic priests have molested 100,000 people in the past few decades.

WE NEED A GREAT CORRECTION, AND WE CAN ACHIEVE IT NOW.

One-fourth of the female population and one-sixth of the male population have suffered sexual abuse as children.

25% of deaths of children are by guns

One-sixth of homocides are committed by adolescents.

The evidence of widespread neurosis is apparent in the rampant and ever-growing societal, cultural, and individual unLawfulness. This short-sighted, self-serving, and dishonorable behavior, which goes against the grain of our inner knowledge of right and wrong, demeans and shames us as a species. The cause of it? Societies and cultures which have become based in intellectual, mechanistic and scientific precepts and which have, in practice, separated themselves from the spiritual context in which all of life occurs. And, even though the word "God" is still used often by the leaders of our neurotic world, the separation is glaring. As Brian Swimme states, in *The Universe Is a Green Dragon*:

> *Our modern western civilization began with a kind of cultural schizophrenia. Our scientific enterprise effectively decoupled itself from our humanistic-spiritual traditions at the beginning of the modern period. All for good reasons, yes, but now the neurosis spreads over several continents. Enmeshed in the most terrifying pathology in the history of humanity, we can perhaps dare to ask if this was such a good idea, this splitting up of the universe.*
>
> *Alert humans could see the danger of our situation from the beginning. Though they could not have predicted the planetary poisons that beset us, nor the threat of annihilation that everyone carries to bed every night of the week, they could see that we were headed for an unhealthy future. Diseased mindscapes only produce diseased landscapes.*[3]

With so many references being made these days to the neurosis which has become so widespread that it pervades the entire spectrum of humanity, we need to have an understanding of what neurosis is in order to begin to transcend its dispositions. Webster's Third New International Dictionary defines neurosis as follows:

> 1) a functional disorder of the central nervous system usually manifested by anxiety, phobias, obsessions, or compulsions but frequently displaying signs of somatic disorder involving any of the bodily systems with or without other subjective or behavioral manifestations and having its most probable etiology in intrapsychic or interpersonal conflict....
>
> 2) individual or group behavior that is characterized by rigid adherence to an idealized concept of the personal or social organism especially when that concept is significantly at variance with reality and that results in interpersonal, cultural, or political conflict and in the development of discomforting intraorganismal tensions....[4]

WE MUST LEARN ABOUT OUR HUMAN EMOTIONAL RESPONSE, OUR HUMAN MIND, AND THE POTENTIAL FOR HIGHER LEVELS OF CONSCIOUSNESS WHICH LIES DORMANT WITHIN US.

Our anxious, phobic, obsessive, and compulsive society, which suffers uncountable forms of somatic disorder, certainly characterizes this dictionary definition of neurosis and attests to the serious disorders of our stressed-out nervous systems. That a large segment of our society still rigidly adheres to a concept of us and of our world which is at variance with the apparent reality, causing interpersonal, cultural, and political conflict is obvious.

As a direct result of the prevailing neurosis, it is common knowledge these days that, to a substantial degree, the fabric of both our national cultures and our world culture is woven with the threads of uncountable lies. Openly or covertly deceiving one another has become the common, to-be-expected, and widely-accepted practice throughout all levels of human relating—from the highest levels of government to the most personal and intimate relationships between family members, lovers, friends, acquaintances, co-workers, employers and employees, and clergymen and their congregations. And, although a constant

[4]By permission. From Webster's Third New International Dictionary ©1986 by Merriam-Webster, Inc., Publisher of Merriam-Webster® dictionaries.

outcry against such deception can be heard, the psychological fabric has been so tightly woven that there may seem to be no way to unravel the tapestry and begin a reweaving with the threads of truth. But there is a way.

That way is the way of individuals discovering their own personal truth and beginning to weave from scratch a new tapestry—a tapestry woven with the threads of high principles which are inherent within their own untwisted psyches. The warp and woof of that new motif are the truthful threads of congruent communications and actions at all levels. We must stand free of the historical fabric and begin to weave a whole new tapestry—one woven with intelligent and humane thoughtforms and behaviors. This new beginning is possible for any of us at any age, once we gain clarity about a few elements intrinsic to our very humanness. We have simply not been educated about our human nature—its various intrinsic aspects and the distinctions which may so easily be made between "right" and "wrong" on a strictly personal level. All of our lives we have been told by our ancestors and by our elders that the secret to life was to *just be ourselves* and to *be true to ourselves*, but our societies and our families have not really given us permission to **do** that, nor have they provided us the space in which to **be** that, nor have they provided us the kind of support necessary to **become** that. Now we will give ourselves permission, we will create the space for ourselves and for others, and we will support each other to discover and express ourselves truthfully.

We must learn about our human emotional response, our human mind, and the potential for higher levels of consciousness which lies dormant within us. We must learn about the human ego and its limited function in which our consciousness has been trapped for many thousands of years. We must learn the distinctions between and the dissimilar motivations of the lower nature and the higher nature of our humanity. We must understand the psychological mechanisms which are always operant within us and the distortion of those mechanisms which have occurred due to the untruthful and inhumane treatment we have received, whose standards we have reluctantly adopted, and by whose methods we have learned to misthink and misbehave. We need a great correction, and we can achieve it now.

The way to save ourselves as a species is to save ourselves as individuals. The way to heal our stricken Earth is to heal our individual psyches. The way to change our grossly unLawful human behavior—from the top levels of leadership to the bottom levels of our *grass roots* cultures—is to change our grossly unLawful individual selves. The way to offer the promise of a better world to our children is to fulfill the promise of our individual potential now.

The truly wondrous uniqueness of our humanness and the amazing potential which is biologically encoded in our human cells await their fuller and ever fuller expression. And these are not just words. Our human capacities and capabilities have been demonstrated in many diverse and stunning ways down through the centuries and throughout the past few decades. We are truly remarkable creatures who have just not yet recognized and realized the God-given faculties with which we are naturally endowed. Our high levels of stress and our widespread neuroses are not the results of our having come too far too fast, but instead are the outgrowth of our being stuck within a context of thoughtforms and behaviors which are much too small for our greatness. Once we break through the hateful walls of the limited mind in which we have been held prisoners for so long, our opened hearts and transformed minds will soar, and our inherent magnificence and dignity will rise to the surface of our everyday lives. Our thoughts will change from thoughts of self-protection to thoughts of self-transcendence. Our actions will change from actions of selfish, self-absorbed, self-seeking to actions of Self-expression. Such profound and noble changes!

The Evolutionary Step Ladder: The Next Rung—Authenticity

What has lain dormant up to now in humanity—which dormancy accounts for the deficiencies in high-minded thought and action—are the higher levels of consciousness at which human beings are potentially capable of functioning. And what seems apparent to many highly intelligent, aware, awakening, and, in some cases, enlightened humans these days, is that we are living in an age of *unheard of* change. This epoch in which we find ourselves seems to be endowed—by our history and by the universal evolutionary mandate—with the necessary "critical mass" of world-level crisis, complexity, and consciousness, which has historically provoked a radical transformation of consciousness within our human psyches. These are the best of times; these are the worst of times. This is an age of apocalypse: the dying of a world order wherein the human ego has reigned and whose life is now coming to an end. This is an age of wonder: the birth of a new world order or universal culture, whose life is in its infancy. There has never been a time exactly like this time. And something truly dramatic and life-changing is occurring and is about to occur. We can feel it in the air we breathe. We can hear it from the tongues of many. We can nearly smell it, taste it, touch it. Something is happening. We can feel the silent rumble throughout the land. Something more is going to happen. We just know it. And, whatever that something is, we all sense that it is sure to be a pivotal and irreversible turn on the evolutionary spiral.

What can we expect of ourselves and others during the crucial and extraordinary times ahead? Can we count on ourselves and each other to rise to this unique occasion and to match our remarkable circumstances with the remarkable responses of which we are potentially capable? Can we strip ourselves of our conditioned responses to change and become the changelings which the times require? Can we turn from the dying consensus reality and lift our faces in innocence to the emerging higher reality which is impressing its vibrant freshness upon our hearts and minds? Can we humbly stand firm in our own sense of truth and justice against the tide of arrogant condemnation which has before caused us great self-doubt? Can we offer ourselves as fledgling emissaries of the dawning of a new paradigm on Earth?

What must we do now in order to begin the preparation of ourselves in order to meet the unique challenges and to fulfill the uncommon demands of this time? We must begin to "get real!" We must begin to discover the truth of ourselves. Really! We must come to understand more about ourselves as human beings and become more fully human. We must vacate the puny identities which we have superimposed upon our vast and potent humanness. We must re-identify more and more with the higher and more expansive aspects of our supra-human nature. We must surprise ourselves and each other with the actual development of latent faculties about which we have only mused before. We must discover and remember what we really are—mysterious mini-expressions of an unfathomable whole expression. We must have the chord of inner knowing struck within us and align our very lives with its frequencies, its pulses, and its rhythms.

We must become a special kind of hero—a champion of things unseen and things unheard by ordinary human eyes and ears. We must champion in this gross realm the realities of the subtle realm. By learning to attune our inner vision and our inner listening so as to see the invisible signs and to hear the silent messages of our deeper Self, we will become adept at wandering the uncharted course of our own destiny path. By truly surrendering our littleness to That Greatness, we will experience the graceful unfoldment of our own transformational process. Like a flower, we will bud and bloom, unfolding the petals of our unique beauty for all the world to see. Like a giant redwood, we will grow very thick and very tall, standing majestically for all to see and holding our branches to shelter all who come near.

All of this begins with the inner journey—the hero's journey through the wastelands of our own troubled, doubtful and fearful minds to the clear, confident and empowered peaks and pools of our greater Self.

> *14 If you would ask me what to study I would say, your selves; and when you well had studied them, and then would ask me what to study next, I would reply your selves.*
> *15 He who knows well his lower self, knows the illusions of the world, knows of the things that pass away; and he who knows his higher self, knows God; knows well the things that cannot pass away.*
> *16 Thrice blessed is the man who has made purity and love his very own; he has been ransomed from the perils of the lower self and is himself his higher self....*
> *21 The only devil from which men must be redeemed is self, the lower self. If man would find his devil he must look within; his name is self.*
> *22 If man would find his saviour he must look within; and when the demon self has been dethroned, the saviour, Love, will be exalted to the throne of power.*[5]

This very personal digression has been symbolically portrayed in the host of mythic tales which make up humankind's rich heritage of mythology. The beginning of the hero's journey has been acknowledged as the ultimate turning point in a human's life and has been characterized by the storytellers of every past human culture. Only in our modern world are we bereft of a mythology which epitomizes modern man's necessary heroic turn from the outer world to the inner vistas of self-discovery. Joseph Campbell's impressive study of world mythology and his creation of a modern library of mythic tales and translations has assisted many twentieth century heroes to understand what our society has failed to impart to us—that we must go beyond the "known" and wander through the inner panoramas of the "unknown" in order to find the treasure of our own heroic Self. Thomas Berry and Brian Swimme are pioneering the beginning of a new mythology which is rooted in the story of the universe. These highly intelligent scientists deliver the magnificence of *The Universe Story*[6] in language that we laymen are not only able to understand, but which makes our cosmic hearts leap to meet the challenges of the cosmic adventure of which we are obviously an integral part.

Within our being, there really is an inner guidance system (spoken of as an *inner guiding factor* by Jung) which is universally referred to as the Self. And, once we become attuned to the guidance and the expression of the Self, our lives are governed by that higher consciousness—and lived with an experience of amazement, fascination, and satisfaction derived from the presence of our own more e-x-p-a-n-s-i-v-e humanity in our daily lives. The turn inward is the requisite revolutionary gesture and it exemplifies our initial conversion experience—an experience which shifts our "spiritual center of gravity" to "a zone unknown."[7] From that unpredictable moment we become like fascinated spelunkers exploring the underground caverns of our own pysche. The relationships and occurrences in our outer world—past and present—are viewed from the deeper perspective of that inner vista—and everyone and everything looks very different than before the *moment of truth*. The inner guiding factor leads us on and on, deeper and deeper into our self and, then, beyond—into our Self. With only a single light to illuminate our way, we are led through the underground adventure of self-discovery and, then, with the exploration complete, up and out into the bright light of a new day—a day of rebirth, of reintegration, of reidentification. Our inner journey recreates us and revitalizes us; it transforms us into a more fully human being who will radiate the depth of the caves he has explored and the heights to which he has since climbed.

There really does abide within us a truth deeper and more real than our surface egoity, and we can discover that truth. Living only from the perspective and agenda of our surface selves will again and again—and always—disappoint us since that perspective and that agenda is no match for the deeper reality which pulses within our humanity with a most persistent need for and a most insistent urge for expression. The deeper truth is what is missing in our lives and in our world today. That missing element—the Principle or Law which is woven into the very fabric of our being—must now be allowed its expression. The surface personality's egoic truth is obviously a hollow shell concocted of self-serving platitudes and clichés. It glibly espouses flat and empty truisms to rationalize its pathetic fear and the awful thoughts and behaviors which are intrinsic to this fragment of the whole. When an "L" is added to "awful," the word becomes "Lawful." The Lawfulness which is the Self must replace the self-generated *awfulness* with which our world is blighted today. That Lawfulness lies within the Self of all humans, and it is that Lawfulness which will set us all free and raise us all out of the quicksand of our present dilemma. It is to our deeper Self that we must turn and to which we must now listen intently.

SOMETHING TRULY DRAMATIC AND LIFE-CHANGING IS OCCURRING AND IS ABOUT TO OCCUR. WE CAN FEEL IT IN THE AIR WE BREATHE. WE CAN HEAR IT FROM THE TONGUES OF MANY. WE CAN NEARLY SMELL IT, TASTE IT, TOUCH IT.

In these apocalytic times, there is still, at least, real hope for us human beings and for our world—and the basis for that hope is our unrealized human potential. In order for us to *real*ize that potential in time, we have some very sincere soul-searching to do; we have some very specific learning to accomplish; we have some very committed physical, emotional, mental, and spiritual practices to fulfill; and we have some very significant choices to make—consciously and in truth. Do we want to change? Are we willing to change, really? Will we do what we must do in order to align with the inevitable changes which must obviously occur in our individual selves, in our relationships with each other, and in our relationship to Mother Earth? Will we turn our attention inward and take the hero's journey to the center of ourselves under the stewardship of our own inner guiding factor—the Self? Will we stop the nonsense and become the sensitive, sensuous, sensational beings that we are, utilizing our five senses, our sixth sense, and our common sense to attune ourselves to our greater Self-sense which abides just below the façade of our surface personality? Will we stand free of our ungraceful, embarrassing and (unL)awful human history and begin anew—weaving a grand new tapestry with the threads of personal and collective truth? Will we recover our senses in time to submit ourselves fully to the evolutionary process, which is about to make a turn on the great spiral, whether we make the turn within its flow or not?

What is truly needed now is the readiness to respond to the call to greatness that is pulsant within the hearts and minds of untold millions of human beings alive on Earth today. The sincere human response which derives from that readiness will so rapidly turn the tide of human thought and behavior that our societies will begin to naturally change at a phenomenal pace and in ways that we can only fantasize about at this juncture. I suggest that the necessary readiness exists among us or the call would not be as powerful and as constant as it is at this time. People everywhere are acknowledging the call within themselves, the dramatic changes that have already begun to reshape their lives, and their distinct sense that major changes are soon to occur in our world. True readiness for change will sustain us while we stand alone as individuals and together as a species during this extraordinary time—the time of the great transition.

We simply must understand that ***we*** are the difference which we genuinely yearn to effect in the world; that ***we*** are the contribution which we really long to make; that ***we*** are the gift which we so sincerely desire to give; that ***we*** are the destiny which we so urgently need fulfilled. We must understand that the difference, the contribution, the gift and the destiny fulfillment all lie within the potency of our God-given humanity. We must realize that our world can accommodate who we truly are—that we do not have to align with the consensus reality in order to be successful as a person. We must know that we can be who and what and how we are—in truth—and much needed miracles will happen!

Getting Started

What is this flame of expectancy, this growth impulse, this frustration which urges us to break through the given patterns of our lives, pulled as though by an irresistible magnet toward each other and toward a desirable yet undefined state of being?

The flame feels like the binding, magnetic force that runs through the process of evolution, the force that drew atoms to atoms, molecules to molecules, cells to cells and now people to people in ever more complex whole systems. It feels like love. Not only personal love for each other, one by one; nor only altruistic love for others; but also, and more so, a transpersonal love, which senses the fulfillment of one's self through deep involvement in the evolution of the world, in connection with a Universal Force.

The flame feels like the attractive and attracted energy that moves the process—the intention of Creation. It represents our contact with the Logos, the Designing Intelligence, the Creative Intention—God.

The flame of expectation is igniting us, animating and attracting us to move beyond our existing life patterns...to do more, to be more, to know more, and above all to connect with each other, to discover what we can do together that none of us can do isolated and alone.[8]

Who are you? Do you have a strong, clear sense of who you are—and what you are here on earth to do, to have and to be? Would you like to feel more peaceful? More confident? More inspired? Would you like to feel more at home and at ease in the world? Would you like to discover your life purpose and fulfill it? All of that is possible through discovering who you really are—in fact, it is guaranteed.

When we are not sure of who we are, the ordinary "problems" of the human experience can consume us, distract us and cause us to run for cover, to seek some security at any cost. They can cause us to hide out in a no-man's land of role-playing, of "acting like." This no-man's land lies in between a deep inner experience and a true outer expression of our authentic selves. It is a land of uncertainty, vulnerability, and dissatisfaction.

Some of us, at some unpredictable point in our lives, become ready to live life very honestly. We become inwardly committed to finding understanding and to becoming greater than the confusion, pain and fear that have dictated our lives up to that point. From that time on, we are never the same. Our lives begin to somehow open up and to take on a form, a direction, and a purpose far different from what has gone before. We begin to be irresistibly drawn into a deeper, richer, fuller experience of who we are, and we begin to be moved by an energy that expresses our individuality in creative, high-minded and personally fulfilling ways.

That shift is evoked by our personal suffering and our recognition of suffering in others. It is fueled by our readiness for true change, and it is supported by the primordial, evolutionary essence of life itself. That shift is the answer to our own particular call to greatness.

The purpose of this book is to acknowledge and discuss that mysterious "calling" and to recognize the strong evidence that many of us are now ready to allow transformation to happen in us—transformation to the next level of consciousness—transformation that will allow fuller expression of our own very unique and amazing selves in this amazing world.

Although it is mysterious, the inner call is very real—and it will not leave us alone. The call has a silent voice; it has an energy that presses outward through us; it has a presence that fills us and surrounds us; it has a constancy that pushes us and pulls us and nudges us and calls and calls and calls to us. And, just as we feel the innate need to answer that call, our troubled world cries out to us to be responsive, to be courageous, to become the great ones that we surely are—which will make the difference that will turn the tide for humankind, for all other life forms, and for our planet.

Down through the ages, it has been the heroes who have answered the call who have captured the attention and applause of all who have secretly yearned to courageously express their truth in the world. Never before has our world been so ready for and so in need of heroic expressions of personal truth. Nearly six billion humans are occupying our planet at this time; but, with most members of our species still captured in their own closed thinking processes, driven by their own fearful, self-serving egoic neediness, and victimized by their own out-of-control or suppressed emotional reactions, very few humans have achieved a laudable degree of personal truth, and, thus, personal freedom. With the populations of the developed countries suffering from nearly every form of stress known to man, our industrialized and high-tech world is now made up of neurotic societies. Tens of thousands of potential heroes of our age remain personally bound up in the preoccupations of physical and psychological survival.

In this remarkable age during which stunning levels of human capability are made possible by highly-evolved levels of scientific know-how and a constant flow of breathtaking scientific breakthroughs—with their as yet unimaginable implications for our world—it is frighteningly obvious that we do not have a generally recognized technology for being human beings. We fall far short of being a match in consciousness for the highly sophisticated levels of technical capability which is at our disposal. As Jean Houston states in *The Possible Human*:

THE WAY TO SAVE OURSELVES AS A SPECIES IS TO SAVE OURSELVES AS INDIVIDUALS.

Never before has the responsibility of the human being for the planetary process been greater... This is a responsibility for which we have been ill prepared and for which the usual formulas and stop-gap solutions will not work...

We find ourselves in a time in which extremely limited consciousness has the powers once accorded to the gods. Extremely limited consciousness can

> *launch a nuclear holocaust with the single push of a button. Extremely limited consciousness can and does intervene directly in the genetic code, interferes with the complex patterns of life in the sea, and pours its wastes into the protective ozone layers that encircle the earth. Extremely limited consciousness is about to create a whole new energy base linking together computers, electronics, new materials from outer space, biofacture, and genetic engineering, which in turn will release a flood of innovation and external power unlike anything seen before in human history. In short, extremely limited consciousness is accruing to itself the powers of Second Genesis.*[9]

We have not been taught to understand ourselves and, thus, each other—and so, whole generations of humans live and die without achieving even a minimal level of true potential fulfillment. That, in itself, is tragic enough, when just beyond the confines of our lower minds lies the unlimited potency of whole dimensions of ourselves in dormancy, awaiting our possible moment of revelation and our subsequent plumbing of its powerful, wise and loving inherencies. More tragic still would be the (now possible) extinction of our species as the result of an irreversible cataclysm caused by highly-evolved technology in the hands of an unevolved consciousness—perhaps to gain power, money, or territory in the name of some self-righteous nationalistic, religious, or ethnic belief system.

A Course In Congruence is an important step in the right direction: it is a clear, fascinating, piece-by-piece working of the puzzle of self-discovery and self-expression. It is a simple way to begin to see ourselves as we have not been able to see ourselves before. It is a method by which we may begin to take charge of our thoughts, to become aware of our ever-changing emotional experience, and to make the high choices on our own behalf rather than making selfish decisions which leave us feeling empty and provide only fleeting experiences of satisfaction. The high choices always support our growth and empower us. They acknowledge and reference the higher, greater, dimension of our being; and they allow the unfoldment of our hidden nature to occur naturally.

What is missing these days in human beings who are otherwise capable, intelligent, and sincerely desirous of healthy and fully functioning lives is a strong sense of self. No one else can give us that self-sense. No *one experience* and no *lifetime of experiences* will give us that sense of self. Only the conscious process of self-awareness, Self-expression, and self-honesty will fulfill the ments of true self-discovery. And for that we need some understanding of the fundamentals of being human, which for so long was considered privileged information and reserved for psychology or psychiatry professionals. At this time, with neurosis lying like a plague upon the psyche of humankind, and with symptoms of that neurosis showing up in ever-increasing aberrated behaviors around the world (such as our children carrying guns and shooting each other), it is obvious that a little understanding can go a long way toward healing our own neurosis and assisting others to become the truth of themselves. *A Course In Congruence* can really help!

Congruence is an accurate matching of our inner experience and our outer expression; and becoming congruent eliminates inner conflict, neutralizes fear, generates self-trust, and puts us in charge of our life—with ease! *A Course In Congruence* is all about getting free—free from limited thinking; free from narrow perceptions; free from conditioned responses to circumstances, to people, and to life itself. It is actually about getting free from the ordinary, selfish, smallness of the damaged ego. This is *the* most important process for us as humans, for until we loosen the tight grip the ego has on us, we are helpless victims, psychologically caught in a world of disillusionment, confusion, pain, and fear. *A Course In Congruence* is about *how to* get free. It is about achieving access to the higher levels of human consciousness in order to experience a wider, higher, expanded sense of ourselves and of our world. It is about discovering our greatness, re-identifying with that greatness, making our choices from that greatness, and ultimately expressing that unique greatness in the world.

The leap in consciousness from the *reactive* third (mental-egoic) level to the *expressive* fifth (existential) level is the long-awaited transformation in humankind to which the great minds have been pointing down through the ages and to which so much attention is being given at this time by those whose lives are devoted to supporting a paradigm shift. As all of the scriptures have said—and as all of the great minds are still saying, the first step toward all that is possible for us in the future is the step of self-knowledge—"Know Thyself."

In his book, *Transforming #1*, Ron Smothermon suggests that for those who are still operating within the limitations of the ego—at the levels of opposition and disloyalty—it is as though they are in a box, "from which it is very difficult to escape, the instructions for escaping being printed on the outside of the box."[10] And, that being the case, they need someone who has been delivered from the box to read the instructions to them. It is this "reading of the instructions" by those who have gone before us which is so important to all of us as we make our journeys into still unfamiliar landscapes of being. As Ouspensky tells us, we need "sufficient help" from "those who began similar work before and have already attained a certain degree of development, or *at least* a certain knowledge of methods."[11] Because I have had those instructions read to me by others who have gone before me and have been liberated from the box, I now turn and read the instructions to others. In the following chapters, I will offer a simple perspective on the limitations which still bind our now quickly-expanding human consciousness. I will also provide an historical overview of the evolutionary process as it has unfolded in the consciousness of human beings. And I will present a methodology with which to process one's self and through which to achieve a level of clear, intelligent, and truthful Self-expression.

A Catalyst for Change

The purpose of *A Course in Congruence* is (1) to support the opening of the lower mind; (2) to bring awareness to the fact that we are imprisoned in our own minds and victimized by our own emotional experience, and to teach the fundamentals for achieving freedom from both conditions; (3) to catalyze a true leap in consciousness to the fifth level—the level of authenticity; and (4) to provide understanding regarding the following aspects of our humanity:

[a] the human emotional response
[b] the split of the ego: persona / shadow
[c] the damaged ego and its reactivity
[d] personal truth {the feeling function}
[e] Self-expression
[f] personal integrity {wholeness}
[g] personal power and personal freedom
[h] the distinctions between the lower self and the higher Self
[i] and more...

The way to heal our stricken Earth is to heal our individual psyches.

The purpose of *A Course in Congruence* is to provide a clear context, intelligent models, and a simple language to use in observing and examining one's inner and outer experiences and in processing oneself to the achievement of personal freedom through authentic self-discovery and genuine Self-expression.

From the tone of this first chapter, the reader may get a strong impression regarding the two ends of the continuum which I suggest must be consistently held in one's awareness: the end which we can call Remembering and the end which we can call LifeActions:

REMEMBERING	**LIFEACTIONS**
Thinking Big	Behaving as novices
The Big Picture	The present moment experience
The Evolutionary Imperative	Our human relationships
The Impulse for Evolvement	The precepts and practices
Our Inherent Greatness	Our daily expressions
Our Cosmic Source	Our earthly opportunities

As we go about our daily lives, we must remember the potential greatness which pulses within our minds and bodies—the higher consciousness awakening within our expanding capacity to receive and accommodate both its blessings and its responsibilities. To **real**ize, or make real, the still unfamiliar reality of evolutionary transformations occurring within our very psyches is a sometimes difficult challenge since we still live within the structures and thought-systems of a consensus with which we no longer agree. But, somewhere deep within, we secretly appreciate the difficulty and challenges in order to prove ourselves strong enough and ready enough to carry the banner for the whole species.

We are truly great beings—with a vast and awe-inspiring legacy of now forgotten cosmic and earthly evolutional epochs under our human belt. We are here on earth to shine forth our greatness for all to see and for all to benefit from. With no exceptions, we all yearn for full expression of that which remains unexpressed within us—that greatness whose brilliance still lies hidden from our hungry eyes.

Toward Expansion and Self-Mastery

1. Make a list of some of the things you notice that indicate that things are changing very quickly in our society.

2. Make a list of some of the things you notice that suggest that things are changing very dramatically in our world.

3. Make a mental note whenever you hear anyone speaking about transformation or the evolutionary Process.

4. Notice how often you would like to say something about the awakening that is occurring in our world.

5. Notice how often you do say something about the awakening that is occurring in our world.

6. Notice your own hesitancy to talk about the awakening that is occurring in our world—and discover what is causing that hesitancy.

7. Make it a practice to speak about the awakening that is occurring in our world on a daily basis. Begin speaking about it to people you already know well. When you have become comfortable with that level of expression, begin speaking about it to people you do not know very well or do not know at all.

8. Contemplate your own place in The Great Chain of Being. See yourself as the present head of a long lineage of evolving beings. Remember your ancestors, known and unknown, stretching back through time.

9. Clarify what it is that you feel a need to know, to understand, and to do at this time in order to move easily and quickly along your chosen path.

Let us remember
that we are the dawn
breaking on the horizon.

CHAPTER TWO

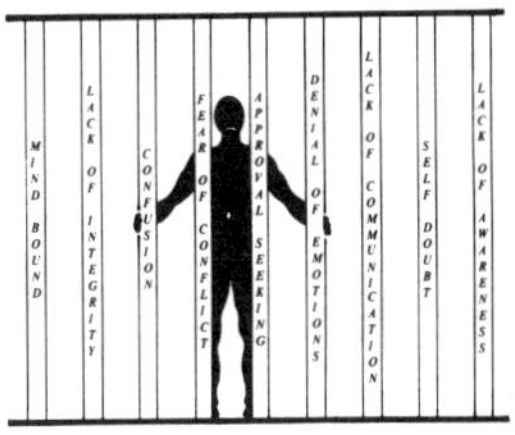

DISCOVERING OUR CAPTIVITY

> *A human being is a part of the whole that we call the universe, a part limited in time and space. He experiences himself, his thoughts and feelings, as something separated from the rest—a kind of optical illusion of his consciousness. This illusion is a prison for us, restricting us to our personal desires and to affection for only the few people nearest to us. Our task must be to free ourselves from this prison by widening our circle of compassion to embrace all living beings and all of nature.*
>
> —*ALBERT EINSTEIN*[1]

A MOMENT OF TRUTH

There comes a moment for some of us when we realize that we have been living our lives in an attempt to *fit in*, to be an acceptable member of whatever group we happen to find ourselves in, and to gain the approval of others. This realization runs deep because it clarifies for us that we have been invalidating ourselves in an unsuccessful series of attempts to gain approval, to achieve success, and to prove to ourselves and to convince others that we are really wonderful human beings who deserve respect.

We see that we have been able to gain the approval of some people, that we have achieved some success in the world, and that we have earned the respect of a number of persons with whom we have related along the way. But we see that, without a doubt, we have not expressed ourselves truthfully; we have not felt easy and comfortable in the world; and, most importantly, we have not achieved a real sense of personal satisfaction, self-fulfillment and self-respect.

From that moment on we are ready to begin to discover our own individual truth and to stop living our lives out of what we feel are other people's expectations, judgments and demands. We actually are able to see clearly that we have been held captive by our own desires to win, to look good, to be right, and to survive—at least in terms of maintaining a sense of security by preserving the status quo.

For many of us, the moment of truth comes sometime in our maturity, after we have had ample opportunity to experience the real-life results of our uninformed approach to the world and to our relationships. But many "twentysomethings" and "thirtysomethings" are now quite conscious that their repertoire of behaviors is producing results which fall far short of fulfillment and a strong sense of self. These days, even adolescents who are given a safe space and the correct information by which to gauge their experiences, are able to clearly see that their own dishonest actions in relationships have caused them suffering, loss of self-esteem and a nagging sense of dissatisfaction.

Once we see what has been going on, we realize that all the sincere desires, all the pulling ourselves up by our boot-straps, and all the "new starts" have been futile in some very real sense. We realize that we, and many others we know, live inside a self-made prison cell, incarcerated by our own fears, misunderstandings, and ineffective behavior patterns. And, we understand that until the prison cell is dismantled, bar-by-bar, we can have no lasting experience of personal freedom and no confidence that we can create and maintain a life that is a congruent expression of our own personality (our individual human identity). The prison cell can be disassembled by achieving understanding about the psychological factors which define our present captivity. And where the bars of our prison cell once stood, we will find an opening for ourselves through which to experience and express our fully-human greatness. As with any other type of learning, we must first have a clear understanding as to the present reality, and then, some specific information about how to effect a change.

As was stated earlier, the purpose of *A Course In Congruence* includes 1) expanding our awareness of the fact that we are imprisoned in our own minds and victimized by our own emotional experience, and 2) teaching the fundamentals for achieving freedom from both conditions. As we have all always secretly known, personal freedom is available only through being the truth of who we are. What we are learning now is that congruence is the discovery of that personal truth and the expression of that personal freedom.

LIKE A FLOWER, WE WILL BUD AND BLOOM,
UNFOLDING THE PETALS OF OUR UNIQUE BEAUTY
FOR ALL THE WORLD TO SEE.

A PERSONAL PRISON

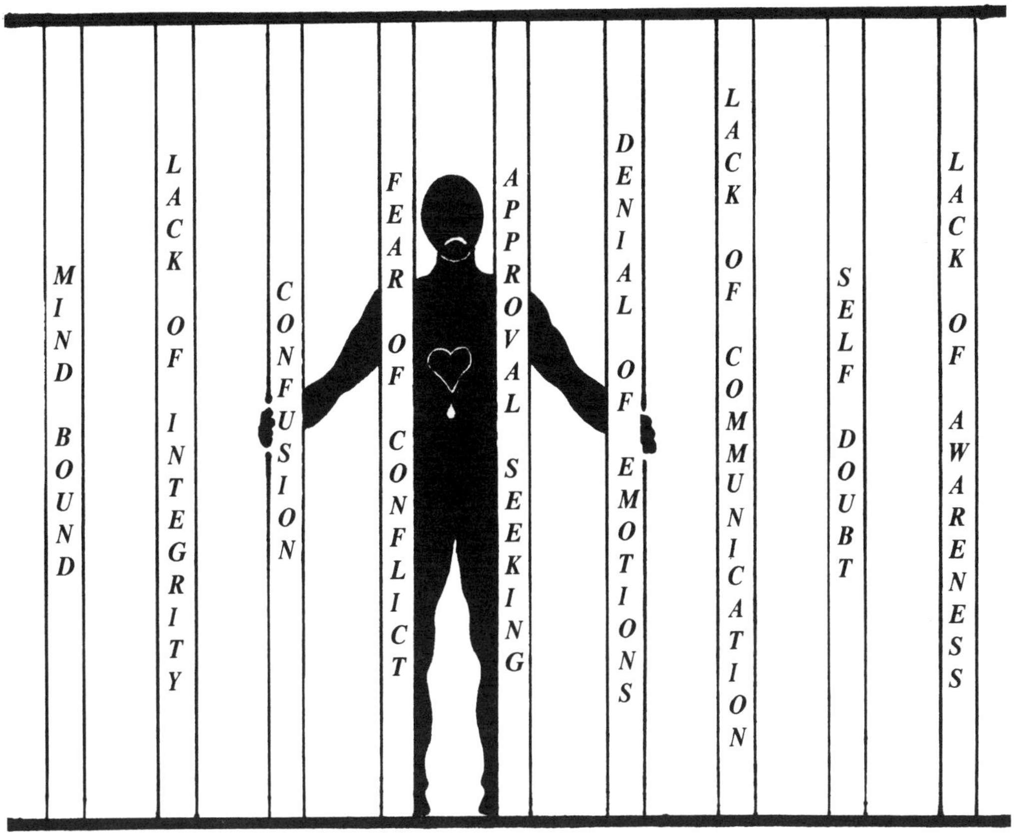

Figure No. 1

The personal prison model [Figure No. 1] is a simple representation of a human being who stands sadly gripping the bars of his own self-made prison cell. The bars of the prison cell represent certain acculturated psychological conditions which are intrinsic to the third level of consciousness—the mental-egoic level. There are other bars which could have been included in the prison, but I have chosen some of the primary conditions which impede easy access to one's greatness to for the purposes of this discussion. Other primary conditions will be given a different treatment later in the book.

What I have depicted in this model is an amazing human being who contains, within his God-given biological and psychological make-up, an encoded potential for greatness way beyond his ability to grasp, to fathom, to imagine, or to express. That vast potential is said to include all of the elements and all of the possibilities that are contained within Creation. That immeasurable potency is said to be the same "stuff" of which the universes, the galaxies, the star systems, and the stars, themselves, are made. That "stuff" is the pulsant evolutionary force of Creation Itself. And since Creation holds within its Infinite Intelligence *infinite* possibilities, this human likewise contains within itself those very possibilities. Because the impulse of Creation is the spiraling impulse toward transformation to the next higher order of consciousness, that impulse is primary in this human being.

But, instead of enjoying the fascinating spiral of the transformational process as the reality of his own life, this despairing human stands alone and impotent, with frowning face and crying heart, behind prison bars which belie his effulgent greatness. Locked in the closed system of his lower mind's limited perceptions, this great being sadly experiences himself as not equal to the circumstances and challenges of his late twentieth-century life. The sadness has become chronic because everyday he arises from his slumber with a sincere desire to be successful in relationships, successful at work, and successful in feeling comfortable here in the world. But that success has eluded his reach; and, as we look at the bars of his prison cell, we can see why that sincerely sought-after success has not been achieved. We can see that there can be no realization of his dreams of success until the light of understanding is shone on the areas of his own human function which presently hold him captive.

WE REALIZE THAT WE LIVE INSIDE A SELF-MADE PRISON CELL, INCARCERATED BY OUR OWN FEARS, MISUNDERSTANDINGS, AND INEFFECTIVE BEHAVIOR PATTERNS.

With the impulse for more growing stronger, with the need for Self-expression becoming urgent, and with the level of personal frustration skyrocketing, this human attempts again and again to "figure things out," to "put things into perspective," and to "examine new strategies" which may cause the changes in his life for which he fervently longs. Although not understood as such, those longed-for changes always equate to longed-for transformations which provide a personal state of being beyond the limited mental-egoic state which now holds him in its confusing, painful and fearful grasp.

Mindbound. Trapped in a condition I call mindbound, this immensely potent being, whose very cells remember the great silence of deep space, now stands by while his overactive mental capacity dredges up memories of its personal past and ruminates on them over and over again in an attempt to resolve the conflicts within himself—or just to reminisce about "the good old days." It also creates plans, spins fantasies and generates scenarios about the future which it then, often, worries about. It pumps out great idea after brilliant idea, which it rarely acts on, since it cannot seem to get past the limited experience of mentalizing its life, rather than living it. It continuously passes judgment on everyone and everything with which it comes into contact or about which it randomly thinks—giving all persons, places, and things its personal rating as to whether they are "good" or "bad" and as to whether it "likes" or "dislikes" them. In this mindbound condition, the innately potent being listens to the inner dialogue of his own mind talking to itself, and unconsciously believes what he is listening to. Rarely is there any intervention from his greaterness to stop, curb, or correct the endless series of random and endarkened thoughtforms which his self-contained mind generates. What a terrible trap!

The more confused we become, the more we live our lives in our minds. The mind works overtime in an attempt to "figure it all out"—to find a solution, to put together the difficult-to-match pieces of the baffling puzzle of our life. We lose touch with the strong signals being sent to us from our own feeling level, from the physical body which begins to manifest discomfort and disease, and from our intuitive self, which knows this is not the way to do it.

The more confused we become, the more questions we generate. The more questions we generate, the more mindbound we become. The more mindbound we are, the more confused we become and the more questions our mind generates. We become prisoners of our own minds.

This is what our prisoner must expect until an opening occurs in his closed mind system and until he makes some conscious, highly-intelligent effort to free himself—a particular type of effort which is based in understanding of himself and the particular methods which do effect a particular type of change.

THE PRISON CAN BE DISASSEMBLED BY ACHIEVING UNDERSTANDING ABOUT THE PYSCHOLOGICAL FACTORS WHICH DEFINE OUR PRESENT CAPTIVITY

Lack of Integrity. Suffering from lack of psychological integrity, this great oceanic being randomly operates out of a tiny piece of his wholeness which we call the ego. The word integrity is a form of the word "integrate," which is a Latin word meaning "to form or blend into a whole." Lack of integrity, then, means that we lack wholeness or union of the different aspects of ourselves. The word integrity further denotes "soundness," "incorruptibility," "completeness," and "honesty." Integration is "coordination of mental processes into a normal, effective personality."[2] In terms of our own captivity, our lives are certainly not sound, unified, complete, and honest expressions of our wholeness until we are a unified personality expressing itself in the world. And the "acting as if," which we do in order to fulfill our little will's agenda, obstructs our growth toward becoming integritous.

As Ouspensky states in *The Psychology of Man's Possible Evolution*:

> *Man cannot move, think, or speak of his own accord. He is a marionette pulled here and there by invisible strings. If he understands this, he can learn more about himself, and possibly then things may begin to change for him. But if he cannot realize and understand his* ***utter mechanicalness****, or if he does not wish to accept it as a fact, he can learn nothing more, and things cannot change for him.*
>
> ***Man is a machine****, but a very peculiar machine. He is a machine which, in right circumstances, and with right treatment, can know that he is a machine, and having fully realized this, he may find the ways to cease to be a machine.*
>
> *First of all, what man must know is that he is not one; he is many. He has not one permanent and unchangeable "I" or Ego. He is always different. One moment he is one, another moment he is another, the third moment he is a third, and so on, almost without an end.*[3]

The point is that the ego has no center, but is, instead, a random accumulation of predictable and always changing thoughts, feelings, sensations, desires, likes and dislikes, which arise on an unpredictable schedule as reactions to outside stimuli.

---

[2]By permission. From Webster's Third New International Dictionary ©1986 by Merriam-Webster, Inc., Publisher of the Merriam-Webster® dictionaries.

As Ouspensky's model [Figure No. 2] illustrates:

> *Every thought, every feeling, every sensation, every desire, every like and every dislike is an "I." These "I's" are not connected and are not coordinated in any way. Each of them depends on the change in external circumstances, and on the change of impressions.*
>
> *Some of them mechanically follow some others, and some appear always accompanied by others. But there is no order and no system in that.*
>
> *There are certain groups of "I's" which are naturally connected....there are groups of "I's" connected only by accidental associations, accidental memories, or quite imaginary similarities.*
>
> *Each of these "I's" represents at every given moment a very small part of our "brain," "mind," or "intelligence," but each of them means itself to represent* **the whole**. *When man says "I" it sounds as if he meant the whole of himself, but really even when he himself thinks that he means it, it is only a passing thought, a passing mood, or a passing desire. In an hour's time he may completely forget it, and with the same conviction express an opposite opinion, opposite view, opposite interests.*[4]

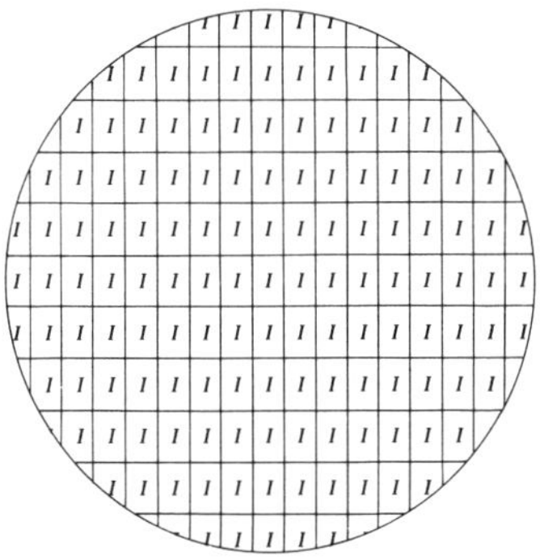

Figure No. 2

The "I's" to which our prisoner gives expression, then, are separate momentary identities which together make up the unintegrated (unhealed) ego. They are pieces of himself. They are fragments that say, "I think," "I like," "I don't like," etc. These are not derived from the central truth of himself. When he says "I think," "I feel," "I like," etc., he is merely giving voice to a transitory opinion and assigning his identity to it. When he acts out of one of these strong opinions, he is acting out of a cursory thought about himself, a meaningless belief about who he is, or a narrow view he holds of his larger personality. At any given time, the fragmented ego is a repository of a random commingling of some of its many accumulated reactions. Since the haphazard selection of thoughts, feelings, sensations, desires, likes, and dislikes changes so quickly and directly influences his decisions, he cannot count on himself to follow through on anything he says he will do. As his moods and focus change, so do his levels of commitment to any previous intention.

Carol Pearson states that "...integrity...means living fully in keeping with one's deepest self."[5] When we become the truth of ourselves and say "I think," the person receiving that communication knows that we really mean it, that we stand for what we say, and that there is no separation between what we say and the central truth of ourselves—that it is not just a little piece of ourselves, but a Truthful expression which is rooted in our wholeness.

Confusion. This exceptional being, whose subatomic structure duplicates the subatomic structure of the universe itself, suffers tremendous confusion about himself as a human being, about others and the way they think and act, about human life and its meaning, and about the world in which he lives. The meaningful questions he has asked since he was a small child—when he first asked, "Mommy, where did I come from?"—have, for the most part been responded to with less-than-meaningful answers. And although he has learned so many things about his country (its early explorers, the Constitution, the Gold Rush, etc.), some things about other countries, some things about the Earth, the sky, and more, he does not have a view that allows him to really understand how it all fits together. And although he has been taught to read, to write, to do mathematics, and even to excel at some profession, his understanding about himself and his life still lacks the kind of context which would make his days and nights meaningful experiences which are a part of an ever-evolving, mysterious, and highly-intelligent unfoldment of a significant lifetime.

We know we are confused about how to do life and how to be in relationships long before we have a full realization that our attempts to get it right have left us unsuccessful and unfulfilled. And, as we reflect on the various strategies we have employed in an attempt to make success happen, we see that we have created a tangle of confusion for ourselves by assuming different attitudes and different behaviors for different lengths of time with the same general result.

Confusion, of course, feeds self-doubt, which feeds the avoidance of conflict, the denial of emotions, and approval-seeking behavior—all of which contribute to our growing sense of overall confusion. It is a vicious and painful, self-perpetuating circle from which we seem unable to escape.

It becomes shockingly apparent that we human beings really need to be taught to understand ourselves as the particular type of psychological beings we are at this time in our evolutionary unfoldment. We need to understand that our mental-egoic level of consciousness represents a limited stage of evolution from which we can access the higher dimensions of being by way of relinquishing control strategies and aligning ourselves with the subtle dimensions of our nature. And from that transcendent point of view, we can perceive ourselves and our world through the eyes of our greaterness.

Conflict is an opportunity to resolve differences in perceptions, expectations, and approaches to producing results.

Fear of Conflict. This ferocious hero, whose very blood contains the elements which make up the mighty oceans, fears conflict! He has often been immobilized by fear of confrontation and does whatever he can to avoid upsetting disagreements with others. An angry clash with another person can cause him to feel bad about himself and sometimes cause him to plunge into protracted periods of depression. And even when episodes of contention are resolved without much strife, he often experiences self-doubt afterward and wishes the difference of opinion had not occurred. He may subsequently be overly "nice" to the other person for some time in order to re-establish feelings of security within himself.

When he loses control to the anger energy which floods his body and mind during a "major upset," he may stay angry at the person or about the subject for days, weeks, months, or years. Since he is not able to "get over it" or to "let it go," he experiences being "stuck in it" and feels helpless to free himself.

When he is confronted by someone who is angry, he sometimes "goes blank," and is unable to respond appropriately in the moment. In those cases, he will usually attempt to defend himself and/or appease the other person during the interval of the confront; but, later, when he is alone, he may be overwhelmed by a sense of outrage way out of proportion to the confront he has received.

His unconscious attitude is that anger ruins relationships and destroys the image of himself that he so conscientiously attempts to put forth to the world. His self-styled image of "being fine" and "having his act together" leaves little room for angry conflicts—so he does what he can to avoid them.

Whether or not we have been exposed to a lot of conflict in our lives, by the time we find ourselves in our young adulthood, with our personal agenda to serve, we have usually built up a real aversion to conflict with others. We have not been taught that conflict is to be expected in our relationships, that conflict is an opportunity to resolve differences in perceptions, differences in expectations, and differences in approaches to producing results. Instead, conflict represents to us nasty encounters which cause upsets and damage already precarious relationships. Conflicts are avoided since we perceive them to be obstacles to achievement of our goals.

In avoiding conflict, we actually avoid truthful relationship, deny our emotional responses, and act like everything is "fine" in an attempt to get what we want. Sometimes we do get what we want in the short term, but whenever we avoid conflict in the outer world, that conflict is stored in our inner reservoir, which causes us personal turmoil on all three levels—physical, emotional, and mental.

In avoiding conflict we withhold ourselves from others, resent the fact that we are unable to be who we really are in the relationship, blame the other person, and assume the role of victim to some degree in that relationship. The next time we find ourselves approaching a point of conflict in the relationship, we remember that we have already been victimized by that person, and most likely repeat the same behaviors used before in order to avoid conflict and get by. The pattern is set.

Approval-Seeking Behavior. This remarkable, unique human being, whose consciousness includes the force of Creation and whose chemistry includes the stuff that giant stars are made of, constantly seeks the approval of others in order to get by and to get what he wants. He deeply desires acceptance and love. His repertoire of approval-seeking behaviors began to be developed when he was a fragile and dependent baby. On through his childhood, adolescence, and young adulthood, he continued developing an assortment of behavioral strategies which he could be fairly sure would evoke in others their approval (acceptance and love) of him. He still falls back on those coping mechanisms today.

The level of approval seeking behavior in our lives is downright shocking when we begin to become aware of it. Even the seemingly most "together" person will find it a revelation when he begins to get honest about this aspect of his human relations. Our fear of rejection is very real throughout our lives until we actually accept that we are going to experience rejection by some people no matter what we do. It is simply not possible for us to satisfy the expectations of all with whom we have relationships, and, thus, gain their approval; and to make the attempt is manipulative and foolhardy.

We do our best as children to gain the approval of our parents and teachers and other grown-up people. We truly need and desire their support. But, even those trusted adults reject some of our attempts to please them, and we suffer the confusion, pain, and fear that such rejection causes in us.

When we become aware that we have been seeking approval from nearly everyone with whom we are in relationship, we are ready to begin to become congruent.

Our pre-adolescence and adolescence is marked by exaggerated attempts to gain the favor of our peer group. We go to extremes, perhaps, in dressing ourselves, in speaking in certain ways, in engaging in "risky business," in listening to the "right" music, and in manifesting other approval-seeking behaviors in order to be "one of the gang."

Young adulthood presents us with a whole new panorama of relationships and motivations for practicing our approval-seeking behavior. The desire to make it in the world and the desire to make it in an intimate relationship drives us to perform by the surefire, certain-to-produce-results method: putting our best foot forward by showcasing only the self-created image of ourselves which we feel fairly sure will be accepted rather than rejected.

By the time we reach our thirties and forties, we are so chewed up inside by the past failures we have experienced, by the conflict which has been generated in our enturbulated psyches, and by our still unmet needs, that our neurosis strongly influences our choice-making, sending us down yet another dead-end run of the maze, where we once again hit the wall of our own disingenuous strategies.

When we become aware that we have been seeking approval from nearly everyone with whom we are in relationship—and that it is an obstacle to our own growth and is causing us tremendous personal conflict—we are ready to begin to become congruent, authentic, genuine, real.

Denial of Emotions. This astonishing human, in whose genetic code resides the creative formulas for the blazing sun and the reflective moon, denies important components of his emotional experience, the capacity for which distinguishes him from all other creatures and all other life forms on Earth. Since he has been victimized by his own emotions (because he was never taught to understand them), he is not able to allow himself to have the whole range of the human emotional response. Because some of his emotions are so painful, so scary, or so confusing to him, he tries to be emotionally "fine" most of the time. And when he is not fine he attempts to appear to be fine in the eyes of others.

Along the way, he gained a strong impression that in order to elicit the acceptance of himself by others, he must deny that he has certain emotions toward people whose disapproval can threaten his security. He overrides his emotional responses with his will to survive and attempts to maintain the status quo at all costs. He actually uses his will to suppress his emotional responses in order to serve his need to fit in and to become successful.

For example, we may recall times when we felt outraged at the demands being placed on us. We may have felt deeply the injustice, the inappropriateness, and/or the abuse of that treatment. But, instead of honoring that strongly felt inner truth, we may have continued to meet the demands of the situation with the hope that we would gain approval, respect, acceptance, and/or love. In many cases, however, meeting the outrageous demands may only have identified us as someone who could be counted on to produce impressive results under unscrupulous duress rather than accruing to us what we had hoped for.

As we continue to suppress our own emotional responses and to act like everything is just fine, we fill ourself with anger and sadness. We become a walking timebomb of emotional suppression, filled to overflowing with pain and resentments. This ticking bomb can be detonated unexpectedly by a clerk at the candy store, by a driver in front of us on the expressway, or by our lover (or anyone) who does not respond in the way we want him or her to respond.

Lack of Communication. Brian Swimme tells us in *The Universe Is a Green Dragon*, "Self-expression is the primary sacrament of the universe. Whatever you feel deeply needs to be given form and released."[6] However, this potent human being, in whom the impulse for Self-expression is overwhelmingly strong, is curiously lacking in communication. He withholds truthful communication in order to gain the approval of others and, so, to get by in the world. So often he wants to tell others how he feels about them and about many things, but he is afraid they will not understand him and/or that they will judge him harshly. Because his sense of self is so fragile and because of his nagging self-doubts, he often fearfully chooses not to take the chance of being misunderstood. Because his need for expression is so strong, he suffers the agonizing condition of being unexpressed. This lack of Self-expression has serious implications for him. It sets him up to exaggerate his feelings for anyone with whom he feels he can express himself—in other words, he may "fall in love" with them even though other important aspects of the relationship are detrimental to his well-being. His lack of Self-expression may also make him an easy mark for political, religious, or social causes which will give him some forum in which to voice an extremist message with which he then becomes identified.

And, in most of his relationships, although he withholds his thoughts and feelings, he expects others to understand who he is, what he thinks, and how he feels; and when they do not (which is most of the time), he experiences hurtful disappointment. The dilemma presents itself once again: How should he *act* in order to get what he wants, while, at the same time, avoiding conflict and gaining approval.

Self-Doubt. This human being, in whom the infinite possibilities of Creation Itself reside, lamentably suffers the debilitating condition of self-doubt. Nagging self-doubt is the psychological sinkhole which undermines all of his relational transactions and is the source of his low self-esteem. Any time this person gains some level of self-confidence, he is easily plunged back into self-doubt either by circumstances which overwhelm him or by other people's expectations, judgments and demands of him. It is self-doubt for which he overcompensates with attitudes of self-important arrogance, defensive rationalization, and pretentious posturing. It is also self-doubt which brings him to his knees in episodes of self-hatred and which oppresses him with experiences of disempowerment—of "I can't."

The more we separate ourselves from others, the more approval-seeking behavior we employ, the more we avoid conflict and deny our emotional responses, and the more self-doubtful we become. As the self-doubt grows, we more often choose approval-seeking behavior, avoidance of conflict, and denial of emotions. As this vicious cycle becomes well-established in our relationships, our loss of self-sense expands and our confusion increases—generating still more self-doubt.

Lack of Awareness. This magnificent being whose heart beats to the rhythm of the universe and in whom the unlimited possibilities of the cosmos abide, suffers a pervasive lack of awareness. He has tunnel vision, the limitations of which make it possible for him to see only narrow segments of what is going on in himself, in others, and in the world. This condition exists simply because his capacities for expanded perceptions have not been developed. In fact, he has been deceived by the narrow perceptions of others from the time he was a baby. Most of the people around him suffer the same debilitation—which is truly a state of blindness to the spacious inherencies of humanity.

With the innate need for expansion into the greatness of his Self, his limited awareness acts as a deficiency which blocks his growth. As a closed system—in a condition of self-contraction—his view gets narrower as he gets older, and he becomes more cynical and hardened. The only way that this human being, or any human being, can free himself from his personal prison is by way of a growing awareness of the "bigger picture" and through expression of truth.

Although we become self-conscious very early in our lives, we lack self-awareness until we begin to become truly honest with ourselves—until we begin to look into ourselves for our own deeper truth: our real thoughts and feelings on the whole spectrum of our experiences and relationships.

Aspirants for Liberation

It is plain to see that even in this land of excessive material abundance and outstanding opportunity to achieve high levels of financial and professional success, we are not supported—either by our democratic society or by our particular culture within that society—to discover and express the very truth of ourselves. It is glaringly evident that in this "land of freedom"—**we are not free**. It is crucial that we now demand of ourselves the disciplines, the high-minded actions, and the effective methods which will provide intelligent support for the transformation of our vast potential to the next higher order of consciousness.

The only possibility we have for creating relationships that work over the long term and for creating lives that are personally satisfying and fulfilling is to become a truthful expression of our own individuality—that is, to become congruent.

The process of self-discovery and Self-expression is a most fascinating one. The healthy changes that begin to manifest quickly in our relationship to ourselves and others is quite surprising and impressive. Once we begin to get the hang of being congruent, an experience of personal empowerment and personal freedom supports us to continue our practice, to give ourselves more permission to be honest, to allow ourselves to become more and more fully human.

Virginia Burden Tower, in *The Process of Intuition*, draws a distinction for us between the "integrated" man and the "aspirant for liberation." This distinction is highly relevant within the discussion of transformation to the next higher order of consciousness—which *A Course In Congruence* implies.

> *But, what, now, is the difference between what the esotericist calls a liberated man...and a mature or well-integrated man as measured by professional psychological criteria? We have devised ways to test the comparative adjustability of human beings; the degree to which one is able to live in a state of relative peace in relationship to the challenge of his environment and the inner struggles which this is likely to produce. Where there is an ability to accept a challenge with poise and equilibrium, to make choices with clarity, and to abide by these choices; and withal, to find an experience of joy and satisfaction in living, then we say that the individual is mature and has mental and emotional health.*
>
> *...Not so the aspirant for liberation. His propensities are such and his will so abnormally strong that he must rapidly evoke all the trials attendant upon the destruction of the barrier which holds him from the universe of reality which he senses within and beyond his immediate environment. There has not been a religious teacher or philosopher throughout history of any stature who has not, in one way or another, alluded to the condition of man as though he were imprisoned.*[7]

The point is that in *A Course In Congruence* we are exploring the psychological condition which is endemic to integration at the extremely limited third level of consciousness and the psychological condition which is endemic to the consciousness which has experienced transformation to the authentic and self-expressive (fifth) level of consciousness. The states of being which the sixth and seventh levels of consciousness represent are only perfunctorily alluded to here as dimensions of being which hold still unimaginable possibilities for us as a species.

It is the thesis of this work that the man who is integrated at the mental-egoic level of consciousness[8] will—due to the implicit nature of that level—experience a nagging *dis-ease*, the subconscious source of which is the sense of separation with which the ego imbues all of his relationships. The split in his psyche which has occurred through the normal course of human growth and development (and which will be discussed at length in the chapter on the ego) has resulted in such a dramatic diminishment of his sense of who he is that he operates out of a fragmented awareness of his greaterness and thinks, speaks, and acts out of tiny pieces of himself. Given this "Fallen" state, he constantly struggles against a stifling experience of captivity at the hands of an invisible captor. Unknowingly, he suspects his parents, his teachers, his friends, his age, his jobs, his lovers, his bosses, his circumstances, his income, (or other people, places or things) to be his captors; and, in various direct or indirect ways, he struggles against them in an attempt to set himself free. Instead, the real captor is the level of consciousness at which he is operating.

The man who is integrated at the existential (fifth) level of consciousness, in contrast, experiences himself, others, and his world through the eyes of his Self and feels an indescribable sense of release for which he has longed. He becomes naturally spontaneous and authentically Self-expressive. The splits within his psyche are healed to the point that he enjoys a self-accepting reunion with huge portions of his humanity from which he has long suffered separation; namely, his previously-rejected shadow and his body.

With authenticity still not well supported in our society, it will take a courageous effort to begin, continue and complete the journey of self-discovery and Self-expression.

Returning to the distinction between the integrated man and the aspirant for liberation and the implications of that distinction in *A Course In Congruence*, the point is that only the type of readiness implicit in the description of the aspirant for liberation will do, if one intends to become one's true Self—one's real, authentic, genuine, congruent self. Only with such an "abnormally strong will" can one "rapidly evoke" and, then, withstand "all the trials attendant upon the destruction of the barrier which holds him from the universe of reality." With authenticity still not well supported in our society and within our cultures, it will take a courageous effort on the individual's part in order to begin, to continue, and to complete the hero's journey of self-discovery and Self-expression. It is for the fearless hero who still stands captive behind those prison bars that I write this book. It is to the silent call within that hero that I add my call to greatness. It is with the inner applause of that hero's Self that I will join in cheering as the bars on his prison cell evaporate in the light of understanding. And it is for the whole world that I will cheer, as that cosmic hero steps forth to give his special gifts to this world-in-need-of-heroes.

> *Lay down your fear. Lay down your reason. Leave the past behind. And prepare yourself for transformation.*
>
> *There are preparatory steps as individuals approach the point where they are open to transformation. But the actual transformation is not a sequential process. It is not a complicated ritual. It can occur in the twinkling of an eye. It only involves one step, one decision, one event. When it takes place, it is as easy as breathing, as simple as a smile. Suddenly, you just know; suddenly, you know on a level of certainty that precludes all knowledge. Your eyes clear, and you see for the first time what lies beyond the prison wall, and you jump. You jump into the unknown: alive, alert, aware for the first time of who you really are. When you are ready to make that leap, you will* ***know****. There will be no other choice.*[9]

We have felt the restrictions and hateful constraints of our personal prison for most of our lives. By consistently bringing our awareness to our self-imposed imprisonment, we begin to neutralize the power of our own conditioned thinking. With a heightened awareness of our tendencies to stand within our self-made prison—behind psychological bars which hold us captive—we can begin to consciously choose to *express* rather than *suppress* ourselves as we move through our days relating to other human beings. As we observe ourselves feeling/thinking one way and acting/saying another, we begin to understand the distinct difference between our inner experience and our outer expression—as well as the psychological conflict which that untruthful way of living generates. As we choose congruent Self-expression over incongruent same-saying or rebellion, we easily notice the experience of personal satisfaction and personal empowerment which naturally results. We feel freer.

By consistently bringing awareness to our self-imposed imprisonment, we begin to neutralize the power of our own conditioned thinking.

YOUR PERSONAL PRISON

1. How are you feeling "stuck," "caught," "trapped" these days?

___By My Circumstances
___By Certain People
___By My Job
___By Choices I Made Some Time Ago
___By My Fear
___By Relationships I Have Outgrown
___By My Own Thoughts and Feelings

2. What are the strongest bars of your prison cell?

___Mindbound
___Approval-Seeking Behavior
___Lack of Integrity
___Lack of Self-Awareness
___Lack of Communication
___Fear of Conflict
___Self-Doubt

Toward Expansion and Self-Mastery

1. Identify which bars on the prison cell are the bars which most serve to keep you separated from others and captured within your own prison.

2. Notice on a daily basis when you begin to employ relational strategies which are directly derived from the bars of the prison cell.

3. Practice consciously intervening to stop all prison-cell behaviors, which have become conditioned responses. For example, if you begin to act in ways which are meant to gain you approval, pause and make the choice not to act like that.

4. Make a list of all of the people whose approval you have been seeking by being less than honest.

5. Make a list of all of the people with whom you fear conflict.

6. Make a list of all of the people who cause you to have serious self-doubt.

7. Begin to bring awareness to how often you are mindbound. When you realize that you have been captured by your own thinking processes, intervene by consciously choosing what it is you will think about. Bring your thoughts to a higher level.

8. Begin to soften your strong opinions and detach your identity from them by saying, "Right now, I think this. I know my opinion may change."

9. Practice expanding your awareness by bringing more attention to what is going on around you as you remain attentive to your inner experience.

10. Practice remaining silent unless you have something of real value to communicate. Notice how often you are tempted to chit-chat or say things just to fill the void when a conversation begins to languish.

LET US RECOGNIZE
THAT WE ARE THE FAINT LIGHT
ILLUMINATING THE DARKNESS.

CHAPTER THREE

Judgments: A Plague on Our House

It is not difficult to relinquish judgment. But it is difficult indeed to try to keep it. The teacher of God lays it down happily the instant he recognizes its cost. All of the ugliness he sees about him is its outcome. All of the pain he looks upon is its result. All of the loneliness and sense of loss; of passing time and growing hopelessness; of sickening despair and fear of death; all these have come of it. And now he knows that these things need not be. Not one is true. For he has given up their cause, and they, which never were but the effects of his mistaken choice, have fallen from him.

—*A Course in Miracles*[1]

Judgments as Lethal Weapons

Our individual and collective human psyches are suffering shock, and our individual and collective human hearts are full of despair these days, as a result of the widespread use of lethal weapons by a broad cross-section of our world community. We subconsciously agonize because the "War Lords" of Somalia and their bands of gun-wielding outlaws brought their whole country to its famished knees. We are anguished because the well-armed and sanctimonious Serbians have militarily filched the rights of the people of Bosnia-Herzegovina and have most-brutally carried out an "ethnic cleansing" before our eyes. We are pained that the hateful neo-Nazis of Germany flagrantly and indiscriminately act out their venomous "rights" to draw down on foreigners. We are tormented because South Africans still shoot to kill each other daily; because Israelis and Palestinians stage genocidal attacks upon each other in the Gaza Strip, and because Irishmen and Englishmen regularly set bombs of destruction against each other, mutilating and killing the innocent people of their lands. We are shocked that two eleven-year-old boys in London abducted and beat to death a two-year-old child for no reason; and we are grievous because of all the other atrocities that mankind is perpetrating upon mankind.

We are, likewise, distressed because our country is most certainly not exempt. In the United States, adults regularly abduct, sexually molest, and violently murder young children, leaving their ravaged bodies in fields, in shallow graves, in rivers or lakes. And "random acts of senseless violence" have become the frightful to-be-expected offenses perpetrated on our citizenry in any location—office, street, automobile, shopping mall, restaurant, commuter train, or home.

We all know that in the grade schools, middle schools, and high schools of our own country, children are arming themselves in preparation for their school day. Otherwise bright, intelligent, and loving children are assuming and acting out the roles of judge, jury, and executioner, by way of the oversimplified judicial process of judging another child wrong, and, then, stabbing or shooting that child for his/her wrongness.

Of course, our children were born neither with the psychological twist nor the practical know-how implicit in their present-day actions. They have learned all they know from adult role models who have demonstrated both the mentality and the behaviors of these most-harmful violations of others—violations which are based solely in their own dispassionate judgment of those they harm. Our children now, as always, mirror us back to ourselves.

Our children, alone and as members of gangs, are shocking us into taking a more direct and more honest look at ourselves. They are causing us to sincerely ask, "Where have we gone wrong?" And the answer resounds with a simple, undeniable, clarity: "We have judged each other harshly." "We have given ourselves the right to violate each other's humanity with our cruel judgments." Our severe judgments of other human beings need only the extension of themselves in the form of cold, hard steel for them to achieve the full expression of their self-righteous anger.

We must evoke the spirit of tolerance, acceptance and respect in those children who have become captured by the power of their own disillusioned anger.

In this Information Age, our media has fed our children's unprogrammed innocence from a database of violence in the forms of comic books, cartoons, television sitcoms, big-screen movies, music videos, and the evening news. In this age of high technology, our children's videos games have taught them to kill. In this age of protests for racial rights, women's rights, mothers' rights, fathers' rights, children's rights, gay rights, life rights, death rights, and the right to choose, some of our children have wrested from their elders the right to determine right and wrong and to implement shockingly violent solutions to what would otherwise be negotiable childhood problems.

Some of our children have learned at remarkably early ages the lessons of retribution through violent acts, which they have been tutored in by their high-tech "games," by the media, and by their elders. They have become conversant in the software or terminology of violence; they have become familiar with the hardware or weapons of violence; and, they have acted out their harsh judgments of each other in the various styles they have seen offered as appropriate means for effecting dramatic resolutions.

Our uncharitable judgments are fraught with the attitude of "I am right, and you are wrong!" and they generate in us a well of seething anger which can only be emptied by true understanding. I recall the childhood defense strategy my brother, sister, and I would employ to protect ourselves against each other's judgmental attacks: "Sticks and stones may break my bones, but words will never hurt me." Some of our children have now demonstrated that words are no longer strong enough stuff for them to use either to attack each other or to defend themselves from one another.

We are now simply seeing the ghastly consequences which accrue when we enhance the power of our judgments by giving these strong opinions strong weapons with which to express themselves. What a horror! Have the children of our species ever been this warlike before? Have generations of human children ever before been so devoid of human conscience? Have generations of human children ever before been so full of hateful reactivity that they are incapable of feeling the "wrongness" of their actions? Have generations of human children ever before been so well-programmed in the mentality of retribution? Have generations of human children ever before been so well-armed?

When I listen to the continuing controversy and debate about the restriction and regulation of the sale of guns, I am amazed that there is never an intelligent reference to or discussion of the surprisingly clear source of the problem: the individual human being's overpowering judgment-driven anger. Not only must gun laws be reviewed in the clear light of intelligent investigation of this awful problem; but, also, our out-of-control tendency to harshly judge other human beings must be acknowledged and drastically changed!

It is indisputable that we have not achieved the level of consciousness globally which would allow us to discuss the possibility of our world being weapon-free. Undeniably there is still a need for the judicious use of military weapons to protect innocent and helpless human beings from the savagery of "malevolent other" human beings. However, something intelligent certainly must be done to disarm both children and adults who *can* learn to thoughtfully deal with their own human emotional responses and who *can*, through understanding, convert their brutal survival-level approach to others to a level of wise and healthy function. We have been teaching our children the wrong lessons! And, now, our world is filled with several generations of humans who have learned those dreadful lessons very well.

We have created a monster! Our schools have been described by some educators as the equivalent of an educational meltdown because huge numbers of our children no longer respect the teachers, no longer care about their grades, no longer are willing to be educated in the basic philosophies, principles, and practices of human society. Our school systems are in a state of near collapse because they, too, have become armed camps, with the halls patrolled by policemen or armed guards, and our school children "scanned" or "patted down" for possible possession of weapons. The doors are kept locked so that gangs from outside cannot "infiltrate" the school building during the school day. In San Francisco, it has recently been suggested by school administrators that because so many children are dying violent deaths at school, the school system should provide the students with burial insurance. What a shockingly grievous reality!

Those of us who can help, must help. We must, most importantly, stop judging each other harshly. We must look upon each other's faces and upon each other's struggles with understanding and with compassion. And, assuming a posture of hopeful helpfulness, we must act upon our heartful desire to bring the light of understanding to those who are so obviously lost in the darkness of confusion, pain and fear. We must evoke the spirit of tolerance, acceptance, and respect in those children who have become captured by the power of their own disillusioned anger. We must do that by teaching them to understand themselves as emotional beings, by teaching them to understand themselves as immensely intelligent beings, by teaching them to understand themselves as much more than their wounded egos and their selfish agendas.

By way of our intelligent, nonjudgmental and *care-full* mentoring, our children can learn these lessons. By being their high-minded champions, we can provide them with an ethical view and a noble perspective of themselves. By being their attentive patrons, we can imbue them with a clear sense of the need for them to function positively within our world. We must let them know that *we* really need *them*! As their wise, humane and caring elders, and, with the loving brilliance engendered in us by our precious relationship with the MoreThanMe, we can lead our children to the truth of themselves.[2]

WHO DO WE THINK WE ARE?

> *...judgment in the usual sense is impossible. This is not an opinion but a fact. In order to judge anything rightly, one would have to be fully aware of an inconceivably wide range of things; past, present, and to come. One would have to recognize in advance all the effects of his judgments on everyone and everything involved in them in any way. And one would have to be certain there is no distortion in his perception, so that his judgment would be wholly fair to everyone on whom it rests now and in the future. Who is in a position to do this? Who except in grandiose fantasies would claim this for himself?*[3]

Enough of us are shocked and frightened these days by the extremes to which our arrogant judging of each other has gone that a true interest in tracing the problem to the source now exists among us. The Age of Information in which we live dispenses to us a steady flow of "news as it happens" which acts as a constant and inescapable mirroring of our enturbulated human psychology. On our television screens and in newspaper and magazine accounts, we daily see ourselves acting out our hateful judgments of each other on the stages of our personal, professional, social and governmental theaters. And even though the stakes are sky high, we see ourselves stuck in the same kind of narrow-minded, self-serving theatrics—judging each other cruelly from our own limited frames of reference—which have brought us to the brink of disaster. When will we see clearly what it is that we are attempting to show ourselves?

As we can see so clearly on our television screens, the acting out of judgments takes many now predictable and many unpredictable forms of expression—abusing babies, maliciously persecuting other issue-oriented groups, beating suspects, gunning down fellow employees, ramming tank turrets through houses, burning and looting whole communities, massacring whole cultures. How awful! At this time the United States and Scotland lead the world in murder rates, but most other "civilized" and "developed" countries also suffer the horrors of out-of-control violent crime—which translates as human beings committing atrocious acts against each other for one self-centered reason or another. These acts are often justified, by way of some judgmental twist which says:

> "**You** are *wrong* and deserve my cruel punishment of you because **my** "rights" are being infringed upon."
>
> "**You** are *wrong* and deserve my brutal retribution because of inequities in **my** personal or cultural past."
>
> "**You** are *wrong* and deserve my unmerciful aggression, and **I** will "do violence unto **you**" before you can "do violence unto **me**."

No matter what face we put on it, no matter how we try to justify the self-centered motives implicit in this predicament, and no matter how much we might wish it were not like this, we have a critical problem which cries out to us to **redefine ourselves** as humans. In this dog-eat-dog world, are we more dog than human? But which breed of dog is so greedy, aggressive, and violent? And what kind of humanity, when it needs sex, just goes out and rapes someone? What kind of humanity, when it wants money, just goes and shoots someone at the ATM machine? And what kind of humanity needs to offer burial insurance to its grade schoolers because there are so many violent deaths at school? Undeniably, the disturbing answer to those disturbing questions is: our kind of harshly judgmental humanity at this terrible time.

In order to support us to understand the psychological mechanisms at work in our societal quicksand, I reference *The White Hole In Time*, wherein Peter Russell distinguishes between two types of judgments:

> *There are the evaluations we make of a person's behavior, appearance, and other personal attributes. This is the kind of assessment we make when, for instance, we weigh up the advantages and disadvantages of employing a particular person for a job.... Such appraisals can be most valuable—without them we might make many errors.*
>
> *The second type is made according to criteria set by our own inner needs. It is the assessment we make as to whether someone might help or hinder us*

in our search for personal fulfillment. Thus I might judge an inflexible bureaucrat who causes me considerable inconvenience and stands in the way of my getting what I want as 'stupid' or 'uncaring.' Conversely, one who goes out of his way to be of assistance I might judge as 'kind' and 'friendly.'

The problem with such judgments is that we all too easily project them onto the other person. We take our reaction to their words and deeds and on that basis make a judgment of them as a human being. In general terms, if we like the person and think they are 'on our side' we categorize them as a 'good' person. Conversely, if we dislike them or think they stand in the way of our fulfillment, we are liable to put them in the category of 'bad'—someone who needs improvement.

Such judgments of another's being are never valid. They are a projection of our own mind; our own hopes and fears. Someone else, with different hopes and different fears, might see the same person in another light....

To judge another person's worth as a human being is never justified.[4]

Using the distinctions which Russell has drawn for us, I call our attention to the fact that in the first kind of judgment there is a relatively **objective** appraisal being made based on established criteria, the purpose of which is high-minded since it is to serve the good of a whole—not just the appraiser's self-centered needs. There is a somewhat objective *weighing* of factors in order to give intelligent consideration to all of the relevant issues and to responsibly match the person being judged to the specific situation.

WE POSSESS WITHIN OUR BEING AN INHERENT DIGNITY WHICH EXPRESSES ITSELF IN MANY CREATIVE AND BEAUTIFUL WAYS.

However, in the second kind of judgment there is a purely **subjective** judgment being made, the purpose of which is not high-minded since it carries an emotionally-charged, self-centered reactivity which makes the person being judged "right" or "wrong" (usually on-the-spot). If the person is "wrong," the judger will most usually write him off—using a well-developed ability to deliver an automatic across-the-board indictment of the person's intelligence, competence, and general worth as a human being. This indictment of the person is then projected onto that person. It is not owned or, in other words, claimed as the sole property of the judger. And the most ridiculous part of this whole ridiculous mental/emotional transaction is that THE JUDGER BELIEVES IT TO BE TRUE, WHEN IT IS SIMPLY HIS OWN AUTOMATIC OR CONDITIONED REACTIVITY TO A PERSON WHO DID NOT DO SOMETHING THE WAY HE THOUGHT IT SHOULD BE DONE. This kind of judging is going on all day long every day in nearly all human beings in this world. And it is precisely this kind of purely subjective, uninformed, unintelligent, and unLawful judging which is at the heart of all of our problems as a species. It is, at its source, nothing more than narrow-minded, self-centered, ego reactivity.

As the above quote from *A Course In Miracles* tells us: "In order to judge anything rightly, one would have to be fully aware of an inconceivably wide range of things; past, present and to come." We simply do not have the capacity to know all that we would need to know in order to take our judgments seriously—and yet we do. And we must stop that!

We all know that we cannot just be told the truth or we cannot just read the truth in a book and suddenly understand and change; we must *learn by experience* and be able to see the truth by way of our **in**sight in order to really *get it* and *be changed* by it. But on this subject, it seems apparent that we as a race—the human race—have had more than enough experience by now to see clearly the error of our ways, to see the truth by way of our **in**sight, to really get it and to be changed by it. Really! But, since that is obviously not the case, we must go to extraordinary lengths now and next in order to make the Great Correction of the ridiculous judging we have been and are still perpetrating on each other. Our mental, emotional, and physical health depends on it. Our lives depend on it. Our future depends on it. Our very world depends on it. Really!

We must ask ourselves:
"Who do I think I am to judge another person?"

We must say to ourselves:
"There is no possibility that, in my own littleness, I can possibly be an all-knowing source of wisdom who can fairly judge others."

We must remind ourselves:
"I am doing the best I can to meet the demands of my own life, and that is enough for me. I am not capable of knowing whether everyone else is "right" or "wrong."

We need to support ourselves:
"I am a good person who fundamentally appreciates other people. I will now correct my perceptions and be more accepting of others."

We need to counsel ourselves:

"I need to pay attention to how I act and react, process my own reactivity to the level of truth, own my own judgments, and treat others with compassion and respect."

Self-sense or Non-sense

Without a strong sense of self, we must rely on a self-image which is derived from our own inconsistent thoughts about ourselves and from feedback which we receive from others. I call this third-level condition "the empty shell" state, since we have no substance to our insides. We feel as though we are made of Jell-O or mush on the inside and constantly attempt to *get* some substance from outside of ourselves with which to fill the empty shell. The "empty shell" state is the case for each of us until we make a real connection with our own Self, until we achieve an experience of being solid on the inside, and until we develop a rich inner life from which we can express ourselves authentically. It is intrinsic to the fragmented character and the mechanical reactivity of the "empty shell" to harshly judge others. Its conditioned self-protective disposition is capable of serving no higher agenda. On the other hand, it is intrinsic to the nature of the Self to express itself authentically, to stand defenselessly confident and free and at the same time capable of including others within its frame of reference. Knowing this to be the case, it is deeply disturbing to watch all of the "empty shells" going at it all day long every day.

Peter Russell calls this pseudo-self the "derived self" since it is derived from the feedback we receive from outside our selves. In describing life lived as a "derived self" in *The Global Brain*, he speaks of our dependency on others for acknowledgement.

> *Deriving our sense of identity from our interaction with others, we need people to recognize and reaffirm our existence and frequently spend considerable effort fulfilling this need. Life becomes a search for personal reinforcement (what are often termed positive psychological strokes).... Some psychologists estimate that as much as 80 percent of our interactions with other people come from the need for reinforcement.*

> *At the same time, our vulnerability to emotional injury is very high; the derived self is extremely fragile. Events are seldom seen as neutral, and what is not reinforcing is usually seen as threatening. As a result, time not spent pursuing positive strokes may be spent avoiding negative strokes.*
>
> *When we do receive negative strokes we feel hurt, and the result is often unhappiness and depression....*
>
> *Another way in which the derived self handles negative strokes, particulary criticism, is to call up its psychological defense mechanisms, such as rationalization, blocking, and retaliation, methods the injured identity uses to make itself strong again.*[5]

He goes on to elaborate ways by which the derived self attempts to meet its always short-term goals and to bolster its identity: accumulating possessions, membership in groups, nationalism, etc. And he reminds us that "...we are more than just biological organisms bounded by skin. We are also unbounded, part of a greater wholeness, united with the rest of the universe. This is the other side of our identity, that aspect of the self that can balance out our sense of individuality and separateness."[6]

In this discussion, we already have moved back away from the initial encounters with others whom we have judged and who have judged us and have gained some perspective on what it is that is the source of our problem. The point is that we must strive to achieve a strong sense of self which derives not from what others think about us, but from what we know to be true. That occurs only when we make a strong connection with our inner feeling-level responses and when we gain some understanding about the other aspects of our humanity and how they all work together to produce a harmonious, healthy, fully-integritous sense of self that we can count on. That includes learning to identify our emotions, translate their messages, disqualify certain thoughts as simply conditioned reactions of our damaged ego, and correct our thinking so as to get at the truth quickly. When secure within our own sense of self, we can be responsive to whatever relational transaction we are having difficulty with and authentically state what we would not have been capable of stating as an empty shell (a derived self) who was so needy of others' approval, unclear, and not equal to the circumstances. For example:

- "I'm sorry. I don't want it to be like this. I want to work this out."

- "I would really rather bring resolution to this issue than to be hurt and wrong or angry and right.

- "I would rather yield my position and really listen to what you are trying to tell me than to resort to my same old boring round of defense strategies—which just generate more upset and conflict in me. I really want us to deal with this, to get through it, and to be free of it."

Included in our analysis is the crucial element of recognition of ourselves as a part of a vast and mysterious greaterness. And although some who do not understand may still hold the opinion that "spiritual stuff" is irrelevant or beside the point, impractical or sheer folly, a careful study of the teachings of the finest minds of any age will reveal the grievous consequences which we can expect to accrue when acknowledgment of this essential aspect of our human nature is not included in our identification. Those consequences have accrued in our society. Without that societal recognition (remembering) of the big picture, we have had no greater context in which to live than the extremely limited agendas of our own self-centered neediness. What a shame!

> *But now listen to the good news: Your body is the result of separation; it is only the visible half of your own true* ***self****. The other half has remained in the unmanifested, unconscious part of your being. By uniting these two complementary halves with each other, you can return to divine* ***unity****! ...Even while your body remains in the visible world of the created, you can merge your consciousness with your own true* ***self****, out of which you have fallen, thus forming the perfect unit.*
>
> *...This striving for reunion is in everything that has been created. Every creature seeks its complementary half in order to re-unite with it.*
>
> *...As long as a creature seeks its complementary half outside itself, in the created, recognizable world, it will never find unity, simply because* ***its complementary half isn't outside itself, manifested, separate from itself, but on the contrary, unseparated from itself, in its own unmanifested part, in its unconscious****! No creature could exist if it did not have its other half in the unmanifested.*[7]

Differences and Distances: Fighting With Ourselves

Implicit in this discussion—or any informed discussion—of judgment is the mechanism of projection which is truly at the heart of the matter. The basic psychological mechanism is that of rejecting (denying) certain characteristics, qualities, or behaviors of our humanness which we do not find acceptable and, then, having them subconsciously projected (or put over there) onto others. Because we have already classified them as "unacceptable," we will react to them as "unacceptable" when we see these characteristics or qualities being mirrored back to us by other human beings. (There are also discussions of projection in Chapters Eight and Nine.) It has been common knowledge for a long time that what we dislike or hate or reject in others are exactly the things we have not accepted in ourselves. Our judgmental reactivity to another person is simply an emotionally-charged repetition of our original rejection of that characteristic, quality or behavior. When we judge another we are actually judging ourselves, since our **denial** that we are **like that** does not mean that we are not like that. The truth is that we hold within our humanness the capacity for **any** behavior that any human being has ever exhibited. The most atrocious and inhumane behaviors that have ever been perpetrated on anyone or anything could also have been elicited in us if a particular set of psychological stresses damaged and twisted our fragile psyche during the formative years of our babyhood or childhood—or if in our adulthood, our inner strength was not developed to the point of withstanding such stresses. There is a shocking body of scientific evidence which was accumulated by Hitler's regime which attests to such a claim.

Can we count on ourselves and each other to rise to this unique occasion and to match our remarkable circumstances with the remarkable responses of which we are potentially capable?

> *What you project you disown, and therefore do not believe is yours. You are excluding yourself by the very judgment that you are different from the one on whom you project. Since you have also judged against what you project, you continue to attack it because you continue to keep it separated. By doing this unconsciously, you try to keep the fact that you attacked yourself out of awareness, and thus imagine that you have made yourself safe.*
>
> *Yet projection will always hurt you. It reinforces your belief in your own split mind, and its only purpose is to keep the separation going. It is solely a device of the ego to make you feel different from your brothers and separated from them. The ego justifies this on the grounds that it makes you seem*

> *"better" than they are, thus obscuring your equality with them still further. Projection and attack are inevitably related, because projection is always a means of justifying attack.*[8]

A Course In Congruence leads us to the truth of ourselves and makes it possible for us to achieve that strength of self-sense which allows us to affirm again and again:

"I have also been like that." or **"I could also be like that."**

As Ken Wilber states in *No Boundary*:

> *When you realize that a projection which appeared to exist "out there" is really your own reflection, is actually part of yourself, then you have torn down that particular boundary between self and not-self. Hence the field of your awareness becomes that much more expansive, open, free, and undefended.*
>
> *...These projected facets will then no longer threaten you because they* <u>*are*</u> *you.*[9]

So, accepting our rejected parts is the healing that must take place. This acceptance is a compassionate reclaiming of parts of ourselves we have denied and hidden away from our consciousness. We can clearly see those disowned parts by noticing the *particular* characteristics we *most often* see in others which *drive us crazy* and which *switch on* our emotionally-energized judgmental reactivity. How interesting!

THE EGO'S PRIMARY MOTIVATIONS ARE BASED IN SELF-DEFENSIVENESS—AND ITS GUARD IS NEARLY ALWAYS UP.

BECOMING DEFENSELESS

> *...lay judgment down, not with regret but with a sigh of gratitude. Now are you free of a burden so great that you could merely stagger and fall down beneath it. And it was all illusion. Nothing more. Now can the teacher of God rise up unburdened, and walk lightly on.*[10]

It is the damaged and isolated ego which is judging everyone and everything and defending itself against all real and perceived threats. The ego's primary motivations are based in self-defensiveness—and its guard is nearly always up. The ego is super-alert as it constantly attempts to see the hidden threats to its survival or to its image, and it is often super-sensitive to the slightest facial expressions, body language, and verbal expressions of others. A raised eyebrow or an involuntary sigh from another person can be misread to mean all kinds of things against which the ego may feel it must defend itself. If the raised eyebrow or involuntary sigh occurs in someone whose racial or ethnic stereotype automatically translates as "unacceptable" due to the ego's conditioning, the volatility of that person's egoic defensiveness will be dangerously high. The ego's defensive stance will make it nearly impossible for there to occur between these two people any meaningful exchange of ideas or any real communication.

By correcting our thinking and training ourselves to become less judgmental, we are undermining the ego's neurotically suspicious thoughtforms about other people and effecting a diminishment of its super-defensive psychological posture. We are beginning the process of becoming defenseless. Being defenseless means being innocently present in the moment, allowing ourselves unprotected listening and blameless speaking with another person. Such a modification of our disposition toward others releases us from the chronic confinement of our own overly-critical evaluations of others. Such a correction also sets others free to be with us defenselessly.

The high degree of personal freedom which is implicit in a state of defenselessness makes well worthwhile all of our conscious efforts to transcend the automaticity of our unconscious responses. In order to consciously intervene between the habituated reactivity which is spontaneously triggered in us and the communication and/or behavior that we express, we must at least discern the underlying condition which is provoked into assuming a defensive stance. The underlying condition is the ego, whose values and function are fear based. In *Terra Christa*, Ken Carey speaks eloquently of that fear.

> *The ego has a set of values that are designed to care for the physical body and protect it from harm. When it is allowed to control decision-making, the ego is overcautious in the extreme; dangers and possible threats become exaggerated; and the individual often finds him or herself functioning out of fear.*

> *...More than any other single factor, fear keeps people locked in unsatisfying behavior. The stress that results from this lies at the root of disease. If we are interested in addressing the root causes of disease and returning to spirit-motivated behavior, we need to look boldly at our fears.*[11]

The process of enlightenment is a process of making the unconscious conscious. Becoming defenseless is a function of personal freedom based on resolution of our subconscious fears by allowing them to rise to the surface of our consciousness so that we are able to deal with them. As Carey points out above, we must make conscious our unconscious or subconscious fears—which are all derived from the fear of death. We must face our fears head on. By facing our fears, we will allow ourselves to experience our greaterness, and we will learn firsthand that we are *so much more* than our trembling little ego, which defends itself against all perceived threats. Only out of that realization will we be capable of constantly undermining the fearfully overcautious and offensively self-defensive ego. Approaching our relational transactions from an authentically defenseless posture will introduce an innocence into our relationships which will engender openness and defenselessness in others. We will not only promote healing within ourselves but will be extending the opportunity for healing to others. What a difference!

CHOOSE AGAIN—AND AGAIN AND AGAIN AND AGAIN AND...

We are willful beings whose free will has been grossly misused. Now we must learn the right use of our will. Never before have the high-minded principles of the Constitution of our country been challenged to interpret First Amendment rights of free speech to the degree they are being challenged today. And the demands being placed upon that source document are demands which are based in self-serving agendas by groups of individuals whose egoic arrogance is blatantly obvious to all who have the eyes to see. From the demands of the pro-life demonstrators, the gay bashers, the right-wing fundamentalists, and the rap music artists, we see its tenets challenged to include the right to aggressively interfere with the life, liberty and pursuit of happiness of others whose beliefs do not match their own. Once again the collective human consciousness is mirroring back to us what has before lain hidden in the subconscious recesses of the human psyche—an arrogant, fear-based expectation that certain personal, narrow judgments should stand as the exclusive law of the land. If the implications of this egoic expectation were not so serious, its pomposity would be laughable. Once again, who do we think we are!?

Until we have gotten right with ourselves; that is, until we have transcended the nonsense of our ego-driven judgments and have discovered the higher planes of perception and function, we are not credible touchstones around whose perceptions others should rally. We should not and others should not take us seriously. Really! And, until that time, we must spend our attention and our energy (which is all we ever have to give) in ways which support that leap in consciousness. To be sure, there is plenty to do.

Based on the information included in this chapter, it is obvious that we need to *real*ize that we are "the chooser." And, whether we choose to live on in a state of mentally lazy fuzziness—subconsciously projecting our rejected parts all over everyone else and having them boomerang back at us—or choose to live in a state of mentally alert lucidity—noticing our conditioned reactivity and intelligently intervening to correct it—we are choosing what we do. That has not been the case before we knew better. Now we know better.

We must choose again each time the conditioned response occurs: choose to correct our thinking, choose to heal the split in our own minds, choose to face the fears of our trembling ego; choose to listen to what is really being communicated by others; choose to remain defenseless; choose to rise to the occasion from a high-minded intention to be the truth of ourselves, now!

> *This was the ego—all the cruel hate, the need for vengeance and the cries of pain, the fear of dying and the urge to kill, the brotherless illusion and the self that seemed alone in all the universe. This terrible mistake about yourself the miracle corrects as gently as a loving mother sings her child to rest. Is not a song like this what you would hear? Would it not answer all you thought to ask, and even make the question meaningless?*
>
> *Your questions have no answer, being made to still God's Voice, Which asks of everyone one question only: "Are you ready yet to help Me save the world?"*[12]

Mentors of Acknowledgement and Validation

Addressing the deplorable level of self-righteous judgments which has infected the human psychology of our species is not an agreeable undertaking. In fact, there is nothing agreeable about judgments. And, in order to turn the negative reality of harsh judgments to informed and hopeful possibilities for positive change, we need only further access and more fully realize our exceptional potential.

The truth is that we are, in our God-given potency, great beings—courageous and noble. We possess within our being an inherent dignity which expresses itself in many creative and beautiful ways. It is obvious that we naturally honor, are deeply touched by, and applaud each other's acts of humane heroism, each other's heartful striving, and each other's enduring attempts to excel. We have a soul! That being the case, it is entirely reasonable to suggest that we are capable of supporting each other, encouraging each other, and cheering each other on, rather than heaping ignominy on each other as we have been doing. We can easily become mentors of acknowledgement and validation of each other. As we make the connection with our deeper Self and accept our full humanity, our perceptions are no longer clouded by the shadowy forms of our own rejected parts. And, from our deeper Self, we are able to see and appreciate the deeper Self of each other, even as we go about our ordinary lives—which, by the way, are ultimately extraordinary.

We are all in this together. At no other time in our history has our world been, to the extent it is now, a global community. At no other time have we been so obviously interdependent in the fullest sense of that word. We truly need each other. We truly depend on each other. We truly appreciate each other. Let us now live together as an expression of those truths. Let us make "random acts of sensitive kindness" our natural expression. And rather than trying to change each other by judging each other harshly, let us change each other by changing ourselves in ways that each other will admire, respect, and strive to emulate.

We must look upon each other's faces
and upon each other's struggles
with understanding and with compassion.

THE LESS WE JUDGE OURSELVES HARSHLY—
THE LESS WE JUDGE OTHERS HARSHLY

THE MORE WE UNDERSTAND OURSELVES—
THE MORE WE ARE ABLE TO UNDERSTAND OTHERS

THE MORE CONGRUENT WE BECOME—
THE MORE FREEDOM WE EXPERIENCE

THE MORE FREEDOM WE EXPERIENCE—
THE MORE WE ARE ABLE TO ALLOW OTHERS THEIR FREEDOM
AND
THE MORE WE ARE ABLE TO APPRECIATE AND SUPPORT OTHERS

THE MORE SELF-EXPRESSIVE WE ARE—
THE MORE CONSCIOUS AND COMPASSIONATE WE BECOME

THE MORE CONSCIOUS AND COMPASSIONATE WE ARE—
THE MORE ALIGNED WE ARE WITH THE UNIVERSAL INTELLIGENCE

Toward Expansion and Self-Mastery

1. Begin to notice just how much judging is going on in your life.

    Notice each time someone judges you harshly.

    Notice each time you judge someone harshly.

        Keep a small notepad with you and keep track of just how often it occurs during your waking hours.

2. Practice remaining silent and defenseless when someone is judging you harshly. Remain alert and notice just what is going on. Observe the other person and observe yourself throughout the experience.

3. Practice disciplining yourself not to say the negative judgments you are thinking.

4. Listen to other people and notice how many negative judgments you hear in the course of "normal" human interaction.

5. Practice acknowledging others for the things you really appreciate about them.

6. Practice validating the good in others whom you have been judging harshly.

7. Practice affirming the good in yourself when you begin to judge yourself harshly.

8. Practice thinking compassionate thoughts about yourself and others to neutralize harsh judgments you have been having.

9. Practice appreciating differences in people, rather than expecting everyone to be the way you have been conditioned to expect them to be.

Let us comprehend
that we are the revolutionaries
and the revolution.

CHAPTER FOUR

Our Evolving Species and The Process of Transformation

I see a change. It is vested in the greatest rise in expectations the world has ever seen. It is so far-reaching in its implications that one might call it evolution consciously entering into time, the evolutionary potential asserting itself. It needed a certain critical mass, a certain merging of complexity, crisis, and consciousness to awaken. Now it is happening.

The change comes slowly. A sleeping giant, it wakes in the hearts and minds of millions. Four hundred thousand years of being humans-in-search-of-subsistence, seven thousand years of being humans-in-search-of-meaning, and two centuries of modern economic and social revolution have prepared the way for the deepest quickening in human and cultural evolution.

And what is happening constellates around the ideas of human freedom and human possibilities. The idea of freedom is expanding because the idea of what it is to be a human being is expanding.

But now the beacons must be tuned to even greater brilliance. The old gleamings are no longer adequate to the time, and to follow them is to fall among the shadows that confound, leading us to shores both dangerous and archaic.

—*Jean Houston*[1]

Tuning the Beacons To An Even Greater Brilliance

The most important element of the hero's journey may well be the recognition of the evolutionary nature of human life, the appearance of which predates us by two and a half million years. With that conscious awareness, we can become sincere students of the process so as to be able to grasp—at least abstractly—the mysterious and seemingly miraculous phenomenon which we speak of as the transformation of the human psyche. The evolutionary impulse and its exceedingly strong influence on us at this time needs to be acknowledged as fact. We must feel the resonant force of its insistent call to us and the strength of our own heartful response. We must prepare ourselves so that we may become capable of somehow capturing the subtle essence and grasping the stunning implications of what transformation is: a leap from one particular sub-species of human being to an entirely different sub-species.

One way that point is brought home to us is the fact that there are several different sub-species of human beings who are living together on the planet at this time. We have seen on television the enduring fragments of still primitive (Neanderthal) cultures of *Homo sapiens* who live in the dense jungles of South America and Africa. These humans—who are evolved only to the early stages of the second (social/emotional) level of consciousness—still live as our early ancestors lived. At the second level, humans began to live in communities and began to engage in primitive toolmaking and rudimentary farming. The brain functions which are higher than the second level of consciousness have obviously not been activated in these archaic humans since they live unimaginatively and with only the simplest tools as their highest technology.

At the other end of the continuum of consciousness, we have present among us individual human beings who have evolved way beyond what is apparently the "normal" level of consciousness—having experienced "enlightenment," "evolution," or "transformation" to the seventh level of consciousness. These beings are truly giants of consciousness—operating primarily at the imaginative or spiritual level—so evolved that they no longer function within the rational world of commerce and ordinary human endeavor as most humans do.

In between the prototypes of these two ends of the continuum of human consciousness, we can observe what are quite apparently different levels of consciousness or different sub-species of humans: the primarily self-centered egoic level, the primarily conceptual or existential level, and the primarily intuitive or metaphysical level. And, because each level of consciousness contains within itself a spectrum of distinctions from low, to middle, to high, and because there are phases of disintegration between levels of consciousness, we can only speculate as to the collage of human consciousness to which we are all exposed in the relational rounds of our daily lives. We must not assume that everyone is functioning at the same level of consciousness nor at the same point on the continuum within any particular level of consciousness. Instead we must continue to strive to serve our own evolvement and continue to strive to bridge the gap in communication and relationship between ourselves and others. We must do this compassionately and non-judgmentally, avoiding the egoic tendency to make ourselves "better than" or "not as good as" others.

We must see ourselves and others as integral links in the Great Chain of Being and honor all of life by sourcing the level of the deeper Self within, at which depth we are all one.

The demand on us awakening humans—at whatever position we find ourselves along the continuum of consciousness—is implicit in Plato's empowered directive "Know Thyself." This evolutionary imperative is intelligently and forcefully impressing itself upon us now by way of the very Information Age in which we live. Any human being who resides within a developed country of this world is offered a wealth of high-minded knowledge at nearly every turn. One only needs the readiness to begin the journey of self-discovery for one's eyes and ears to open to a steady flow of fascinating information about ourselves from the immense and ever-growing databanks of knowledge. Both the vast profusion of enlightened teachings to which we are privy at this time, as well as the convergent concentration of distinguished intellectuals on the unprecedented and seemingly unsolvable crises of this epoch, are meaningful testimonies to the portentous possibilities which are rushing to meet us earthlings as we approach the third millennium of human history. Having seemingly neared the end of a dead-end road in our attempts to progress and evolve in the ordinary sense, it has become indisputable to both the mystically awakening ones and to the purely rational intelligentsia that something extraordinary must happen soon in order to set our world straight in time to redirect the course of our destiny.

As a species we already live as the world community which was prophesied thousands of years ago by our spiritual forefathers. As we know, those ancient prophesies also described what are still unimaginable changes in our times.

As spiritual beings who long ago became disenfranchised from our multidimensional natures, it may well be that recapturing those lost dimensions will provide us, as a species, with the fundamental perceptual fields and truly brilliant creative abilities to elegantly finesse not only the problems we have created, but the beginnings of the metamorphosis of our entire species.

AN UNCOUNTABLE NUMBER OF HUMANS IN THE WORLD TODAY ARE ALREADY OPERATING FROM THE HIGHER CENTERS OF THE PSYCHE, WHICH ARE REFERRED TO AS THE HIGHER SELF.

AN HISTORICAL PERSPECTIVE

After existing as humans for over two million years at the first level of consciousness—at which our animalistic nature was dominant and our physical survival was the primary motivator and reason for our living—our consciousness experienced a leap to the second level. After existing for tens of thousands of years at the second level of consciousness—at which a natural inclination for socialization (emotional relationship and community living) emerged and developed and commingled with our focus on physical survival—our consciousness experienced a leap to the third level. According to Ken Wilber in *Up From Eden*, the transformation of human consciousness to the mental-egoic (third) level, which "set" the modern world, occurred "sometime during the second and first millennia B.C., when the exclusively egoic structure of consciousness began to emerge from the ground consciousness...and crystallize out into awareness." Wilber further identifies this as "the last major stage—to date—in the collective historical evolution of the spectrum of consciousness."[2]

Drs. Thomas Berry and Brian Swimme in *The Universe Story*, in their discussion of the emergence and developmental phases of human beings since their first appearance 2.6 million years ago, say:

> *After these centuries of development through the period of Homo habilis and Homo erectus, a decisive new development occurred some* ***two hundred thousand years ago*** *in north-central and east Africa: the appearance of Homo sapiens, the human species that succeeded these other forms and from which all contemporary humans are descended.*[3]
>
> ***Four million years ago*** *in Africa, humans stood up on just two limbs, and by two million years ago they began using their free hands to shape Earth's materials into tools.* ***One and a half million years ago*** *these restless hands were controlling fire, shaping the Sun's energy that had been stored in sticks, to advance their own projects. Beginning around* ***thirty-five thousand years ago****, as if unable to restrain any longer their astonishment at existence, humans began a new level of celebration that displayed itself in cave paintings deep within Earth, that filled the nights with festivals and music-making, that shaped ceremonials around the passing of friends and seasons, that captured in the artistic depiction of the animals some of the beauty that had seized the depth of their minds.*

> ***Twenty thousand years ago*** *Earth, through its human element, entered conscious self-awareness of the patterns of seeds, and seasons, and the primordial rhythms of the universe. Although some of these patterns had been set into existence by Earth billions of years ago, and although the first humans had organized themselves for millions of years within these patterns,* ***twelve thousand years*** *ago humans began consciously shaping these patterns by domesticating plants and animals—wheat and barley and goats in the Middle East, rice and pigs in Asia, corn and beans and the alpaca in the Americas.*[4]

Within this articulate and coherent unfoldment of consciousness in human beings, there occurred, at some particular point in time, an obvious dramatic leap forward and upward in brain function and mental capacity. As Christopher Hills tells us, this leaping is part and parcel of the evolutionary imperative.

> *Evolution works slowly and its influence cannot be felt by any one individual person. A hundred thousand generations may pass before a big change becomes obvious. Yet there are times in the billions of years of our history where the subtle advance has been dramatic and sudden, where the preparations over a million years provide the ground for a million-year jump which takes place in one event, in one generation. This leap ahead represents a change in the nuclear structure of the guiding field of the organism. The physical changes follow this nuclear change by releasing the intelligent energy accumulated over a million years into one moment of realisation, one great moment of thrust into new understanding of man's role in the vast cosmos, one great change in his purpose.*[5]

According to Peter Russell, the term *Homo sapiens sapiens* has been used by some anthropologists to identify a new sub-species of *Homo sapiens* which emerged some fifty thousand years ago.[6] And, although their timelines do not agree (50,000 years ago as compared to 3,500 years ago), we must assume that Russell and Wilber are pointing to the same phenomenal occurrence—the full emergence of the exclusively egoic structure of mind—when they specify a time when a radical (unheard of) transformation of consciousness occurred in the human psyche.

Also pointing to a specific time for this radical, evolutionary leap in consciousness, Berry and Swimme mark the beginning of "modern *Homo sapiens*" at

40,000 years ago, during the Upper Paleolithic period.[7] The archaic *Homo sapiens* is known as Neanderthal and the modern *Homo sapiens* is known as Cro-Magnon. The term *Homo sapiens sapiens*, to which Russell makes reference, obviously draws a distinction between the modern humans (the Cro-Magnons) from their immediate predecessors (the Neanderthals)—in whom the egoic structure was still in its low (or earliest) stage of evolution. As Drs. Berry and Swimme tell us:

> *Immediately upon their arrival in the European region the Cro-Magnon peoples manifested an artistic and inventive genius completely missing in what we know of earlier peoples. Both in the volume of their technological inventions and in their artistic skills the Cro-Magnon were an overwhelming presence on the European scene. This can be observed in over two hundred caves with these people's wall paintings and engravings, while their individual sculptures and engravings might be in the range of ten thousand or more.... More than one hundred different types of stone implements were fashioned in this period.*[8]
>
> *...Since these artistic abilities were associated with a new capacity for the understanding and use of spoken language, we are meeting here not simply with another change in methods of stone working or the processing of some physical material, but with a transformation of human consciousness on a scale and with a dramatic impact such as we seldom encounter in this narrative of our emergent human development.*[9]

The difference between *Homo sapiens* (Neanderthal) and *Homo sapiens sapiens* (Cro-Magnon) has to do with the development of higher levels of brain function and the ways in which the complex human brain was used. Furthermore, Russell tells us that our present environmental, economic, and social problems result from "a crisis in our thinking, perception, and values," which can be directly traced to the emergence of *Homo sapiens sapiens* (or full emergence of the ego). He states:

> *This crisis has been coming for a long time. Its seeds were sown some fifty thousand years ago, when* **Homo sapiens**, *the creature with an enlarged neocortex, began to use its complex brain in new ways. Something different was walking on the Earth — a species whose future was determined not by its genes so much as by its ideas. A species that could understand the Uni-*

> *verse in which it found itself. A species with unprecedented creativity. So new were these developments that some anthropologists gave this species a new name,* ***Homo sapiens sapiens*** *— variously translated as the 'wise human being' or 'man that knows it knows.'*[10]
>
> *This is the real opportunity nestling within our global crisis: the opportunity to develop a new consciousness, a new way of seeing, a new way of thinking. What is being called for is a new sub-species. A species that can manage the creativity of* ***Homo sapiens sapiens*** *with true wisdom—a* ***Homo sapiens sapiens sapiens.***[11]

In attempting to reconcile Wilber's transformational moment with that of Berry and Swimme, we must look at their discussions of the dramatic shift from female to male deities within the mythology of our ancestors. Berry and Swimme point out that at the end of the revolutionary Neolithic period and the beginning of the Classical period (3,500 years ago), something very significant occurred. They tell us: "there was a change at the end of the fourth millennium B.C.E. from the dominant female deities to a dominance of male deities."[12] Similarly, Wilber marks the emergence of the ego structure by this shift from female-dominant to male-dominant deities:

> *If we now look closely at the collective mythologies of the beginning of this egoic period, what we discover is unequivocally clear: an entirely different form of myth begins to emerge, a myth never before seen to any great extent.*
>
> *...in the new myths, we find an extraordinary occurrence: the individual triumphs over the Great Mother—breaks free from her, transforms her, defeats her, or transcends her. And this is the "Hero Myth," the myth that is this period of history.*[13]

I suggest that it is not important that we know exactly when the leap to the egoic level of consciousness took place; but, it is important to know that it did take place in order to understand more clearly the reality of the evolutionary imperative in our own times and in our own lives.

It is the third level of consciousness—what Ken Wilber terms the mental-egoic level[14]—which suddenly appeared in *Homo sapiens* (Neanderthals), transforming them into Homo sapiens sapiens (Cro-Magnons) or "man that knows it knows." Obviously, mental capacities which had not been present in earlier humankind suddenly awakened. The Cro-Magnons began the process of mentalizing every aspect of life, further awakening and developing the mental level of human function. And, it is this mental-egoic level of consciousness at which most of the human species has been functioning for this long time.

It is due to the very nature of the self-reflexive consciousness of the mental-egoic level that we have literally gotten "stuck" in it. The remarkable self-reflexive capabilities of the third level have distinguished us from all other (or nearly all other) living creatures and life forms on earth and have provided us humans with the amazing aptitude for reflecting on—and, thus learning from—our past actions. (There is some indication that the dolphins and whales may also have evolved to—or even beyond—the level of the self-reflexive mind.) This faculty has made it possible for us to contemplate our options for the future so as to make intelligent, **conscious** choices (rather than instinctual responses) which increase our chances for growing and thriving. In a very real sense, when our species experienced the leap in consciousness which held within itself the ability to consciously reflect, we were afforded the possibility of becoming the *masters of our own lives* to an *unheard of* extent. This self-reflexive faculty did, however, put us at risk; because inherent within the nature of self-reflexiveness was the danger of becoming excessively self-conscious and self-absorbed. Needless to say, the magnitude of excessive self-absorption and self-serving power mongering which has historically taken place and is still taking place within our world today is a testament to the fact that a high percentage of our species has fallen victim to that implicit danger. Based on the earlier "timely" leaps in consciousness which have been identified from our human history, it seems that this level of conscious function may well have fulfilled itself in many who are now alive on earth. If that is the case, another stunning transformation to higher levels of consciousness and, thus, expanded states of awareness and capacity, is destined to fulfill itself in those who are ready.

What has become apparent to many who are knowledgeable and intensely interested in what is occurring in our world today is that human consciousness is very possibly approaching another leap in consciousness—a leap to the higher levels of capacity and function, which will so dramatically change our perceptions of ourselves, others, and our world, that to many of us the limitations of the lower level already appear shockingly anachronistic and tragically unnecessary. Our world has changed and is changing at such a high rate of speed these days and decades that we can all be certain that, at some unpredictable moment, something unheard of is going to happen in our world which will irrevocably alter everything. No one can really guess when that "something" will occur or what provocation will activate the alteration of our very psyches, on a sweeping scale. Many of us who are alive on the earth today have been being prepared for some time for the moment of transformation toward which we are rushing. Three of the most important things we can do at this time are: 1) become intelligently informed about the essential aspects of our humanness; 2) discover the truth of ourselves and begin to relate from that authentic level of our being; and 3) provide openings in our own minds and in our hearts through which the graceful work of transformation may be accomplished.

WE MUST CONTINUE TO STRIVE TO SERVE OUR OWN EVOLVEMENT AND CONTINUE TO STRIVE TO BRIDGE THE GAP IN COMMUNICATION AND RELATIONSHIP BETWEEN OURSELVES AND OTHERS.

THE PSYCHE, THE SOUL, AND THE HIGHER SELF

> *The nature of this transformation comes from within our psyches, our souls. Like a flower bursting forth, our unfoldment, our maturation, is pushed outward from within...*[15]

Because we are psychological beings, the transformational process is a psychological process; that is, the irrevocable changes which occur in us occur within the hidden dimensions of our own complex psychic (or soul) structure. That being the case, we need to have at least a simple understanding of what the psyche is. That the psyche is both hidden and complex is attested to each time we attempt to gain a concise and easily understandable definition of it. Even our most trusted authorities in these matters have difficulty getting a hold of it conceptually and languaging their conceptions in a way that allows us to really understand. Frances Vaughan's discussion of the psyche and psychology in *The Inward Arc* is most helpful. She quotes the work of Sigmund Freud to tell us, "'Psyche' is a Greek word and its German translation is 'soul.'"[16] She further states that "Bettelheim claims that Freud himself insisted on thinking in terms of the soul when referring to the whole psyche."[17] From her discussion, we see that Freud designated the ego, the id, and the superego as three parts of the total psyche, or soul; and that, in its totality, it "includes both the conscience that imposes reasonable moral values and the irrational, demanding, and punitive aspects of introjected societal values."[18]

For Freud the soul was not a religious phenomenon but a psychological concept meaning 'that which is most valuable in man while he is alive.' The soul was thought to be the seat of both the mind and the passions. In the absence of careful investigation one is likely to remain largely unconscious of the soul.

Psychology, as the study of the ***psyche****, originally meant a study of the soul, but this original meaning has been lost in most Western psychotherapy. The word* ***therapy****, derived from the Greek word meaning healing, has also lost some of its original meaning.*[19]

Vaughan draws an important distinction for us between the psyche (or soul) and the higher Self (transpersonal Self). She says that "while the transpersonal Self includes *awareness* of the soul, it is not exclusively identified with it. ...Awareness of the transpersonal Self, then, designates the specific stage of development wherein the soul remembers itself and its prior unity with the Absolute."[20]

Because there are so many references made throughout *A Course In Congruence* to both the lower self and the higher Self, some clear statements about these two halves of our wholeness is in order, if at least a simple understanding is to occur. It is widely stated that the lower self is the "conscious personality" or "ego" and that the higher Self is a subtle aspect of consciousness, transcendent to the ego, which includes awareness of the soul. As Vaughan states,

In analytical psychology, the Self as the center of the psyche is differentiated from the ego as the center of the conscious personality. This Self is defined as:[21]

...an inner guiding factor that is different from the conscious personality...[it is known as] the regulating center that brings about a constant extension and maturing of the personality. But this larger, more nearly total aspect of the psyche appears first as merely an inborn possibility. It may emerge very slightly, or it may develop relatively completely during one's lifetime. How far it develops depends on whether or not the ego is willing to listen to the messages of the Self.[22]

This "inner guiding factor" and "regulating center" is the organizing principle to which we also refer as our higher Self, transpersonal Self, inner Self, deeper Self, inner Guide, deeper Personality, subtle Self, guidance, center, center of our being, and more. Brian Swimme, in *The Universe Is a Green Dragon* names it *"the unseen shaping."*[23] Matthew Fox in *The Coming of the Cosmic Christ* tells us that "The spiritual tradition proposes that the Cosmic Christ is the '*pattern that connects.*'"[24] All of these ways of naming and speaking about the "invisible something" which lies beyond the limits of our conscious mind are most helpful to us in our attempts to envision and trust the mysterious Intelligence which so responsibly and so brilliantly shapes our destiny by moving us onto and along the path of our own unique journey.

Just as the new mental capacities of *Homo sapiens sapiens* somehow sprang forth into existence and expanded the capabilities of human beings way beyond what they had known before, a higher level of consciousness has begun to spring forth in the psyches of modern man. An uncountable number of humans in the world today are already operating from the higher centers of the psyche, which are referred to as the Self. And many others, in whom the higher nature has not yet fully awakened, are very aware that there is a higher Self and are striving to support a fuller awakening within themselves and others. The fact that we are capable of supporting our own awakening is mind-boggling. Of course, that capability carries within it both a tremendous privilege and a tremendous responsibility—that of helping to raise ourselves out of the limitations of the lower levels of consciousness. One of the ways we can surely help ourselves is through learning what we can about ourselves as psychological beings. Since our own lives are the battlefields on which our struggle for transcendence is being waged, we can best learn about ourselves by learning how to translate what has occurred and is presently occurring in our own lives—in psychological terms.

Before the process of transformation can begin, there must be an opening of the mind.

The Opening of Consciousness and The Impulse for Growth

From some moment in our infancy or early childhood, most of us suffer an acute psychological shock which introduces a subconscious fear about our survival and causes a pervasive sense of personal disillusionment and distrust of others, the world, and life itself. This often results from a real or perceived threat to our survival or to the fulfillment of our basic needs. This "Fall"—from innocence into disillusionment—is sometimes due to insensitive, neglectful or abusive treatment by those on whose care we depend. It may occur from our own misinterpretation of an experience due to our fragility and dependent need for reassurance. The psychological suffering which this unresolved confusion generates acts as a driver in our struggle to protect our tender selves, to find our way in a big and often scary world, and to find love (which is experienced as safety). This psychological pain underlies our search for a meaningful function or role in the world and our earnest attempts to achieve a level of comfortability in relationship to ourselves, to others, and to the world at large. About this Fall from innocence, Carol Pearson, in *The Hero Within*, says:

> *The Innocent lives in an unfallen world, a green Eden where life is sweet and all one's needs are met in an atmosphere of care and love... To Innocents, other people, the natural world, everything exists to serve and satisfy them. God's whole reason for being is to answer prayers. Any pain, any suffering, is an indication that something is wrong—with them (God is punishing them) or with God (maybe God is dead)...*[25]

The Fall from innocence, then, is the plunge into the preheroic archetypal Orphan, with its inherent experience of powerlessness and fear of abandonment.

> *The archetype of the Orphan is a tricky place to be. His or her accomplishment is to move out of innocence and denial to learn that suffering, pain, scarcity, and death are an inevitable part of life... To move on, the Orphan must fully be in the Orphan stage, and that means confronting one's own pain, despair, and cynicism; and it means mourning the loss of Eden, letting oneself know that there is no safety, that God is dead (at least that childish notion of a 'Daddy God')... Orphans, more than any other archetype, need help crossing the threshold and embarking upon their heroic journey.*[26]

At some point—most usually after unsuccessfully seeking relief and consolation in the ordinary experiences of life—we admit to ourselves that we are suffering, that we deeply desire relief from that pain, and that we need help. At that time, we have become ready to listen to others who have preceded us on the hero's path; we have become ready to surrender our selfish willfulness in hope of future understanding; and we have become ready to begin the turn inward in our search for truth. Ken Wilber tells us in *No Boundary* that the dissatisfaction we experience is a good sign.

> *The movement of descent and discovery begins at the moment you consciously become dissatisfied with life. Contrary to most professional opinion, this gnawing dissatisfaction with life is not a sign of "mental illness," nor an indication of poor social adjustment, nor a character disorder. For concealed within this basic unhappiness with life and existence is the embryo of a growing intelligence, a special intelligence usually buried under the immense weight of social shams. A person who is beginning to sense the suffering of life is, at the same time, beginning to awaken to deeper realities, truer realities. For suffering smashes to pieces the complacency of our normal fictions about reality, and forces us to become alive in a special sense—to see carefully, to feel deeply, to touch ourselves and our worlds in ways we have heretofore avoided. It has been said, and truly I think, that suffering is the first grace. In a special sense, suffering is almost a time of rejoicing, for it marks the birth of creative insight.*
>
> *Suffering should neither be denied awareness, avoided, despised, nor glorified, clung to, or dramatized. The emergence of suffering is not so much good as it is a good sign.*
>
> *We must correctly interpret suffering in order to enter into it, live it, and finally live beyond it. If we do not correctly understand suffering, we simply get stuck in the middle of it—we wallow in it, not knowing what else to do.*[27]

Joseph Campbell identifies the hero's emergence as the moment of submission of one's will to the journey and the simultaneous turn inward.

> *The hero is the man of self-achieved submission.... The first step, detachment or withdrawal, consists in a radical transfer of emphasis from the external to the internal world, macro- to microcosm, a retreat from the desperations of the waste land to the peace of the everlasting realm that is within.... In a word: the first work of the hero is to retreat from the world scene of secondary effects to those causal zones of the psyche where the difficulties really reside, and there to clarify the difficulties, eradicate them in his own case.*[28]

By way of the journey into ourselves, we wend our way through the wastelands of self-doubt and eventually reach the fertile plains of self-acceptance. We slog through the swamps of self-absorbed unworthiness and one day find ourselves standing on the solid ground of confident self-love—for the first time truly available to love others and to be loved in return. We fight our way through the heavy undergrowth of harsh self-judgment and self-protective arrogance and find our way to the clearing of humility and selflessness. We cross the valleys of disempowerment and helplessness and one day find ourselves scaling the sheer walls of what had once seemed to be impossible heights, with a strength that seems to grow the higher we climb. Eventually, we stand tall at what seems to be a summit of ourselves—free at last. The air is thinner, the sun is brighter and our perspective on our world seems greatly changed. Instead of feeling as though we are separate from our world and others, we feel naturally at-one-with all we see and sense and know. Our newfound sense of self is somehow large enough to encompass all the world.

LIFE AS A FLOWING, CHANGING PROCESS

When I speak or write about the transformational process, a deep sense of reverence and tender devotional feelings spontaneously arise in me. I am undeniably awed by the mystery of The Great Process and hold it precious beyond the ability of words to measure or describe. The essential richness and miraculous nature of life lived as spiritual process continually imparts to life a resonant depth and a feeling of boundless freedom. Living as the unfoldment of one's own process of transformation reinstates the underlying sentiment of innocence and the faculty of fascinated anticipation inherent to early childhood. Released from the attitude of disillusionment, one becomes starry-eyed, trusting, renewed.

Carl Rogers describes so well the experience of living life as a process:

> *Life, at its best, is a flowing, changing process in which nothing is fixed. To experience this is both fascinating and a little frightening. I find I am at my best when I can let the flow of my experience carry me, in a direction which appears to be forward, toward goals of which I am but dimly aware. In thus floating with the complex stream of my experiencing, and in trying to understand its ever-changing complexity, it should be evident that there are no fixed points. When I am thus able to be in process, it is clear that there can be no closed system of beliefs, no unchanging sets of principles which I hold. Life is guided by a changing understanding of and interpretation of my experience. It is always a process of becoming.*[29]

Before the pivotal moment in my own life—after which I began living life as a spiritual journeyer—I had experienced life as a series of disparate and disjointed experiences that did not seem to hang together very well no matter how hard I tried to make them do so. My life seemed to be a continuous, though ragged and jerky, sequence of stops and starts in which my high hopes and strategic plans turned again and again to disappointment, heartache and unfulfilled expectations. Since that moment, however, I have experienced myself, my life, and life itself as a process of unfoldment that is always and only mysterious, unknowable, and flowing from some unfathomable Source that is so much greater that we are. Living always in closest contact with that realization, I have become peaceful, certain, and free—in a way and to a degree that is indeed astonishing—given my painful disposition for all the years before that moment.

It was as if, by some miracle, I had become connected with a part of myself that was always in open communication and perfect synchronization with the flow of the Intelligent Universe—which included me and my unfoldment in Its own plans. Instead of having to fretfully figure out what to do next or having to scramble to do certain "smart" things in order to serve the future of the burden that my own life was, I merely had to wait and watch and listen for the guidance which would let me know what to do and when to do it. I had to merely "...let the flow of my experience carry me, in a direction which appear[ed] to be forward, toward goals of which I [was] but dimly aware." Amazing!

Spiritual process is a process of surrender to the Divine. It is a process of giving up the hold on our lives in order that our lives may become radiant expressions of the Higher Consciousness. Our lives then become endowed with the richness of the flow of that higher expression. Everything before that mystical moment loses its significance as we become fully alive in moment-to-moment communion with the Unknown More Than, the precious All. This flow of richness and radiance is but one way that the Unlimited Love reaches out to all those who are reaching out in an attempt to know It fully.

SPIRITUAL PROCESS IS A PROCESS OF SURRENDER TO THE DIVINE. IT IS A PROCESS OF GIVING UP THE HOLD ON OUR LIVES IN ORDER THAT OUR LIVES MAY BECOME RADIANT EXPRESSIONS OF THE HIGHER CONSCIOUSNESS.

Mapping the Mystery: Personalizing the Process

The process of transformation is a process of dis-identification of ourselves from a lower level of consciousness and a re-identification of ourselves with a higher level of consciousness—with all that that implies. The capacities of the lower levels are not lost, but are reordered in their degrees of importance for use within the context of the higher levels. As we are opened into the more intelligent and, thus, more creative dimensions of our being, we may use certain capabilities as much or more than we have used them at lower levels of function, but, perhaps, in a decidedly different manner or for a dramatically different purpose. Ken Wilber, in *The Atman Project*, describes this dis-identification and re-identification process:

> *The point is that as each higher-order structure emerges, the self eventually identifies with that structure—which is normal, natural, appropriate.*
>
> *As evolution proceeds, however, each level in turn is differentiated* ***from*** *the self, or "peeled off" so to speak. The self, that is, eventually* ***dis-identifies*** *with its present structure so as to* ***identify*** *with the next higher-order emergent structure. More precisely (and this is a very important technical point), we say that the self detaches itself from its* ***exclusive*** *identification with that lower structure. It doesn't throw that structure away, it simply no longer exclusively identifies with it. The point is that because the self is differentiated from the lower structure, it* ***transcends*** *that structure (without obliterating it in any way), and can thus* ***operate*** *on that lower structure using the tools of the newly emergent structure.*
>
> *Thus, at each point in psychological growth, we find: 1) a higher-order structure emerges in consciousness (with the help of symbolic forms); 2) the self identifies its being with that higher structure; 3) the next-higher order structure eventually emerges; 4) the self dis-identifies with the lower structure and shifts its essential identity to the higher structure; 5) consciousness thereby transcends the lower structure; 6) and becomes capable of operating on that lower structure from the higher-order level; 7) such that all preceding levels can then be integrated in consciousness, and ultimately as Consciousness.*[30]

A simple model of the never-ending, living process is shown in Figure No. 3. In this very simple map of the hero's journey, I have shown human consciousness as a flow upwards from a **lower** to a **higher** level. In between **integration** at the lower level and the higher level, there is a large open space, in which the dis-identification from the former level of perception is accomplished. For purposes of *A Course In Congruence*, the process of transformation is represented as flowing upwards from the third level of consciousness (mental-egoic) to the fifth level of consciousness (existential).

Before the process of transformation can begin, there must be an opening of the mind. In the model, that opening is depicted by the broken lines which indicate the boundaries of the two distinct levels of consciousness. The opening of the mind to unknown possibilities is caused by an intensification of the inherent evolutionary impulse and may be triggered by any number of different factors, once one's level of disillusionment is sufficient to precipitate seeking outside known prescriptions for relief of psychological pain. It is important to emphasize that **the opening is the single most-important element** in the process of transformation. Without the opening, we remain locked up within our own minds—prisoners of our own unenlightened thoughts and of our unresolved past, which continuously pulls at us for resolution. And, in the early stages of accelerated process, it is the opening which must be served most heartfully so as to allow the evolutionary process to transform our psyches as only it can.

Once that opening occurs, there will be, at some unpredictable moment, an inspiration (stimulus) strong enough to provoke an appropriate action (response) which will cause movement out of the psychological status quo. There may be several or many inspirations before one actually takes an action which demonstrates the legitimate strength of the impulse. Stalling denotes lack of readiness to begin the life-changing process.

First there is an **inspiration.**
Then there is an **action of will.**

The strength of the both the impulse and the response are
measures of one's readiness for a genuine (irrevocable)
surrender to the Process.

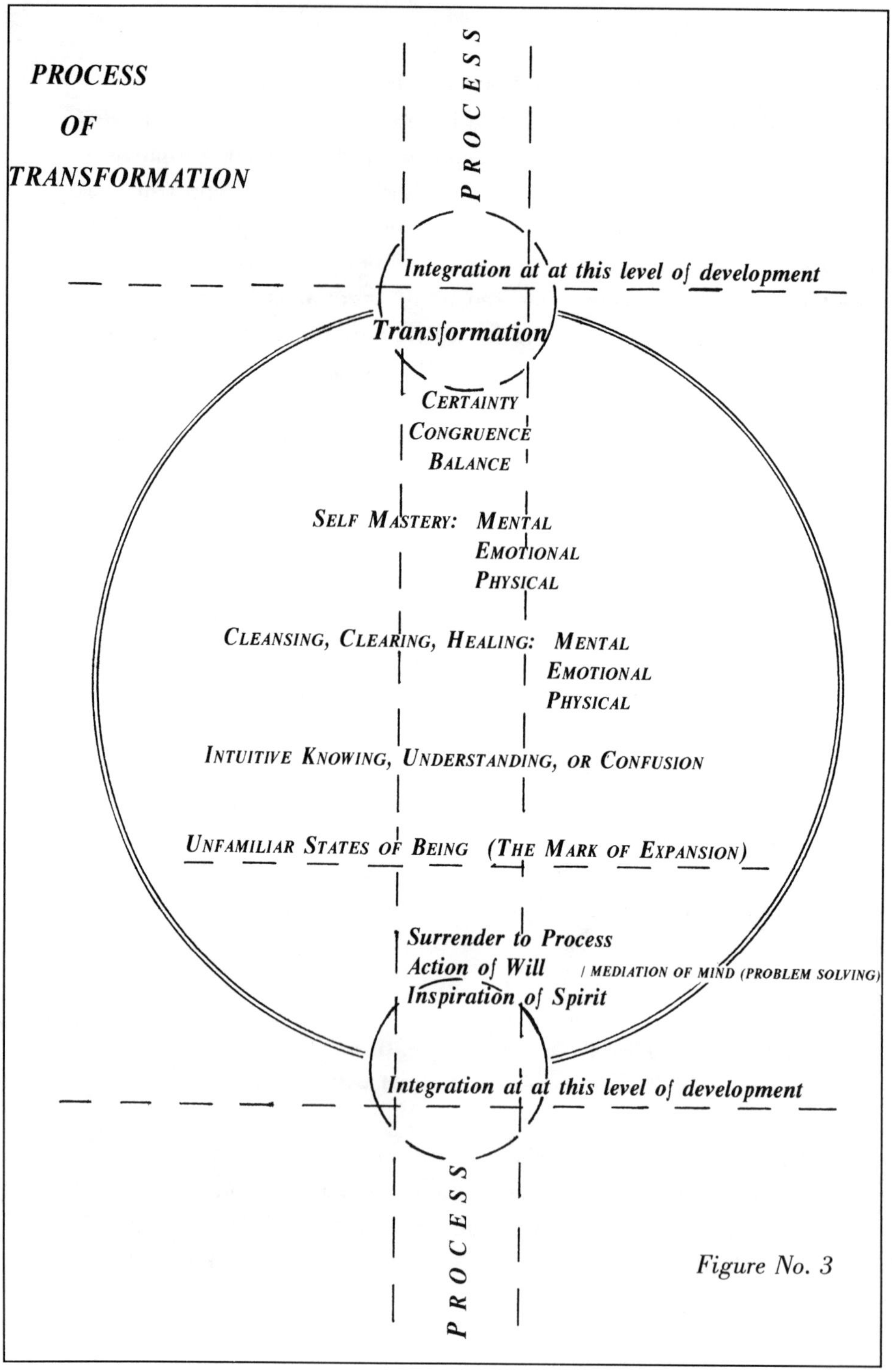
PROCESS
OF
TRANSFORMATION
PROCESS
Integration at at this level of development
Transformation
CERTAINTY
CONGRUENCE
BALANCE
SELF MASTERY: MENTAL
EMOTIONAL
PHYSICAL
CLEANSING, CLEARING, HEALING: MENTAL
EMOTIONAL
PHYSICAL
INTUITIVE KNOWING, UNDERSTANDING, OR CONFUSION
UNFAMILIAR STATES OF BEING (THE MARK OF EXPANSION)
Surrender to Process
Action of Will / MEDIATION OF MIND (PROBLEM SOLVING)
Inspiration of Spirit
Integration at at this level of development
PROCESS
Figure No. 3

Responsiveness: A Willful Action Once there is an evocative inspiration, an act of will follows. This will be a meaningful demonstration in response to the inspiration. All of a sudden we begin to act in response to the growth impulse.

Surrender To The Process: That act represents a certain degree of surrender to the process of transformation. By that act, we know that we are giving up the habituated ways of living, or, at least, trusting the unknown to some degree, in order to go beyond them.

The Mind Aligns: With readiness for change, the ego does not resist, but, instead, supports what is occurring. In response to the inspiration and the willful action, the mind mediates or problem-solves for us. It goes to work figuring out how we can get the money, how we can get off work, how we can reschedule trips or appointments, etc. In other words, the logical mind strategizes how we can manipulate the ordinary circumstances of our lives in order to serve our seemingly illogical process.

We actually use the mind in order to transcend the mind. That being the case we will need to speak to the ego regularly to assist it to understand so that its fears will not rage out of control—resulting in strong resistance or a closing down to the Process. With some reassurance the ego will continue to align with the high purpose of transcending its narrow perceptions and its conditioned reactions.

The process of transformation is a process of dis-identification of ourselves from a lower level of consciousness and a re-identification of ourselves with a higher level of consciousness —with all that implies.

Dis-identification and Re-identification. Once we have experienced surrender to the Process of Transformation—an actual giving up control over our lives—we can expect to experience a variety of UNFAMILIAR STATES OF BEING. These unfamiliar states of being are THE MARK OF EXPANSION, in that we begin the dis-identification phase of process. We begin to feel different in ways we are unable to or barely able to describe. We are no longer the same person we have been; we are not yet the person we are becoming; and, yet, we do not have any clear idea of who we are instead. We experience ourselves as somewhat amorphous beings whose previous choices are no longer attractive, whose previous preferences are no longer important, whose previous activities are no longer interesting, and whose previous relationships are no longer satisfying. Rather than looking outward for satisfaction and fulfillment, we begin to find the search for understanding of and re-identification of ourselves irresistible.

As amorphous non-identities heartfully seeking understanding, we can expect to have random and uncontrollable moments of clear INTUITIVE KNOWING, periods of clear UNDERSTANDING, and degrees of CONFUSION ranging from slight to nearly overwhelming.

As the open systems we have become—but still full of and fascinated by our personal past—we are mysteriously guided through the discovery stage of a variety of different approaches to reflecting on and reprocessing those experiences. Those approaches which will really work for us are obvious in that they evoke a high level of interest in learning about them. We take them to our hearts and quickly begin to use them in the service of our own transformation. Our crystallized conceptions and perceptions of the past begin to rise to the surface for our inspection by way of our newfound methods of thinking and viewing events. Our past is the rich source material utilized in the all-important reformation of our psychological posture. In the privacy of our own psyches we live out the CLEANSING, CLEARING AND HEALING OF THE PHYSICAL BODY, THE EMOTIONAL BODY AND THE MENTAL BODY. We notice—and others may notice—that we feel, act, and look lighter, better, clearer, and freer for periods of time; and all of the time, we are aware of an underlying sense of hopefulness and a growing sense of certainty.

After some indeterminate period of time, as we continue in the process, we will begin to experience SELF-MASTERY at higher levels than we have experienced before, PHYSICALLY, EMOTIONALLY, MENTALLY. The conditioned compulsive responses of our bodies and minds lose, to a significant degree, their power over our choices. Our choices are all invariably made based on what we perceive to be our highest good in every case—the choice which will best serve our own unfoldment. As the high choices are consistently made, our new identity begins to be sketched in lightly—and then drawn with bolder strokes.

With our new identity actually beginning to emerge, we unknowingly approach the unforeseeable moment of transformation, with a growing natural sense of BALANCE; a growing, natural EXPERIENCE OF CONGRUENCE; and a strong, though indescribable, FEELING OF CERTAINTY about ourselves, about our lives, and about our destined fulfillment.

Then, at some mysterious, unpredictable moment transformation will occur—by the Grace of God. That transformation of consciousness will take place only if we have RISKED IT ALL (our past) and have CONTINUED TO PARTICIPATE every step of the way in the process.

The Price: Responsiveness, Participation, Demonstration: Our conscious role in the process of transformation is an all-important one, even though we must remember that we cannot transform ourselves. We can only submit ourselves to the process, support ourselves to remain one-pointed in our intention, be highly responsive to the signs and demands of our own personal process, and demonstrate our readiness on a schedule that is, and in ways that are, appropriate and timely. In relationship to this model, there are some things that we must be continuously aware of due to the weight of their importance to our unfoldment:

First — Willingness to Participate. Our willingness to participate is the sure sign that our surrender is real. The process of transformation is a graceful flow only as long as we are willing to participate by honoring our deeper (evolutionary) impulses. We demonstrate this willingness by engaging the conscious practices which assist re-identification to occur, and by making the demonstrations we are given the opportunities to make: the higher choices which serve our own unique unfoldment.

The flow is impeded and we experience struggle when we attempt to control the circumstances of our lives and strive to make things turn out a particular way or on a schedule that we think is "right" or "good" or "appropriate."

It is worthy of note here that, although the model of transformation looks very neat and all of the stages appear to be distinct and easily recognizable, in the living of it the process will most probably be messy, chaotic, and oftentimes unreadable, as our identifications of ourselves are interfered with, as our perceptions are turned inside out, and as our manifest worlds are turned upside down. Most usually, only after we have completed a specific phase of the process are we able to reflect and see clearly what was really occurring in our process during that time.

Second — Having Our Experiences Fully. The transformational process ultimately depends on our not closing down on (thus stopping, diluting, or adulterating) our experiences before they are completed. We must learn to live each experience of the process *completely* in order that we receive every ounce of value from each incident or event, even though it may seem unimportant to us or incongruent with what we think should be occurring.

It is valuable for us to be aware of the ego's tendency to stop in the middle of the cycle of action—which includes beginning, continuing, completing—leaving its commitments uncompleted. Because the ego is a constellation of thoughts, when a "better idea" presents itself, it is the ego's normal behavior to jump to a new conclusion as though it were a train jumping its tracks. Because the ego does not want to do anything it does not feel comfortable doing, or anything which does not obviously forward its own strategies, its uncompromising "No" is a definite factor to be contended with. In order to have our experiences fully, then, we must override the ego's tendencies to sabotage and subvert our continuing participation in order to live our relationships and circumstances to their real completions.

Security: The Illusion. At the third level of consciousness, there is no security. Any feeling of security that we create for ourselves from our possessions, our relationships, our ideas, and our circumstances is a lie, an illusion. We are holding onto air. When we transcend the level of the logical, rational mind, we begin to feel secure out of our Self—not because of circumstances, not because of money, not because of relationships, not because of anything but the reality of the Self. When we become established at the next level of consciousness, we become inwardly comfortable in a much more real and meaningful way—the result of the higher state of being we now enjoy.

Dealing With Resistance. Our inner "Yes" must be stronger than the ego's fearful "No" in order for us to continue to participate. So, an important part of our practice is supporting the ego's alignment with our High Intention. We can expect the ego's resistance in several forms: arrogant judgments, thoughts and feelings of "I can't," self-righteous reactions, know-it-all attitudes, laziness or inertia, and denial of the possible value of an experience before we even have the experience. Whatever form it takes, resistance can close us down and keep us in our cozy comfort zone (lower level of consciousness). We all desire the freedom of "Yes." So, when we are thinking "I can't," "I don't want to," or "I won't," we simply must change our thinking to "I will."

Before the New Reality Is Real. Until our process of transformation becomes "real" to us and *unequivocally* the single most-important focus of our life, we will suffer some conflict. We will often have the experience of living in two separate realities—an experience which I call "doing the splits." Before our re-identification has been completed, we will sometimes find the ways and means of the consensus reality to be "real" when we are engaged in things of the world; and, we will most often find the very different ways and means of process to be "real" when we are alone, when we are with others of like mind, or when we are studying the high teachings which make our hearts leap.

Using the scale of justice as a metaphor for ourselves is effective in attempting to understand what is going on and what phase of process this experience of living in two realities represents. If we see the scale (ourself) as heavy on the left-brain (rational) side when our awakening begins, and recognize that the right-brain (subtle) side of the scale (ourself) takes on more and more weight as we proceed along our path, we will realize that at some point our right side will have more weight. We can conclude that the moment the accumulated weight causes the scale (us) to shift downward on the right side, our re-identification is well-enough established to alleviate whatever conflict we were experiencing during the stage wherein we were "out of balance" in the ordinary or mental-egoic way.

WE WILL NEED TO SPEAK TO THE EGO REGULARLY TO ASSIST IT TO UNDERSTAND SO THAT ITS FEARS WILL NOT RAGE OUT OF CONTROL.

THE CHAKRA SYSTEM AND THE LEVELS OF CONSCIOUSNESS

The levels of human consciousness as the chakra system are presented in Figure No. 4—a model by Christopher Hills. The chakras are shown with the corresponding functions of the brain.[31] By way of this model we see that there are seven primary "chakras" or energy centers—which represent levels of consciousness—in the etheric field of the human body. They may be identified as follows:

Seventh level	— the Crown Chakra	— Imaginative or Spiritual
Sixth level	— the Brow Chakra	— Intuitive or Metaphysical
Fifth level	— the Throat Chakra	— Conceptual or Existential
Fourth level	— the Heart Chakra	— Self or Surrender
Third level	— the Solar Plexus Chakra	— Intellectual or Mental-Egoic
Second level	— the Splenic Chakra	— Social or Emotional-Sexual
First level	— the Root Chakra	— Physical or Survival

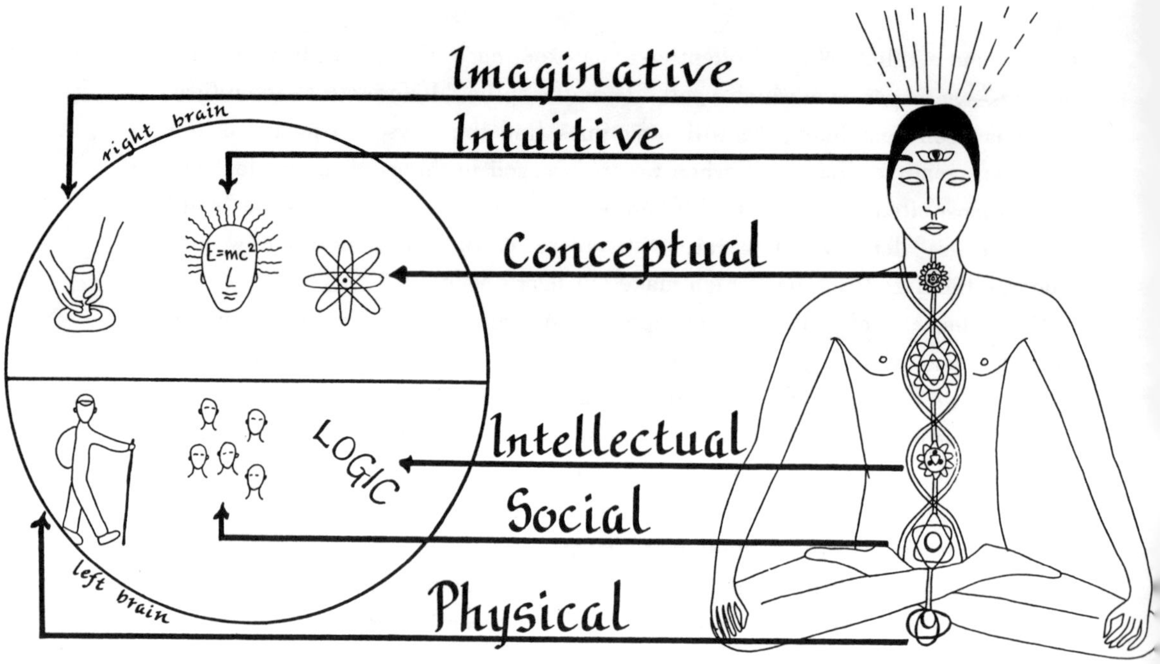

Figure No. 4

The lower self is represented by the three chakras which lie below the level of the heart. The higher Self is represented by the three chakras which lie above the heart. As we will see represented in Figure No. 7, the heart chakra is the place where the consciousness of the higher centers commingles with the consciousness of the lower centers—the place where transformation actually occurs.

Each higher chakra represents a higher-order of potential with which the human being is biologically, psychologically, and spiritually endowed. And, the awakening of the higher centers is the breakthrough for which all human beings unconsciously yearn. This *breakthrough* in consciousness is the *breakout* from our personal prison. It is the only true escape from the limitation of the lower levels of consciousness which have held us captive and have left us feeling dissatisfied, unfulfilled, frustrated, and incomplete for too long. This breaking through the walls of the robotic mental structures into the higher realms of being is the aim of all forms of spiritual practice which have been ordained for and enacted by seekers throughout our history.

In Figure No. 5 Jacquelyn Small identifies for us the motivating forces of the lower self,[32] which evolve within each of us, bringing us to a point of readiness for sincere conscious participation with our own transformational process. She identifies the first level of consciousness as the level of fear, which drives the need for self-preservation, which then evolves to a desire for physical well-being, and gradually, evolves to the will to live. She identifies the second level of consciousness as the level of passion, which drives the desire for self-gratification, which then evolves to a desire for emotional balance, and gradually evolves to the will to feel. She identifies the third level of consciousness as the level of desire for identity, which drives the desire for self-definition, which then evolves to a desire for mental clarity, and eventually evolves to the will to know.

The Motivating Forces of the Lower Self

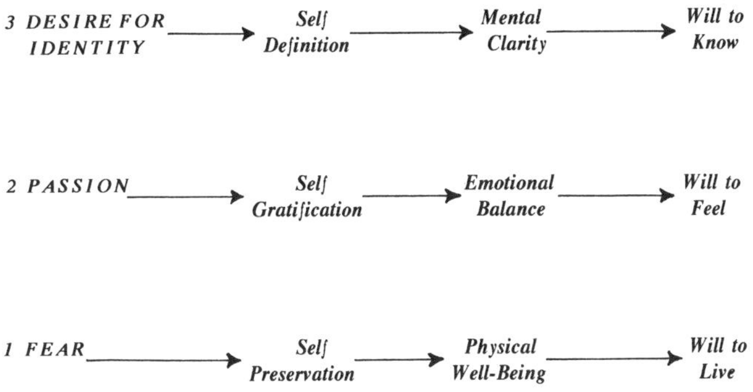

Figure No. 5

On Earth As It Is In Heaven. The centers of consciousness which are represented by the chakras are interrelated and have an influence on each other. In the following model [Figure No. 6], we see that by way of the transformational process, the higher (heavenly) centers of consciousness (or the higher chakras) influence and, thus, change the consciousness of the lower centers. Through this depiction by Jacquelyn Small[33] we are able to see that as the higher centers become activated and receptive to the inflow of higher intelligence (or higher consciousness), a direct effect of that activation is experienced in the lower centers, eventually transforming them to a condition of enlightenment, in true alignment with the higher Self. The fear-based motivations of the lower chakras arise from a personal desire to feel secure physically, emotionally, and mentally and are self-centered. The evolution-based motivations of the higher chakras originate in the drive toward true wholeness and are Self-centered.

THE VITALIZATION OF THE SEVENTH LEVEL INFLUENCES THE FIRST LEVEL:
The Love of God (Self) commingles with the Will to Live, transforming Fear into Courage.

THE ENERGIZING OF THE SIXTH LEVEL INSPIRES THE SECOND LEVEL:
The Love of Life commingles with the Will to Feel, transforming Passion into Compassion.

THE ACTIVATION OF THE FIFTH LEVEL ILLUMINATES THE THIRD LEVEL:
The Love of Truth commingles with the Will to Know, transforming the Desire for Identity to Understanding. Self-Acceptance—which occurs by way of the transformational process in the heart—opens the heart to our full humanity and the fullness of humanity in others.

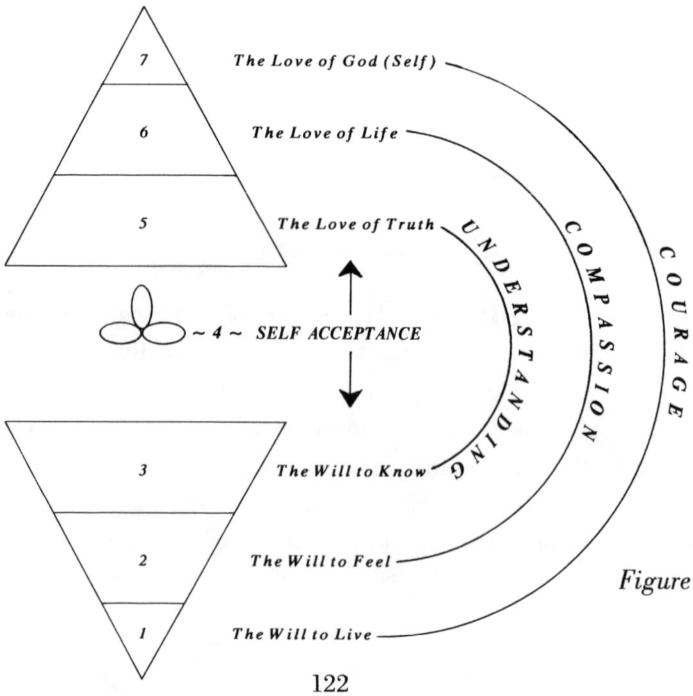

Figure No. 6

As we see in the Christopher Hills' model[34] [Figure No. 7], the enlightened consciousness flows into the higher centers and through the heart chakra, where the connections with correspondent lower chakras are made. So, it is within the human heart that the process of transformation is centered and mysteriously effected. Dr. Hills' model of the flow replicates the unbroken shape of infinity within the human body.

By way of this model, Dr. Hills indicates the color which represents each chakra or level of consciousness, and identifies the lower self as objective (exclusionary) consciousness and the higher Self and subjective (inclusionary) consciousness. As is discussed at length in Chapters Eight and Nine, the experience of separation, which is the plight of the lower self, creates perceptions of an object-filled world that is "different than" the self. The condition of at-one-ment, which is the natural state of the higher Self, engenders an experience of a world of unity, togetherness, and essential relationship. The heart—through which the seven levels of consciousness flow and in which they commingle—is the direct correspondent of the mid-brain, which is the regulating center for the flow of higher consciousness to the entire body.

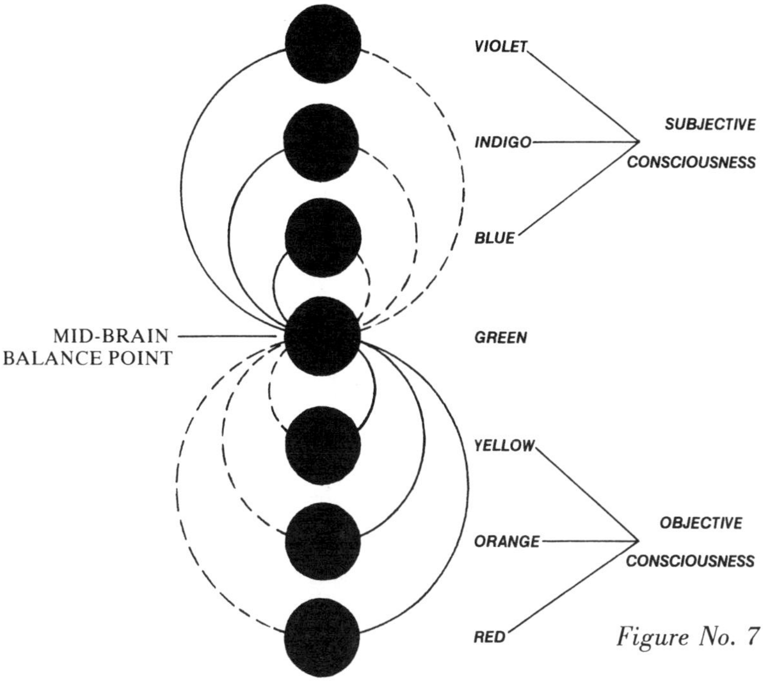

Figure No. 7

Those of us who are so obviously being changed by the graceful flow of higher consciousness can at least begin to grasp the concepts which provide us with a way to translate our amazing metamorphosis. As Da Avabhasa states in *The Holy Jumping-Off Place*:

> *Enlightenment is a literal change of the whole body. When you have acquired the human form, the literal change that must occur in the body is not really so much in its outward appearance, because you already have the necessary structure. But the changes that must occur are literal, psycho-physical changes, just as literal as if you were to acquire more legs and arms, except that the most dramatic changes occur in dimensions different from the outward shape of the body. The change is as literal as evolving from a dinosaur to a human being, and it is as dramatic as that, but it principally occurs at more subtle levels of the physics of the bodily being. There are literal changes in the nervous system, literal changes in the chemistry of the body, literal changes in the structural functioning of the brain.*[35]

By way of this discussion, and, certainly by a closer study of the referenced teachings, we can begin to get a clearer idea and a better understanding of what transformation actually is: a process of real psycho-physical change. Of course, no words nor diagrams could ever approximate the truth about this mysterious, invisible, and silent metamorphosis of a human consciousness.

TOWARD EXPANSION AND SELF-MASTERY

A VISUALIZATION: SWIMMING WITH THE CURRENTS

Close your eyes. Straighten your spine. Tell the holding in your body to let go. Allow your breath to breathe you freely.

Imagine a bright and glorious day in a mountain setting.
Imagine a beautiful crystal clear stream flowing down from a hidden height.

Notice that the stream is making joyful gurgling and bubbling and rushing sounds as it flows.

Notice that the stream expresses a purposeful intention to reach an unknown destination. And realize that the stream cannot be stopped from flowing.

Now imagine an exquisite fish, sleek and colorful, swimming against the flow of the stream. In your mind's eye see the magnificent fish swimming upstream against the forceful currents of the stream's intention.

See the graceful fish thrash about awkwardly, knocking up against the rocks in the stream, struggling to move through the downrushing flow. Name the fish—your name.

Now imagine that the exquisite fish, sleek and colorful, just lets go, stops trying to swim, and notice what happens.

Notice that the currents of the stream turn the fish around in the water. Notice that the movement of the waters sweeps the fish along in its rushing flow to an unknown destination.

Notice that the fish begins to gracefully ride the currents of the clear, cold stream. Imagine that it begins to share the joyful gurgling and bubbling and rushing feelings that the stream generates. For a few moments, swim as that exquisite fish in the beautiful stream and experience the freedom and natural innocence of it.

Notice that by merely allowing your attention to become one with the water, you easily able to swim along. And, with a slight movement of your fin, you can skillfully glide around the large rocks in the stream bed. Feel the peace.

LET US, WITH GREAT ANTICIPATION, ENTHUSIASM, AND HUMILITY, TURN OUR ATTENTION TO THE ENCODED PROMISE WHICH PULSES MYSTERIOUSLY WITHIN OUR HEARTS AND MINDS.

CHAPTER FIVE

THE RISK FACTOR

The heart is an adventurer, the explorer of the mysteries, the discoverer of all that is hidden. The heart is always on a pilgrimage. It is never satisfied, it has an innermost discontent, a spiritual discontent. It never settles anywhere. It is very much in love with movement, dynamism.

—BHAGWAN SHREE RAJNEESH[1]

CLIFF-JUMPING

Through my many experiences of choosing the high road, I have discovered that the risk factor is an inherent and all-important catalyst in the transformational process. Again and again I have found myself standing at the edge of the cliff; and, again and again, I have flung myself over that edge into the thin air of the unknown with complete self-abandon. And each time I have experienced being held aloft, as though I were strapped onto the frame of a hang glider, my floating flight over the abyss assured. Completely at risk in earthly terms, my heart's allurement to the Divine has always been intensified by the riveting views of my inner vistas. And, always, I have felt deeply the great adventure of it all. Always have I been deeply touched by the privilege of living my life "on the edge" and "hanging in thin air" in a most subtly intimate relationship with the Great Adventurer Itself.

I strongly suggest cliff-jumping as the only way to live. I highly recommend "The Way of the Heart" because it is life lived courageously, but, surprisingly, effortlessly. It is life created, not out of the ordinary presumptions of our mind's narrow views, but, instead, out of the extraordinary possibilities and the unimaginably broad panoramas of the Great Mind Itself. As such, it is a life of fascinating twists and turns, awe-inspiring synchronicities, and miracles by the score. It is a life which designs itself as a richly-patterned tapestry, with the meticulous interweaving of the golden threads of Universal Principle, which our limited thinking can neither grasp, translate, nor equal.

The great adventure is a life, not of "figuring it out," but, of participating fully, in truth, with the circumstances and relationships of our life at any given time. This intuitive life is a life of continuous change—change within ourselves and in the circumstances and relationships of our manifest world. This flowing life is a life of innate spontaneity and instinctive responsiveness to the signals which reveal to us the necessary components of the flow: what, when, where, and who. Somewhere along the way, without really knowing "how," we realize we have done what we were called to do.

The cardinal principles on which the life of cliff-jumping is based are trust and letting go; and, in fact, these are the same. To let go, we must trust; and, to trust, we must let go. This elemental aspect of becoming a great adventurer lays outside the veil of our rational mind, and is given to us by God. It lies in wait for our first precious moment of realization, when, with our heart soaring, we leap beyond the confines of the known into the Great Unknown. That initiatory leap is life-changing; and, before we know it, we are hooked on cliff-jumping.[2]

To let go, we must trust; and, to trust, we must let go.

How Could You Refuse?

> *This first stage of the mythological journey—which we have designated the "call to adventure"—signifies that destiny has summoned the hero and transferred his spiritual center of gravity from within the pale of his society to a zone unknown.[3]*

The model of risk-taking [Figure No. 8] gives us a way to view ourselves as cliff-jumpers, to reflect on our present level of desire to leap beyond the confines of our own pseudo-security, and to mentally test ourselves against the challenges which our process is calling us to meet.

The Territory of Consolation—also the heights of reason and doubt—is shown here to be integration at the third level of consciousness. This territory is *consoling* since it is a psychological province wherein denial of the fragility of our very life allows us to feel just secure enough to get by. It is a territory which perpetrates our illusion of standing on solid ground, allowing us to operate most of the time at a manageable level of fear.

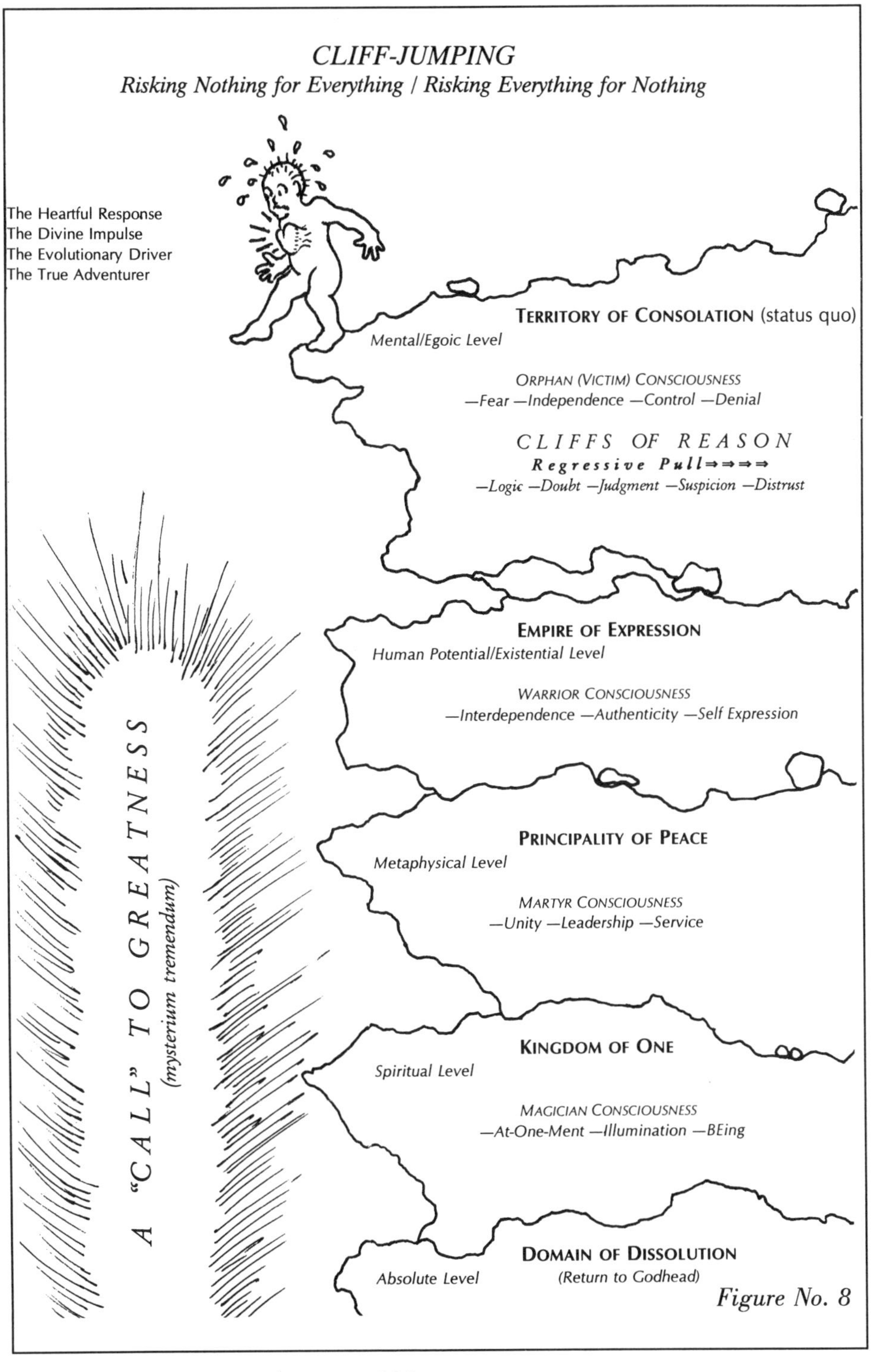
CLIFF-JUMPING
Risking Nothing for Everything / Risking Everything for Nothing
The Heartful Response
The Divine Impulse
The Evolutionary Driver
The True Adventurer
TERRITORY OF CONSOLATION (status quo)
Mental/Egoic Level
ORPHAN (VICTIM) CONSCIOUSNESS
—Fear —Independence —Control —Denial
CLIFFS OF REASON
Regressive Pull⇒⇒⇒⇒
—Logic —Doubt —Judgment —Suspicion —Distrust
EMPIRE OF EXPRESSION
Human Potential/Existential Level
WARRIOR CONSCIOUSNESS
—Interdependence —Authenticity —Self Expression
PRINCIPALITY OF PEACE
Metaphysical Level
MARTYR CONSCIOUSNESS
—Unity —Leadership —Service
KINGDOM OF ONE
Spiritual Level
MAGICIAN CONSCIOUSNESS
—At-One-Ment —Illumination —BEing
DOMAIN OF DISSOLUTION
Absolute Level
(Return to Godhead)
A "CALL" TO GREATNESS
(mysterium tremendum)

Figure No. 8

> *The usual person is more than content, he is even proud to remain within the indicated bounds, and popular belief gives him every reason to fear so much as the first step into the unexplored.*[4]

In *A Course In Congruence* we are interested in the freedom which lies beyond the bounds of this consoling neverland—the freedom which we will experience when we leap beyond the present limitations of mind, emotions, and body.

Having achieved a level of psychological comfortability (however precarious), we will begin to feel the limitation of that level of function sooner or later. And, although we may *fight for our lives* to maintain the status quo which that level represents, we will, at the same time, be unconsciously desiring dramatic change—growth, transformation, evolution. We are evolutionary beings; and we are never being true to ourselves unless we are experiencing the flow of that dynamic process as it changes and changes and changes us. In learning to read ourselves and arrive at the level of truth, it is valuable to know that a comfort zone acts as a pit of quicksand in that it sucks us in and holds us until the unbreakable lifeline of our higher nature pulls us out and thrusts us into the next phase of our dangerous and exciting evolutionary cycle.

As we see in the model, the third-level Territory of Consolation is a self-created illusion which is built on the ego's faulty assumption of its separation from others and a view of itself as an independent agent—in other words, its rightful duty and ability to do it "my way." This self-created illusory world is one of denial of whole parts of its humanity and of subconscious characteristics which are too frightening for it to face—namely, its irrational terror of death (and, so, of life). This illusion is constructed on the cliffs of logic and reason, the face of which is marred by cracks and crevices of fearful self-protective doubt. This is the level of the pre-heroic "Orphan," who experiences being a victim of circumstances and being victimized by others. The Orphan, however, is really victimized by its own limited perceptions and its sense of helplessness, weakness, and inability to rise above its own limitations.

We see, by the hair standing on end and the gaping eyes, that the "call" to begin cliff-jumping has struck a strong chord of fear in this journeyer. But we see, too, the hero heart with its vibrant response to the "call" from the Great Mystery. The heart represents for us the divine impulse, the great adventurer, the evolutionary spark which has been ignited.

We also see our journeyer's arms flapping as he stands immobilized by the fear in which his feet are stuck. And as he stands at the cliff's edge, we can imagine that he is contemplating the risks inherent in his imminent leap. What does he risk? Everything!

He risks:

- The loss of his present level of comfort;
- The loss of self;
- The loss of his belief systems;
- The loss of his relationships;
- The loss of his ability to *hide out* and to *just get by*;
- The loss of his material possessions;
- The loss of his lifestyle;
- The loss of approval;
- Being wrong;
- Making a fool of himself.

WE ARE EVOLUTIONARY BEINGS; AND WE ARE NEVER BEING TRUE TO OURSELVES UNLESS WE ARE EXPERIENCING THE FLOW OF THAT DYNAMIC PROCESS AS IT CHANGES AND CHANGES AND CHANGES US.

Before that initial leap, we are afraid—even terrified—of the consequences of our actions. But there comes a point at which we become willing to suffer the consequences of our clear conscious choices in order to be free. And once we become the truth of ourselves we will experience ourselves as being **equal to** the circumstances of our life—and **greater than** the circumstances of our life. Such freedom!

With this high level of risk, will our hero fling himself off the cliffs of reason and into the Unknown More Than? Perhaps he will realize that he is going to be fearful until he leaps beyond fear. Perhaps he will realize that fear is a natural part of being human, and that fear's counsel is not the wisest counsel he can seek when making choices about cliff-jumping.

> *...it is a deliberate, terrific refusal to respond to anything but the deepest, highest, richest answer to the as yet unknown demand of some waiting void within: a kind of total strike, or rejection of the offered terms of life, as a result of which some power of transformation carries the problem to a plane of new magnitudes, where it is suddenly and finally resolved.*[5]

Willingness. Anyone who uses the word willingness in relationship to change is talking about risking. After the all-important opening of the mind, willingness to risk becomes the basic determinant of our process since without that willful alignment of the ego, we become stuck in our own conflict: desiring change but lacking the willingness to risk. What we must realize is that the transformational process is THE BIG DEAL of our life. As Joseph Campbell has shown us through his voluminous research, it is the essence of our existence; it is the central core of meaning for humans; it is the purpose for our being here; it is the source of our concealed discontent; it is the theme of all myths; it is the thread which runs through all of humanity's history. And, when the scale is finally tipped by the weight of our own inherent desire for transformation, the "NO" which has held us in place will become the "YES" which will move us to the cliff's edge, which will set our wings to flapping, and which will, at some unpredictable moment, propel us over the brink into the thin air of the great adventure.

> *Having responded to his own call, and continuing to follow courageously as the consequences unfold, the hero finds all the forces of the unconscious at his side. Mother Nature herself supports the mighty task.*[6]

Resistance. In speaking of willingness and readiness, it is important to also speak of resistance—another element of our humanity about which we most certainly need some understanding. We can expect that our entire life will include the element of resistance, no matter how enlightened we become. Resistance is a normal part of our being human, and we need only learn how to perceive and translate resistance in order to deal with it in truth. Resistance can be spoken about in a variety of different ways, some of which are quite technical. For our discussion here we only need to realize that resistance is the ego's fearful reluctance to give up control of its hold on our life—control which it conceives to be absolutely necessary for our survival. When we open and allow the deeper personality to emerge, the ego's resistance is easily overcome again and again. We will still suffer the weight and drag of resistance on us; but it will not stop us, and it will not slow us down anymore.

Another form of resistance which is a fact of life is called "regressive pull."[7] Regressive pull is the influence of lower evolutionary stages—"stages not outgrown and integrated, but disowned and dissociated."[8] Since an earlier stage has not really been outgrown, it "erupts today as neurotic symptoms and emotional obsessions: conflict-ridden obsessions which conceal a hidden wish for emotional-sexual impulses and gratifications. Those bodily...impulses, when not outgrown, transformed, and integrated, remain lodged in the recesses of an otherwise higher-order self, and there disguise themselves as painful neurotic symptoms, compulsions, obsessions."[9]

The impulse for change, for transformation, for evolution is the creative force of Life Itself. And the tension between the resistance to change and the genetically-encoded potency of our humanity is creative tension—the tension which causes change to occur. Without resistance, no creation happens. Resistance is what we press up against and what we press through as we go beyond the limits of the Territory of Consolation. So, resistance is good and necessary! The whole idea that enlightenment is only about being wonderful and joyful and peaceful is simply not the truth. There is always more resistance to overcome since there are always more levels of transformation. As the power of the transformational process increases in us and as our surrender becomes more and more profound, our natural resistance may sometimes increase. However, it will have less influence on our choices. Once we have gotten the hang of cliff-jumping, we can be assured that resistance will only make the leap over the edge more thrilling.

> *The adventure is always and everywhere a passage beyond the veil of the known into the unknown; the powers that watch at the boundary are dangerous; to deal with them is risky; yet for anyone with competence and courage the danger fades.*[10]

The Empire of Expression—also the existential (fifth) level of realization—is shown here to be the level of consciousness to which the wandering hero must leap in order to be freed from the extremely limiting parameters of the mental-egoic stage of human evolution. This ledge on the cliffs of the transformational process—as represented in this model of risk—is characterized by a greatly expanded self-awareness, authentic Self-expression, full acceptance and actualization of natural interdependence and personal empowerment.

This is the level of the archetypal (spiritual) Warrior—the journeyer who was once a disillusioned Orphan, became an open-minded Wanderer, and arrived at the Empire of Expression equipped to "have an impact on the world, and to avoid ineffectiveness and passivity."[11] The Warrior discovers that with courage and hard work people can take a stand and can make changes—for themselves and for others.[12] The Warrior's lessons have to do with confronting fear and bringing the hope and meaning they have found to the world.

When we have become comfortable at this level, we will, at some point, become aware of the "call" to leap again into more profound levels of our vast potential. The "spontaneous will" of the evolutionary impulse will again begin to move, and we will find ourselves once again hugging the edge of the cliff, as our heartbeat quickens at the prospect of another high adventure. And once again we will risk it all!

> *The hero is the man of self-achieved submission....[13] The hero, therefore, is the man or woman who has been able to battle past his personal and local historical limitations to the generally valid, normally human forms. Such a one's visions, ideas, and inspirations come pristine from the primary springs of human life and thought. Hence they are eloquent, not of the present disintegrating society and psyche, but of the unquenched source through which society is reborn. The hero has died as a modern man; but as eternal man—perfected, unspecific, universal man—he has been reborn. His second solemn task and deed therefore...is to return then to us, transfigured, and teach the lesson he has learned of life renewed.[14]*

The Principality of Peace—the metaphysical (sixth) level of realization—is the leap in consciousness which the Warrior hero must make in order to proceed beyond the earthly freedom which authentic Self-expression has afforded him in order to fulfill his hidden desire to become an "explorer of the mysteries." This is the level of the archetypal Martyr, who is characterized by a personal experience of unity with others and the world-at-large as well as selfless service and leadership.

As Carol Pearson tells us "...the Martyr is not trying to bargain to save its self but believes that the sacrifice of the self will save others. This is what the Christ story is about: sacrificing to save others.... The decision to care, even at the cost of self-sacrifice, is a choice here for life and against despair. Heroes...not only endure hardships, they maintain their love of life, their courage, and their capacity to care for others. No matter how much suffering they experience, they do not pass it on to others. They absorb it and declare: Suffering stops here."[15]

And, when our hero has become masterful and comfortable at the metaphysical level, he will once again experience the "call" to adventure and will once again be up to risking everything for whatever lies within the unknown reaches of the great process.

> *...we have not even to risk the adventure alone; for the heroes of all time have gone before us; the labyrinth is thoroughly known; we have only to follow the thread of the hero-path. And where we had thought to find an abomination, we shall find a god; where we had thought to slay another, we shall slay ourselves; where we had thought to travel outward, we shall come to the center of our own existence; where we had thought to be alone, we shall be with all the world.*[16]

The Kingdom of One—the spiritual (seventh) level of realization—is the leap in consciousness which this pilgrim hero must make in order to achieve true enlightenment. This is the level of the archetypal Magician and is characterized by an impersonal experience of at-one-ment with All That Is and true illumination of all levels of his being. Pearson tells us "...the Magician learns to move with the energy of the universe and to attract what is needed by laws of synchronicity, so that the ease of the Magician's interaction with the universe seems like magic."[17] She further states: "...the Magician gains what the Orphan longed for, the return to the lost Eden, first on a microcosmic, personal level, and later on the cosmic level; but instead of experiencing plenty from a childlike, dependent position, the Magician enters the garden on the basis of interdependence—with other people, with nature, and with God. The last lesson the hero learns, then, is happiness."[18]

> *Those who know, not only that the Everlasting lives in them, but that what they, and all things, really are <u>is</u> the Everlasting, dwell in the groves of the wish-fulfilling trees, drink the brew of immortality, and listen everywhere to the unheard music of eternal concord.*[19]

The Domain of Dissolution—the realm of Absolute Consciousness.

> *The bounded, shackled centers of consciousness, myriadfold, on every plane of existence (not only in this present universe, limited by the Milky Way, but beyond, into the reaches of space), galaxy beyond galaxy, world beyond world of universes, coming into being out of the timeless pool of the void, bursting into life, and like a bubble therewith vanishing: time and time again:*

lives by the multitude: all suffering: each bounded in the tenuous, tight circle of itself—lashing, killing, hating, and desiring peace beyond victory: these all are the children, the mad figures of the transitory yet inexhaustible, long world dream of the All-Regarding, whose essence is the essence of Emptiness: "The Lord Looking Down in Pity."[20]

The point is that the high adventure of spiritual process is a risky business. It is so risky that it requires the hero heart—the heart of the true adventurer in order to meet the challenges along the way. And the risks are experienced as very real, very personal, and very scary. There is no talking them away. There are no reassurances which will make them seem less risky. There are no guarantees. There are no predictable outcomes in ordinary terms. There is only the adventure of giving up control of our lives, of surrendering ourselves to the Invisible Reality, and of trusting the Great Intelligence which calls to us: **LEAP**!

Our society has not bred a population of heroes. Instead the consensus reality of our culture has encouraged us to "play it safe," "to do it right," and "to fit in" to the existing societal structures, which are, in reality, obvious aberrations of an originally-conceived society which would accommodate heroes. Our forefathers risked it all, leapt off the ledge of their own Territory of Consolation, flung themselves from the cliffs of reason and doubt, experienced transformation to the level of authentic high-minded expression, and together intelligently set up a system based on spiritual principles which would promote truth, freedom and love. But, somewhere along the way, uninspired and unheroic leaders translated their vision through their own untransformed perceptions. Things became all about shoring up the walls of the Territory of Consolation, filling in the eroding crevices of doubt, and making the status quo the god to which we were all to submit ourselves. Independence, logic and reason became the watch words for a whole society of potential heroes.

We set out with the best of intentions: to reduce suffering and be more at peace. But unwittingly we fell into assuming that the inner needs we were now developing could be met in the same way as our physical needs—through having or doing the right things. ...we let ourselves be seduced by the material world and by all its fruits.

But then, at the very time we most needed to change, we found ourselves unable to let go. Clinging to our comforts, we seemed unwilling to bear the modest discomforts that would enhance our chances of survival. Too many people preferred to risk annihilation rather than give up their attachments and illusions.[21]

FACING FEAR AND FEARING FORWARD

Our inability to let go can be traced directly to the ego's clinging to the past, its strong resistance to sacrificing its creature comforts, its attempts to maintain the status quo, and its fear of the unknown. In order to answer our individual and collective *call to greatness*, we must now face our fear, and, with informed intention, we must override the ego's self-serving approach in order to make the leap into the invisible flow of the evolutionary process. Ken Carey speaks eloquently of the ego's fear in *Terra Christa*:

> *The ego will often present fear in a guise of responsible concern, making it appear logical and reasonable. But fear is fear; the body always knows the difference. No matter how convincingly the ego may justify fear, the body that has to live with it will not be healthy. Fear is designed to play only a minuscule role in a healthy life.*
>
> *On those few occasions when fear serves some useful purpose, its appearance is brief and to the point.*
>
> *The use and protective appearance of fear is more aptly called fright. Fright is what one may feel on a street corner at the sudden approach of an automobile. It may cause one to jump back and so save the body from damage. However, fright has only momentary usefulness. It was never intended to be a permanent state of existence.*
>
> *In our modern world, fright has become institutionalized under a thousand and one poorly-understood brands of subliminal anxiety. This is a devastating condition, robbing us of vitality, awareness and good health. Becoming aware of our anxieties is the first step toward removing their subliminal influence from our lives.*
>
> *Fear is a parasite, sapping vitality, destroying health, and diminishing consciousness. We do not need to accept it as a part of our lives. Subconscious fears will remain to trouble us so long as they are repressed or ignored; their only exit point is through the conscious mind. Taking time out*

> *to look at our fears, inviting them up out of the subconscious realm into the light of day, may not be a particularly enjoyable exercise, but it is necessary if we are to return to healthy, spirit-motivated function.*[22]

In *Up From Eden*, Ken Wilber assigns fear to two major categories:

> *What has been so very difficult for Western psychology to grasp is that there are at least two major but quite different forms of fear and anxiety. One form is pathological or neurotic terror: any type of anxiety that can legitimately be traced to 'mental illness,' pathological defense mechanisms, or neurotic guilt. But the other form of terror is not due to a mental aberration or a neurotic illness—it is a basic, unavoidable, inescapable terror inherent in the separate-self sense. Man's prior Nature is Spirit, the ultimate Whole, but until he discovers that Wholeness, he remains an alienated fragment, a separate self, and that separate self necessarily is faced with an awareness of death and the terror of death. It is not a circumstantial terror. It is existential, given, inherent, and it remains so until Spirit is resurrected and the self is one with all possible others."*[23]

With these articulate statements about fear, it becomes clear that in our own personal journeys toward a leap in consciousness, we must be able to achieve a high level of informed self-honesty. We must also develop certain proficiencies:

1) an ability to recognize the type of fear which is "the basic, unavoidable, inescapable terror inherent in the separate-self sense"—the ego's experience of existential terror and its hidden desire for a return to the innocence of "Eden;" this type of fear generates timidity out of its fear of change (which it equates with ego death);

2) an ability to recognize the type of "anxiety that can legitimately be traced to 'mental illness' (neurosis), pathological defense mechanisms, or neurotic guilt;" and,

3) the ability to acknowledge that damage has been done to our ego and the willingness to do whatever is necessary to support the healing of that damage.

THE EVOLUTIONARY RISK-TAKERS: RISKING IT ALL

The basic tenet of *A Course In Congruence* is that personal transformation is not just a personal choice for personal reasons at this time in our history. The heroes of this time must risk it all for the good of the whole. As Russell says, "A new situation is at hand. And the old mode of consciousness is no longer appropriate. Once again there is great danger. And once again Life is being driven to respond. One way or another, the old way—our outdated egocentric thinking—has to go."[24]

We must recognize that life is risky. Every moment of our lives we are but a heartbeat and a breath away from death. With that awareness and the courage to face our own physical mortality, we must live our lives in such a way that they become meaningful expressions of the amazing adventure that being human really is. For those who are ready, that adventure now most certainly includes leaping from the promontory of our own fear-based, small-minded, security-seeking, self-centeredness into the ethers of the Universal Intelligence which is obviously penetrating our consciousness in uncountable ways at this time. We must learn trust by trusting. We must learn letting-go by giving up control of our creeping lives and allowing the invisible force of SuperNature to imbue them with Its All-Knowing blueprint of high-minded articulation. We must realize that we cannot capture the Intelligence of that Greater Something with a stretch of our logical minds. Its ways and means are too complex and all-encompassing for our puny reasoning faculties to comprehend.

THE RISK FACTOR IS AN INHERENT AND ALL-IMPORTANT CATALYST IN THE TRANSFORMATIONAL PROCESS.

It is only by detaching ourselves from all that we have held dear that we can stand free enough to qualify as a potent candidate for the magic and majesty of the transformational ordeal. It is only by living courageously that we may feel the stretching of our very souls. It is only by truly surrendering our little willfulness to the Great Will that we can hope for the painful descent into the fiery abyss where personal death and rebirth occurs. It is only by allowing the divine impulse—which has been urging us to be responsive—to refocus our attention, to change our direction, to change our perceptions, and to change our intentions, that we will find ourselves suspended over that seemingly bottomless chasm for whose secrets we secretly yearn.

> *It costs so much to be a full human being that there are very few who have the enlightenment or the courage, to pay the price... One has to abandon altogether the search for security, and reach out to the risk of living with both arms. One has to embrace the world like a lover. One has to accept pain as a condition of existence. One has to court doubt and darkness as the cost of knowing. One needs a will stubborn in conflict, but apt always to total acceptance of every consequence of living and dying.*[25]

IS "SURRENDER" MORE THAN A WORD?

The word "surrender" falls so easily from the tongues of the awakening ones of today—and that is a very good sign! That so many are speaking in terms of surrender signals us that the mysterious *meaning behind that word* has risen to the level of our surface consciousness to such a degree that we must now think in terms of surrender and speak about surrender to each other. And, beyond that, it signals that many are now ready to do more than *think in terms of* or *speak about* surrender. Many are now approaching a level of readiness to really surrender. And, as we all know, there is quite a distinction between the former and the latter. Although I am delighted that so many awakening ones are up to thinking in terms of and speaking about surrender, I have seen very few who have truly surrendered themselves, their lives, and all that they hold dear. Really!

As Morris West says in the above quote, "It costs so much to be a full human being that there are very few who have the enlightenment or the courage, to pay the price...." And, although I am gratified that so many people are now able to include surrender in their database of concepts which are fundamental to the understanding of the great process, I must state that understanding the concept is not the same as the *state of being* which is true surrender. I have too often seen and heard and felt the arrogance in people who perceive themselves as having surrendered. I have too often been the target of or witnessed others being the target of egoic judgments on the part of someone who still suffers the painful captivity of his own conditioned rigidity while pridefully espousing a state of surrender. I have too often observed a silly, surface attitude about surrender in some who have little spiritual depth and who take an "airy-fairy" approach to all things spiritual. I have too often heard people "talking the talk" who are not truly "walking the walk." The walk is real and the walk is a deeply personal experience which is animated from the deepest reaches of our deepest Self. The walk is humbling. The walk makes one open and ready to listen and compassionate and brotherly/sisterly. The walk heals the separation and halts the hateful judging.

So what is surrender? It is a dis-identification from ourselves as the egoic mentalness by which we actually know ourselves. That being the case, it is practically an impossibility. How can we possibly dis-identify from ourselves? The only thing that makes it possible is our own *willed action* to stop the incessant judging and controlling by our own ego mechanism and open to receive the power of Divine Grace in our minds, in our bodies, and in our lives. It is a big deal! It is really difficult! If it was easy, the whole world would already be transformed. And, because it is really difficult, it requires a real readiness on the part of the potential journeyer. It takes a level of readiness which allows the breaking down of the psychological mechanisms which have heretofore held us together as a personality. It takes a level of readiness which will allow the transformational process to have its way with us, no matter what! It takes a level of readiness which will override all fears and all temptations to turn back.

In the following model [Figure No. 9], Jacquelyn Small depicts the lower consciousness (Outer World of Experience) and the higher consciousness (Inner World of Wisdom) as two triangles, with the lower self containing the ego ("I" or "me")—the part of us which must surrender to the true Self in order that the process of transformation may unfold. The true Self, or Fourth Force, resides in the heart. Small tells us that the Act of Surrender is a Willed Action. She says, "Letting go is an *active* force that *wills* our ego to release its perpetual judging and accept things exactly as they are."[26] This vigilant and active *willing* of the ego to give up control creates a condition of open-mindedness in us which allows us to learn to see things in a "different light" by opening our minds into surprising new ways of perceiving and behaving.

As we continue to *will* the ego to surrender its hold on our mind and our life, we become available to a flood of high-minded teachings and thoughts which serve to feed and strengthen the deeper personality—at the same time, they serve to undermine the self-centered agendas of the ego personality. Courageous demonstrations are required of us—heartfelt expressions which represent our strong intention to offer ourselves like an acorn which has fallen upon the ground and within which the potential for a great oak abides. By the Grace of God a complete surrender of the lower self to the higher Self is achieved. By the Grace of God the transformational process completes itself in us, leaping us to the next higher level of consciousness.

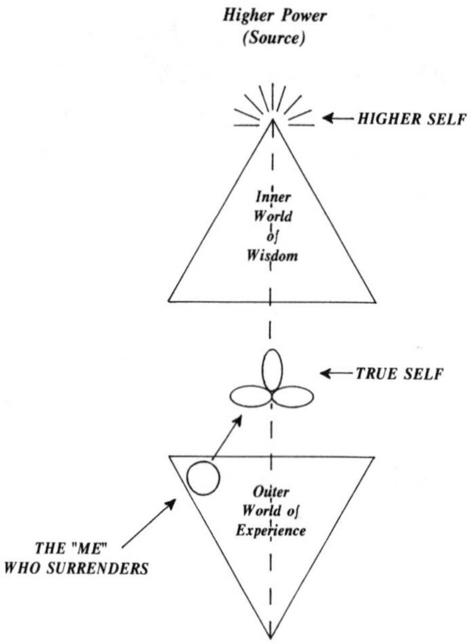

THE ACT OF SURRENDER, A WILLED ACTION

Figure No. 9

LIFE IS RISK

In order to support risk-taking as a way of life and in order to prepare for real cliff-jumping, I offer the next model [Figure No. 10] as a touchstone for daily living. In this model we simply see risk as a constant possibility. We see that risk lies waiting in many small increments or degrees, which gives us constant choice as to how much we *desire to* or are *capable of* going beyond our present Territory of Consolation or level of comfort. We see that we can risk a little or a lot and that it is our own choice.

LIFE IS RISK

The Great Process Is Life Transforming Itself Through Authentic Self-Expression

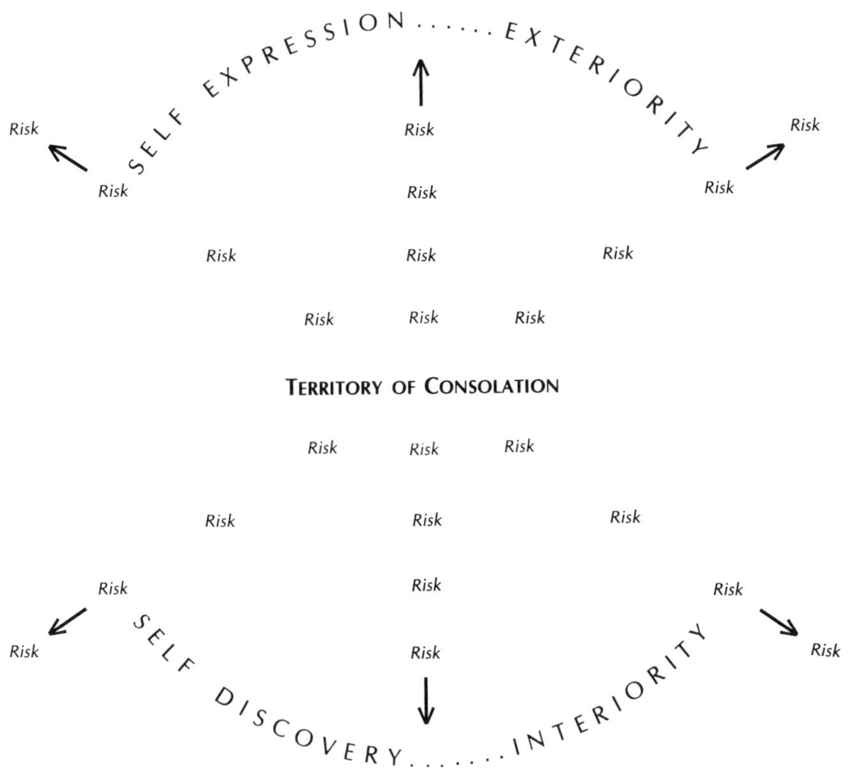

Figure No. 10

Our risks do take many forms of expression and are a significant part of every relationship, every relational transaction, and every choice we make. By way of this model we can subjectively assess ourselves continuously in regard to our level of risk-taking as compared with our tendency to seek the security of our present comfort zone. The more we risk and learn from that risk-taking, the more inner strength we acquire. The more inner strength we acquire, the more willing we become to continuously risk in order to engage the Process of self-discovery and Self-expression.

Once we get the hang of how it works, we stand upon the solid foundation of self-trust through Self-referencing, expressing ourselves ever more freely and fully—and changing rapidly as we grow in self-confidence based in self-knowledge. Our once tentative maybeness becomes a required "Yes" in order for us to feel the stretch of risk-taking as a normal and healthy part of our lives.

SOMEWHERE ALONG THE WAY, WITHOUT REALLY KNOWING "HOW," WE REALIZE WE HAVE DONE WHAT WE WERE CALLED TO DO.

TOWARD EXPANSION AND SELF-MASTERY

1. Make a list of the really risky things you have done—the things which required a clear choice, a real commitment, and courage. Which of these things strongly influenced or dramatically changed your life for the better?

2. Make a list of the things you would really like to do but are afraid to do. Also record how long you have wanted to do each thing but have not done it because of the risks involved. Make your list as complete as possible; include all the small things and the big things you would really like to do.

3. Write down what risks are involved in each of the things you really would like to do.

4. Mark the one thing on the list that you would most like to do, but are afraid to do.

5. Rate the other things on your list as to the strength of your desire to do them (1-2-3, etc.).

6. Based on your willingness to risk as a part of your own unfoldment, choose the one thing that is most appropriate for you do begin to do or work toward doing within the next three months.

7. Make a list of the actions you can take in order to approach the time when you can start doing what it is you want to do.

8. Take some action within three days from the list of actions on your list. Make a commitment to yourself that you will continue to do whatever it takes in order to realize doing the one thing you have chosen to do that you have been afraid to do.

9. Check up on yourself on a regular schedule, so that you do not lose consciousness about your intention and your commitment to fulfill it.

10. Remain very self-aware during the entire process of working toward and attaining your goal.

    Notice your fear.
    Notice your resistance.
    Notice how you feel when you overcome your resistance.

    Notice the impetus that begins to build as you continue to do what you need to do in order to achieve your goal of doing something you really want to do.

    Notice how you feel actually doing what you have wanted to do.
    Notice how you feel after having achieved expression.

Let us accept
that we are the harbingers
of what is to be.

Part Two

STANDING ON THE LEDGE

The death of the seed will be the birth of the tree, and there will be great foliage and flowering and fruits, and birds will come and sit on the branches and make their nests, and people will sit under the shade of the tree; and the tree will talk to the clouds and the stars in the night, and will play with the sky, and will dance in the winds; and there will be great rejoicing. But how can this be known to the poor seed which has never been anything else? It is inconceivable. That is why God is inconceivable.

—BHAGWAN SHREE RAJNEESH
I Say Unto You[2]

Let us offer ourselves to the
evolutionary process that we may change,
be changed, and cause change within our world.

CHAPTER SIX

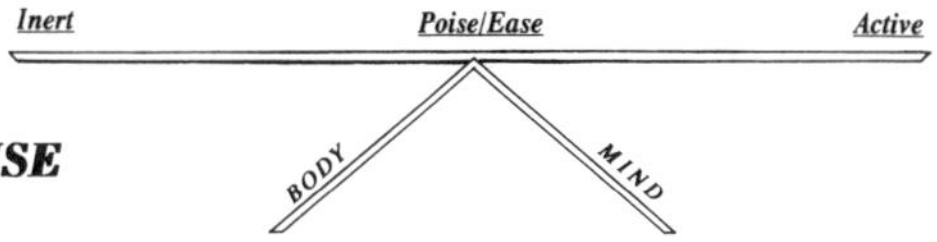

THE HUMAN EMOTIONAL RESPONSE

21 My mother taught that grief and selfish love, and hopes and fears are but
reflexes from the lower self;
22 That what we sense are but small waves upon the rolling billows of a
life.
23 These all will pass away; they are unreal.
24 Tears flow from hearts of flesh; the spirit never weeps; and I am longing
for the day when I will walk in light, where tears are wiped away.
25 My mother taught that all emotions are the sprays that rise from human
loves, and hopes, and fears; that perfect bliss cannot be ours till we have
conquered these.

AQUARIAN GOSPEL OF JESUS THE CHRIST[1]

BEING HUMAN IS BEING EMOTIONAL

Human beings are uniquely emotional beings. Our emotional life is, by its very nature, so rich, so sensitive to outside stimuli, and, thus, so changeable, that we simply must be educated about its character and its messages in order to experience life as *fully human* beings—without our emotions being a constant personal problem that we must attempt, in our ignorance, to deal with.

We remain confused victims of our emotions until we attain an understanding about ourselves as the amazing emotional beings that we are. We are understandably perplexed by the emotional dimension of being human until we learn to accept our emotions; until we learn to accurately identify and process ourselves about our emotions; and, until we learn to express our emotions freely.

The nearest thing to a "formal" education about our emotions we have received piecemeal from our parents, from our teachers, from our priests or ministers, and from other elders who themselves have not been well-schooled in the nature and nuances of the human emotional response. They were confused since they also received their instruction piecemeal from their elders who, themselves, also were lacking in understanding. To one degree or another, they were emotionally conflicted and at the mercy of their own emotional responses. That being the case, they have been able to provide us with only incomplete and contradictory information about our often disturbed and disturbing emotional life; in other words, how to interpret it, how to identify with it, and how to dis-identify from it.

For example, we are taught that Jesus "acted out" with great force the anger he felt toward the merchants and money-changers in the temple.[2] Exhibiting the highest levels of anger energy (incensed and fierce opposition), he yelled at them and furiously strode about turning over tables and throwing their things around. This story in the Bible, and the priestly reiterations of it, unmistakably infer that this angry display was "good." And, yet, our own angry words and acts are nearly always admonished, with either strong inferences or clear communications as to their "badness." As children, our knuckles may have received the cruel smack of a ruler because of our anger—or our angry faces may have been turned to the wall until they could be turned into "happy faces." How confusing!

In our movies and television dramas and sitcoms, we see the reflection of our own emotional life. The actors and actresses "emote" their inner responses to the outer stimuli of their private and professional lives. The degree to which they are capable of "emoting" that inner personal experience is the degree to which we are able to understand them and relate to them. It is the degree to which they can touch us and move us. The degree to which they can touch and move us determines the level of success or failure of their "art."

And, yet, within our own lives we continue to make ourselves and each other very wrong for our deeply emotional responses. We continue to expect that we will maintain ourselves within the "feeling fine" category, emotionally, and we continue to subconsciously judge the emotional expressions of ourselves and others as being pathological rather than healthy.

WE REMAIN CONFUSED VICTIMS OF OUR EMOTIONS UNTIL WE ATTAIN AN UNDERSTANDING ABOUT OURSELVES AS THE AMAZING EMOTIONAL BEINGS THAT WE ARE.

EVEN THE GODS GET ANGRY AND WEEP

The volatility of the emotional body is a factor which needs some emphasis in order to support our acceptance of this "embarrassing" aspect of our human life. I use the word embarrassing only because the more "civilized," "proper," or "intellectual" individuals and sub-societies of our world have broadly inferred that our emotionality falls into the same category of our humanity as our need to defecate or urinate. That is, it is inferred that emotionality is just as private and uncivilized a function of our humanity as going to the bathroom and should be done behind closed doors where others do not have to see it. The inference is that "polite" society controls its emotions—just as it controls its bowels and bladder functions until it can make it to a bathroom—until it can make it to an "emotion room." It is interesting to note that so many of us have run to the bathroom in times of emotional crisis in order to hide our upset from others.

In terms of levels of consciousness, the physical (first) level is the level which controls the involuntary systems of the body, including defecation and urination. The social (second) level is the level of consciousness which controls the involuntary system of the emotions. And, the mental-egoic (third) level of consciousness is the level which controls the involuntary systems of the mind, including the function of the intellect. Granted there are important distinctions which can and must be made between the lower- and higher-order levels of consciousness. And the higher-order levels most certainly are to be celebrated as evolutionary developments which have raised humanity out of its more animalistic lowness. However, it is absolutely imperative that we understand that the lower levels of function cannot be left behind—and that to attempt to dispossess ourselves of them is not only foolhardy, but is devastating to our psychological well-being, which depends on the acceptance of and the intelligent inclusion of our full humanity.

The depths of emotional dysfunction to which our families have fallen during the past several decades—decades which epitomize impressive heights of human intellectual function—are shocking testimonies to the unrealistic attempts to move our species ahead without taking along important parts of itself. Over the past ten years, the very "proper" and "civilized" royal family of Great Britain has become a tragic symbol for the pervasive psychological dysfunction which distinguishes our times. We all stood helplessly by as two intelligent, privileged and well-meaning people reacted to each other again and again out of their own individual *activity* and *inertia* emotions. As the years passed, they both obviously spent nearly all of their time *stuck* in one or the other extreme of the continuum of the human emotional response. Their rages and their depressions became their hallmark as the heirs apparent to the British throne. How sad! And how awful that in this modern era we can expect no better from our brightest and best, because they have not been taught to understand themselves in all ways—including emotional ways.

Repressed and suppressed emotions have not "disappeared" simply because we have controlled them and/or denied them—Prince Charles has shown us that. Emotions whose messages are not responded to in a manner which relieves the emotional stress will eat holes in our psychological armor and generate inner conflict which will turn in upon ourselves in brutally self-destructive behaviors—as Princess Di has shown us. And we have been fascinated because we have understood their pain through our own experiences of emotional pain. We, too, have been like that!

The point is that we are emotional beings who have now accumulated an impressive body of evidence out of our own history which unquestionably supports the fact that we must learn about our emotional dimension. We must become truly "civilized" by becoming authentically physical, emotional, and mental beings who understand the very real and very serious implications of those facets of our personalities. We have gone way past the time when we can run to the bathroom and hide our emotions, return to the parlor acting as though we are "fine," and expect that we will live happily ever after. It won't happen!

Becoming more human (really civilized) requires that we feel more of our emotions, not less. It requires that, instead of experiencing only a few of our emotions and suppressing, denying and avoiding the rest, we become capable of experiencing the *entire* range of human emotions easily and naturally as they arise. And, instead of being an emotional "case," it requires that we become well-integrated physical, emotional, mental and spiritual beings, whose different facets and functions work together to produce that more fully-human condition. How royal!

A MISS IS AS GOOD AS A MILE

L. Ron Hubbard, in *Self Analysis*, states: "Emotion monitors or regulates the endocrine system. The perceptions and the central nervous system call for certain emotional secretions to catalyze the body to meet the various situations in the environment. Emotion is one of the easiest things to aberrate."[3] By introducing the notion of "misemotions," Hubbard provides us with a point of departure by which we may begin to review our emotional reactions. He continues:

> *Most people are not emotional—they are misemotional, in that they do not react to the situations in their environment with the emotion which would be most rational to display. The social order has confused irrationality with emotionalism.*
>
> *Inhibited or excessive misemotionalism is one of the most destructive things which can occur in the human organism. A person who is so aberrated is unable to experience happiness and so enjoy life. His physical body will not thrive.*[4]

Our present-moment awareness is clouded by a subconscious perceptual filter coated with a residue of memory fragments. These remnants of previous similar experiences become referents to which we compare our present experience; and, in this way, they directly influence or dictate our emotional response. If the present experience seems similar to a previous "safe" and/or "agreeable" experience, we will most likely "open up" and allow our emotions their full response and allow ourselves our authentic expression. If, however, the present experience subconsciously reminds us of a previous "threatening" and/or "disagreeable" experience, we will most likely "close down," block the full emotional response to some degree, and withhold our truthful expression.

BECOMING MORE HUMAN REQUIRES THAT WE BECOME CAPABLE OF EXPERIENCING THE ENTIRE RANGE OF HUMAN EMOTIONS EASILY AND NATURALLY AS THEY ARISE.

In order to protect ourselves from a perceived psychological threat, we will become misemotional; that is, we may become "warm" when the appropriate response would be to become "hot" emotionally—displaying emotional balance when high emotional activity would obviously be the authentic emotional reaction. If we actually *experience* the "heat" of anger and, instead, *act as though* we are experiencing the "coolness" of fear or the "warmth" of peace, we are said to be suppressing our emotions. If we actually *experience* the "warmth" of moderate interest when we, instead, *certainly ought to be* "red hot" with anger, we are said to be repressing our emotions—since we are literally experiencing the wrong emotion.

Suppression is a psychological defense mechanism—a conscious choice based on subconscious fear. The choice to suppress is the choice to stuff the emotion back down once it has begun to arise. Suppression is an *overriding* of the emotional experience for purposes of perceived self-protection.

Repression, however, is not a conscious choice. It is a defense mechanism which is subconsciously controlled so that we do not even experience the emotion. We actually have no idea what our natural emotional response would have been, since the mechanism of repression—in order to protect us from what seems to be a psychologically devastating incident (like a traumatic previous similar experience)—prevents us from experiencing the normal energy cycle by blocking what would have been a deeply emotional response.

Our ego is the psychological commingling of our physical, emotional and mental levels of consciousness, including subconscious aspects of our mentality. Together they make up our *person*ality. The primary drive of the physical level is our physical survival. The primary drive of the emotional level is relationship. The primary drive of the mental-egoic level is the satisfaction of our basic psychological (physical, emotional, mental) needs. Emotional weakness, fragility, or oversensitivity arouses physical fear for survival and mental-egoic fear of not achieving fulfillment of our basic needs. The commingling of the three levels of reactive fear requires an intelligent sorting out and translation of levels in order to truly understand from what level we are primarily responding. For this discussion, however, it is important to recognize that being misemotional may often result from our fear of rejection by others—which may alert the survival level fears about being able to *get by* in the world. Misemotional responses may also occur simply because we are frightened by our own emotions and the emotions of others, since we do not understand their messages or their meaning in our lives.

The point is that we must become adept at responding with authentic emotional expressions to present-moment stimuli in order to correct the distorting of our emotional life. This tendency to attempt to feel *a certain way*, or to act as though we do, in order to "play it safe" or to meet the limited criteria of a self-made image, generates a tangle of psychological confusion from which we find it more and more difficult to extricate ourselves.

What's What?

There are some important distinctions which must be drawn in order to provide clear guidelines by which we can view, translate, and intelligently monitor our own emotional life and by which we can observe, interpret, and intelligently respond to the emotional messages of others. Without those distinctions we will remain handicapped by being emotionally repressed, suppressed or out-of-control.

Where do we begin? 1) We begin with a general understanding of what our emotions are and the exceedingly important function they serve in the fullness of our humanity. 2) We proceed by gaining an awareness of the primary emotions we experience continuously and an awareness of the categories into which our emotions may be divided. 3) We then practice identifying our emotions as we live out our days until we become adept at recognizing, classifying, and distinguishing our emotions in the moment. A general understanding of our emotions, an expanded awareness of the relationships emotions have to each other, and an ability to identify emotions as they arise, enable us to get an intelligent grip on our own emotionality and to become congruent in all our relational transactions. What a relief! The following are dictionary definitions of the word "emotion:"

1) a: a physical or social agitation, disturbance, or tumultuous movement b: turmoil or agitation in feeling or sensibility c: **a psychological departure from homeostasis that is subjectively experienced in strong feeling (as love, hate, desire, or fear) and manifests itself in neuro-muscular, respiratory, cardiovascular, hormonal, and other bodily changes preparatory to overt acts which may or may not be performed** d: **an instant of such a turmoil or agitation in feeling or sensibility: state of strong feeling (as of fear, anger, disgust, grief, joy, or surprise)**

2) a: the affective aspect of consciousness: FEELING b: a reaction of or effect upon this aspect of consciousness[5]

Using the dictionary definitions as a point of reference from which to draw distinctions, I have added emphasis to 1)c and 1)d since the *psychological* character of emotions, the consequent *physical manifestations*, and the dimension of *feeling* are therein stated.

---

[5]By permission. From Webster's Third New International Dictionary ©1986 by Merriam-Webster, Inc., Publisher of the Merriam-Webster® dictionaries.

The human psyche is understood to be the soul of man and the physical body is the vehicle through which the soul lives and relates here on earth. There is literally no separation between the psyche and the physical body, although the subtle dimensions of the psyche may live on after the physical body is dead. The psycho-physical body is a highly complex organization of the various systems which together receive, process, and express energy at seven different levels. As mentioned in the definition above, the emotions cause changes in the nervous system, the musculature, the respiratory system, the cardio-vascular (heart and blood) system, and the hormonal system. Although the definition goes on to say "*and other bodily changes*," it is common knowledge that **ALL** systems of the body are involved in and affected by the human emotional response. They are, in fact, the very systems which *produce* the response by way of their changes. In other words, *they are the emotional response.*

For our discussion of the human emotional response, only the most rudimentary understanding of this massive subject is necessary. It is important to know that emotions are an inherent part of our psychological make-up, that they produce measurable changes in the physical body, and that we experience them as what we call *feelings*. In the next section, I will draw some helpful distinctions between feelings and emotions.

BECOMING MORE FULLY HUMAN REQUIRES THAT WE BECOME WELL-INTEGRATED BEINGS WHOSE DIFFERENT FACETS AND FUNCTIONS WORK TOGETHER TO PRODUCE AND SUSTAIN THAT CONDITION.

The dictionary definition states that all emotions are "disturbances" and a "departure from homeostasis" which, by its standards, must be a completely emotionless state. In my presentation of the categories of human emotion, you will notice that I regard only the inert and active emotions as disturbances. In my use of the word homeostasis, I mean emotional balance.

With only the most cursory investigation of dictionary definitions, it becomes obvious that there is no clear, commonly agreed upon, explanation of precisely what the emotional response in humankind is. A likewise cursory examination of books which address this subject also uncovers an absence of clear, specific information by which we may gauge our own emotional responses. The following is one way which we may approach such a personal understanding of our uniquely *human* emotional dimension. Its purpose is merely to provide a general comprehension of some of the all-important aspects of our emotions that we may awaken to the truth which lies beyond them and, thus, escape the unnecessary afflictions to which a lack of understanding condemns us.

Which Is Which?

In *The Practice of Personal Transformation*, Strephon Kaplan Williams, a Jungian therapist, says,

> *For the full development of the human psyche, for the total functioning of our human abilities, and for the full experience of human life, we must have our feeling function activated. Feelings are the inner experiences of energy expression, either positive or negative.*
>
> *Feelings let us know where we stand, what we like and what we dislike, who we are and who we are not, whether we are fully living life or are half living it in a repressed state.*
>
> *Feelings are not emotions. Emotion is strong positive or negative affect which transcends immediate feelings of the moment.*[6]

Once we are able to clearly identify our emotions and become keenly aware of the always-changing energy cycles which the emotions are, we realize that there is an obvious distinction between *feelings* and *emotions*, although we will still most often refer to our emotional experiences as feelings. This realization is all-important to the development of our ability to process ourselves to the underlying truth which has previously lain hidden beneath our emotional reactivity. This distinction is the key to discovering the truth of ourselves over and over again as we continuously engage in relational transactions with others.

Carl Jung addresses the difficulty inherent in attempts to categorize the subtle characteristics and functions of our psychological (including emotional) nature:

> *We can readily agree that physiological characteristics are something that can be seen, touched, measured. But in psychology not even the meanings of words are fixed. There are hardly two psychologies that could agree, for instance, about the concept of "feeling." Yet the verb, "to feel" and the noun "feeling" refer to psychic facts, otherwise a word for them would never have been invented. In psychology we have to do with facts which are definite enough in themselves but have not been defined scientifically. The state of our knowledge might be compared with natural philosophy in the Middle Ages—that is to say, everybody in psychology knows better than everybody else. There are only opinions about unknown facts.*[7]

It is from Jung's presentation of his views and distinctions regarding *feeling* and *the feeling function* that I draw a distinction of my own in order to assist us to process our emotional responses to discover precisely which, more self-revealing, *feelings* lie beneath them. In *Psychological Types*, Jung states:

> *I count feeling among the four basic psychological functions. Feeling is primarily a process that takes place between the ego and a given content, a process, moreover, that imparts to the content a definite* **value** *in the sense of acceptance or rejection ("like" or "dislike"); but it can also appear, as it were, isolated in the form of "mood," quite apart from the momentary contents of consciousness or momentary sensations.*
>
> *Feeling, therefore, is an entirely* **subjective** *process, which may be in every respect independent of external stimuli, although chiming in with every sensation....Hence feeling is also a kind of* **judging**, *differing, however, from an intellectual connection but is solely concerned with the setting up of a subjective criterion of acceptance or rejection. The valuation by feeling extends to* **every** *content of consciousness, of whatever kind it may be. When the intensity of feeling is increased an* AFFECT *(q.v.) results, which is a state of feeling accompanied by appreciable bodily innervations. Feeling is distinguished from affect by the fact that it gives rise to no perceptible physical innervations, i.e., just as much or as little as the ordinary thinking process.*[8]

Jung's elaborations of his thoughts on the subject are most certainly worth one's careful study. However, for our discussion, the basic assumptions serve to adequately educate us as to the differences between our emotions and our feelings.

Out of the awareness of my own feeling and emotional processes, and with the validation of my observations by Jung's assertions, I identify the Feeling Function to be our personal psychological (soul-level) response which discerns for us what is truth or not-truth. This function is a *feeling* that what is occurring is "as it should be" or that "something is wrong." And although Williams, above, asserts that "we must have our feeling function activated," I say it must be RE-ACTIVATED. My assertion is that as children we innately *felt* the *rightness* or *wrongness* of whatever was occurring; and that, only as our perceptions became distorted as to what was right or wrong, based on our confusing conditioning, did we fall out-of-touch with—or into doubt about—our natural ability to discern for ourselves truth and not-truth. As a result of either being out-of-touch with this faculty of discernment or constantly having our discernments undermined by our culture, we became incapacitated and self-doubtful in our attempts to respond to our manifest world in a way which produced psychological comfort and a growing confidence in ourselves. We became crippled in our ability to source ourselves. How sad!

The implications of having lost touch with our own simple truth are serious ones. These implications encompass all of the forms of neurosis and other pathologies which have shown and are showing up in our individual and collective consciousness today. Left to read ourselves from the *symptomatic* emotional level, we have missed the hidden messages which emanate from our deeper, instinctively wise, dimension of being. Even the animals are far more truthful than we have become.

The search for the truth of ourselves in the process of becoming congruent is a search which will always lead us to the feeling function of our private reality. That *realness* will prove to be the essential guidance system with which we are naturally endowed. It is one of the unique and necessary faculties which define us as human beings. Without it we are missing an indispensable part of ourselves. No wonder that as a species we are in such a spin!

There will be a deeper discussion of the Feeling Function in Chapter Eleven. Therein the purpose will be to teach the wandering hero HOW TO go beyond the emotions in order to *get down to* that deeper feeling response and HOW TO interpret its meanings. At this time, however, it is most important that we achieve a broader understanding of our emotions.

WE MUST BECOME ADEPT AT RESPONDING WITH AUTHENTIC EMOTIONAL EXPRESSIONS TO PRESENT-MOMENT STIMULI IN ORDER TO CORRECT THE DISTORTING OF OUR EMOTIONAL LIFE.

EVERYTHING IS ENERGY—EVEN EMOTIONS

Emotions are energies in our bodies. Since our egos are rooted in the muscles of our bodies, and since our emotions are the ego's energy responses to inner thoughtforms and outer stimuli, we can easily feel the effects of our ego's emotional responses in our musculature. We can feel our muscles become tense and ready for flight if there is danger from which we may have to flee; we can feel our muscles lose their tone when we fall into despondency; we can feel our muscles become relaxed when we feel safe and loved. We can all remember many times when our bodies have been racked with the sharp-edged energy of emotional pain and weighed down with the heavy energy of grief; when our bodies have been flooded with and animated by the dynamic energy of anger; and when our bodies have felt light and aglow with the energy of love.

The experience which we call our emotional response is the energy produced by certain combinations of physiological changes which occur as reactions to outer stimuli. In *The Relaxation Response*, Herbert Benson, M.D., says:

> *Humans, like other animals, react in a predictable way to acute and chronic stressful situations, which trigger an inborn response that has been part of our physiological makeup for perhaps millions of years. This has been popularly labeled the "fight-or-flight" response. When we are faced with situations that require adjustment of our behavior, an involuntary response increases our blood pressure, heart rate, rate of breathing, blood flow to the muscles, and metabolism, preparing us for conflict or escape.*
>
> *Man's ancestors with the most highly developed fight-or-flight reactions had an increased chance of surviving long enough to reproduce. Natural selection favored the continuation of the response. As progeny of ancestors who developed the response over millions of years, modern man certainly still possesses it.*
>
> *In fact, the fight-or-flight response, with its bodily changes of increased blood pressure, rate of breathing, muscle blood flow, metabolism, and heart rate, has been measured in man. But the response is not used as it was intended—that is, in preparation for running or fighting with an enemy. Today, it is often brought on by situations that require behavioral adjustments, and* ***when not used appropriately, which is most of the time, the fight-or-flight response repeatedly elicited may ultimately lead to the dire disease of heart attack and stroke.***[9]

Although Dr. Benson's focus in his research on stress is the fight-or-flight response (anger-or-fear), we know from experience that emotions enjoy a broad range from very low-level energies to very high-level energies. The low or inert energies slow us down or stop us physically. The word inert means "not having the power to move itself."[10] The high or active energies move us into action. The inert energies are turned inward and cause us to become introspective. The

[10]By permission. From Webster's Third New International Dictionary ©1986 by Merriam-Webster, Inc., Publisher of the Merriam-Webster® dictionaries.

active energies are turned outward and cause us to become extroverted. And, between these two extremes of low and high energies, lie the center or middle energies which provide us with an experience of emotional balance, emotional poise and emotional comfort or ease. Within this range, our interiority and exteriority find a point of perfect balance.

The point is that any one of our emotions is a *transitory* energy experience which involves the interconnected physiological systems of our bodies. We could not have human emotions without human bodies. We are not to attach our identities to fleeting energy occurrences. Instead, we are to realize the temporary nature of our emotional responses, take notice of them, translate them to the level of truth, and make ourselves ready for the next emotional experience—which is sure to occur soon.

The absence of understanding about our emotions has created a conflicted dichotomy within us which places either too much or not enough emphasis on emotions. Emotions are an all-important component of our wholeness, but they are not to be the dictators of our sensibilities, our choices, our very lives. They are neither to be hidden away and denied their essential function nor glamorized and dramatized to the point of being made disproportionately significant. By way of the process of achieving understanding of our emotions, we find the answers to some essential, unspoken questions about ourselves as human beings.

The very real requirements of our present-day society include an informed perspective on these forceful energies and the part they should be playing in our search for truthful, healthy, and harmony-producing relationships at all levels: personal, professional, community, city, state, nation, and world.

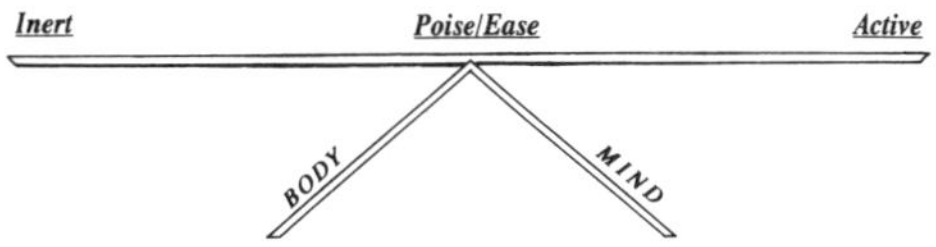

It's Not a Rollercoaster—It's a Teeter-Totter

The Human Emotional Response model [Figure No. 11] provides us with a simple metaphoric representation of the structure and the workings of our emotional dimension. The human emotional response is presented here as a teeter-totter, the center of which rests precariously on the junction at which the body and the mind meet—with the active and inert energies on either extreme. The tilt of the teeter-totter is always changing as our emotional experience fluctuates—as it does all day long every day. For example, we may be feeling *fine* as we walk down the street on a beautiful sunny day with our emotional experience being that of peaceful/content. With our love life just the way we want it, with our professional life very secure and interesting, with our checkbook balanced and some extra money in the bank, we have not a care in the world, so to speak. Then, suddenly, we spot a child being abused by an older child, who is obviously intent on hurting him physically, destroying his books and papers, and humiliating him. In a flash, we will experience the dramatic fluctuation of our own emotional teeter-totter, as we are flooded with emotions which might understandably include sad/grieving and anger. Our emotional experience will switch from mid-balance to mid-inertia and mid-activity within a second or two. Wow! What a fluctuation. What we *do* or *do not do* about what we have seen will determine the next fluctuations of our emotional teeter-totter.

This model grants us an overview of our emotional selves and offers us a degree of clarity from which our self-awareness may expand and our self-understanding may begin to grow by leaps and bounds. As we see in the model, the emotions are divided and arranged into three categories: inert energies, poise/ease energies, and active energies. As a general rule of thumb, a human being will spend only about twenty percent of his time in balance and about eighty percent of his time in either inertia or activity until he stops attempting to control his emotions and allows them to rise freely and to change easily; that is, until his awareness is such that he is able to identify his emotions as they occur, until he is able to hear the messages of his emotions, express himself at the level of truth, and complete the energy cycle. We must give up our silly and unfounded expectation that we should be in a state of emotional balance all the time.

The Inertia Scale. The inert energies are all fear-based emotions. Reading down the scale from the highest energy to the lowest energy, the spectrum includes uncertainty, pain, fear, sad/grieving, undeserving, bad/evil, failing and numb/powerless. The lower end of the scale is so low energetically that we may become unable to function or barely functional. At their lowest ebb, the inertia energies of numb/powerless may incapacitate us to the point that we cannot seem to stay out of bed or off the couch. The inert energies represent the experience of self-doubt and produce an attitude of "I am wrong. They are right."

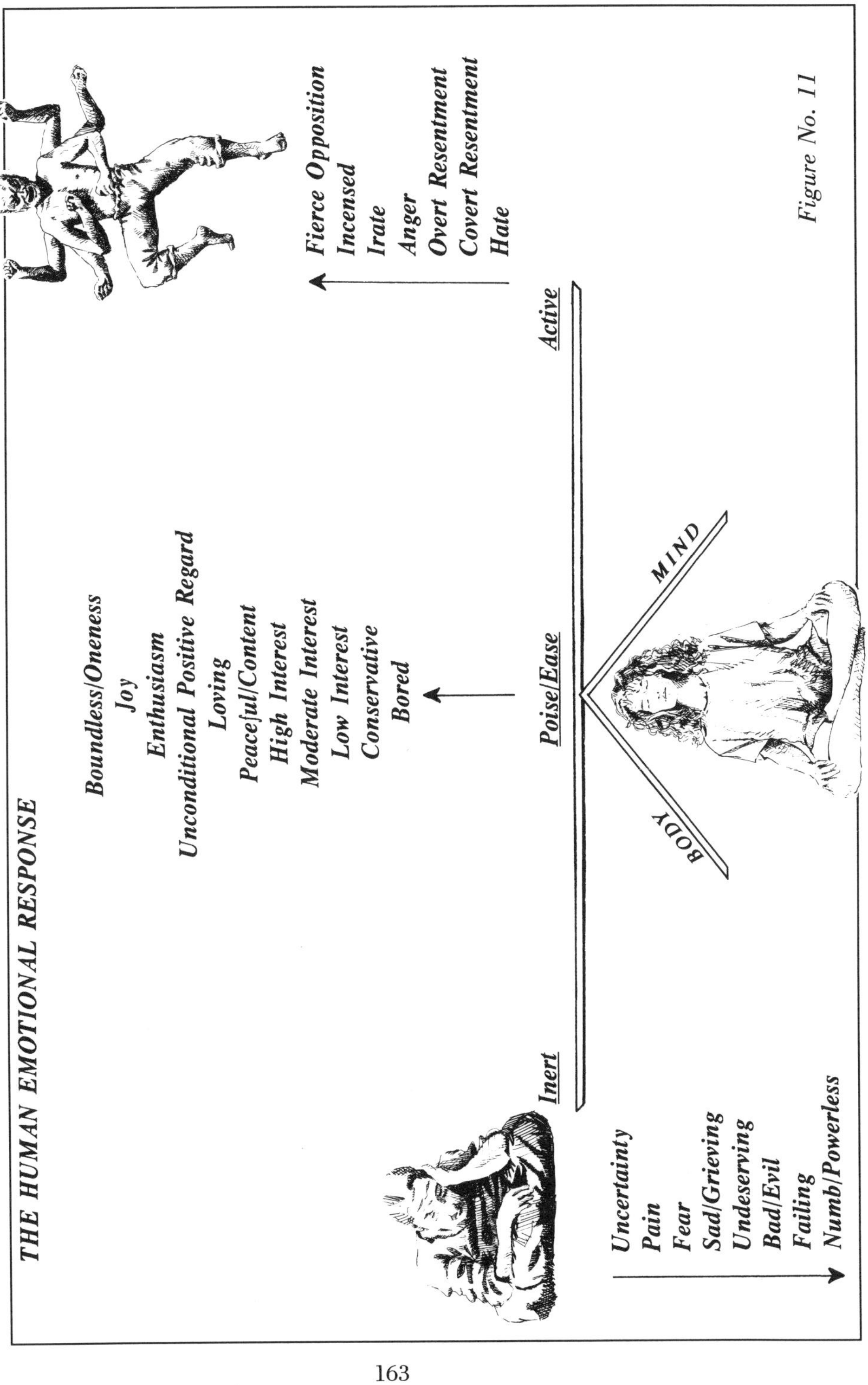
THE HUMAN EMOTIONAL RESPONSE
Boundless/Oneness
Joy
Enthusiasm
Unconditional Positive Regard
Loving
Peaceful/Content
High Interest
Moderate Interest
Low Interest
Conservative
Bored
Fierce Opposition
Incensed
Irate
Anger
Overt Resentment
Covert Resentment
Hate
Inert
Poise/Ease
Active
BODY
MIND
Uncertainty
Pain
Fear
Sad/Grieving
Undeserving
Bad/Evil
Failing
Numb/Powerless

Figure No. 11

The Activity Scale. At the other end of the board, we have the active emotions, which are all anger energies and which progress from lowest to highest levels, energetically. Reading up the scale from the lowest energy to the highest energy, we encounter hate, covert resentment, overt resentment, anger, irate, incensed, and fierce opposition. The scale of active emotions is experienced as producing progressively more energy in the body as we move out of the **motion**less (inert) emotions and move up by degrees through the e**motion**al (active) responses. As we go higher on the scale of active energies, we are less and less able to hide, to suppress or to control our thoughts and actions. The active energies are generated from attitudes of make-wrong and from feelings of having been somehow violated. They produce a self-righteous sentiment of "I am right. They are wrong."

Emotions are an all-important component of our wholeness, but they are not to be the dictators of our sensibilities, our choices, our very lives.

The Balance Scale. In the center we have the balance energies. Reading up the scale from lowest to highest energies, our emotional choices include bored, conservative, low interest, moderate interest, high interest, peaceful/content, loving, unconditional positive regard, enthusiasm, joy, and boundless oneness. The balance energies are generated from feelings that everything is as it should be and produce (to varying degrees) an attitude of non-threatened "inclusion" and "wellness." Within this scale we experience ourselves all the way from "fine" to "terrific."

We can have a combination of emotions from the different categories at the same time. For example, we may at any given moment be experiencing residual sad/grieving from the death of a friend and at the same time be carrying anger energy from an encounter we had at work yesterday. With both inertia and activity energies in our bodies, we can also experience strong interest or love or some other balance energy as a result of some good news we just received.

After taking a brief look at "the base" on which the teeter-totter balances, we will return to explore the "ups" and "downs" of the three emotional scales.

Who's Who?

We are not our bodies. We are not our minds. We are not our emotions. We are so much more than any one or all of these aspects of our lower nature. And yet, these three powerful aspects of our being—which together constitute what is known as our personality—are constantly producing separate conditions which directly or indirectly affect the attitudes and well-being, of the other two bodies or facets of our humanity. It is important to place great emphasis on the very real influence which the body has on our mind and on our emotional experience, as well as the influence our mind has on our body and on our emotional experience.

The Physical Body. As we have all experienced many times, when we feel physically strong and healthy, our minds naturally tend to generate positive thoughts about the present and hopeful thoughts about the future. These positive and hopeful thoughts generate balance emotions—perhaps strong interest and peace. When we are physically ill, our mind tends to generate negative thoughts about the present and doubtful thoughts about the future. These negative and doubtful thoughts generate inertia emotions—perhaps sadness and fear.

The Mental Body. As Brian Swimme says in *The Universe Is a Green Dragon*, "Diseased mindscapes produce diseased landscapes."[11] And in between the mindscapes and the landscapes exists the physical body, which experiences incredible stresses and debilitations as a direct result of strongly negative thoughtforms, which can chronically flood the physical body with inertia and/or active emotional energies.

It has become common knowledge that our mental health does affect our physical health. So, even a healthy body can experience a breakdown in its condition as a direct result of the thoughts which dominate the subconscious and conscious domains. We have been supported for years now to change our habits of thinking in order to change our physical health and our emotional condition.

The Emotional Body. When the physical body is strong and healthy and the mind is filled with positive thoughts, emotional reactions which produce a deluge of especially low inertia energies or especially high activity energies *directly undermine* both the physical and mental well-being of the individual. The physical body does undergo a definite reposturing as a direct result of the emotional experience. The mental body does undergo a reordering of its perceptual capacities as a direct result of the emotional experience.

The point is that we cannot achieve a condition of true psychological well-being by addressing only physical issues, only mental issues, or only emotional issues. We must approach our physical, emotional and mental selves from a transcendent perspective which acknowledges their inherent unity and addresses the issues of all three bodies with equal attention.

Nature's Ways

As with everything else in nature, the principle which underlies the volatile character of our emotional being *naturally* returns us again and again to a state of homeostasis or balance. And, in order to accomplish that emotional *return*, an opposite and equal reaction must be experienced energetically in order to create energetic harmony out of energetic opposites. To a certain degree, until we gain understanding about our emotions and consciously see to it that we have our emotional experiences fully—and thus complete the natural energy cycles—our bodies and minds are along for the ride. As we know, our emotional condition is in a constant state of fluctuation, since it is highly sensitive to stimuli from the outside world, as well as highly sensitive to the influences of our mind and physical body. If we, however, become chronically depressed or chronically angry, an intentional triggering of the opposite and equal emotional reaction can be therapeutic in that it will reactivate the natural motion of the energy cycle. It is the active energies which will pull us out of our inertia and allow homeostasis to be once again achieved. It is the inert energies which will decrease the energetic levels of the activity scale and allow balance to be once again attained. Any chronic emotional state will be a direct result of not having had our emotional experience fully—whatever it may be. It so quickly becomes obvious that *only* the *full* experience of an emotion will free us from its energy, from the thoughts it will cause our mind to generate, and from the physical condition it will produce. In *Everything Is Energy*, Robert and Loy Young tell us:

> *In the Vedas, the oldest writing known to man, the evolution of energy is described as a cycle of action called START — CONTINUE — COMPLETE. In the Hindu teachings of the Bhagavad Gītā, we were again taught about energy, this time called gunas, which were considered to be the qualities and substance of nature. The Hindu description of the energy cycle was INERTIA — MOTION — RHYTHM. Today, our version of the cycle of energy is INERTIA — ACTIVITY — BALANCE.*

'Inertia' and 'activity' are two extremes or 'polar opposites.' We go back and forth many times experiencing the extremes of the energy until finally we unite the best of the two extremes. The narrow middle path is called 'balance.'[12]

Realizing that energy moves in cycles of action assists us to understand the "motion" of our emotions. Once begun, a cycle of action must be allowed to complete itself in order for us to be returned, naturally, to a state of homeostasis or balance. If we interfere with or subvert the cycle, we will only postpone the release of emotions generated in that incomplete emotional cycle. Those emotions will either be delegated to our own inner stockpile of unresolved emotional conflicts or released inappropriately as reactivity toward someone who has no idea what is bothering us. We are learning about the human emotional response so that we may experience the full range of human emotions easily and quickly—spontaneously—and with clear awareness in the moment. We are gaining understanding about our emotions so that we may complete the energy cycles more quickly and return to homeostasis fast, without accumulating more unresolved psychological conflicts as a by-product of unexpressed emotions. The test is always: "How quickly can we return, in truth, to love (or center or balance)?"

TAKING THE PLUNGE ⇓ : THE INERTIA ENERGIES

We must be capable of and willing to suffer the **pain** of loss when it attempts to rise within us. We must "let it rip." We must be willing to allow it its full, aching, raw, sore, tender, bitter, sorrowful expression in our bodies. We must be willing to roll around on the floor in great distress, if necessary, in order to have our emotional experience fully instead of denying the pain, instead of closing down on the pain, and instead of attempting to control the quality or quantity of the pain. We must allow our heart to break and spill its grief all over the floor, if necessary. When we have had the painful experience fully, we will be "fresh" and available for the next lessons and tests with which our journeys are so richly endowed. To attempt to go forward with the pain of loss still hanging in our space, we will have neither the attention nor the energy necessary to consciously attend to the relational transactions or the messages from our own emotional selves. We will remain stuck in our pain, whether or not we are willing to admit it.

We must be willing to "get down" emotionally into our experience of **failure**. We must **FEEL** ourselves reduced to the disappointing dud, flop, loser that we experience ourselves to be at the time. We must allow ourselves the collapse—the breakdown—that failure implies, rather than attempting to "keep it together" and/or "put on a happy face.☺" On the other side of this energetic cycle, we will be restored to balance with an emotional footing which will allow us to take our next step along the path.

ANY CHRONIC EMOTIONAL STATE WILL BE THE DIRECT RESULT OF NOT HAVING HAD OUR EMOTIONAL EXPERIENCE FULLY—WHATEVER IT MAY HAVE BEEN.

Within the inertia scale, the emotions of **uncertainty**, **pain** and **fear** "hold hands," so to speak. If we have become emotionally confused (uncertain) we will naturally also experience emotional pain and emotional fear to some degree. If we drop first into fear, we will simultaneously suffer the effects of uncertainty and pain. When we enter the scale at the level of emotional pain, we will suffer, to some degree, the effects of emotional fear and emotional uncertainty.

The emotions of **sad/grieving** are generated by feelings of disappointment—due to unfulfilled expectations—and are well-described by the thought, "I didn't want it to be like this."

The emotion of **undeserving** is an experience of loss of self-worth and unequivocal self-doubt. **Bad/evil** takes us beyond self-doubt to self-loathing and an experience of there being something wrong with us. We feel that there may well be a hidden facet of us which is hateful, base, vile, sinful, immoral.

The lower-energy emotions of **failure** and **numb/powerless** are more deeply introverted experiences of self-doubt and self-hatred. They say, "I can't." At this lower end of the scale, we have, so to speak, imploded into ourselves. In that sense we are rather like an emotional black hole. In this state, we experience the extremity of aloneness. Our space is so small that there is room for no one else.

The entire scale of inertia emotions represents varying degrees of depression. The lower end is a state of heavy depression. Once in a state of heavy (non-chronic) depression, it will generally take us about three days to rise out of that condition, if we do nothing to clear ourselves or to transmute the energy.

"I Hate Your Guts" and Other Furies ⇑ : The Activity Energies

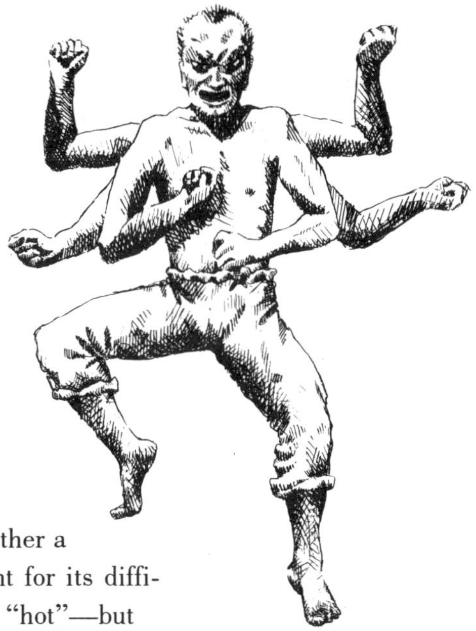

We must, likewise, be willing to FEEL our anger fully. Although there is great confusion in our society about all of our emotions and their "appropriateness" or "inappropriateness," no other emotion generates as much confusion and controversy as does anger. And in this case, I refer to the whole range of anger, as epitomized by the activity scale. We are able to love only to the degree that we are able to hate, so it is to our highest good that we experience our hate fully.

Hate is an amalgam of high inertia and low activity emotional energies. We see that hate lies energetically just above the inner-directed emotions of inertia, and just below covert resentment on the scale of outer-directed emotions. Its placement on the scale implies that it is neither a depressive nor an expressive emotion, which may account for its difficult-to-get-hold-of messages. Being an anger energy, it is "hot"—but who or what it wants to burn, often remains a mystery. Hate is most often experienced more as an emotional *condition* rather than an emotional *reaction* which is provoked by a particular person or situation. Its attitudes and messages are pervasive and intrude upon our perceptions and responses to all areas of our life. In other words, we hate everything equally!

HATE IS AN EXPERIENCE OF EMOTIONAL FRUSTRATION. Hate seems to contain some of the confusion, pain and fear of the upper inertia scale and some of the covert resentment of the lower activity scale, which allows it to be likened to a pot of hot liquid which has not reached—and cannot reach—its boiling point. In order to become more fully human we must **FEEL** the hate when it raises its ugly head; we must allow it its "say" to us; and, we must make a clear, conscious choice as to what, if anything, we need to do in order to either *propel* ourselves into the higher levels of anger or to *fall* into inertia. If we do nothing, one of these movements will be evoked by an encounter or a circumstance in our life—we will either be provoked into an explosion of anger or plunged into the middle to lower levels of self-doubt. Either way, it will be a relief, as it triggers the action of the energy cycle for an eventual return to emotional balance.

With **covert resentment**, rather than allowing the hostility we feel for the other person to capture our attention, as it usually does, we must FEEL the dull or sharp edge of our resentment and let it speak to us of the mistreatment it perceives, which have caused such disaffection.

The energetic levels of **hate** and **covert resentment** are "sticky" and can hold us for periods of time, unless we *consciously* move out of them and into expression. Covert resentment is the killer of relationships because we withhold ourselves and withhold our communications about the judgments we are harboring. By so doing, we inhibit the natural action of the energy cycle and block the avenues by which our relationship can flourish. When indulging in covert resentment, we will either "put a good face on it" and act as though everything is fine or we will remain aloof from the other person while he or she tries to figure out what, if anything, is wrong. Try as we may to cover-up our resentment, cynicism begins to drip out of the sides of our mouth and run down our chin as we attempt to relate to the person who is the target of our unspoken resentment.

By the time our hostility has reached the energy level of **overt resentment,** we are no longer able to keep it in, and we find ourselves becoming *outwardly* cynical toward and finding fault with the other person, rather than just taking silent exception to the other person. This level of expression is often characterized by the use of cynical barbs or hostile humor laced with coded messages.

The higher we go up the activity scale, the more energy we experience in our body. By the time our resentment has risen to the level of **anger**, we can no longer contain it. The energy begins to express itself through our actions. We may be able to stay seated, but we may begin to push papers around, slam down the phone, speak in louder tones, and outwardly blame the other person.

At the level of **irate**, we are seething, hot, more active physically, and exuding the menacing energy of "You ain't seen nothing yet." When irate we are obviously an *explosion* just waiting to happen.

At the level of **incensed**, we are up out of the chair, performing large muscle actions which are more dynamic and sweeping in their expressions. We may kick things, slam doors, throw things, and speak in very loud tones, with great emphasis and with forceful attitudes which broadly condemn the other party.

When we reach the level of **fierce opposition**, we have *lost our mind* and we have *lost control*. We are *up to* picking a fight; and we really want to fight—the energy in our body is a perfect match for a physical fight. We are an emotional experience of raw aggression—fearless in our self-righteous stance. Our rational mind is unable to reason beyond the situation of the moment, and its focus becomes laser-like as a result of the "case" it has built against "the enemy."

To the degree that we go up the activity scale, we may plummet down the inertia scale. Unless we acknowledge and authentically express the highly-charged **anger, incensed, and fiercely oppositional** energies, we can be sure that we will find ourselves plummeted into the lower to lowest energies of the inertia scale at some point in the near future, as the natural energy cycles begin the process of returning us to homeostasis. If we tip the teeter-totter high enough to reach the top of the active scale, we will notice that the other end is positioned just as low on the inertia scale—and it becomes a sliding board down which we may slide into inertia energies. Due to the limitations of this metamorphic model, the tilt will certainly not be precise, but we can get a general idea of how the inertia and activity energies relate to each other and transmute within our psychic structures.

The test is always: "How quickly can we return, in truth, to love?"

Experiencing, Translating, and Expressing Anger. We must always remember to bring our attention back to our own inner responses, so as to feel the experience fully and to listen to the messages of our emotional self. Only when we have gotten a handle on what is actually going on inside are we able to 1) sort it out, 2) process it to a high level of truth, and 3) intelligently choose what communications we need to make or what actions we need to take in order to complete our experience and, once again, be fully available for relationship.

From the level of **overt resentment** on the activity scale, on up through **fierce opposition**, we come face to face with not only our own personal conflict about anger, but also with the deep-seated conflict which permeates the collective consciousness of our society. So, before we are capable of experiencing, processing, and expressing our anger, we must recognize this conflict and free ourselves from its tangled jumble of cliché-level logic. Because of this conflict, a supposedly pure "intellectual" discussion of the oblique controversy surrounding the expression of human anger—which obviously *rages* within our society—can quickly evolve, instead, into a *furious debate* between fiercely opposed factions. How shocking!

Like it or not, we all get angry. And, believe it or not, being angry is just as psychologically healthy as being peaceful/content. From this model, we can see clearly that we can expect to experience anger on a regular schedule as we move through the energy cycle over and over again—from inertia to activity to balance. There simply is no way humanly possible to have the human experience without regularly responding angrily to this or that stimulus. So anger is not wrong!

What about the *expression* of that anger? Should our expressions of anger be kept at a particular decibel of sound? Should our expressions of anger be elegant and/or pleasant to watch? Should our expressions of anger be "highly-civilized" attempts to contain the energy of anger as we report being "fine" or speak about the weather? None of the above!

- Anger sounds angry—the tonal quality of which often requires a decibel level which is higher than "normal."

- Anger looks angry—which does not fall into the "elegant" or "pleasant to watch" categories.

- And the energy of anger cannot really be contained. It expresses itself whether we give it permission or not—no matter how much we attempt to make it "civilized."

In our *ignorance* about anger, it is pathetic that we argue with each other about its expression. In our *poorly-informed* condition, it is silly for us to act as experts on the subject of anger. In our *confused* state, it is nonsensical for us to judge ourselves and each other harshly about our experiences and expressions of anger.

It is true that anger has gotten out-of-control in our country and in our world—and something simply must be done now to counter the dangerous and frightening displays of angry self-righteousness which destroy not only good will, but also human life, the earth's surface, private and public property, governments, and whole cultures. Whether viewing the situation from the big picture or from the more mundane level, the implications of anger gone out-of-control in our world today are extremely serious. And, with our society's children carrying guns and shooting each other, it is obviously high time we begin to personally experience, process, and express our anger in ways which empty our reservoirs of anger rather than filling them to overflowing. The intelligent way to approach that end is by achieving understanding of ourselves and by expanding our awareness of our own emotional responses. Let us continue. . .

The first important thing, then, is to understand and accept that we are going to get angry and that anger is *not bad*. Then, we must give ourselves permission to raise our voices, if necessary, in order to give expression to the anger which has risen in us. And, we must be willing to look "upset" instead of elegant in order to authentically express ourselves. We must disengage ourselves from the conflict and controversy which has been generated in our society about anger and simply follow a few clear and simple guidelines in our recurring experiences of the scale of activity energies.

1) We must allow the energy to rise as we consciously bring our awareness to its natural escalation;

2) We must translate our emotions to discover the feeling level truth which has generated the response;

3) We must address only the particular issue which has been evoked in us by the other person's action and not allow ourselves to use our present upset to bring up "old" issues which were not cleared. Those unresolved issues need to be cleared in a different way and during another meeting;

4) We must remember that this is our own personal anger, which ultimately has little to do with anyone else—that if this person and this circumstance can evoke this strong response from us, then other people and circumstances can also evoke the same response. So we must "claim" it as *our very own* anger;

5) We must honor our anger and at the same time honor the other person. We do this by giving ourselves permission to be angry without closing down on the relationship. In other words, we must say "I am angry." "I am very upset with you." "We need to talk about this." "I do not understand." In this way, we remain relational, rather than separating ourselves in self-righteous attitudes of superiority;

6) We must *report* our anger as being *our* anger and describe the *effects* which the betrayal or unfair treatment is having on us, instead of simply judging the other person to be "wrong" and heaping blame on him or her;

7) We must remember that, underlying the anger, we truly want to understand and we truly want to work this out;

8) We must remember that this angry experience and exchange is a normal part of healthy human relationship and that the integrity of the relationship can be well served by having an authentic exchange of anger; and

9) We must remember that beyond the anger is sadness and beyond the sadness is love—and that what we are attempting is the return to love as quickly as possible.

In addition, our awareness needs to include the fact that our subconscious minds are literally full of old, unresolved conflicts with people from our past until we empty them through **particular** *conscious* efforts, which include authentic Self-expression in the present. Before we begin the work of self-discovery, we are barely able to keep our nose above the waterline of the cesspool which our subconscious mind has become. We are swimming in our own "stuff;" and during emotional storms, we often nearly drown in the infested waters of our own hidden and uncleared past. Metaphysically, our world is the reflection of our own collective consciousness; and, as such, we now see our rivers, lakes, and oceans polluted with the poisons of man's "civilized" living. Like our subconscious, the polluted waters of our manifest world are grievously influencing our present, and are profoundly endangering our future. That is no way to live!

One of the methods we can utilize in order to honor the anger which rises in us and to allow it to tell us what it is really saying, is to write all of the emotionally-charged thoughts on a piece of paper. Let the anger speak through your pen and say on paper all the hurtful, blaming, and nasty things it wants to say rather than attempting to override those reactive thoughts with "nice" thoughts. Once again, *let it rip*! Hold nothing back. Do not monitor or change any of the ugly, awful things the anger wants to say. Then tear up the paper. After a while, do it again. Notice if and to what extent the anger has dissipated. Notice the difference in the level of energy with which the words are imbued. Tear up the paper. By the third writing, you should realize a shift in your emotional experience and a recognition of the real issue which has generated such an angry response.

A Precarious Balance ⇔ : The Poise/Ease Energies

As is true of the other categories, the emotions which comprise the scale of balance energies have a broad range and a graduated increase/decrease of emotional force. The emotion of **bored** shares some of the same qualities of hate in that it is a hybrid of the low-energy balance energies above and the violent activity energies just below. It is said that if you scratch boredom, you will uncover anger. But, because the energetic cycle has entered its balance phase, we will more easily ascend the balance scale than fall back into anger. Being bored has a quality of nothing much happening emotionally and waiting for something to happen. In that way it is uncomfortable and causes us to feel a gnawing sense of low-grade agitation at the same time that everything seems to be "fine." Being **conservative** emotionally is a relief from being bored in that we experience a neutrality which allows us to just go through the motions with a sense that everything is "okay."

Low interest, moderate interest, and **high interest** move us up the scale toward the mid-point which **peaceful/content** occupies. As we move up the scale, things in our life will most probably not have changed much from the time when we were experiencing the lower energies, but our interest level will make everything seem more fascinating. We need to recognize, too, that as we rise energetically on the scale, we become more and more expressive or emotive. And, as we compare the lower emotions to the higher emotions on the scale, we notice that the lower emotions create in us a introspective experience, while the higher emotions cause us to be more extroverted with our attentions and expressions.

From **loving** through **boundless/oneness**, our experience of relationship with others and with the whole world are greatly expanded and expanding. Our attention is freed from our own problems since we are feeling "great." We see the beauty and the wonder all around us, and we truly appreciate our friends, relatives, co-workers, and humankind-at-large. At the level of **unconditional positive regard**, we have become naturally able to depersonalize the behaviors of others; and, so, we find no fault with them. Some people have a very difficult time experiencing the emotions above unconditional positive regard simply because they are so energetic. The energy level of **enthusiasm** is so similar to the energy level of *incensed* that it can make us vulnerable to a surprising shift into that activity energy—which is obviously quite a plunge—until we become accustomed to sustaining a high degree of emotional well-being for extended periods of time. As an example of how easily that shift can be made, I refer to the recent rash of violent and destructive mob scenes involving sports fans after their teams have achieved victory. In obvious energetic frenzies, these sports enthusiasts trash whole urban areas, breaking into stores, looting, turning over and wrecking cars in the street, etc. These highly-charged emotional outbursts seem to be obvious anomalies of the high balance emotions.

EMOTIONS ARE NEITHER TO BE HIDDEN AWAY AND DENIED THEIR ESSENTIAL FUNCTION NOR GLAMORIZED AND DRAMATIZED TO THE POINT OF BEING MADE DISPROPORTIONATELY SIGNIFICANT.

At the level of **joy**, we experience a delicious sense of aliveness which seems to dance within every cell and celebrate each moment, each ray of the sun, and each raindrop. At the level of **boundless/oneness** there is an experience of our boundaries having become transparent, which allows us to *know* our unity with everyone and everything, including the unknown reaches of space.

How Frustrating!

There is a hidden relationship which exists between the activity scale and the inertia scale of emotions which shows up often in episodes of emotional frustration. Frustration occurs when a situation elicits both an inertia scale response and an activity scale response at the same time. For example, we may have an angry response and an experience of undeserving, bad/evil, and/or failure concurrently. This occurrence causes us to simultaneously experience superiority and inferiority, self-righteousness and self-doubt. Awareness of the effect of these commingled emotional responses assists us to separate them in our processing of the incident so as to glean the full value of the experience.

I Am Not An Island

It is important to realize that our emotional energies have an effect on the emotional experiences of others. When we are angry others may get angry—or they may fall into confusion, pain, and fear. When we are sad, others may get sad—or they may be provoked into anger by our sadness. When we are happy, others may feel happy—or they may become resentful. It all depends on where they are in their own personal energy cycle, and which of their subconscious "stuff" is activated by our emotional condition. How interesting! So we need not take it personally if someone we are relating to does not respond in a way that matches our own emotional experience. In fact, with this understanding we can observe the changes in others which our own emotional states effect, thus gaining important insights into our relationships.

Chameleons, Powder Puffs and Tyrants

As a part of this discussion, it is beneficial to mention that to some degree we have been, in our ignorance, what I call emotional chameleons, emotional powder puffs and/or emotional tyrants. Oversensitive "to the max" to the emotional experiences of others—and always supporting our self-made image—like **chameleons** we have sometimes changed emotional colors over and over again by abandoning our own emotions and going into agreement with the emotional experience of others. We have done this—which I refer to as EMOTIONAL MERGING —in order to seem caring, sympathetic, empathetic, and, above all, a *good person*.

If that has not been our forte, we may have been an **emotional powder puff**, powdering the noses of those who came to us in distress with the fairy dust of platitudes and clichés, which were supposed to make them feel better and which were supposed to make us seem like a *wonderful and wise person.*

If our persona was more one of "tough guy," we may have assumed the role of **emotional tyrant** wherein we huffed and puffed and acted "mean" about every little shortcoming or turned each foible in others into a serious deficit or enormously improper action which had to be dealt with by punishing indictments of their character, which was meant to *straighten them out* for their own good and to make us seem authoritative and very *"BAD"*. Enough has already been said to make it obvious that this type of emotional play-acting is silly and serves absolutely no useful purpose. Get real!

Lower What? Higher Who?

Emotions are the ego's reactions to occurrences which are to some degree influenced by subconscious memories of previous similar experiences in which we were or were not able to express ourselves authentically. This being the case, while we are still captured by the damaged ego's perceptions and uninformed survival strategies, the circumstances and events of our lives dictate our relative levels of psychological comfort and discomfort. If things are going our way, we feel *good*; that is, we are positive, hopeful, and emotionally *happy.* We have a hard time if a relationship or situation is not going our way.

The point is that life lived at the mental-egoic level of consciousness is life lived primarily out of the selfish agendas of our lower self. The level of psychological well-being which we experience will be in direct relationship to how well things in our manifest (outer) world are going; that is, to what degree the circumstances of our life match our expectations and perceived needs and to what degree others respond to our strategies to *get what we want.* Our available attention and energy (whatever is left over from our ruminations on the past and concerns about the future) is concentrated on attempts to make things turn out in *certain* ways. This level of living makes us "sitting ducks" for the disappointments which accrue from both our *obvious* and our *hidden* attempts to control people and circumstances—who and which are way beyond our ability to control. A continuous succession of relational and circumstantial episodes will take us, again and again, to the "heights of hopefulness" and to the "depths of despair" emotionally. With a general understanding of the ego's motivations and with a growing awareness of the emotional implications of its "personal" experiences of happiness (balance), anger (activity), and confusion/failure (inertia), we begin a most important part of the journey of self-discovery, self-transcendence, and Self-expression.

It is not until we have become opened into the higher Self, have become adept at decoding our emotional messages, and have become able to express ourselves congruently that our overall psychological well-being is not interrupted for prolonged periods of time by the ups and downs of our emotional life.

As a result of expressing ourselves congruently, our subconscious is gradually emptied of the emotional residues of past experiences in which we felt overwhelmed, overpowered, and unable to express ourselves. When we discover the truth and the natural confidence of the higher Self, we are able to respond consciously *in-the-moment* to all occurrences. Our responses become bright, intelligent, and devoid of the neurotic twists which characterize subconscious "stuff." This capacity assures that the subconscious remains clear, which, in turn, insures that present relationships remain free of past disturbances, and which allows the all-important starting, continuing and completing of the emotional energy cycle.

We must give up our silly and unfounded expectation that we should be in a state of emotional balance all the time.

Wandering Heroes

As we continue on our path towards emotional self-mastery, emotions eventually become unrooted, free floating, and as spontaneous as a child's. In *The Path to No-Self*, Bernadette Roberts provides us a distinction between living as a subjective experience of our ego as compared with living at "the center" of our Being.

> *...outside (the center), the mind and emotions were roaming about, unable to enter this deeper dimension, and they were therefore at a loss for an object to which they could become attached. Their continual movements were disquieting and distracting: they drew attention away from the center.*

> *...By remaining passive, however, we learn the knack of being objective about our thoughts and feelings, and come to see them for what they are—superficial, without depth, perishable, fickle, disturbers of peace, and totally incompatible with life-at-the-center.*
>
> *...the center gradually frees us from the tyranny of the lower faculties; once we are no longer slaves to mind or emotion, we have come upon the essence of human freedom.*[13]

Although, as wandering heroes, we must traverse the wastelands of our own lower faculties (minds and emotions), it is imperative for us to remember that it is to the higher Self we are headed. And, although only the glistening summits of the high Self will fulfill our aspiration for liberation, we must not attempt to jump over the lessons and tests which are implicit in the valleys and swamps of our early process.

With a growing understanding and an ever-expanding awareness, we can become adept at **identifying** our emotional responses, **interpreting** their messages, and **consciously choosing** the intelligent, sensitive, and appropriate communications and behaviors we make—instead of allowing the emotions, themselves, to dictate our words and actions. Our own sense of self will begin to grow strong and our relationships with others will begin to take on an entirely new complexion. We most certainly will begin to experience a solid sense of hopefulness based on changed perceptions of ourselves and others.

In the name of heroic wandering through the wastelands of our distressed and distressing emotional selves, we must discard our own make-wrongs of emotions which do not fall into the "fine" (balance) category. We must recognize that to be able to experience fully the energies of **all** of the emotions is healthy, instead of continuing to harbor the misconception that we are only as healthy as we are "fine" emotionally. It simply is not true!

TRANS-WHAT?

Transmuting energy is the work of those who have gained high degrees of awareness as to the workings of the energy cycles and who have become highly sensitive to the fluctuations and the levels of their emotions and the emotions of others. With those awarenesses and sensitivities well developed, they are able to transmute (convert) their own emotional energies at will. That is, they are able to move energetically up and down the energy scales and back and forth between the energy scales by consciously duplicating the energy levels of the various emotions. They no longer need be stuck in any particular energy in order to have it complete its normal cycle. And, they are able to raise or lower their own emotional energy in order to match the energy levels of others. This ability denotes true emotional self-mastery only when it is done *consciously* and *at choice*, rather than occurring as an automatic (conditioned) response to the emotions of others. And, of course, the person is able to easily and quickly identify the emotion's messages and the underlying truth.

This ability is not meant to subvert the natural rhythm of the energy cycle just for the sake of undermining or avoiding the experience of any particular emotion or group of emotions. The skillful raising and lowering of the emotional energy in order to meet another person at his or her level and bring him or her into balance enables the two to come together at the same emotional level, rather than having the disparity in their emotional experiences be a distraction or hindrance to their communication. This level of emotional self-mastery also equips us to "go down" and to "go up" in order to meet others at the level at which they are operating and to "be with" them there. If, for example, a person is grieving the loss of a loved one, we would not attempt to bring them to balance, but could join them at that level at least long enough to really be with them. If a person came at us with the energy of fierce opposition, we could spontaneously match that energy in order to meet him on his own ground, stand him down, or at least keep ourselves from being overwhelmed by the force of his emotional energy. This deliberate raising and lowering of our emotional energy is the conscious opposite of the before-mentioned emotional chameleon, whose emotional agreement depends on a blurring of the lines of his identity and an irresistible merging with the other person's emotional experience.

When we discover the truth and the natural confidence of the Higher Self, we are able to respond consciously, in-the-moment, to all occurrences.

"I" AND THE HIGHER EYE

Within the complex structure of our psyche there are distinct levels, each of which represents particular capacities not intrinsic to the other levels. This being the case, it is obvious that we will not be "whole" until we have become operant at the highest level and, thus, have had all of the levels of our humanity activated and integrated with all the other levels.

The sixth level of consciousness is the level wherein lies the capacity to view the conditioned tendencies of our lower selves. Located at the brow level just above and between the physical eyes, it is universally known as the third eye—our Observer Self or Witness Self or Impersonal Self. (There are also other names which are used to identify this remarkable function.) Remarkable, too, is the fact that we can actually employ the services of that higher level before we have actually been raised up to and established at that loftier, metaphysical level. Amazingly, we can activate the function of the third eye while we are still captured in the third level of consciousness, which otherwise is an extremely subjective experience of whatever physical conditions, emotional energies, and mental thought processes happen to be occurring.

WITHOUT THE PRESENCE OF THE WITNESS CONSCIOUSNESS OR SELF, OUR LEVEL OF SELF-AWARENESS IS ABYSMALLY LOW OR NON-EXISTENT.

Without the presence of the Witness Consciousness or Self, our level of self-awareness is abysmally low or non-existent, and we are reduced to a level of grossly inauthentic thoughts and behaviors which are no more than robotic reactions straight out of our past conditioning. And without the benefit of this Impersonal Self, the cycles of emotional energy become uncomfortable and prolonged periods of anger and depression with only brief periods of balance. Since our angry and fearful attitudes generate an undercurrent of self-threatened insecurity, we take everything personally.

If we will pause and take another look through the eyes of the Witness Self, we will be able to see objectively what has really been going on. We will be able to provide ourselves with an OVERview of our own thoughts and our own actions. How helpful! If we will replace the pronoun "I" with the pronoun "he" or "she" and rethink things from a third person perspective, we will be able to objectively view what has before been a purely self-centered experience of victimization at the hands of some menacing monster of a person who seemed to deserve the hateful recriminations which we have heaped upon him—at least in our own minds.

With the sharp edges of harsh judgment blunted by the Witness Self's higher view, we are freed from the emotional intensity we have been suffering as the subjective experience of an angry or depressed ego. Given the eyes of intelligence and discernment, we are able to confess to ourselves the incitive, irresponsible, or downright unacceptable words and/or actions on our part which may have caused the incident to occur in the first place or which may have caused it to escalate to the point of real upset. With the return of high reason to our mental capacity—which results from an infusion of wisdom from the Witness Self's larger context—we experience a restabilizing of our sense of self and our desire to work it out rather than to remain upset and self-righteous. What a healing!

> *Only when one has succeeded in observing thoughts, emotions, and sensations as contents of consciousness and seeing that one has them but is not identical to them, can one begin to know the Self.*[14]

WHISPERS AND SCREAMS

What are the emotions saying? How are we to know? And what are we to do about it? Good questions. Perhaps if we think of ourselves in the same way that we think of amoebas—those lowly lifeforms which lie in puddles of solution on glass slides under the unblinking gaze of the microscope—we will be able to see the simple, instinctive reflexiveness of the emotional response in humans. Supposing that the amoeba does not have an emotional life, we can still see that it has the remarkable ability to respond to outside stimuli. Touch it with a sharp instrument and it moves. It is highly responsive in that way. In humans, the emotional response can, in order to make a point, be likened to the amoeba's response to being touched or jabbed. The "probe" which elicits a human emotional response is not a laboratory instrument, but, instead, most often, some other person's words or actions.

Whether they say THIS, THAT, or THE OTHER, we involuntarily respond emotionally to the stimulus more or less as the amoeba responds to the scientist's probe. This awareness helps us to notice how sensitive we are emotionally to what others say to us; and, it gives us a way to begin to listen to the messages of the emotions—OUCH!—and to understand their whispers before they become screams.

They say **THIS** and we respond from the inertia scale:

1) "I don't know how I feel about this." = UNCERTAINTY
"I hurt so much. I feel like I cannot stand this loss." = PAIN
"This is scary. What is going to happen?" = FEAR
2) "I am so sorry. I didn't want it to be like this." = SAD/GRIEVING
3) "I am so dumb and useless and awful." = UNDESERVING
4) "I am so mean and insensitive." = BAD/EVIL
5) "I just can't do it any more." = FAILING
6) "It's all so hopeless. There's no use trying." = NUMB/POWERLESS

They say **THAT** and we respond from the activity scale:

1) "I hate my life and myself and everyone." = HATE
2) "She is such a phony; I can't stand her."
"Oh, hi, I'm so glad to see you." = COVERT RESENTMENT
3) "You think you are so smart." = OVERT RESENTMENT
4) "You lied to me and I have had it with you!" = ANGER
5) "You liar! You will pay dearly for this!" = IRATE / INCENSED
6) "You !#!%* fraud. You pitiful excuse for a human. Get the !#!%* out of my face before I break every bone in your body." = FIERCE OPPOSITION

They say **THE OTHER** and we respond from the balance scale:

1) "This is so boring. Everything is so boring." = BORED
2) "Hmmm...is that so." = CONSERVATIVE
3) "Hmmm...is that so. I might be interested in that." = LOW INTEREST
4) "That's interesting! Tell me more." = MODERATE INTEREST
5) "Amazing! I really want to find out more about that." = HIGH INTEREST
6) "I am glad to be alive. Everything is really fine." = PEACEFUL / CONTENT
7) "I love the stars and the trees and you." = LOVING
8) "You are a great being." = UNCONDITIONAL POSITIVE REGARD
9) "Life, you and the world are so incredibly magnificent." = ENTHUSIASM
10) "I feel alive, happy, and so ecstatically playful!" = JOY
11) "The grass and the sky and I are one." = BOUNDLESS / ONENESS

The remaining question: "What are we to do about it?" For purposes of this discussion, we need only to 1) identify our emotions; 2) claim them as our own personal responses; 3) decipher what they are saying to us with real self-honesty; and, if appropriate, 4) report them to the person with whom we are relating. The report most often should be a simple statement that allows the other person to understand what is going on inside us so they can factor that into their assessments of us at the time. "*I am feeling very sad (or angry)(or peaceful) right now*" says a lot.

We are discovering the truth of ourselves; and, in the search for the greaterness that we are, the attainment of a vastly expanded awareness of our human emotional dimension is an all-important aspect of our hero's journey. As a result of our lack of understanding, lack of awareness, and self-doubt, we have developed neither a rich and healthy emotional response nor the ability to consciously process that response to its deeper meaning. Without such clarity, we have been unable to communicate the heart of the matter regarding our emotional upsets and downsets. This handicap has kept us operating on the surface of ourselves and has limited even our close relationships to the shallow waters of what is a deep ocean of human experience and meaning. As we begin to dive below the surface, explore the depths, ride the undercurrents, and rise to the surface again, we will discover things about ourselves as emotional beings that we have not known before. And on that self-discovery we will stand—more confident, less fearful, more aware, and much more capable of expressing the truth of ourselves.

In order to become congruent expressions of our real Self, with a consistent experience of inner peace and a underlying sense of purpose and meaning, we must achieve freedom from the prison in which our emotions have held us for too long. Being emotionally out-of-control, emotionally suppressed, and misemotional has caused us extreme psychological pain and serious dysfunction. We are now ready to learn to have our emotions, rather than our emotions having us. And freedom awaits us just the other side of misunderstanding, misinterpretation, and misconception.

OUR OWN SENSE OF SELF WILL BEGIN TO GROW STRONG AND OUR RELATIONSHIPS WITH OTHERS WILL BEGIN TO TAKE ON AN ENTIRELY NEW COMPLEXION.

Playing Sherlock.

The following questions will help you to gain understanding about what is going on with you emotionally at this time. I suggest that you give careful attention to what is being asked, contemplate the question, and be sincere and honest with yourself when you answer.

1) **Which emotions are you spending a lot of time with these days?**

   Are you easily shifted into the inertia scale and tending to remain there for several days at a time? Or, are you more easily provoked to anger and tending to remain somewhere on the activity scale for days at a time?

2) **Which emotions are you withdrawing from/avoiding these days?**

   Do you notice yourself resisting the experience of one of the high anger energies or, perhaps, the uncertainty/pain/fear trio at the top of the inertia scale?

3) **Which emotions do you sometimes deny you have?**

   Do your make-wrongs of certain emotions cause you to sometimes lie to yourself and/or others and disavow your experience of them?

4) **Which emotions stop you or slow you down noticeably?**

   In fact, at what point on the emotional scale do you noticeably begin to lose clear purpose and high productivity?

5) **Which emotions scare you?**

   Perhaps because of their high or low energy level or your history of getting stuck in them, you may be frightened of certain emotions.

6) Which emotions do you experience when someone you respect *shows disapproval* of something you think or feel?

The strength of your sense of self and the degree to which you are still dependent on the favor of others will determine your emotional responses in this case.

7) Which emotions do you experience when someone you respect *flatly disagrees* with something you think or feel?

Your ability to trust your own thoughts and feelings—to withstand the judgments of others and not fall into self-doubt—is measured here.

8) If you could eliminate one emotion from your experience of being human, which one would it be?

This emotion will in some way be the most unacceptable and difficult to cope with. It may be one of those you attempt to avoid.

9) Which person in your life has the ability to effect a change in your personal emotional experience *the most*?

Your relationship with the person who can "push your buttons" the most is a relationship which will transform as you gain understanding and become congruent.

10) Which person in your life is most affected emotionally by you?

Your understanding of yourself will assist you to understand and more easily relate to this person.

11) With whom do you pretend to agree in order to maintain peace?

Is there an emotional tyrant in your life? Or is it just that you fear conflict?

12) Against whom do you rebel because of their thoughts, feelings, or actions?

Is someone reminding you of your parent(s) and are you slipping back into adolescent reactivity?

13) Which emotional energy do you feel most comfortable with?

Have you become comfortable being angry? Or sad? Or does conservative fit like an old shoe?

14) Do you normally choose to spend your time with emotionally "intense" persons or with persons who are "mellow" emotionally?

You may be an "intense" type who enjoys feeling your intensity compared to the mellowness of others—or vice versa. Or you may attempt to spend your time with those who match your own emotional type. Either way, your answer will be informative.

15) Whose expectations, judgments and/or demands are you trying to satisfy these days?

Be honest. Make sure your list is complete.

16) Which emotions do you have a difficult time feeling?

Since when?

17) Which emotions are you unable to experience?

Can you easily and regularly experience the emotions just below or just above them on the scale?

TOWARD EXPANSION AND SELF-MASTERY

1. Practice identifying your emotions from time to time throughout the day.

2. Make lists of the emotions you are having most frequently and most infrequently.

3. Record your day's emotional experience before you go to bed at night. Track your emotional life in this way for three months.

4. Notice which emotional scale you spend most of your time in these days: inertia, activity, or balance.

5. Rate the intensity of your emotional experiences on a scale from 1 to 10 (10 being the highest intensity).

6. Begin to notice to what degree your own thoughts affect your emotional experience.

7. Begin to notice to what degree your physical condition affects your emotional experience.

8. Begin to notice to what degree your emotional experience affects your thoughts and your physical condition.

9. Begin to report your emotional experience to others—when it is appropriate—and notice the effect your report has on the success or failure of your relational transactions.

10. Begin to increase your own acceptance of your emotions. Notice which people in your life do not accept your emotional experience.

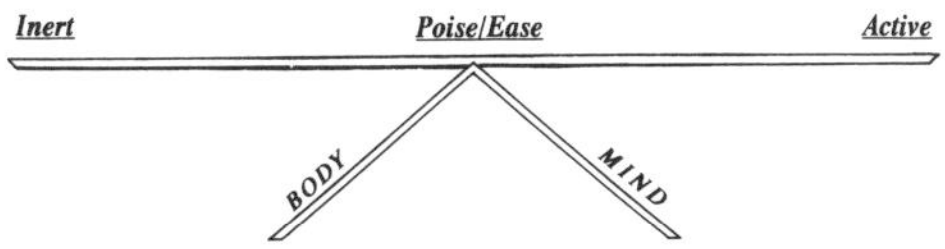

Let us understand that
we are cosmically-endowed links
in The Great Chain of Being.

CHAPTER SEVEN

THE HUMAN BEHAVIORAL RESPONSE

> *...(the star-child) waited, marshaling*
> *his thoughts and brooding over his still untested*
> *powers. For though he was master of the world,*
> *he was not quite sure what to do next.*
> *But he would think of something.*
>
> —*ARTHUR C. CLARKE*[1]

MASKS AS COPING MECHANISMS

For the purposes of this teaching, coping mechanisms are simply two categories of behaviors which we chose to utilize as very young children in order to get by in the world. Because of real or perceived threats to our physical or psychological well-being, we actually began to choose at a very early age to behave in particular ways with particular people in order to strengthen our chances of survival and to gain attention and/or approval. Because our behavioral strategies proved to be effective—in that we survived and, perhaps, became established members of a family—our identities became bound up with behavioral responses which we elected as babes. We earned a reputation for being either a *good little boy or girl* or a *difficult child*. Since we fell back on these behaviors again and again during times of relational stress, as we grew into childhood, into adolescence and into adulthood, our identities were drawn more and more boldly, and we came to know ourselves and be known by others as the adult rendition of the childish behaviors: *wonderful person* or *tough guy*.

In *The Celestine Prophecy*, James Redfield tells us, "Everyone manipulates for energy either aggressively, directly forcing people to pay attention to them, or passively, playing on people's sympathy or curiosity to gain attention."[2] He further states:

> *Before we can connect with the (Universal) energy on a permanent basis there is one more hurdle we must pass. We must face up to our particular way of controlling others. ...our particular style of controlling others is one we learned in childhood to get attention, to get the energy moving our way, and we're stuck there. This style is something we repeat over and over again. I call it our unconscious control drama.*
>
> *I call it a drama because it is one familiar scene, like a scene in a movie, for which we write the script as youths. Then we repeat this scene over and over in our daily lives without being aware of it. All we know is that the same kind of events happen to us repeatedly. The problem is if we are repeating one particular scene over and over, then the other scenes of our real life movie, the high adventure marked by coincidences, can't go forward. We stop the movie when we repeat this one drama in order to manipulate for energy.*[3]

Redfield distinguishes four masks or control dramas: interrogator, intimidator, aloof, and poor me.[4] The interrogator and the intimidator control dramas fall into the difficult child/tough guy category and the aloof and poor me control dramas fall into the good little boy or girl/wonderful person category.

Similarly, Virginia Satir, in *Peoplemaking*, identifies four masks: placater, blamer, computer, and distracter.[5] Her blamer and computer compare to the difficult child/tough guy category; and her placater and distracter can be classified as the good little boy or girl/wonderful person category.

And, as Redfield tells us, "The first step in the process of getting clear, for each of us, is to bring our particular control drama into full consciousness."[6] So, in the process of self-discovery, it is necessary to recognize which behaviors we have chosen to use as our primary response to stressful situations in order to get by—and how we have identified ourselves by these behaviors. The following are some simple guidelines for identifying the two types of behavior.

> **The good little boy or girl** is consistently *agreeable* in response to the judgments and expectations of others. He or she seems to roll with the punches of life; seems to be very flexible; and seems to absorb shocks and disappointments remarkably well. The good little boy or girl *withholds* expressions of *disagreement* and suppresses his or her emotional responses. This approach to life gains an inordinate amount of approval

from parents, teachers, and other adults since the child is so easy to get along with. If they could only see that the child is strategically choosing to act this particular way just to get along, perhaps his elders could assist the child to feel safer and to express him or herself more truthfully. In adulthood, this *wonderful person* has developed a whole list of charming and self-aggrandizing nuances which makes the original versions of this category of behavior look like child's play.

The difficult child is consistently *disagreeable* in response to the judgments and expectations of others. The difficult child seems to resist unpleasant turns of events; seems to be inflexible and rebellious; seems to react strongly against shocks and disappointments; and may act out in negative ways or may be sullenly silent and withdrawn. The difficult child *withholds* expressions of *agreement* and suppresses his or her loving and tender emotions. This approach to life gains an inordinate amount of uninformed disapproval from parents, teachers, and other adults since the child is so difficult to get along with. If his elders could only see that the child is strategically choosing to act this particular way just to get attention or to attempt to meet his or her basic needs, perhaps they could assist the child to feel safer and to express him or herself more truthfully. In adulthood, this *tough guy* has developed a whole list of firm, unyielding, uncompromising, and stern attitudes which makes those who know him or her wish that someone had done something to help during childhood.

We all move back and forth between these two roles throughout our childhood, our adolescence, and our adulthood—responding one way with some people and responding the other way with other people. Sometimes we will change behavioral strategies with a person with whom we have been consistently one way or the other in order to test the relationship or because of some particular set of circumstances which elicits our changing masks.

Without delving deeply into the convincing statistical findings which have been accumulated over the past few decades, it can be stated here with confidence that the *nice guy* syndrome of behavioral strategies results in psychosomatic *dis-ease* which turns in on oneself; for example, anorexia, bulimia, ulcers, just to name a few. The *not nice guy* syndrome—often manifesting as Type A Behavior—likewise takes its toll and results in hypertension, stroke, and heart disease, to name just a few. The causes of these serious physical conditions are easily traceable to the fact that coping mechanisms are not truthful expressions of who we are. The physical *dis-ease* is only symptomatic of the intense psychological *dis-ease* which the *wonderful person* or *tough guy* has experienced over a prolonged period of time. The coping mechanisms allow us to get by in a world of untruth and role playing, but the dramatic results of suppressing our authentic human responses have obviously become a very high price to pay.

In order to discover and express the truth of ourselves, we must put away these childish ways and stand forth as the richly-endowed and vastly-capable beings that we really are.

When we are ready to begin to express the truth of ourselves, it is imperative that we be able to identify which of these two coping mechanisms has been our mainstay and to notice each time we find ourselves falling back on this, now comfortable, approach to manipulating others in an attempt to satisfy our own needs. It is crucial that we see how much of our sketchy and uncertain identity has been formed as a direct result of our choice of coping mechanisms. In order to discover and express the truth of ourselves we must put away these childish ways and stand forth as the richly-endowed and vastly-capable beings that we really are. We must create the space to be who we are that we could not create as children. We must innocently and intelligently relate with others outside the fear of survival mentality which has so obviously caused us so much confusion and pain. In order to discover and accept ourselves, we must take the chance that others will judge us harshly and will reject us. It is well worth the risk.

The Ego Defense Mechanisms

As only a fragment of our vast wholeness, the ego is always experiencing itself as *thin, insubstantial, small, frail*, and *weak*, at the same time that it imagines its role to include the central function of our mind and full responsibility for figuring out, managing, and causing everything in our life. In order to defend itself from the threat it feels from its own subconscious fears and from what it perceives to be a hostile world, the ego ingeniously devises and implements strategies which can disguise its self-doubts. Over time, these strategies have been discovered, categorized and described by clinical psychologists. By gaining understanding about these defense mechanisms, which we have been using all along, we can intervene in our ego's conditioned (defensive) responses to others. By bringing conscious awareness to what has been unconscious reactivity, our ability to relate with others authentically will naturally and quickly begin to thrive.

Projection. Projection is the mechanism of attributing to others the hidden (repressed) parts of ourselves which we have stored in what is referred to as the shadow—and then either making them "wrong" or making them "right." The rejected parts of ourselves will show up in other people continuously and will evoke a highly-energized response from us until we have accepted them as part of our own humanity. Our emotionally-charged reaction of indignant self-righteousness because of someone else's behaviors are a dead give-away that we are experiencing a projection. Anytime we say, "I would never be like that," or "I could never do that," we are denying a very real part of our own humanity. We may be sure that if we **hate** some quality in another human being, it is because we have not accepted it in ourselves. We may also be certain that if we obsessively **love** some quality in another human being, we are loving it "out there" because we have not been able to accept it as a part of ourselves. Strephon Kaplan Williams, in *The Practice of Personal Transformation*, states:

> *WE PROJECT WHAT WE HAVE NOT YET MADE CONSCIOUS.*[7]
>
> *PROJECTION IS EXPERIENCING AS OUT THERE WHAT IS REALLY WITHIN OURSELVES.*[8]

Reaction Formation. In order to counteract its feelings of weakness or inadequacy and to block their rise to the conscious level, the ego implements a system of overcompensation by which it exaggerates, magnifies, and/or overdevelops certain conscious tendencies as a defense against unconscious dispositions which are opposite and unacceptable in nature. This strategy of reaction formation was studied with great interest by the great psychologist, Alfred Adler. In *Why Am I Afraid to Tell You Who I Am?*, John Powell, S.J., discusses this phenomenon:

The extremely dogmatic person, who is absolutely sure of everything, consciously cultivates this posture of certainty because of demoralizing doubts in his subconscious mind. His self-image isn't strong enough to live with these doubts. People who are overly-tender, to the point of exaggerated sentimentality, are usually suspected of assuming this attitude in compensation for harsh and cruel tendencies which have been repressed into the subconscious mind.[9]

Compensatory attitudes are a leaning over backwards to avoid tipping forward. The dogmatist is never wrong. The prude is hyper-chaste. The reformer-type, preachy and self-righteous, viciously hates sin and sinner alike without any recognition of normal human weakness.[10]

Displacement. Powell explains that displacement is "the indirect expression of an impulse that the censoring conscience (Freud's super-ego) prohibits us from expressing directly."[11] For example, in defending itself against its own strong feelings of hostility and anger toward its mother, for which its acculturation denies direct expression, the ego may *place* that anger on some other person and vent its feelings in a way that is culturally acceptable, such as yelling angry remarks at an athlete during a sporting event. Father Powell says,

'Scapegoating' is a common form of displacement. We react with uncalled-for violence when someone looks at us the wrong way, because there is a hostility in us that we cannot express directly. For some reason the person to whom we would like to express hostility seems too formidable to us.[12]

Another interpretation of displacement is the tactic of masking facts which cause us discomfort by magnifying something else which is not so humiliating to the ego. For example, we may profess to worry about something trivial to hide a greater anxiety simply because we cannot admit our fear. We defensively *place* our fear on something else. In a relationship, we may *place* our deep feelings of overall discontentment with our partner on certain well-chosen minor qualities and become quarrelsome about them.

Introjection. Powell defines introjection as "the ego defense by which we attribute to ourselves the good qualities of others."[13]

> *Introjection is prominent in what we call 'hero worship.' We identify with our heroes. Also, we identify our possessions with ourselves. We take great pride when someone praises our home, or we think that we are 'bigtime' because we come from a famous city, belong to a well-known fraternity, or have traveled to many places. Many women identify with the tragic heroines of soap-opera programs on television.*[14]

Rationalization. The ego defense most commonly utilized is that of rationalization. This defensive strategy is simply thinking up a "good reason" for our actions when we fear that the real reason may make us vulnerable to the judgments of others. When it is simply too risky to our ego to disclose its real motives, strategies, and tendencies, it reverts to rationalization. As Father Powell explains:

> *Rationalization is not only self-deceit but eventually corrupts all sense of integrity (wholeness). We rationalize our failures; we find justification for our actions; we reconcile our ideals and our deeds; we make our emotional preferences our rational conclusions.*
>
> *...Rationalization is the bridge which makes my wishes the facts. It is the use of intelligence to deny the truth; it makes us dishonest with ourselves, and, if we cannot be honest with ourselves, we certainly cannot be honest with anyone else. It consequently sabotages all human authenticity. It disintegrates and fragments the personality.*[15]

Up With the Masks. Down With the Defenses. Let's Get Real!

What is demanded of us as we stand on the ledge over the abyss is a dropping of all of the coping mechanisms and all of the defense mechanisms which we have used as psychological crutches to hobble along through the *Territory of Consolation*. Those crutches have seemed to be necessary since we have been seriously disabled by our fears and doubts and terribly burdened by our perceived need to "pull ourselves up by the bootstraps," "play our cards close to the vest," "keep up a good front," "fit in," and "get by" at any price. Standing alone without the crutches is a fascinating, though disconcerting, proposition in the beginning, but one we relish and treasure. It is what we have always wanted to do; we just have not known how to do it. This book provides several substantive and meaningful replacements for those time-worn crutches—methods which will make it possible for us to walk tall, to run with grace, and eventually to fly like an eagle on the wings of our own true expression.

To leap us beyond the less-than-authentic forms of communication which we have utilized since infancy, the next step is the development of authentic communication based on emotional courage, emotional self-discipline and emotional gracefulness. With what will soon become a natural methodology based on our own personal feelings, thoughts, ideas, and beliefs, this approach to truthful expression will speed us along our path.

Emotional Courage, Self-Discipline, and Gracefulness are crucial elements which must be a part of our basic understanding and, then, an essential part of our practice in order for us to "clear up," in order for our lives to become authentic, and in order for us and our relationships to thrive. I first heard these potent terms in 1984, when, in the early stages of my own conscious process, I was exposed to the teachings of Loy and Robert Young. Just hearing them made a real difference for me. Even before I knew for sure what they meant, it was as if a cloudiness in me cleared up, as if a simple and strong structure were put in place in my understanding. I have seen the same effect occur in others to whom I have said these words. Out of my own experience, I now offer these elaborations of what may become a cornerstone for Self-expression in other journeyers, as it did in me.

> EMOTIONAL COURAGE IS THE WILL, THE DETERMINATION, THE COMMITMENT, TO BE THE TRUTH OF OURSELVES IN THE WORLD.

> EMOTIONAL COURAGE IS THE WILL AND THE ABILITY TO EXPRESS OURSELVES TRUTHFULLY. IT IS NOT REBELLION (WHICH IS REACTIVITY).

EMOTIONAL COURAGE IS THE WILL, THE DETERMINATION, THE COMMITMENT, TO EXPRESS OURSELVES AT THE RISK OF REJECTION, AT THE RISK OF NOT LOOKING GOOD, AT THE RISK OF BEING HARSHLY AND NEGATIVELY JUDGED BY OTHERS.

EMOTIONAL COURAGE IS THE WILL AND THE ABILITY TO CONFRONT THE DISHONESTY IN OURSELVES AND IN OTHERS.

EMOTIONAL SELF-DISCIPLINE IS THE ABILITY TO CONSCIOUSLY CHOOSE OUR COMMUNICATION AND OUR BEHAVIOR NO MATTER WHAT OUR EMOTIONAL EXPERIENCE IS—RATHER THAN HAVING OUR EMOTIONS DICTATE WHAT WE SAY AND HOW WE BEHAVE.

EMOTIONAL GRACEFULNESS IS THE ABILITY TO EXPRESS OURSELVES IN SUCH A WAY THAT OTHERS CAN HEAR US NO MATTER HOW POWERFUL THE COMMUNICATION IS. IT IS THE ABILITY TO EXPRESS OURSELVES IN SUCH A WAY THAT THE OTHER PERSON DOES NOT CLOSE DOWN, EVEN THOUGH THE COMMUNICATION MAY BE CONFRONTIVE.

Having just reviewed the coping mechanisms and defense mechanisms which are *digressions into dishonesty*, it is easy for us to see that an untwisting of our conditioned (unconscious) responses is sorely needed if we are to become our true selves—real, genuine, authentic, congruent human beings. And, although the simple formula for straightening out all those tangled distortions includes all of the chapters of this book, I want to emphasize here that the development of emotional courage, self-discipline and gracefulness is *central* to the Self-expression which is our goal.

Emotional Courage. One of the misconceptions which many of us have is that emotional courage means being tough or mean or loud or rude. It does not. There are many times when our most emotionally courageous choice will be to remain silent, to speak softly, or to reveal our own tender thoughts and feelings. It will, of course, depend on the particular relational transaction, the existing circumstances, and all of the subtle nuances relevant in the moment. Being emotionally courageous, then, does not always mean being assertive. It means being truthful with ourselves and dealing with situations in truth. Being emotionally courageous does mean that we no longer sell out on ourselves because of our fear of conflict, our fear of rocking the boat, or our tendency to defer to others who are playing their *tough guy* role to the max or who are more assertive than we.

The *tough guy* behaviors are not models for emotional courage. These coping mechanisms are fear-based, as are the *wonderful person* behaviors. We must become capable of differentiating between the "in-your-face" or "behind-your-back" behaviors—which epitomize adolescent reactivity—and real emotional courage. It does not take courage to vent our disappointment and anger on others. It only takes sufficient disappointment and anger to trigger old familiar tough guy behaviors, which are, as we have seen, based in childish coping strategies. It takes emotional courage to meet another human being as an equal, to speak truthfully about something which may cause each of us to feel uncomfortable, to say what it is that we really need to say without wimping out and without crucifying the other person. It takes emotional courage to give up being right and to attempt to really understand what the other person thinks and feels and perceives. It takes emotional courage to discard our attitudes of superiority and inferiority and to become vulnerable as human beings who are seeking the truth of ourselves. It takes emotional courage to abandon our combative attitudes and victim attitudes in order to rise to the occasion and honor our humanness.

It does take emotional courage to express our anger, if we have been loath to or unable to do so before. For the *wonderful person* who is still frightened by his own and others' anger, the practice of emotional courage in the form of expressing anger, if done in incremental stages, will result in swift and dramatic changes in his sense of self. For the *tough guy* who has been regularly unleashing his hostility on others, the practice of emotional courage in the form of giving up being right and approaching others as credible equals will quickly result in the creation of a whole new experience of himself.

Realizing that we have been hiding behind masks and using defense mechanisms to keep us "separate" and "safe," we begin by raising the masks and dropping the defenses so that we can begin to show up as who we really are. Remembering that the goal is personal freedom and the vehicle is Self-expression, we continue by disclosing, when appropriate, more of what we have before withheld from others—our personal thoughts, ideas, feelings, beliefs. Knowing that we have withheld these deeply personal parts of ourselves from others because we were not sure they would be accepted and/or approved of, we now must take the risk of disclosing ourselves and taking the consequences of that disclosure. It is the only way we will ever achieve authenticity, and, thus, freedom. In this way, we discover others with whom we have much in common; and, we no longer attempt to fit ourselves into relationships where there is little commonality. We need to be with others who will celebrate our uniqueness. We need no longer wear the mask of a square peg, if, instead, we are really a round hole (and vice versa).

Emotional Self-Discipline. Withholding ourselves from relationship with others and withholding our communications because they are judgments of others is not emotional self-discipline. In fact, the more emotionally self-disciplined we become, the more relational we will become, because we are confidently and comfortably able to trust ourselves to deal with our own emotions and to respond in truth to whatever the other person says or does. Emotional self-discipline very simply means that, in order to serve the truth in an interaction, we are able to withhold the spiteful, hurtful, and blameful words which our distressed ego may want to say. Or, if we are a wonderful person, in order to serve the truth in an interaction, we are able to withhold the charming, manipulative, ego-stroking words which our frightened ego may want to say. Or, if, in the thick of a painful separation, we are able to withhold the shameful, pitiful, clutching, grasping pleas of the ego, which is willing to try any tactic in order to subvert change. The ability to discipline ourselves in order to override the ingrained tendencies of the reactive ego sets us free over and over again and acts as a source of personal empowerment.

A distinction must be drawn between *controlling* or suppressing our emotional experiences and *disciplining* ourselves so that our emotional responses do not dictate what we say and how we behave. When we control ourselves, we actually "lose our nerve," "cave in," and "wimp out." By suppressing ourselves we put the mask back on and fall back into the unconscious, fear-based behaviors which either tell others what they want to hear or attack them with our make-wrongs. When we discipline ourselves, we remain conscious and courageously say what we feel and think and believe to be true, or we courageously choose not to say anything because we know that it is to our highest good to remain silent. But we do not sell out on ourselves by falling back on behaviors motivated by subconscious fear.

When we realize that our struggle is with ourselves and not with the other person, we become very different. When we realize that we actually make a unique and valuable contribution to the lives of others and to the world-at-large by being who we are in the world, we become equal to the circumstances of our lives. When we realize that there is *another more appropriate response in this case* and are able to choose it *on the spot*, we become more self-confident and more available for relationship than we have ever been before. The ability to consciously choose what we will say and when we will say it—even in the thick of a highly-energized relational transaction—is the stuff of which congruence is made.

Emotional Gracefulness. Being "charming" in a way that fosters one's reputation for being a *wonderful person*, in a way that attempts to make everything "nice," in a way that strokes another's ego for one's own self-serving purposes, or in a way that deflects the difficult truth of a situation, is not emotional gracefulness. The ability to be emotionally graceful includes the ability to read the situation and express the truth with a decibel level, a tonal quality, a facial expression, and word and body language which will make it possible for the listener to receive the communication.

A Spoonful of Sugar Makes the Medicine Go Down. Many times in our attempts to communicate truthfully with others it will be necessary to introduce a touch of gracefulness by, perhaps, introducing a touch of humor. Many times in our attempts to communicate truthfully with others, we may need to use tones of voice and body language which indicate calmness, security, compassion, and good will—which are not likely to evoke angry reactions from our listener. As we become more experienced and more confident in expressing ourselves congruently, we will be capable of appropriately introducing these practices of emotional gracefulness more and more often.

> **A laser through the concrete wall.** Many times in our attempts to communicate truthfully with others it will be necessary to introduce a touch of gracefulness by, perhaps, introducing a touch of stunning directness and crystal clarity. In this form of gracefulness our sense of self, our emotional integrity, and our intention to communicate become laser like energetically, and we say the simple truth in a well-modulated, impersonal, loud and clear voice in order to penetrate what is obviously the hard wall of a mind that does not want to hear us and cannot hear us over its own loud inner (and, perhaps, outer) chatter. And, though our listener may not be immediately "cleared" by our clear communication, he will have heard it and will hear it ringing in his ears for a long time. What makes this form of emotional gracefulness elegant is 1) the conscious use of emotional courage, self-discipline and gracefulness all at once, 2) communicating clearly and simply from the center of ourselves, 3) the conscious timing of the communication, and 4) delivering the communication in such a way that we know the listener will hear it.

Where should we begin our practice? In which order should we practice these three crucial elements of communication? A simple rule is that without emotional courage we will not get very far in becoming the truth of ourselves; so I suggest that everyone begin their practice with emotional courage. (Remember that tough guys have not been being courageous. They, too, have been hiding behind a mask of fear-based bravado.) When we are ready to introduce another element into our practice, I suggest we choose between emotional self-discipline and emotional gracefulness based on whether we have, primarily, taken the role of *wonderful person* or *tough guy*. The *wonderful person* will find it challenging to discriminate between old ways of "acting like" everything is okay and self-discipline and old ways of "turning on the charm" and authentic emotional gracefulness. The *tough guy* will find it challenging to develop both self-discipline and gracefulness. Both will find the practice very interesting and the results extremely rewarding. The abyss awaits!

LIFE LIVED AUTHENTICALLY
IS NEITHER A GAME OF HIDE AND SEEK
NOR A POPULARITY CONTEST.

CONGRUENCE
Emotional
Courage
At
Choice
Inertia
Confront
Self
Activity
Self
Discipline
Communication
Self
Trust
Resistance
Balance
At
Risk
Gracefulness
Satisfaction

Figure No. 12

Toward Expansion and Self-Mastery

1. Determine which coping mechanism you chose to use most often in order to get by and to establish yourself as an identity among your family and friends. Difficult child? Good little boy or girl?

2. Determine (on a scale from 1 to 10) to what degree you have moved beyond the limitations of that coping mechanism or self-protective mask.

3. With which people do you feel most free—most able to take off the mask?

4. With which people do you feel most in need of relating from the pseudo-identity you created—most unable to take off the mask?

5. Become more and more aware of when you automatically slip into the Difficult Child or Good Little Boy or Girl role-playing.

6. Begin to consciously practice emotional courage in relating to the people in your life. Notice your own inner experience as you take off the mask you have been wearing; and notice the different effect you have on the others with whom you relate. If you have a difficult time in changing your image, don't give up. Try again...and again.

7. Begin to consciously practice emotional self-discipline in relating to the people in your life. Combine your practice of becoming more aware of your emotional experiences with the practice of consciously choosing not to allow your emotions to speak in order to lash out at others. Notice your level of empowerment when you practice emotional self-discipline.

8. Begin to consciously practice emotional gracefulness in relating to the people in your life. Do not allow the charm of your Good Little Boy/Girl role to override the primary purpose of your life—expression—but practice communicating at the tolerance level of others. Help them to understand what you mean.

Let us perceive
that we are weaponless warriors
whose lives are the battlefield
on which the struggle for
transcendence is being waged.

CHAPTER EIGHT

THE DIMINISHED SELF

The ego is literally a fearful thought.
The ego is your belief.
The ego is a confusion in identification.
This fragment of your mind
is such a tiny part of it that,
could you but appreciate the whole,
you would see instantly
that it is like the smallest sunbeam to the sun,
or like the faintest ripple on the surface of the ocean.
In its amazing arrogance,
this tiny sunbeam has decided it is the sun;
this almost imperceptible ripple
hails itself as the ocean.
Think how alone and frightened is this little thought,
this infinitesimal illusion,
holding itself apart against the universe....
Do not accept this little, fenced-off aspect as yourself.
The sun and ocean are as nothing beside what you are.

—*A COURSE IN MIRACLES*[1]

THE SUNBEAM WHICH THINKS IT IS THE SUN

An awakening is an expansion of awareness. When we begin to awaken, it is as if our eyes have opened wider and we are able to see more of what has been and is occurring all around us. We are also able to see ourselves more clearly and with more perspective. An expanded awareness brings with it an intense desire to gain understanding about our ourselves and others, about our world and other realms of being, and about life and death.

One of the signs of the great awakening that is occurring in our world now is the fact that so many people have become aware of the ego, have gained some

THE EGO HAS...
...EYES IN THE BACK OF ITS HEAD
...CLEAR VISION INTO THE PAST
...DIM VISION IN THE PRESENT MOMENT
...TINY EARS / POOR, IMPAIRED HEARING
...BIG, NOISY MOUTH / CONSTANT CHATTERING
THE EGO WANTS...
...TO WIN
...TO BE RIGHT
...TO LOOK GOOD
...TO SURVIVE
THE EGO HAS...
STRONG ATTITUDES:
COMBATIVE
VICTIM
SUPERIOR
INFERIOR
THE EGO HAS...
EXPECTATIONS
JUDGMENTS
DEMANDS
PAST

Figure No. 13

understanding of what the ego is, and view themselves and others in terms of the ego's agenda. However, even though the word ego falls so easily off the tongues of people representing a broad spectrum of divergent socio-economic, ethnic, educational, and professional categories, as a society I feel we still lack a simple and clear understanding of what the ego is and how it functions. This simple and clear understanding will assist us to reclaim our lives from the neurotic tendencies and limiting strategies of the ego.

Our western culture has generally accepted Sigmund Freud's translation of the term "I" to mean *the rational mental life*[2] and his identification of the sense of "I" as the *ego*. For several decades only psychiatrists and psychologists were educated about the ego. And since Freud's school of psychoanalysis caused as much controversy as it brought clarity, there has been no generalized agreement among the psychiatrists in our society about the ego and how we can begin to deal with it. Having undergone psychiatric and psychological therapy during my thirties and having spoken to psychiatrists, psychologists and therapists over the past years, I have realized that clarity about the ego is not widespread. Because of the disparity among the teachings about the ego today, there is confusion in the minds of many seekers as to how to hold the ego, what attitude to have about it, and how to deal with it. Is it a monster which must be struggled with and slain? Is it a fragile child-like aspect that needs to be comforted and reassured?

I do not presume to outdo Freud or presume to be as well-informed and knowledgeable about things psychiatric or psychological as the well-trained professionals whose shingles dot our land when I present my simple model of the ego. I simply offer this depiction [Figure No. 13] and elaboration of some of the clear and easily understandable aspects of the ego in an attempt to bring clear understanding about this aspect of our humanity which holds us captive as a species.

WITH ONLY SMALL SLITS FOR EYES, THE EGO HAS DIMINISHED AWARENESS OF WHAT IS HAPPENING RIGHT IN FRONT OF IT.

In this model, the ego is depicted as a small, endarkened, partial self. It has **eyes in the back of its head**—with unclouded vision into the past and dim vision in the present moment. With only small **slits for eyes**, it has diminished awareness of what is happening right in front of it; yet, it sees clearly and in great detail what happened to it in the past. In fact, it relives previous experiences over and over again in its well-developed and overactive memory.

The ego has **tiny ears** which impair its ability to correctly hear what is being said to it. In fact, nearly all incoming communications are distorted by its memories of previous communications or experiences which seem somewhat similar to what it is hearing in the present. The ego's hearing is also influenced by prejudices it has already acquired regarding different races, colors, and types of people and ways of behaving, as well as strong opinions it has developed about different places and things. So when it is being spoken to the ego has difficulty hearing precisely what is being said.

Besides the fact that it has tiny eyes for seeing and tiny ears for listening in the present, it has a **big, noisy mouth**. Its disproportionately big mouth chatters incessantly, as if having a conversation with itself. Its inside chatter consists primarily of judgments of whether someone or something is *good* or *bad* and whether it *likes* or *dislikes* them or it. It also produces all kinds of scary and worrisome thoughts about what might or might not happen in the future. The damaged ego feels separated from the universe, from the environment, from its body, and from the shadow part of itself; and that separation makes it feel alone, lonely, and unsafe in the world. It is most often worried, and it is frequently filled with either self-doubt or self-righteous indignation.

Its big, noisy mouth also chatters out loud. When it speaks to others, it says things to make itself feel better, to report its wonderful life, to report its difficult life and unfair treatment, and to make itself seem to be *right*, or *fine*, or mistreated in their eyes. The damaged ego personalizes nearly everything and says very little of real substance.

In any disagreement with another, the ego wants to **win** the argument. If it cannot win, it wants to **be right**. If it cannot be right, it wants to at least **look good**. And if it cannot look good, it wants, at least, to **survive**.

The ego has strong attitudes. It has a **combative attitude** and a **victim attitude**—which are two ends of the same continuum. And it vacillates all day long every day between these two attitudes. It either reacts from an attitude of superiority (as though it is "better than" others or "too good to be treated like this"), or it exhibits an attitude of inferiority (as though it is "not equal" to others, "unworthy," "not good enough"). It fluctuates back and forth between these two attitudes throughout the day, depending on the different relational circumstances in which it finds itself.

The ego has **expectations, judgments, and demands** of everyone and everything. It constantly generates expectations, judgments, and demands of itself, of others, of all experiences and circumstances. It continuously creates scenarios of what it wants, how it thinks things should be, and how others should respond in thought and action—even in the way they dress or comb their hair. The ego even expects that the weather meet its expectations, and it can become quite disconsolate if there is rain on a day that it expected to be perfect for an outdoor event. The ego **judges everything** based on its own expectations of how things should turn out and formulates its demands on others based on how it thinks they should be and what they should do. It judges everything based on its own experiences, on its acculturation (societal mores) and on its conditioning (judgments of its elders and peers). It constantly compares itself to other people—judging itself either "better than" or "worse than" them. The ego is not the truth of ourselves. It is a peculiar mixture of accumulated prejudices and opinions—out of which it reacts to the people and circumstances in its (our) life.

The ego is **damaged**. In the model, that psychological damage is represented by a band-aid, a scar, some stitches, and a bruise. When this person was very small and dependent on others for its care, it experienced shocking disappointment due to unfair and/or abusive treatment (real or perceived) by someone—most probably its parent. Whether or not the treatment was cruel in some way, the child actually experienced a psychological shock and was traumatized to some extent. That shock to its innocent and fragile babyhood or childhood frightened it because it caused the baby or young child to realize its dependency and the threat(s) to its very survival. The shock acted as a wake up call in that it put the child on alert to its need to protect itself, to find some way to get by in a dangerous world in which even its most trusted allies could not really be trusted. Instinctively ingenious at conceiving survival strategies, the child began to find ways to act in order to avoid what it perceived as threats to its survival.

As the years went by, the child suffered still other shocking experiences of hurtful treatment in some of its relationships with others it trusted—parents, grandparents, uncles, aunts, teachers, ministers, priests, policemen, siblings, and friends. Each startling experience of hurtful disappointment produced a contusion on its tender surface. With these disillusionments as its subconscious reference, every time one of these bruises or cuts or scars is touched (recalled) by an experience in the present time, the ego reacts: OUCH! And that OUCH! is an ego reaction—the words, tones of voice and behaviors which result are forms of ego reactivity and are based on past hurts.

All humans, no matter how carefully they are handled as babies, do suffer this experience of psychological shock and the resultant "Fall" from innocence. If a child has known only trustful and loving care, for example, his shock and disillusionment may occur at the time his beloved pet dies. Since the ego personalizes all of its experiences, the death of a pet can trigger the shocking realization of one's mortality—the wake-up call to which I refer.

The ego has real needs that have not been met and that must be met somehow. It needs attention, approval, a sense of security, and love. Being completely self-conscious, self-absorbed, and self-serving, the ego tries its best to meet its needs. It employs approval-seeking behavior, emotional manipulation of others, and justification of its thoughts and actions as it seeks acceptance, safety and love.

THE EGO HAS EXPECTATIONS, JUDGMENTS, AND DEMANDS OF EVERYONE AND EVERYTHING.

The ego in the model holds a **bag of the past** in one hand all the time. However, it never knows for sure which highly energized memories the bag contains until it is triggered into reactivity by something or someone. For example, the triggering may occur while the ego is standing at the check-out line at the supermarket. It may see an interaction between two people it has never seen before which activates an old unhealed wound—and its "stuff" will come up. From its own emotional reaction, it will remember a previous similar incident. It may, for example, see two people who are very much in love and who are being very sweet and loving to each other, which may cause the ego to feel a rush of sadness and grieving for a lover that it had in the past. That relationship was never completely resolved in the ego; and, so, it still hangs around in the bag of its past. The bag is always full of surprises from the past—experiences which caused the ego confusion, pain and fear, and with which the ego dealt by utilizing its limited repertoire of strategies in order to win, to be right, to look good, or to survive, and by employing its attitudes of combativeness and victimization, superiority and inferiority.

The ego's other hand reaches out into the world in futile **attempts to control circumstances and people** in its struggle to get what it wants. And it holds on! It grabs on to people and to things and holds on tight. The ego is very possessive and very proud of its possessions. Whatever it has claimed as belonging to it is perceived as in need of constant protection from the threat of being taken by others. As a result of its feelings of aloneness, it identifies itself by its relationships, its jobs, its experiences, and its possessions. Since its whole identification of itself is bound up in its materialistic view of the world, the ego is keenly aware of and often jealous of the possessions and positions of others, since more possessions or a more prestigious job equate to a better identity in its way of thinking. It becomes deeply attached to people, places and things and fears the loss of anyone or anything to which it has become emotionally attached, since they actually represent important parts of the ego's self-created image or identity. A loss of a loved one or a loved thing is experienced as a loss of self, and the grieving it does is really a grieving of its own loss.

The higher Self is represented in the model by the circle which lies behind or beyond the head of the ego. I have characterized its harmonious nature by way of the straight lines inside the circle, and have implied the relationship of the unhealed ego to the higher Self by placing the ego out in front of the higher Self. Relative to the process of transformation, strong emphasis must always be given to the relationship of the ego to the higher Self. Returning to the quoted material from Franz' "The Process of Individuation," we are reminded that the higher Self "appears first as **merely** an inborn **possibility**." The encoded potential in all human beings lies dormant as a possibility only. Franz tells us that the possibility for transformation to higher levels of consciousness actually **depends on** *our ego's willingness to align itself* with the impulse for evolvement of our higher Self. He says of the higher Self: "It may emerge very slightly, or it may develop relatively completely during one's lifetime. How far it develops depends on whether or not the ego is willing to listen to the messages of the Self."[3] That being the case, it is of ultimate importance that we assist our egoic consciousness to relax and trust the greater process of which it is a part and to which it is an obstruction. The ego acts in its robotic manner as our "free will" in that it is the "naysayer." At the mental-egoic level, its hold on and domination of our consciousness is undeniable. Until, with its permission to proceed, we have moved beyond its fearful hold on our life, our destiny is in its hands.

As with all aspects of ourselves, our lives, and our Processes, I suggest that we must be two-headed in our attitudes about our ego and in our approaches to dealing with it. We must get the hang of employing different strategies to undermine the ego's attempts to control people and circumstances in ways which serve to slow down or thwart the "irrevocable transformations" for which the inherent cosmic qualities of the higher Self hanker. From the Observer or Witness level, we must learn to act, at times, as loving parents and caring friends to our own egos. At other times, we must relate to our own egos as teachers or trainers. At times, we will need to assume the role of unwavering disciplinarians, demanding that the ego release its fearful grip on our lives. By listening to the messages of our deeper personality, we gain confidence in our ability to maintain alignment from the ego in order to sustain ourselves upon our chosen path to freedom.

THE EGO: CONSCIOUSNESS BECOMES CONSCIOUS OF ITSELF

> *...and then, at the mental-egoic stage, around the second millennium B.C., an absolutely unprecedented cry of anguish, guilt, and sorrow screams out from the world's myths, narratives, and records, for at that point, mankind had finally emerged from its great sleep in the subconscious, and was faced with the stark awareness of its own mortal and isolated existence. No longer protected by the subconscious, and not yet awakened to the superconscious, mankind—stuck in the middle—cried out to the gods that would no longer answer and wailed to a goddess no longer there. The world, quite simply, was never to be the same.*[4]

As Ken Wilber tells us, the emergence of the ego structure in humans was actually our "Fall" from innocence. The appearance of the ego was an absolutely amazing leap in consciousness. All of a sudden, in the mind of man, an awakening occurred at a level of consciousness in which the being could look back upon itself. The self-reflexive nature of this new consciousness made it possible for human beings to contemplate the past and learn from their previous actions. But as amazing as it was, it marked the moment at which humans became aware of their own mortality and terrified of their own certain death. As we can now imagine, the incredible expansion of awareness which the advent of the mental-egoic level of consciousness introduced was so shocking to humans—who were previously unconscious of their mortality—that instead of celebrating their new capacity to reflect upon themselves and the ways of the world, they were sorely aggrieved because of what they were now able to see. The Garden of Eden had at its center the Tree of Life[5] (symbolizing the nervous system of the human body which was attuned to the life of the universe). Humans who lived in the Garden lived in a natural condition of inner bliss and the ability to "know" God through the unobstructed intuitive resonance within the intelligence of their own bodily systems. Having lived in the Garden of Eden (the two brain centers below the mental-egoic level of brain function) in total trust of the beneficence of the universe, the consciousness of those first humans who "ate of the fruit of the Tree of Knowledge of Good and Evil" by that "eating" became centered in the lower level of the third brain and became self-reflexive "thinkers." Now operating primarily as mental beings, their new mind systems denied them access to the "the Garden." They experienced their new self-consciousness (represented by the fig leaves which they placed over their genitals) as a strange and difficult affliction—as a cruel and frightening obstruction to the Divine Realms.

The "Fall" or awakening from the Edenic dream of trust and a sense of security **repeats itself** in each of us as our ego begins to emerge sometime after our first year of life. Besides this disillusioning loss of innocence which shocks us into a separate and mortal self-sense, many of us also experience damage to our fragile egos by the hurtful treatment (intentional or unintentional) by our caregivers. The wounds inflicted by such treatment distort our perceptions of ourselves and others and remain unhealed unless and until we consciously resolve them as adults. The resolutions to these distorted perceptions are oftentimes hard won victories which come long after we have attempted to achieve relief from the psychological pain they breed through the addictive use of drugs, alcohol, sex, food, etc. The "inner child" therapeutic work which has become so popular today is a testimony to the widespread awareness of psychological pain which has been directly caused by ill-treatment during our formative years.

The more wounded or damaged our ego is, the more defensive (self-protective) it will be in relationship with others and with its environment. The more defensive it is, the more egomania it will exhibit in terms of pride, self-righteousness, harsh judgments of others, compulsive competitiveness, and on and on. The more wounded or damaged our ego is, the more self-doubting it will be—which will show up as overcompensating, isolating, and self-destructive behaviors.

IN ANY DISAGREEMENT WITH ANOTHER, THE EGO WANTS TO WIN THE ARGUMENT. IF IT CANNOT WIN, IT WANTS TO BE RIGHT. IF IT CANNOT BE RIGHT, IT WANTS TO, AT LEAST, LOOK GOOD. AND IF IT CANNOT LOOK GOOD, IT WANTS TO SIMPLY SURVIVE.

So, it is of utmost importance that we become aware of the behaviors we subconsciously choose to repeatedly compensate for the confusion, pain and fear which derive from our ego's wounded condition. We must learn to recognize our own egoic tendencies so that we may intelligently serve the healing/strengthening of our own egos. Truthful Self-expression in the present moment effects amazing healings of our injured egos and corrects our twisted perceptions of ourselves.

The Work of the Ego: Stability and Evaluation

The ego is the ego is the ego. It is not a monster. It is not a demon. It is a particular and remarkable structure within the human psyche which appeared thousands of years ago, and which transformed the human species into "man who knows it knows." The ego mechanism has particular functions which only it is capable of and responsible for performing—and it performs those functions automatically or naturally or involuntarily. Once we have at least a rudimentary understanding of the mechanism which the ego is, we can begin to observe its functions and choose to consciously intervene in what has before been an unconscious process. Meher Baba states:

> *The process (that is ego) implies capacity to hold different experiences together as parts of a unity and the capacity to evaluate them by mutual relation....*
>
> *The part played by the ego in human life may be compared with the function of the ballast in a ship. The ballast keeps the ship from too much oscillation; without it, the ship is likely to be too light and unsteady and in danger of being overturned.... The formation of the ego serves the purpose of giving a certain amount of stability to conscious processes, and secures a working equilibrium which makes for organized life.*[6]

One of the primary functions of the ego is to maintain the status quo—as the ballast on a ship does. The struggle we feel as we take our journey is the ego's resistance to change. This natural resistance will be a factor with which we must contend, even if the status quo is repressive and miserably unfulfilling and even if the impending change is undeniably positive and potentially liberating. The ego is just doing what it does best—attempting to insure that nothing rocks the boat, to avoid the possible dangers of the unknown, and to see to it that we (it) survive(s). The ego figures that the easiest—and, so, the best—way to assure its survival is to achieve an even keel (safety and security) and, then, to maintain that course. As Ken Carey says, "The ego has a set of values that are designed to care for the physical body and protect it from harm. When it is allowed to control decision-making, the ego is overcautious in the extreme; dangers and possible threats become exaggerated; and the individual often finds him or herself functioning out of fear."[7]

In its role as evaluator of what is "good" and what is "bad," the ego creates its own criteria based on its particular acculturation, its personal conditioning, and its accumulation of personal preferences (which are often influenced by past and present peer groups). But even though the ego sits on the throne of judgment, assessing what is "right" and what is "wrong," its evaluations reek of personal preferences and vested interests in *certain* outcomes. In other words, it is not a wise and objective judge.

Da Avabhasa has pointed out that, "essentially, the (untransformed) human is both passionate and lazy,"[8] so he will strive to effect change in his life only if he feels somewhat assured that the change will fulfill some of his desires and provide it with security. It will elect to allow change to occur in its life only if its efforts to do what it must do to support the change seem fairly sure to pay off in the currency of enhanced chances for attaining acceptance, security, and love.

The fearful, overly cautious, overburdened, and sluggish ego is afraid that it will have to do something that it really does not know how to do, something that it really cannot do, or something that it just does not want to do. Basically, the over-burdened ego, feeling weak and helpless, just wants to get by. So, even though it often displays emotional passion in regard to its strong opinions, it will most usually create strategies based on what will bring it the most security and the most approval from its culture, society, family, or peer group. Even wildly rebellious, "in-your-face" behaviors will have their passionate roots in attention-getting or approval-seeking motives, with the trembling source of the psychological twist being a particular peer culture.

Since we need the ego's alignment in order to change our course and set sail for the high seas, our understanding of its basic functions and attitudes will assist us to compassionately and dispassionately observe its reactions, feel its emotions, and apply high reason to its emotional and logical approach to life. By comprehending its logic, we can influence the ego's attitudes, persuading it to elect higher choices than is its custom by choosing higher reasons for its actions. This high-minded influence can neutralize the ego's resistance and ease its eventual alignment with the high purposes of the greater Self.

A NEW BEGINNING IS POSSIBLE FOR ANY OF US AT ANY AGE, ONCE WE GAIN CLARITY ABOUT A FEW ELEMENTS INTRINSIC TO OUR VERY HUMANNESS.

The Ego: A Set of Thoughts

In the following quote, Ram Dass describes the ego in such a way that we may really begin to understand it so that we may become less fearful of losing our identity, and so that we may begin to venture beyond its narrow confines.

> *Your ego is a set of thoughts that define your universe. It's like a familiar room built of thoughts; you see the universe through its windows. You are secure in it, but to the extent that you are afraid to venture outside, it has become a prison. Your ego has you conned. You believe you need its specific thoughts to survive. The ego controls you through your fear of loss of identity. To give up these thoughts, it seems, would eliminate you, and so you cling to them.*
>
> *There is an alternative. You needn't destroy the ego to escape its tyranny. You can keep this familiar room to use as you wish, and you can be free to come and go. First you need to know that you are infinitely more than the ego room by which you define yourself. Once you know this, you have the power to change the ego from prison to home base.*[9]
>
> *We need the matrix of thoughts, feelings, and sensations we call the ego for our physical and psychological survival. The ego tells us what leads to what, what to avoid, how to satisfy our desires, and what to do in each situation. It does this by labeling everything we sense or think. These labels put order in our world and give us a sense of security and well-being. With these labels, we know our world and our place in it.*[10]
>
> *Our ego renders safe an unruly world. Uncountable sense impressions and thoughts crowd in on us, so that without the ego to filter out irrelevant information, we would be inundated, overwhelmed, and ultimately destroyed by the overload. Or so it seems.*
>
> *The ego has convinced us that we need it—not only that we need it, but that we are it....*
>
> *The path to freedom is through detachment from your old habits of ego.*[11]

THE TRULY WONDROUS UNIQUENESS OF OUR HUMANNESS AND THE AMAZING POTENTIAL WHICH IS BIOLOGICALLY ENCODED IN OUR HUMAN CELLS AWAITS ITS FULLER AND EVER FULLER EXPRESSION.

The Price of Understanding: Thoughts, Words, Actions Based in Truth

Before "Adam and Eve," there were no humans around predicting that a leap might take place simply because there was no human consciousness which was conscious of itself on earth. At this time, however, there are so many intelligent and articulate humans who are pointing to and predicting and supporting what seems to be a possible imminent leap to the next level. How amazing! Until that leap actually occurs, however, it is the ego's perceptions which human beings experience as real. Until the ego has been transcended, our expanded awareness and our intensified need for understanding require that we search for clear definitions and descriptions of the ego's ways and the ways of the higher Self. As our understanding grows, we must hold ourselves responsible for correcting our thoughts, words, and actions in order to pull ourselves up and out of the quicksand which our automatic egoic reactions have come to represent as a species.

With awareness of the earlier stages of evolution which still impinge upon our consciousness, and with an understanding of some of the reasons for the development of certain obvious egoic tendencies in all of us, it is clearly possible to begin to undermine those tendencies and to replace them with thoughts and behaviors which will assure the steady growth of healthy self-acceptance and empowerment out of the inclusion of an entire part of ourselves which we have not recognized and sourced before—our higher Self.

Can we offer ourselves as fledgling emissaries of the dawning of a new paradigm on Earth?

When we look out into our world, we can clearly see that disaffected and disempowered egos are lashing out at other disillusioned and impotent egos based on their own strong opinions and prejudices. Between the members of all generational sub-groups, ethnic sub-groups, racial sub-groups, nationalistic sub-groups, religious sub-groups, gender sub-groups, sexual preference sub-groups, political sub-groups, socio-economic sub-groups, and more, the level of wrathful judgment is sky high. And within those sub-groups, battles for power and position rage unabated. At any level and within any struggle to cause a particular outcome, we can clearly see the ego's strongly held opinions and its desire to win. We can see its inability to yield as its combativeness, its empty arrogance, and its self-righteousness raise their ugly self-serving heads. To the thousands of relevant issues of our times—with all of their sophisticated complexities—the grandiose ego again and again declares that it is sure that *it knows* the "right" answer. That pathetic allegation provokes a backlash of cruel judgments from egos on the other side of the argument who, filled with their own combative, arrogant, and self-righteous hatefulness, proclaim that *they* know the "right" answer.

And, at the personal level, individuals struggle in much the same way, daily attempting to impose their personal opinions on others—opinions which have their roots in the consciousness of separation and the conditioned prejudicial judgments which they have absorbed like sponges from the opinions of others. Even in the most loving relationships this silliness is enacted and re-enacted *ad nauseam*, until, most often, the love has become tainted with the impurities of selfish striving and the relationship has become less important than the rightness to which both parties cling. Then, so often, they fight it out in court over possessions to which they both are strongly attached. The loss of their partner and their loss of some of their possessions is experienced as a loss of self, and profound episodes of depression may ensue for years after such a "split."

> *Poor Much-Afraid tried to pull her hand away, for now she began to understand the meaning of his presence there and his bitter hatred of the Shepherd, but as she struggled to free her hand, he only grasped it tighter. She had to learn that once Pride is listened to, struggle as one may, it is the hardest thing in the world to throw him off. She hated the things that he said, but with her hand grasped in his they had the power to sound horribly plausible and true.*[12]

We must become masterfully capable in our ability to recognize the ego's easily recognizable motives, strategies, and tendencies. We must become masters at recognizing them in **ourselves**, as well as in others. Only by seeing the ego operating within ourselves, can we begin to choose to think and act differently. Like Much-Afraid in the above quote, we must become aware of the ego's prideful hold on us, the influence its convincing arguments have had on us, and the difficult effort it sometimes takes to wrench ourselves free from its strong grasp. With awareness of that freedom of choice and with a *learned ability to choose* firmly fixed in our understanding, our ability to see the ego operant in others helps us to move out of reactivity and relate at the level of truthful Self-expression rather than to merely react from our ego's threatened sense of self.

The point that needs to be made here is that in this exceedingly amazing and astonishingly beautiful, abundant and intelligent world, we unique humans, with all of our unrealized multi-dimensional inherencies, remain stuck at a level of consciousness which is so limited that its inherent dispositions allow us only this distorted and painful experience of life. What a shame! What a tragedy, given that there is so much more capacity awaiting its unfoldment in us, just beyond the limited structures of the ego mind.

Multitudes of us must now see what is going on. We must see that all day long every day our potency as humans is being wasted in the simple (and boring) self-seeking of the ego as it struggles to survive in a world it cannot clearly see and with which it can never feel at-one. Innately unaware of the vast reaches of the higher Self which lies just beyond the sketchily drawn boundaries of its false identity, the frightened ego's repetition of its ineffective strategies to gain the impossible—loss of its isolation—has become a luxury our world can no longer afford. We must transcend the limitations of the ego now. We must!

THE CONTINUUM OF HUMAN CONSCIOUSNESS

In order to understand ourselves and, thus, develop the ability to support ourselves to rise above the acculturated perceptions and conditioned reactivity which have defined our views and relationships with others and with the world-at-large, we can and must reference the teachings of high-minded others who have preceded us along the path of self-discovery. One of the brilliant minds of our time, Ken Wilber, has presented us with a model which clearly shows us how, through the normal course of human growth and development, we come to a point wherein we begin to "accept (a) little fenced-off aspect of (our)self" as who we are. From that time in our lives, things can only go badly for us in psychological terms. By then, our mental health has been ravaged by the virus of denial of important aspects of our own humanity, and that virus spreads as we continue to identify ourselves within the narrow confines of an extremely limited image of ourselves, which we create. The invention of our fictional selves is supported by our culture, our parents, and all others who have also fictionalized themselves by entering the maze constructed by our modern world for all to run—and who have ended up with their backs to the wall of the same psychological dead-end.

Reading up Ken Wilber's model of The Spectrum of Consciousness [Figure No. 14] we see a clear and enlightening representation of the splitting of the human psyche—which we have been calling human growth and development. Once we are able to see the diminishment of our human potential in this way, our potent billions no longer need take the dead-end run in the maze, generation after generation. I strongly recommend the serious student of the transformational process to study Mr. Wilber's book, *The Spectrum of Consciousness* wherein this model is dealt with in a most scholarly and comprehensive manner by "the expert." For purposes of supporting the teachings of the ego within *A Course In Congruence*, however, I have chosen to reference Mr. Wilber's presentation of this model from his book, *No Boundary*, as follows:

> *It's obvious that each successive level of the spectrum represents a type of narrowing or restricting of what the individual feels to be his 'self,' his true identity, his answer to the question, 'Who are you?' At the base of the spectrum, the person feels that he is one with the universe, that his real self is not just his organism but all of creation. At the next level of the spectrum (or 'moving up' the spectrum), the individual feels that he is not one with the All but rather one with just his total organism. His sense of identity has shifted and narrowed from the universe as a whole to a facet of the universe, namely, his own organism. At the next level, his self-identity is narrowed once again, for now he identifies mainly with his mind or ego, which is only a facet of his total organism. And on the final level of the spectrum, he can even narrow his identity to facets of his mind, alienating and repressing the shadow or unwanted aspect of his psyche. He identifies with only a part of his psyche, a part we are calling the persona.*
>
> *Thus, from the universe to a facet of the universe called 'the organism'; from the organism to a facet of the organism called 'the ego'; from the ego to a facet of the ego called 'the persona'—such are some of the major bands of the spectrum of consciousness. With each successive level of the spectrum, there are more and more aspects of the universe which appear to be <u>external</u> to the person's 'self.' Thus, at the level of the total organism, the environment appears outside the self-boundary, foreign, external, not-self. But on the level of the persona, the individual's environment <u>and</u> his body <u>and</u> aspects of his own psyche appear external, foreign, not-self.*[13]

Always in humble deference to Mr. Wilber's translation of his model, I have also translated it in my own words in order to assist others to see the limited identity from which they have been living and to show them the way out.

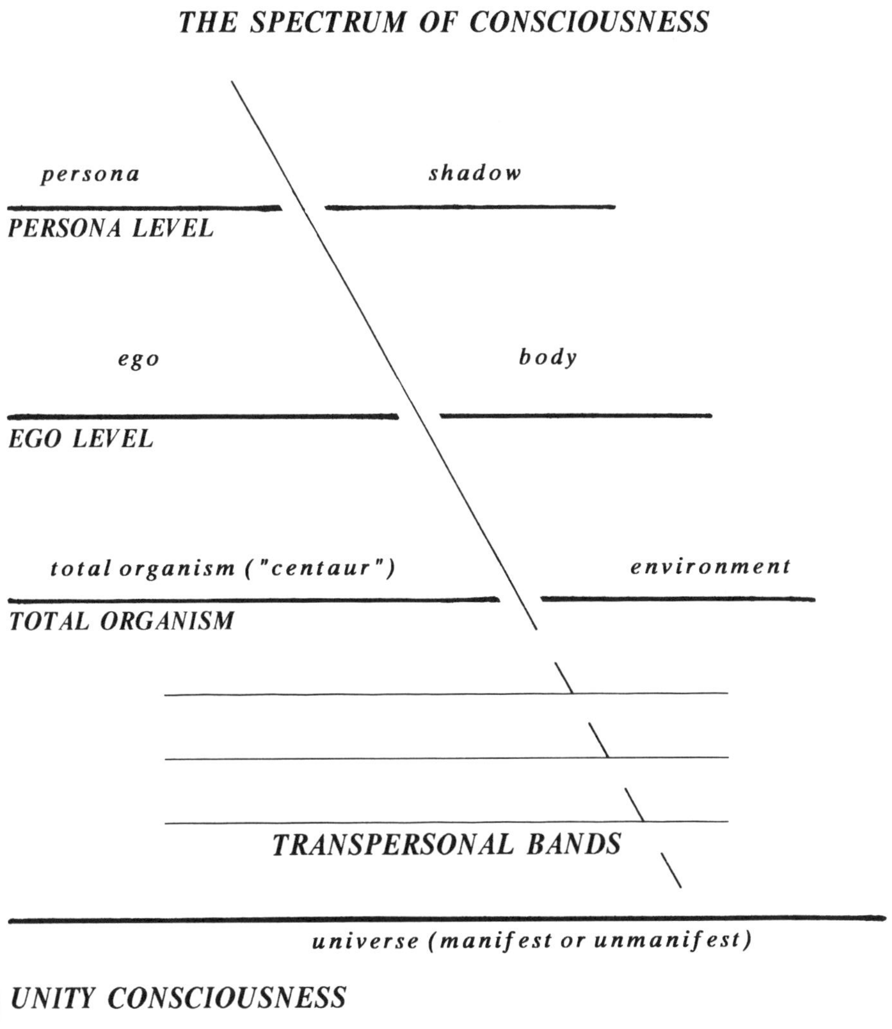
THE SPECTRUM OF CONSCIOUSNESS
persona
shadow
PERSONA LEVEL
ego
body
EGO LEVEL
total organism ("centaur")
environment
TOTAL ORGANISM
TRANSPERSONAL BANDS
universe (manifest or unmanifest)
UNITY CONSCIOUSNESS

Figure No. 14

A Baby Is Born. As I perceive the model, a human baby is born into this realm from the unlimited consciousness of the Universe, still in an experience of unity with All That Is. Within the first few days or weeks of life the baby passes through the Transpersonal Bands to the fifth level of consciousness, the consciousness of the total organism, wherein it experiences itself as at one with the environment, although having lost consciousness of the Universal All. But, fairly soon, the baby will perceive that there is something *over there*, separate from its own body. It will notice that its body ends and then that "something else" begins. It may occur when its mother withdraws her breast from its mouth or lays it down and leaves the room. It may occur when it reaches out and touches the bar on its crib or tries to reach a mobile hanging above its head. Whenever it occurs in any particular baby's experience, a split in that baby's psyche occurs. It realizes that it has a body which is separate from all other bodies and all other things. From that moment on it always experiences its environment as "other than" and "outside of itself." This is the first split of the psyche.

The Ego Appears. The baby grows and develops and a burgeoning ego begins to appear. As soon as that ego begins to form there is another experience of separation. At some stage in its early development of language, the young child perceives its mind as separate from its body and there occurs another splitting of the psyche—the child identifies its "self" as its ego mind and experiences its body as outside its "self." So now the child has a much diminished perception of who it is: it perceives that it is not the Universe, that it is not the Spirit of the Universe, that it is not its environment and that it is not its body. Instead of being any of that, it perceives itself to be its "personal" thoughts.

Denial Begins. Soon after that—and, again, at some unpredictable moment—there occurs a final splitting of the child's psyche. This time the split occurs within the ego. The ego splits into two parts: one part—the *persona*—contains only the thoughts, feelings and behaviors which the child judges to be acceptable for him or her to have; the other part—the *shadow*—contains all the thoughts, feelings, and behaviors which the child judges to be unacceptable to the self image he or she has begun to create. This final split may be triggered by something as simple as a trip to the mall with "mommy."

How It Happens. Let us suppose that a mother had a nerve-wracking experience the last time she took her little boy to the shopping mall because he was nearly unmanageable and cried a lot while she attempted to shop. So just before they leave the house to go to the mall again, she tells him, "Good little boys don't cry at the mall." With only a little prompting the little boy promises that he will not cry at the mall—that he will be "a good boy." And let us suppose that during that visit to the mall, the little boy sees another child crying. Remembering his promise, wanting to be a "good little boy," and wanting to gain his mother's approval, the little boy proudly states, "Mommy, I'm a good boy. I don't cry like **that bad boy**." In that statement, he denies a very real part of his "self," his very humanity. At that moment, he begins to create a diminished image of himself. If he ever cries at the mall in the future, he will rationalize his crying by making it somehow different than the crying the other little child was doing. He will generate good reasons which defend his crying and which will somehow legitimize his crying to himself—because now he holds "crying at the mall" as repugnant, repulsive, and unacceptable to the persona he identifies himself with now—namely, a "good little boy who does not cry at the mall."

The Shameful Shadow. The aspect of himself which "cries at the mall" is a very real threat to his self-image, so he subconsciously puts that into the dark closet of the shadow and quickly closes the door so that he will not have to see it. Since he will not look at it in himself, he will see it "out there" and will make himself "right" because he *does not* cry at the mall; and he will reaffirm his persona image by making the "other" child wrong because it is crying. And as the child judges other thoughts, feelings, and behaviors as unacceptable to the image he has begun to identify as his "self," he will again and again open that closet door, stuff in another piece of himself and slam the door tightly shut. And before he knows it, most of his humanity will live behind that closet door, strongly rejected by an egoic need to "be good" in order to please others and to feel good about himself.

A Fragment of the Whole. So now the child has a drastically diminished perception of who it is: it perceives that it is not the Universe, that it is not the Spirit of the Universe, that it is not its environment, that it is not its body, and that it is not even *all* of its "personal" thoughts, feelings and behaviors. Instead, it identifies its "self" as only a tiny piece of its wholeness; and, as that tiny piece of its "self," it perceives the world and others through its rigid and narrow views. As years go by, the boy, the adolescent, the man denies more and more of his fullness as a human being; again and again he subconsciously says to himself, "I am not like **that bad boy**!" He puts another piece of his humanity in the closet and closes the door. And he only opens the closet to put more of his denied humanity into that shadowy place. He lives out of a tiny part of his personhood or personality. When he gets up in the morning, the fragment of himself is what he assumes, what he identifies with. He is *not* like *THAT*. He is separate from his shadow, he is separate from his body, he is separate from his environment and he is separate from the All-Encompassing Universal Consciousness. With the tightly closed closet door bulging with the unaccepted parts of his "self," which are pressing to get free, his carefully created persona image presents its "bright" and "acceptable" face to the world throughout his adolescence and on through his adulthood, hoping against hope that no one will suspect the presence of those "darker" aspects of himself, which still frequently poke their heads out of that shadowy closet in his psyche.

This is the odyssey of Everyman and the psychological tale of Everywoman. This is what has occurred in all of us—even those of us who have lived privileged lives of "freedom" in democratic countries of our world during times of abundance and relative peace. This is the simple story of "normal" human growth and development at the third level of consciousness, with or without traumas caused by child abuse or other psychologically traumatizing experiences. And, this is where we must start the process of reclaiming our wholeness. In becoming congruent we experience the healing of the psychological splits by way of self-discovery and Self-expression. By speaking and behaving at what Wilber refers to as the *centaur level*—authentically—we heal the splits in our psyche which have been incurred through the process of growth and development and which have been exacerbated through incongruent reactivity and role-playing. We heal the splits in the psyche at the *persona/shadow level* and at the *ego/body level* so that we may become established at the *centaur level* of consciousness, wherein we begin to experience the integrity of our minds and our bodies once again. When we have become re-established at this level of consciousness, with our minds opened to the flow of higher Intelligence, that Intelligence (Spirit) can pull us back into Unity Consciousness while we are still in human form and within the human reality. In this way it is possible for us to become our amazing, fully human, selves.

The Reordering of Our Psyche: Putting the Sunbeam In Its Place

Since the transformational process is a reformation of our very psyches, what are the psychological changes we are supporting and what resultant differences may we expect from the leap in consciousness to the fifth level which will provide us with an experience of personal *freedom*? A metaphoric reference to the reversal of roles in the relationship between the sun and an orbiting planet lends some understanding to the scope and meaning of this question.

Imagine that the planet (ego) at some point begins to believe that it is the center of the universe and believes the sun (higher Self) (and everything else) to be orbiting around it. In so doing, the ego's sense of overwhelming responsibility and self-importance becomes a primary factor for it to deal with in that this wrong perception begins to generate conflict. The conflict is between an overrated sense of self-importance and a growing sense of self-doubt about its ability to fulfill the demands of this all-encompassing role. The root of the conflict is the ego's fundamental sense of separation from a life-giving and information-giving Source and the absence of a larger context in which to identify itself.

We must have the chord of Inner Knowing struck within us and align our very lives with its frequencies, its pulses, and its rhythms.

Given its exalted role as the center of all it surveys, the ego begins to assume that its opinions and motivations are the messages to be listened to—rather than the messages from the higher Self, which it regards as holding a secondary role in the whole scheme of things. This self-aggrandizing attitude also pervades its perceptions of its role in relationships with other people. There, too, its frightened arrogance presumes that others should honor its opinions—which are based on its limited perceptions—as though they were "law." With others likewise wrongly assuming that their egoic drives and desires are the Central Truth of themselves, it is easy to see why relationships built on the foundation of these faulty assumptions are ill-fated since both persons are psychologically conflicted— plagued by a duality of self-importance and self-doubt.

By way of the process of transformation, the ego is simply put into its proper place: its orbit around the higher Self. This reordering of the psyche relieves the ego of its heavy burden of responsibility and allows it to perform its necessary functions with ease, as outlined in Ram Dass' description above. Its limited thoughts and selfish desires are overridden by the more intelligent thoughts and larger context as the higher Self shines through the limited "me, me, me-ness" of the ego's self-serving agendas. The tendencies of the ego to greedily grab what it wants are undermined as the larger context of the higher Self automatically includes the needs of others. The tendencies of the ego to hold a hard and unyielding line based on its own opinions are undermined by the higher Self's wider view and unthreatened ability to listen to others. The tendencies of the ego to judge others harshly are undermined by the higher Self's inherent compassion and selfless understanding. The tendencies of the ego to react emotionally to any perceived affront to its fragile sense of self are undermined by the higher Self's ability to express itself with confident strength in the face of even harsh and hurtful judgments.

> *We simply must break through the veil of the mind at this time. We simply must free ourselves from the prison of our lower minds now. We simply must leap beyond the wall of the closed system of our own thinking at once. We simply must break through the membrane of our tiny partialness into our Vast Wholeness immediately. We simply must stop our foolish identification with the boringly predictable perceptions and reactions of our self-reflexive minds and become finely tuned receivers of the Unlimited Intelligence of the Unlimited Mind. We must allow Creation to flow through our minds as it flows through our veins and through our loins. As we allow Ultimate Intelligence to breathe us, so must we allow it to think us, to animate us, to BE us.*
>
> *In our frightened littleness, we have been unwilling to relinquish control of our lives to Life Itself. We must relinquish control now! In our confused arrogance, we have been unwilling to confess that we cannot create a world of peace and healthy function. We must confess that now! In our selfish desire for satisfaction of our own personal needs, we have been unwilling to take responsibility for what is going on in this world. We must take that responsibility now! In a conscious and unconscious attempt to avoid having to shine forth, we have remained aloof. We must Shine Forth now!*[14]

TOWARD EXPANSION AND SELF-MASTERY

1. Consciously identify your egoic motivations to win, to be right, to look good, and to survive in each of your relational transactions. Notice what

you say and how you act. Notice how your communications and behaviors affect the other person and their interactions with you. Notice how you feel about yourself afterward.

2. Notice each time you have ego-driven thoughts and feelings of superiority and inferiority. Notice what you say and how you act. Notice how your communications and behaviors affect the other person and their interactions with you. Notice how you feel about yourself later.

3. Notice each time you have ego-driven thoughts and feelings which are combative (argumentative). Notice each time your thoughts and feelings have to do with being victimized. In both cases, notice what you say and how you act. Notice how your communications and behaviors affect the other person and their interactions with you. Notice how you subsequently feel about yourself.

4. Notice each time you make an attempt to control other people or circumstances (through other people). Notice what you say and how you act. Notice how your communications and behaviors affect the other person and their interactions with you. Notice how you feel about yourself as a result.

5. Once you can identify the conditioned egoic reactions above, begin to consciously choose to relate non-judgmentally and unselfishly. Begin to choose to communicate and behave more honestly, less defensively, and without attempting to control others. Notice how your communications and behaviors affect the other person and their interactions with you. Notice how you feel about yourself as a result.

6. Become more and more aware of the ego's constant chattering: inside your own mind, coming out of your mouth, and coming out of the mouths of others. Notice its constant judging. Tell it to stop. Begin to halt the chatter on a regular basis by saying a strong silent or strong audible "STOP!" Then choose which thoughts you will think, and think them.

Let us discern that
we are the powerful undercurrent
in which oceanic mysteries
are being carried
to the shores of our world.

CHAPTER NINE

Changing Our Perceptions

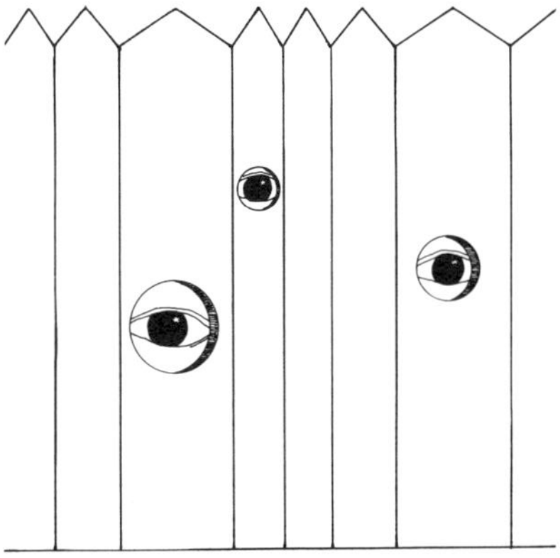

What would you see?
The choice is given you.
But learn and do not let your mind
forget this law of seeing:
You will look upon that which you feel within.
If hatred finds a place within your heart,
you will perceive a fearful world,
held cruelly in death's sharp-pointed, bony fingers.
If you feel the Love of God within you,
you will look out on a world of mercy and of love.
Learn how to look on all things
with love, appreciation, and open-mindedness.

—*A Course In Miracles*[1]

The Softening of Perception

Have you ever looked out at the world through soft eyes? Eyes which see the same world but in a different way? What did you see? Or rather, how did it seem different than the *normal* way of seeing? Through those soft eyes did you see harmony where you usually see conflict? Did you see flow where you usually see struggle? Did you see unlimited possibility where you usually see obstacles and uncertainty? Did you see "yes" where you usually see "no?" Did you see yourself as part of a great and wonderful world—somehow mysteriously bonded with the rest of *the human family*—where you usually see yourself as separate from that big, bad world and all of those "other" *strange* people? What is that "soft" way of seeing? What causes it to happen? And how can you recreate it for yourself? Is it possible to consistently see the world through soft eyes?

Hard eyes are the eyes of the negative ego—that part of the mind which processes all incoming data through the distortion of memories of past experiences. The negative ego is the repository of our own personal fears, judgments, disappointments, outrage and confusion. This *damaged* or *unhealed* ego is epitomized by the cynical attitudes with which it processes its experiences. When we have "one of those days" we can be certain that this minuscule part of our vast Self has had what is commonly known as a "field day"—that is, it has run roughshod over all higher translations of the day's events.

Soft eyes are the eyes of the *healed* ego in a bonded relationship with the higher Self—a mighty combination which processes all incoming data through its disposition of neutral observation, high thoughts and compassion. This unlimited Self waits patiently and hopefully for the opportunity for expression in our lives—which expression we experience as a "magical day" or as a life that is a steady unfoldment of our own true nature. The *mystical* life of the Self makes sense in this world of random events, but is caused outside the realm of the *ordinary* world.

How are you seeing right now? Are you viewing what is going on around you through hard eyes? Or through soft eyes?

The work of self-discovery, based on a deep desire for understanding, personal freedom and a sense of ease, is the focus of attention in ever-increasing numbers of humans at this time. We are assured by many great minds that at this time in human history there is an unprecedented possibility for a *shift* from the lower levels to the higher levels of consciousness among a significant segment of the world population—ordinary people who are reaching the level of readiness required for an "opening" into the higher Self to occur. That *opening* is the single, most-important occurrence in a person's life, in terms of personal growth, evolution, fulfillment of potential, discovery of life purpose, psychological well-being, an experience of clarity and ease—and the ability to look out at the world through "soft eyes."

Once we have achieved a level of true readiness for transformation there is "movement" (or what is called "spontaneous will") at the deepest psychological levels in response to the soul's true intention—evolution itself. The negative ego then relinquishes its powerful grip, its fearful hold, its service to its own smallness—and the higher Self emerges in its majesty, its rhythmic harmony, its wondrous *soft* certainty.

The moment the "shift" occurs, the very reason for living becomes a reality in our human life: to move beyond the limitation of the lower self and into the mystery and unknown possibilities of that "other" part of our being. This is the beginning of the accelerated process which will flow in an articulate and coherent manner toward full expression of the Self through our individual consciousness.

Having relinquished control, the negative ego attempts to reclaim its supremacy by projecting fearful distrust onto the higher Self's trustful ways. For this reason, most of us need some form of support in order to continue to let go and let the higher Self guide us on our way. That support will be provided by the higher Self in a form that is appropriate and timely for our own particular needs.

This very precious phase of accelerated process is experienced with a sense of wonder, a quickening of spiritual desire, a sometimes overwhelming feeling of vulnerability, and a "softening" of our view of the world. The *softening* is a hallmark of the spiritual journey, an indication that extraordinary possibilities lie just ahead. All that is required of us from this point on is the simple response of "Yes" to the guidance which is the presence of the higher Self—the soft Self.

> *Interpretations are what stand between you and the clarity of perception that you will need to do the work that lies ahead. You must release them with your thoughts, with your dreams, with your hopes and with your fears. They may seem to be insignificant, ethereal things, floating gently through your mind, but do not be misled by their apparent lack of substance. They are the stuff that wars are made of, the harbingers of death, the agents of disease and destruction. With the energy that you give them through your attention, they have the strength to cripple a planet.*[2]

As I emphasized in Chapter Five, we must do the nearly impossible: dis-identify from our prepackaged selves. We must realize again and again that our conditioned patterns of thinking—our very thoughts themselves—are not the truth of who we are. We must recognize—even while that "automatic" thinking is occurring and while we are behaving in "robotic" ways—that the truth lies deeper than our surface withdrawal and reactivity, to which we have become so accustomed and by which we have become so defined. We must become open thought systems which respond from a deep well of inner resonance. In this way, we become courageous, compassionate and understanding journeyers whose perceptions have a wider field, whose mental structures have a less rigid posture, and whose responses mirror the high-minded principles upon which our lives are now being built, day by day. Although dis-identification is *nearly* impossible, by Grace the miraculous process becomes possible.

Holes In The Fence

Expanding Our Horizons. The purpose of this simple model [Figure No. 15] is to evoke in us awareness of the fact that "there is another way to look at this"—no matter what it is that we are perceiving at any given time. Its purpose is to support us in our practice of changing our thoughts in order to change our perceptions. The model is a drawing of a portion of a fence with three holes in it—holes which represent our views (perceptions) of the world at different times.

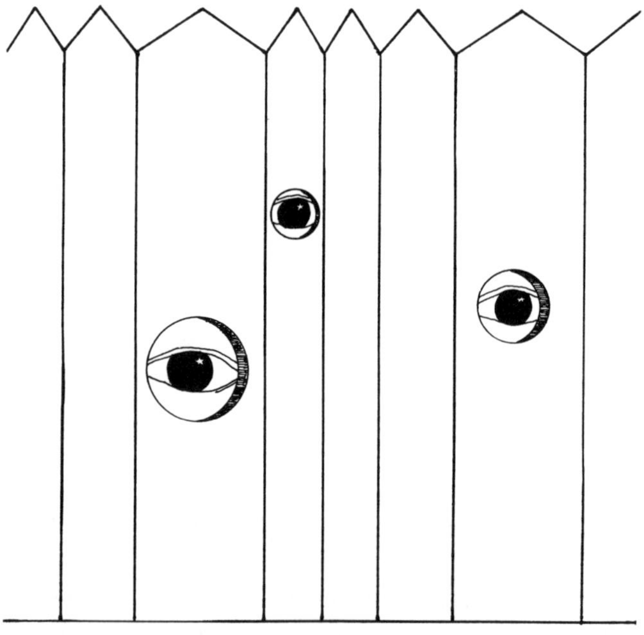

Figure No. 15

At some stage in our life we may have been looking out at our vast, complex, and mysterious world through a very small hole in the fence. Our thinking then was limited by the conditioning to which we had been subjected by others who were accustomed to perceiving the world through a small hole in the fence. What we saw through that hole validated our preconceived notions about the world. Our limited view always reinforced our beliefs about how the world is, how life is, and how things *should be* according to our perceptions of *right* and *wrong*.

Somewhere along the way we were exposed to higher, more expansive and more inclusive thinking, and we also had experiences which disproved our earlier limited perceptions of life. As a result, our view enlarged, and we began to better understand ourselves, others, and life in a way that can be represented by the next larger hole in the fence. The achievement of still larger perceptual fields—epitomized by the much larger hole in the fence—obviously allows us an experience of freedom and truth way beyond the uncompromising narrowness of our previous views.

The continuous enlargement of our "window on the world" is the undisputed function and the to-be-expected consequence of the process of transformation. And transformation, itself, will ultimately grant us a view from *over the fence*. We will actually be able to see what is on the other side—true liberation! Each step of the way (each phase of the process) concedes to us an enhanced capacity to see more clearly and to be more aware than we have ever been before about the multi-dimensional natures of ourselves, of others, of the world, and of life itself.

WE MUST DO THE NEARLY IMPOSSIBLE: DIS-IDENTIFY FROM OUR PRE-PACKAGED SELVES.

You have no conception of the limits
you have placed on your perception,
and no idea of all the loveliness that you could see.[3]

The Limitation of Others' Perceptions. This model also supports us to pause and contemplate what size hole in the fence "significant others" in our lives may be looking through. A disparity in levels of perception can only cause continuous relational conflict as there is no match between the realities perceived and responded to by the two individuals. At different times in our lives we have actually given our power away to people who had a narrower view of the world—because we were in love with them or because we were dependent on them in some other way: physically, emotionally, or mentally. We allowed them power over us although we may have suspected or we may have known that their view of the world was smaller, narrower, more limited than ours. For some reason, we did not feel that we were free to express ourselves authentically, and we were afraid to rock the boat. In those relationships, we suppressed and/or distorted our own personal truth, and we paid the price in a number of psychologically painful ways.

Having raised this point, it is only fair to say that the essential problem in those relationships was that we were not really clear about our personal truth. We did not really understand or *know* ourselves. And when the messages from the feeling function urged us to take a stand on this or that high principle, our own weak sense of self, our considerable self-doubt, and our fear of the possible consequences of our actions often held us in check. Because we have not known ourselves, it is true that others have never really known us. It is now time that we begin to discover the truth of ourselves and express ourselves in ways that allow other people to know us as they have never known us before.

BECAUSE WE HAVE NOT KNOWN OURSELVES, IT IS TRUE THAT OTHERS HAVE NEVER REALLY KNOWN US.

Perception is a choice and not a fact.
But on this choice depends far more
than you may realize as yet.
For on the voice you choose to hear,
and on the sights you choose to see,
depends entirely your whole belief in what you are.[4]

The Perceptual Fields of The Lower and Higher Natures. Until we are established in the higher Self, we operate from the limited perceptions of the ego, which fearfully peers out at the world through a narrow opening which epitomizes the third level of consciousness. Sometimes we look out through only a slit of an opening and at other times our vision is temporarily broadened somewhat to include more of the big picture. We are constantly expanding and contracting based on what kinds of things are "going on" and whether things are "going our way." Very often when we have a transitory experience of safety, peacefulness and unity—which the broader view permits—we think we have finally "figured it out;" we think that everything is going to be "all right;" and we think that we finally have learned how to "do life" successfully. We feel great!

But when we contract back into our old familiar separated and self-protective ways of being, we angrily or sadly stare at the world once again through a tiny opening. Our perceptions validate our attitudes of being victimized by life, and we once again become overwhelmed by confusion, pain and fearful doubt. We see struggle and difficulty. We feel awful!

But, then, we have a "good day" and we feel "great" again!

The point is that until we take responsibility for changing our perceptions of the world we see, we remain victims of uncontrollable circumstances, and our level of well-being depends almost entirely on the unforeseeable fortunes and misfortunes of the life our level of consciousness creates.

> *Misperceptions produce fear*
> *and true perceptions foster love.*
>
> *You respond to what you perceive,*
> *and as you perceive*
> *so shall you behave.*
>
> *Everything you perceive is a witness*
> *to the thought system you want to be true.*[5]

Healing The Split. Speaking of perception in her discussion of mental health in *The Inward Arc*, Frances Vaughan tells us:

> *Perception itself may be recognized as a selective, differentiating function based on subject/object dualism. Nothing can be perceived without separating the observer, as subject, from what is observed, as object... Perception is invariably influenced by conditioned patterns of thoughts, beliefs, and expectations, in addition to being colored by emotional states.*
>
> *Perceptions and beliefs tend to be mutually reinforcing. When one believes something to be true, perception will selectively reinforce it.*
>
> *...We know that the mind can be re-programmed, but conditioned patterns of perception tend to persist in the absence of self-awareness and conscious intention to change.*[6]

It has been widely proven and is now common knowledge that when we are viewing a particular situation or relational transaction we simply must consciously enforce a correction of our highly-subjective thinking processes in order to change our limited perception and, thus, move out of our highly-predictable reactions to others. We must realize the truth that we are at one with all other persons, all other creatures, all other life forms, the Earth itself, all other life systems, the air we breathe, the sky, the stars, and the deepest reaches of space. And we must keep that realization alive in us by conscious recall and conscious practices which will heal the separation we experience between ourselves and the rest of life. In *Up From Eden*, Ken Wilber tells us:

According to the perennial philosophy, this "discovery of Wholeness," the removal of the optical delusion of separateness, is not merely a belief—it is not a dogma one accepts on mere faith. For if the Ultimate is indeed a real integral Wholeness, if it is equally part and parcel of all that is, then it is also completely present in men and women. And, unlike rocks, plants, or animals, human beings—because they are ***conscious****—can potentially discover this Wholeness. They can, as it were, awaken to the Ultimate. Not believe in it, but discover it. It would be as if a wave became conscious of itself and thus discovered that it is one with the entire ocean—and thus one with all waves as well, since all are made of water. This is the phenomenon of transcendence—or enlightenment, or liberation, or moksha, or wu, or satori. This is what Plato meant by stepping out of the cave of shadows and finding the Light of Being; or Einstein's "escaping the delusion of separateness." This is the aim of Buddhist meditation, of Hindu yoga, and of Christian mystical contemplation. That is very straightforward; there is nothing spooky, occult, or strange in any of this—and this is the perennial philosophy.*[7]

In *The Global Brain*, Peter Russell says:

The one phenomenon that directly challenges the skin-encapsulated model is the personal experience of unboundedness, of oneness with the rest of creation, the immediate awareness that "I" and everything else are, at their most fundamental levels, of one essence. This direct personal experience of unity is the anomalous observation that cannot be incorporated within the skin-encapsulated model. This is the crisis for the old identity, revealing the model's incompleteness and starting the shift toward a new self-model.[8]

In order to heal the split between ourselves and everything other than ourselves, we must continuously remind ourselves that "There is another way to look at this." We can ask ourselves the following questions as a way of supporting the opening of our field of perception:

"What is the higher (more transcendent) way to look at this?"

"What is here that I have not seen yet that I can seek to see?"

"How can I look at things through a larger hole in the fence?"

As a result of this practice, our minds open and our boundaries become irrevocably extended to include other ways of thinking, behaving, and relating. As we shift our gaze to a larger hole in the fence, we literally begin to be recreated. By being willing to overcome our conditioned rigid thinking patterns, which spawn limited and limiting judgments of everything we view, and by being willing to give up our prideful positions of being right, we become capable of a softer and more expanded view of all we see.

Perception can make whatever picture
the mind desires to see.
Remember this.
In this lies either Heaven or hell,
as you elect.[9]

The transformation itself will ultimately grant us a view from over the fence.

The Open Mind

...a new type of awareness opened up and...I began the long trek, a trek of many years, to what I call "the open mind" which is a goal, an exercise, a movement that I found continually insightful and enlightening. This was the path through space that I had been looking for, had prayed for. And, as it turned out, what may have begun as an intellectual exercise ended as a medium of grace.[10]

I have often told my students: "The opening is everything! The opening is everything! The opening is everything!" By that powerful and unequivocal statement, I mean that the opening of the mind is the single most-important element in the process of transformation, simply because without an opening of the closed system of the lower mind no process of unfoldment can occur, and we will remain locked within our own mindbound prison—separate, robotic in our responses to others and to circumstances, unconsciously talking nonsense to ourselves all day long and believing that nonsense.

In reporting her struggle to achieve a state of open-mindedness, Bernadette Roberts speaks of the "basic structure of mind" and the obstacle it presents.

> *...it occurred to me that the basic structure of the mind was like a computer in which all incoming data had its place; everything fit, and as long as everything fit, no change was possible—thus no challenge.*
>
> *I realized my particular mentality or basic structure of mind had been formed long before I came to the university, formed by past experiences and influences, so that much of my thinking, along with values and judgments, was a fairly ingrained response. I all but knew the answers before the questions were asked, because I could predict the answers within the framework of my own mind. Thus all incoming ideas and information were automatically interpreted, adjusted, and incorporated into this pre-formed structure, and if something did not fit, well, naturally I could not understand it at all. From this I concluded that* ***I did not grow because I had no trouble incorporating new information, and therefore, the standstill was an intrinsic, not an extrinsic problem.*** *Having realized this much, however, it was necessary to find out how this existing structure could change in order to permit growth, which meant finding the particular challenge that would bring this about.*[11]

On the verge of dropping out of the university curriculum, she was guided to a professor who challenged his students to step outside the boundaries of their own individual frame of reference in order to really understand the characters in the literature they were assigned to read. As a result of the strategies to which he introduced her, her life would never be the same.

> *The first tendency, he said, would be to interpret and judge them in our own light, by our own standards, which would do nothing more than reinforce our own way of thinking; in which case, we would have learned nothing. He warned us, however, that stepping outside our usual way of thinking would not be easy...*
>
> *From the outset, I met a mountain of obstacles; obstacles not due to a prejudiced or unwilling mind, but to an unconscious single-mindedness, an automatic habit of judgment I had never noticed before. Initially, I wondered if I would ever be able to step outside my structured mind in order to see into other—perhaps equally structured—minds. Certainly this was a challenge to be reckoned with, and something in me responded with energy....*
>
> *Striving for the open mind is vital to the unitive life because it means* ***stepping outside the self and our unconscious habitual ways of thinking and judging****. In some respects, it means putting aside the content of personal*

consciousness, which seems to be a necessary preparation for eventually going beyond the personal or "I" consciousness.[12] *[Emphasis added.]*

The point is that a state of open-mindedness requires *conscious* struggling against the "ingrained responses" which have become so automatic and which are so easily (unconsciously) triggered in us by all outside stimuli. We must actually become conscious of the unconscious "pre-formed" mechanism which habitually generates unceasing judgments and reactive thoughts and behaviors. And as Bernadette Roberts teaches us, we must become capable of overriding the chronic tendencies of our well-developed mental structures in order to escape the prison of our own minds. And we must expect to come up against our limited selves over and over again as we attempt to understand others through *their* particular perceptual fields.

There is no other intention which is more important in our list of sincere intentions to support our process of transformation. It is the open mind which allows all other conditions, all other states of being, and all leaps to the higher levels of consciousness to occur. We actually must *use* our mind in order to *transcend* our mind. We must remember to elicit the Witness Self in order to bring consciousness to what will otherwise be unconscious responses. We must remember to remind ourselves that "There is another way to look at this." We must realize when our perceptions are the perceptions of our hard eyes and correct our thinking in order to once again shift our gaze so as to peer through a larger hole in the fence, where only soft eyes can see the bigger and softer picture. Bernadette Roberts speaks of the results of our conscious efforts:

THE OPENING OF THE MIND IS THE SINGLE MOST-IMPORTANT ELEMENT IN THE PROCESS OF TRANSFORMATION.

I discovered the true key to the open mind was nothing more than ***the cessation of judgment itself****....*

When we can listen nonjudgmentally to others with a selfless, objective mind, the door opens to an understanding of the ways of God in each soul, which automatically gives rise to charity. Thus the greatest result of the open mind is a charity that knows no prejudice, is beyond the need of mere tolerance, self-sacrifice, patience, beyond a noncommittal silence, and certainly beyond any subtle feeling of self-enlightenment.

This type of objectivity takes us beyond likes and dislikes, and enables us to meet others with an open, clear mind, without preconceived images and with no defensive stance wherein we use our judgment as the standard of measurement for everyone. This allows others the freedom to be themselves and find their own way, without our mentally or silently imposing our way on them. In leaving others free we also become free, and in this mutual freedom there is true relationship and communication.[13] *[Emphasis added.]*

We must realize that our mind needs a great correction, a great healing; and we must with great conviction and great desire change our own thoughts—again and again and again. We will quickly reap the benefits of changing our negative thoughts to positive thoughts. We will promptly experience the marked difference in our mental attitudes, our emotional cycles, and our physical condition. We will immediately notice the relief of release from our own addictive thinking patterns and the freedom and hope which that implies. We will soon feel the sense of personal empowerment which our practice produces in us. We will come to understand firsthand the pivotal role the open mind plays and its on-going significance in our journey toward liberation and ascendancy—for which we so earnestly yearn.

As a man thinketh, so does he perceive. Therefore, seek not to change the world, but choose to change your mind about the world. Perception is a result and not a cause.... Everything looked upon with vision is healed and holy. Nothing perceived without it means anything. And where there is no meaning, there is chaos... Say only this, but mean it with no reservations, for here the power of salvation lies:[14]

I am responsible for what I see.
I choose the feelings I experience, and I decide
upon the goal I would achieve.
And everything that seems to happen to me
I ask for, and receive as I have asked."[15]

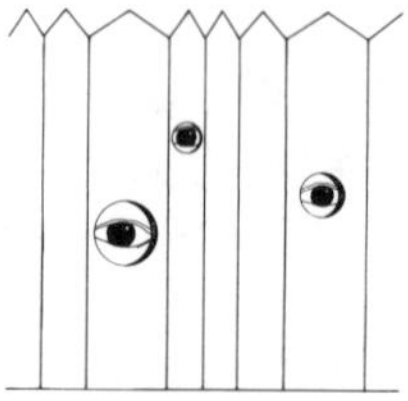

Projections of Our Rejected Selves

> *The ego identifies with its PERSONA and rejects and represses the SHADOW. We build persona by identifying with positive qualities and repressing negative qualities into the shadow.*
>
> *But to build the personality we need to live our shadows as well as our personas. We need to relate to all the opposites within and without.*
>
> ***What I consider positive is what I identify with. What I consider negative is what I repress and reject.***
>
> *When I adopt a wholeness perspective,* ***I integrate the positive and negative, sacrificing only the extreme aspects of both. Integration is creating a new unity by including both opposites.***[16]

There are two books in particular which make our projections easily apparent: *The Hero Within* by Carol Pearson and *Hinds' Feet on High Places* by Hannah Hurnard. A careful reading of Pearson's book reveals to us that each level of consciousness at which we function is a perceptual field which translates our experiences of life and from which we evaluate all persons, places and things. A careful reading of Hurnard's book shows us both our ego mind's fearful, sad, angry, and prideful thoughtforms and agendas and our high mind's yearning for the "High Places" and the *liberation* which those "High Places" represent.

Pearson's elaboration of the pre-heroic Orphan describes a disillusioned innocent who experiences being overwhelmed and victimized by life. She says:

> *The Orphan's story is about a felt powerlessness, about a yearning for a return to a primal kind of innocence, an innocence that is fully childlike, where their every need is cared for by an all-loving mother or father figure. This yearning is juxtaposed against a sense of abandonment, a sense that somehow we are supposed to live in a garden, safe and cared for, and instead are dumped out, orphans, into the wilderness, prey to villains and monsters. It's about looking for people to care for them, about foregoing autonomy and independence to secure that care; it's even about trying to be the all-loving parent—to their lovers, or children, or clients, or constituencies, anything to prove that that protection can be or is there.*[17]

From this description we can clearly see that the Orphan lives out of a self-perception or self-image which is decidedly narrow and one-sided. Having identified with a sense of helplessness and a childlike need for dependency, he has *disowned* his own ability to do and to operate independent of a parentlike caregiver. Those attributes of himself which he has rejected he projects out onto others (villains and monsters) in his world (the wilderness)—and experiences being victimized by them. This is what Ken Wilber refers to as "the boomerang effect"[18] of projection. Not until the Orphan accepts the world as it is and overcomes the denial of his rejected power will he be ready to assume the role of heroic Wanderer. As Warrior he will slay the dragon of his own fear, and, by so doing he will be made ready to fulfill the heroic role of Magician. That *slaying* is the actual reclaiming of his own rejected power.

WE MUST BECOME OPEN THOUGHT SYSTEMS WHICH RESPOND FROM A DEEP WELL OF INNER RESONANCE.

Hurnard's description of Much-Afraid's painful, but heroic journey to the High Places includes several examples of her projection of the contents of her shadow onto her manifest world. She is assisted on her way by Sorrow and Suffering which "had always seemed to her the two most terrifying things which we could encounter."[19] She is taunted and tormented by the personifications of Craven Fear, Pride, Resentment, Bitterness, Spiteful and Self-Pity. When she has reached the High Places, Sorrow and Suffering are transformed into Joy and Peace, the influence of the other shadow personalities have been undermined and overcome, and within the heart of the transformed Much-Afraid—who is now Grace and Glory—grows Acceptance With Joy. Joy and Peace explain to Grace and Glory how her acceptance of the rejected parts of her own ego caused the transformation to occur.

> *Two radiant, shining figures stepped forward, the morning sunshine glittering on their snowy garments, making them dazzling to look at. They were taller and stronger than Grace and Glory, but it was the beauty of their faces and the love shining in their eyes which caught at her heart and made her almost tremble with joy and admiration. They came toward her, their faces shining with mirth and gladness, but they said not a word.*
>
> *"Who are you?" asked Grace and Glory softly. "Will you tell me your names?"*
>
> *Instead of answering they looked at one another and smiled, then held out their hands as though to take hers in their own. At that familiar gesture, Grace and Glory knew them and cried out with a joy which was almost more than she could bear.*

"Why! You are Suffering and Sorrow. Oh, welcome, welcome! I was longing to find you again."

They shook their heads. "Oh, no!" they laughed, "we are no more Suffering and Sorrow than you are Much-Afraid. Don't you know that everything that comes to the High Places is transformed? Since you brought us here with you, we are turned into Joy and Peace."

"Brought you here!" gasped Grace and Glory. "What an extraordinary way to express it! Why, from the first to last you dragged me here."

Again they shook their heads and smiled as they answered, "No, we could never have come here alone, Grace and Glory. Suffering and Sorrow may not enter the Kingdom of Love, but each time you accepted us and put your hands in ours we began to change. Had you turned back or rejected us, we never could have come here."

Looking at one another again, they laughed softly and said, "When first we saw you at the foot of the mountains, we felt a little depressed and despairing. You seemed so Much-Afraid of us, and shrank away and would not accept our help, and it looked so unlikely that any of us would ever get to the High Places."

...With that they came up to her, put their arms around her, and all three embraced and kissed one another with a love and thankfulness and joy beyond words to express.[20]

From this meeting between the transformed Much-Afraid and two parts of her own humanity which she had previously denied, we get the full impact of the healing which is inherent in accepting our rejected selves. From this brilliant and touching allegory we are able to see that it is our perceptions which change as we take our journeys. The deserts, cliffs, rivers, plains, swamps, forests, mountains and valleys—which are symbolic of our own life experiences—remain the same; it is our perceptions of them which change. It is our ability to rise to the occasion and to meet the challenges which they present to us which becomes strong and well-developed. And it is on the reclaiming of our rejected selves that transformation depends.

I will accept the truth of what I am,
and let my mind be wholly healed today.[21]

THE THREE SELVES

Perception is a mirror, not a fact.
And what I look on is my state of mind,
reflected outward.[22]

The model of the three selves [Figure No. 16] is yet another way to present a simple, at-a-glance, overview of the structures of the psyche—and it may help us to see that our unconscious or conscious translations of events determine our perceptions and, thus, the *low* or *high* or *true* character of our experiences. The model is meant to stand as a reference by which we may consciously choose again and again to serve the highest and best in ourselves—by which we may be supported to make the highest choice in every case. With awareness that the higher Self exists out-of-time and stands free of and undisturbed by occurrences within the daily round of our ordinary experience, we can easily draw a comparison to the ego's bondage to and subjective involvement in each and every incident. What a difference!

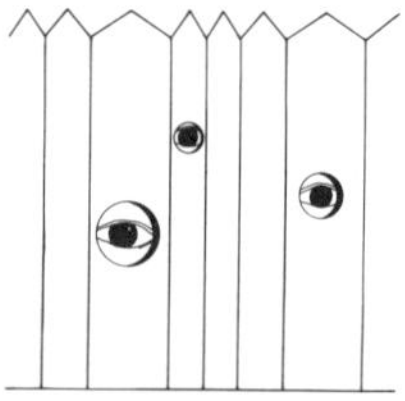

AS WE SHIFT OUR GAZE TO A LARGER HOLE IN THE FENCE, WE LITERALLY BEGIN TO BE RECREATED.

The model also shows the true Self as a distinct level of consciousness which represents an obvious healing of the lower condition. This expressive fifth level is the level of congruent Self-expression which, by way of the model, we can see is a real leap from the level of the reactive ego. And, as we read across the columns of characteristics accorded each self it is easy to see that the selfless influence from the higher Self has effected the transformation from self-centered to Self-centered in every instance. And, by way of this oversimplified prototype of the psyche it becomes obvious that it is upon the higher Self that transformation depends; it is the higher Self from which the transformational process derives; and it is the transcendent reality of the higher Self which makes possible the whole evolutionary unfoldment in humankind.

We simply need to expand our awareness of the qualities inherent in each level of consciousness and make the critical (causative) choice to serve the highest and best in ourselves by way of our thoughts and our actions, including our conscious surrender and our intelligent study and practice.

THE THREE SELVES: The critical choice: Which self to serve!

This model of the human being represents us as three selves. We must be aware of the states of being experienced by these three selves in order to allow real human growth to happen in an articulate, coherent fashion.

The Lower Self	The True Self	The Higher Self
he unhealed ego)	*(The healed ego in bonded relationship with the Higher Self)*	*(Unlimited Self)*
Reactive	Expressive	Creative
Stuckness	Freedom	Flow, Evolution
Controls	Allows	Rejoices
Opposes	Accepts	Causes Change
Extreme	Balanced	Detached
Negative	Positive	Neutral
Separate	Communal	At-One
Confused	Clear	Pure Awareness
Grabs, Holds On	Lets Go	Is
Mindbound, Helpless	Empowered, Inspired	Power
Timebound	Timeless	Timeless
Reasons	Intuits	Knows
Fearful, Angry	Peaceful	Bliss
Threatened	Safe	Certain
Disillusioned	Realistic	Reality
Underlying Depression	Underlying Aliveness	Life Itself

Figure No. 16

THE FOUR FUNCTIONS OF THE MIND

Swami Muktananda, in his book, *The Mind*, presents us with a model of the psyche which provides us with a clear view of the ego's relationship with the other functions of the mind, "the inner psychic instrument." It also provides us with a reference for the other functions, which up to now we may have considered egoic functions. By being aware that the other systems exist, we may well be able to allow them their essential processes without identifying with them from our egoic point of reference.

As we have seen, the word "psychic" comes from the Greek "psyche," which means "soul." Psychology is, thus, the study of the soul. So the psyche, the inner soul instrument, is made up of these four parts:

1) FILLED WITH THOUGHTS

2) CONTEMPLATION

3) DECISION-MAKING

4) SENSE OF "I"NESS[23]

Filled With Thoughts. The thoughts which drift about in our psyche are just random thoughts. They may be thoughts generated by our own individual thought-producing brain structures, thoughts from the collective human consciousness, or thoughts that we are picking up from other people. They are not to be identified with and invested with our conscious energy by worrying about them, elaborating them *ad infinitum*, or attempting to figure out what they really mean. Neither are we to try to control or stifle them. Instead, we can just notice them, choose what we really want to think about—and think about that.

Contemplation. This faculty ponders questions and issues and should be consciously employed to consider the meaningful matters of our life. Contemplation is the amazing faculty which allows us to reflect upon previous experiences in order to decipher their significance, to survey our present options, and to comprehend our own deeper sense about things.

Decision-Making. This function of our mind problem-solves the little issues (how to buy shoes next week when we have no money in our checking account) and the big issues (how to reorder our lives in order to serve our transformational process). The *more consciously* we live our lives, the *more honestly* we face the realities of our lives, and the *more intelligently* we approach the challenges of our lives, the *more well-defined and well-developed* our decision-making ability becomes. When our decision-making is based on conscious contemplation and includes intuition, it becomes highly effective in serving our unfoldment.

Although dis-identification is nearly impossible, by Grace the miraculous process becomes possible.

Sense of "I"ness. This function is the ego, which is the organizing structure of our surface personality and which includes the physical, emotional and mental aspects of our lower self. The ego's sense of itself as the whole is so obviously erroneous, but must be corrected by way of what is referred to as "a revolution of the psyche"—which amounts to a transformative sublimation of its role to that of supportive ally of the higher Self.

By way of this discussion we are again able to see the important role which awareness and understanding of ourselves as human beings play in our on-going process. Only with the *tools* which awareness and understanding become are we able to intelligently reflect upon ourselves from a perspective which allows us to view the overall panorama of our lives and by which to intelligently make the hard choices which will speed us on our way toward the higher levels of consciousness and function.

> *Say not, "I have found the truth," but*
> *rather, "I have found a truth."*
> *Say not, "I have found the path of the soul."*
> *Say rather, "I have met the soul walking*
> *upon my path."*
> *For the soul walks upon all paths.*
> *The soul walks not upon a line, neither*
> *does it grow like a reed.*
> *The soul unfolds itself, like a lotus of*
> *countless petals.*[24]

Eternal Mind / Temporal Mind

The model of the Eternal and Temporal Minds [Figure No. 17] provides us with yet another way to view the structure of the psyche and, thus, gain understanding as to the attributes and qualities of the higher Self and the lower self.

We see that the Eternal Mind, which is timeless essence, is defenseless, intuitive, innocent, free. In the realm of Eternal Mind, we enjoy aliveness, happiness, safety, certainty, love, harmony, peace. Our underlying experience is one of union with everything or "I am THAT."

In sharp contrast, the Temporal Mind, which is timebound individuality, is defensive, reasoning, judgmental, captive. In the realm of the ego we experience fear, pain, anger, separation, conflict, worry, misery, depression, death. In the Temporal Mind our underlying sense is one of separation or "I am not that or THAT."

By way of the transformational process our spiritual center of gravity is transferred from the illusory realm of the Temporal Mind to the reality of the Eternal mind. And in the transition from one state-of-being to the other we go through a period which is exemplified by great confusion, since we are no longer who we were and we are not yet who we are becoming. This transitory state of confusion distinguishes the dramatic process of personal dis-identification and impersonal re-identification. Once established in the consciousness of the Eternal Mind we enjoy a state of expanded awareness and profound levels of acceptance of ourselves and all other beings and things.

Despair, the categorical affect of the Temporal Mind, metaphysically finds evidence in our outer world which supports our perceived reasons for despair. The Temporal Mind also magnetizes experiences which match and validate our despairing thoughts and feelings (perceptions) about life. Likewise, our lower mind's despair manifests (produces) more despair out of its very nature.

Confusion (the underlying affect of the transformational process) and acceptance (the categorical affect of the Eternal Mind) metaphysically evidence, magnetize, and manifest our stage-specific perceptions in the form of experiences and circumstances in our outer world. When our perceptions change, our life changes!

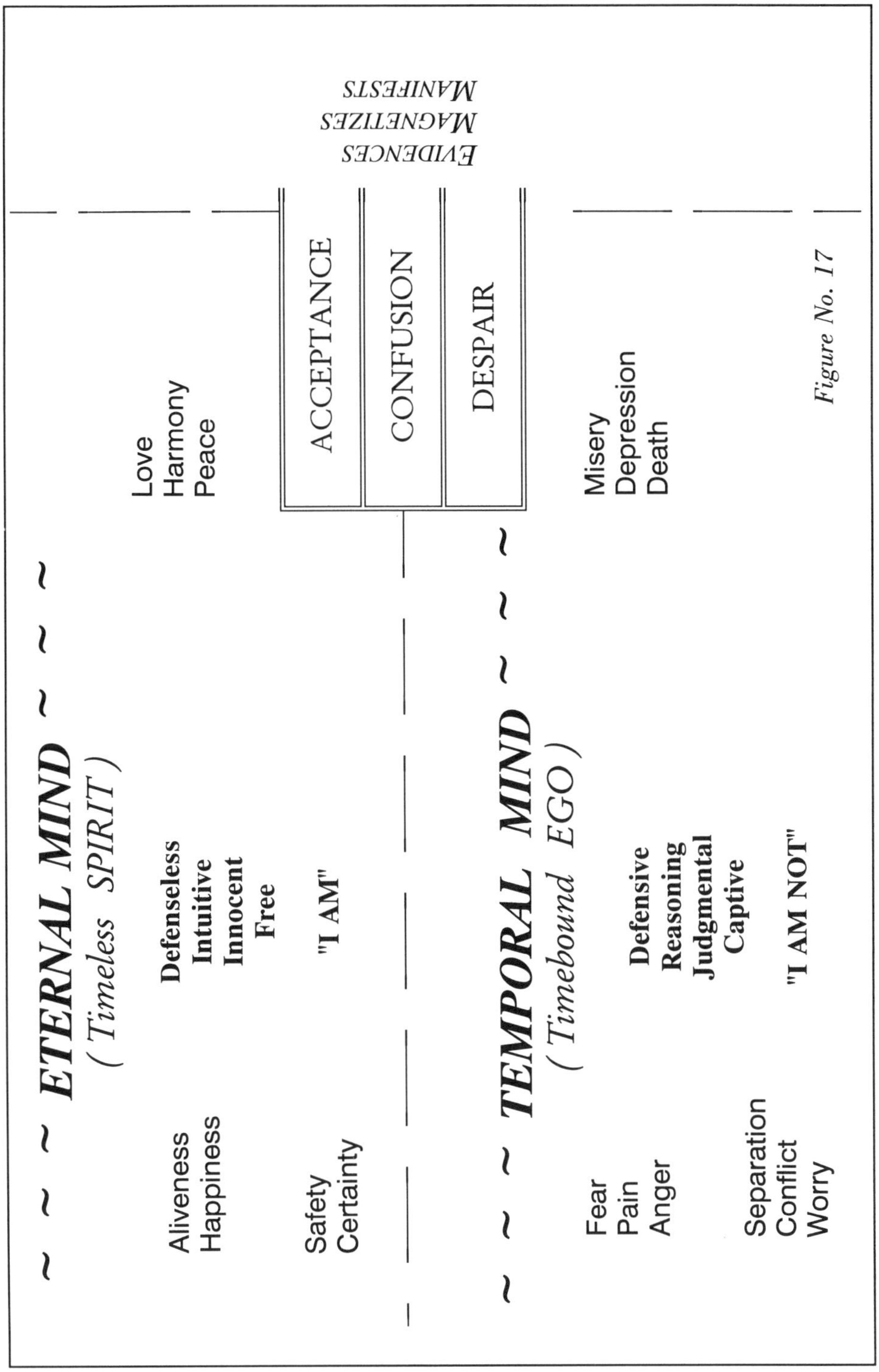
ETERNAL MIND
(Timeless SPIRIT)
Aliveness
Happiness
Defenseless
Intuitive
Innocent
Free
Love
Harmony
Peace
Safety
Certainty
"I AM"
EVIDENCES
MAGNETIZES
MANIFESTS
ACCEPTANCE
CONFUSION
DESPAIR
TEMPORAL MIND
(Timebound EGO)
Fear
Pain
Anger
Defensive
Reasoning
Judgmental
Captive
Misery
Depression
Death
Separation
Conflict
Worry
"I AM NOT"

Figure No. 17

Remember that you too are a natural process. Being aware of how things happen includes being aware of yourself. Your life unfolds according to the same principle that governs every other unfolding. You are rooted in the common ground of all creation.

Being like everything else means that you are ordinary. But consciously knowing that you are like everything else is extraordinary. And knowing how that universality works and having the sense to act accordingly is the source of your power, your endurance, and your excellence.

Consciousness or awareness, then, is the source of your ability. Learn to become increasingly conscious.[25]

TOWARD EXPANSION AND SELF-MASTERY

1. When relating to others, bring your attention into the present, open your eyes a little wider and tune your listening to a clearer channel so as to be able to see and hear what is actually occurring right there and then. Notice when you begin to slip back into unconscious listening and seeing. Notice the difference in your communications and behaviors. Notice the difference in the way your relational transactions develop and conclude. Notice how you feel about yourself afterward.

2. Throughout the day, as the ego's judgments spontaneously occur, remind yourself: "There is another way to look at this." Then look at the person, place, or thing in a different way—a less judgmental way—a more open-minded way. Notice how you feel about the person, place, or thing as a result of changing your perception. Notice how you feel about yourself.

3. Begin to consistently bring consciousness to your projections, both negative and positive. Each time you judge someone harshly, remind yourself: "I have also been like that" or "I could also be like that."

Having healed the separation between yourself and the person you were judging (at least at the level of thought), generate thoughts of understanding and compassion for that person (and yourself).

Each time you judge someone with lavish praise, remind yourself: "I have also been like that" or "I could also be like that." Having healed the separation between yourself and the person you were praising (at least at the level of thought), generate thoughts of appreciation for that person (and yourself).

4. Observe your thoughts for periods of time every day, without attempting to change them and without becoming captured by them. Just notice them. Dis-identify yourself from your thoughts. Realize that they are just thoughts and they are not who you are. Remember that they will change to other thoughts soon. You can do this practice in a formal sitting—in a meditation position and in the quiet—or you can do this practice as you take a walk, a run, a bike ride. You can practice this discipline as you ride on the bus or train, or as a passenger in a car.

   Each time you become captured by the thoughts and begin to seriously apply your thinking to them, pause, and then say "Start again." Then begin again to observe the thoughts that are floating around in your mind.

5. Practice stepping outside your own frame of reference and attempt to see the world and circumstances through the eyes of the person to whom you are listening. Allow the lines of your identity to become transparent for a short time and remain as neutral as you possibly can as you allow the other person to show you by way of their words and actions just how they are perceiving things. Listen carefully and without judgment. Give them unspoken permission to be exactly how they are. Notice the effect your practice has on the relational transaction. Notice how you feel during and after this practice.

Let us grasp that we are
the metamorphosing caterpillars
being given wings by which
all humans shall fly.

Part Three

INTO THE ABYSS

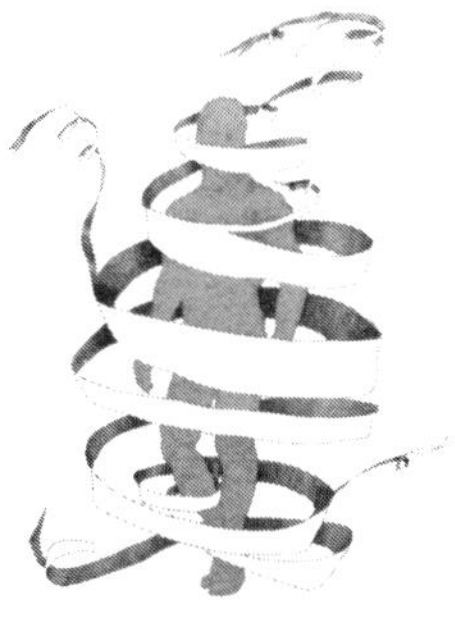

...the butterfly can never rejoin the caterpillars as long as he lives. The butterfly is not an extra-ordinary caterpillar; rather, he is a different type altogether.

—BERNADETTE ROBERTS
The Path To No-Self[3]

Let us now dispense with all
arrogance and all fear—and relax
into the experience of Innocent Trust
which lies at our core.

CHAPTER TEN

The Concept and Context of Congruence

Our fundamental idea shall be that man as we know him ***is not a completed being;*** *that nature develops him only up to a certain point and then leaves him, to develop further,* ***by his own*** *efforts and devices, or to live and die such as he was born, or to degenerate and lose capacity for development. Evolution of man in this case will mean the development of certain* ***inner*** *qualities and features which usually remain undeveloped,* ***and cannot develop by themselves.***

Experience and observation show that this development is possible only in certain definite conditions, with efforts of a certain kind on the part of man himself, and with ***sufficient help*** *from those who began similar work before and have already attained a certain degree of development, or* ***at least*** *a certain knowledge of methods.*

We must start with the idea that without efforts evolution is impossible; without help, it is also impossible.

After this we must understand that in the way of development, man must become a ***different being,*** *and we must learn and understand in what sense and in which direction he must become a different being; that is, what a different being means.*

Then we must understand that ***all men*** *cannot develop and become different beings. Evolution is the question of personal efforts, and in relation to the mass of humanity, evolution is the rare exception.*

—P.D. Ouspensky[1]

The Code and The Key

It is my strong and sincere conviction that self-honesty and authenticity of expression will heal us, will deliver us from our aimless drifting (individually and collectively), will set us securely on the path to self-knowledge, and will ultimately save us. No matter from what angle we observe our world today, we see the lack of truth and the profusion of dishonesty, deception, duplicity and fraud at every level of relationship. And, though it is important that we see this condition in our political, religious, educational, and professional leaders, it is much more important that we see it in ourselves. As "the public" we continuously denounce the unethical and unscrupulous actions of our leadership, all the while denying our own lack of ethics and scruples in our dealings with each other and with our societal systems. In America we could "throw the bums out" if we were really ready to be honest ourselves and to demand honesty in our leadership. Once again, we gaze into the mirror of our own psyches wherever we look.

All of my life I inwardly denounced the two-faced nature of our society's accepted standard of socialization. I clearly perceived and felt an unspoken agreement among us which discouraged self-honesty and prevented interrelational integrity. It was as if there existed, somewhere outside my range of understanding, a secret reason for this duplicitous mode of behaving—a secret that I expected to uncover some day. I sensed it to be an *extremely important* reason that must never be spoken about—a reason which was loaded with frightening implications for us all. I felt that everyone else knew the secret and that my not having broken the code was symptomatic of a deficiency in me. So as I went through the motions of accepted behavior, feeling as though I were lost in a fog, it was with anticipation of a moment of revelation after which I would be able to clearly see **why** we needed to behave in this way.

In being congruent, we live more fully as a human being—spontaneously, thoughtfully, and confidently.

As a mature adult, unknowingly living out a pivotal phase of my transformational process, I one day stepped beyond the invisible and ill-defined bounds of the societally accepted ways of behaving—never to return. I became, in an instant that I will never forget, unwilling to play by unspoken rules I did not understand, did not esteem, and which did not make any sense to me. The implications of that spontaneous choice were serious and included a loss which caused me tremendous personal pain for some years; but I have never regretted crossing over to a life of self-honesty and congruent Self-expression. In an unexplainable moment of revelation, I knew that I had just corrected the error of my ways. And, at the same time that I felt I had somehow let go and that I was breathlessly free-falling within a boundless realm of freedom and unburdened lightness, I also experienced being filled by the intangible stuff of personal empowerment that had spontaneously begun to rise up within me. I had finally broken a code! It was just not the code I had, all those years, expected to break. What a relief! What a rush! What a prophetic moment!

Never again did I suffer an uncomfortable conflict within myself about whether or not to relate to others out of my own sense of self. Never again did I include myself in the superficial charade of agreeable samesaying in order to fit in. Never again did I dishonor myself by allowing the consensus behavior of any group to override my own sense of what is authentic and high-minded behavior. Never again did I allow others' judgments of me undermine my own sense of right and wrong. Never again did I defer to others at times when I had to make difficult personal choices—either to have them make the choices for me or to allow them to influence my choices in any way. And never again did I find it necessary to rebel against anything or anyone. Instead, I stayed in close touch with my own sense of self, processed myself to the underlying truth for me, and expressed myself from that source of inner counsel. What a difference! What a miracle!

Having taught the principles and practices of becoming congruent for some years now, I have discovered that I was not the only child, adolescent, or adult who had not broken the code of the societal mystery. In fact, we can be assured that there is no high-minded principle being served by a code of personal and cultural conduct which pays homage to the unspoken suppression of truth and the "free speech" of judgments, blame, self-centered excuses and lies by the score. We can build more and more prisons, create more and more therapeutic models and approaches, and contrive more and more rehabilitative programs for our troubled citizenry, but it will be to no avail until we have a moment of truth about truth itself. Not until we consciously choose to abandon the amorphous nature of our dishonest drifting will we begin to hit the mark of the target of all our problems. Not until, in the name of all that is *wholly*, we truly face ourselves (and so each other)—with understanding based in compassion—will we be dealing with the real source of our uncountable problems.

It has become apparent to me that an impressively large segment of our population is now really ready to forsake the unintelligent patterns of behavior which have literally brought us to our knees—if we would only bend them. There is now strong evidence that tens of thousands of us are now ready for a moment of truth, are now eager to break the code of personal freedom, are attentive to the signs that this is **the** pivotal time in our collective transformational process, and are available for the "sufficient help" of which Ouspensky speaks.

I have seen again and again what occurs when a person is shown the way to become self-honest and Self-expressive. They come alive with a deep and spirited response that is truly heart-wrenching, as it unself-consciously conveys the confused groping which has epitomized their lives up to that time. There is real hope; and I see among those who are now prepared to make the "efforts of a certain kind" a hopefulness with which I have never seen others imbued. This hopefulness includes the willingness to do *whatever it takes* in order to pierce the armor of self-protection with which we have disguised ourselves. This willingness includes the desire to raise our carefully fashioned masks and to "become a different being." This desire includes deep gratitude for having found the way out of this land of freedom's consensual prison—by simply stepping out of our own personal prison cell. Becoming congruent is the key that opens that cell door!

The Concept of Congruence

Congruence is an accurate matching of inner experience and outer expression.

Carl Rogers was one of America's most distinguished psychologists, a central figure in the field of humanistic psychology, and the originator of what is called "client-centered" therapy. In a chapter titled "A Tentative Formulation of a General Law of Interpersonal Relationships" in his book, *On Becoming a Person*, Dr. Rogers defines his concept of the term "congruence." He qualifies his definition by saying "...it (this document) endeavors to look at a perceived underlying orderliness in all human relationships, an order which determines whether the relationship will make for the growth, enhancement, openness, and development of both individuals or whether it will make for inhibition of psychological growth, for defensiveness and blockage in both parties."[2] By this statement we know that Dr. Rogers was attempting to distinguish for us the principles by which relationships will thrive. He, too, was a breaker of codes.

> *Congruence is the term we have used to indicate an accurate matching of experiencing and awareness. It may be still further extended to cover a matching of experience, awareness, and communication. Perhaps the simplest example is an infant. If he is experiencing hunger at the physiological and visceral level, then his awareness appears to match this experience, and his communication is also congruent with his experience. He is hungry and dissatisfied, and this is true of him at all levels. He is at this moment integrated or unified in being hungry. On the other hand if he is satiated and*

content this too is a unified congruence, similar at the visceral level, the level of awareness and the level of communication. He is one unified person all the way through, whether we tap his experience at the visceral level, the level of awareness, or the level of communication. Probably one of the reasons why most people respond to infants is that they are so completely genuine, integrated or congruent. If an infant expresses affection or anger or contentment or fear there is no doubt in our minds that he ***is*** *this experience, all the way through. He is transparently fearful or loving or hungry or whatever.*

For an example of incongruence we must turn to someone beyond the stage of infancy. To pick an easily recognizable example take the man who becomes angrily involved in a group discussion. His face flushes, his tone communicates anger, he shakes his finger at his opponent. Yet when a friend says, "Well, let's not get angry about this," he replies, with evident sincerity and surprise, "I'm not angry! I don't have any ***feeling*** *about this at all! I was just pointing out the logical facts." The other men in the group break out in laughter at this statement.*

What is happening here? It seems clear that at a physiological level he is experiencing anger. This is not matched by his awareness. Consciously he is ***not*** *experiencing anger, nor is he communicating this (so far as he is consciously aware). There is a real incongruence between experience and awareness, and between experience and communication.*

Another point to be noted here is that his communication is actually ambiguous and unclear. In its words it is a setting forth of logic and fact. In its tone, and in the accompanying gestures, it is carrying a very different message—"I am angry at you." I believe this ambiguity or contradictoriness of communication is always present when a person who is at that moment incongruent endeavors to communicate.[3]

So Dr. Rogers has drawn essential distinctions for us in the matter of personal congruence. He has shown us that congruence includes:

1) **Experience** at the visceral level. The level of the viscera is the level of the vital or body organs, hence, gut level. It is also referred to as our innards or inwardness. Visceral also denotes our instinctive, intuitive and/or emotional level.

2) **Awareness** of our visceral level experience.

3) And **communication** of our experience based on our awareness.

He has shown us by his examples that without awareness of our inner experience, we are not congruent. So the first order of business must be to expand our awareness of our inner experience as outlined in the chapters on the personal prison, the human emotional response, judgments, and the ego.

He has gone on to teach us that unless there is an accurate matching of the inner experience and the outer expression, there is no congruence. So the second order of business is to become emotionally courageous, emotionally self-disciplined, and emotionally graceful in order to communicate at the level of inner experience. These criteria for congruent relating are elaborated in Chapter Seven.

I sincerely refer the reader to a careful study of Dr. Rogers' full discussion of this subject; and having said that, I will point out other aspects of congruence and incongruence from his discussion which will be essential for understanding congruence within the context of this *Course*.

Dr. Rogers also submits that at times we are not a good judge of our own degree of congruence and suggests that *defensiveness* is the smoke screen which blocks our awareness of the inner experience which is occurring and which is made obvious to others by our tone of voice and our body language.

Dr. Rogers also points out another type of incongruence; namely, the type wherein we are well aware of our inner experience, but we consciously attempt to deceive others by falsely communicating a completely different experience. He uses the example of being bored at a party and then telling the hostess, upon leaving, that we had a wonderful time.

He goes on to explain that when we are being entirely congruent our communication could not express external facts; but, instead, we would need to always express ourselves from the level of experience, which means feelings, perceptions, and meanings from our inner response. He emphasizes that the implications of this are important ones.

Having said that, he further states that speaking from the context of personal perceptions does not necessarily indicate that we are being congruent, since we may use that way of speaking as a defense. (This is one of the ways I have seen the teachings of congruence distorted).

Dr. Rogers concludes by stressing what was pointed to above; namely, that we can see and feel when another is being the truth of himself and when he is not.

> *To conclude our definition of this construct in a much more commonsense way, I believe all of us tend to recognize congruence or incongruence in individuals with whom we deal. With some individuals we realize that in most areas this person not only consciously means exactly what he says, but that his deepest feelings also match what he is expressing, whether it is anger or competitiveness or affection or cooperativeness. We feel that "we know exactly where he stands." With another individual, we recognize that what he is saying is almost certainly a front, a facade. We wonder what he really feels. We wonder if he knows what he feels. We tend to be wary and cautious of such an individual.*[4]

As Dr. Rogers indicates, "this concept of congruence is a somewhat complex concept with a number of characteristics and implications."[5] It is important to remind ourselves of this fact as we approach our study and practice of congruence. Gaining a clear understanding of what congruence is and achieving the necessary awareness and the ability to communicate authentically is no small matter. In fact, it is a big deal. It is the remedy for our lack of self-sense and our present interpersonal dysfunction. So we must not jump to conclusions, toss off a superficial retort with an "I know that" attitude, and expect to turn that key in our prison cell door. If the man who grappled so long and so sincerely to clarify congruence for us cautions us that it is somewhat complex, let us first understand **that**. I place special emphasis on this because I have watched some people who initially saw the possibilities which the achievement of congruence offered them later slip back into denial and fall far short of self-discovery. But they used the language of the congruence teachings to do what they had done before: judge others harshly, make others wrong, defend themselves, and blame others. In this chapter I will attempt to put together the pieces of the puzzle of becoming congruent in a way which makes it possible for the sincere student to avoid the pitfalls and booby traps which might distort the central principles of congruence.

IN BEING CONGRUENT, WE EXPERIENCE CONFIDENCE, EASE, AND A PROFOUND SENSE OF PERSONAL FREEDOM.

The following is a summarization of Dr. Rogers' definition of congruence:

1) Congruence begins with an inner experience which we can feel in our bodies. It is an instinctive, gut-level response.

2) Congruence includes **awareness** of our inner body-level experience.

3) Congruence also includes **communication** of our inner experience based on our awareness.

4) Incongruence occurs when our awareness does not match our inner experience, making our communication inconsistent with our tone of voice and body language.

5) Incongruence also occurs when our awareness matches our inner experiences, but our communication is not a match, as when we consciously choose to deceive others.

6) Ambiguous and unclear communication results whenever we are incongruent.

7) We are sometimes not a good judge of our own level of congruence as defensiveness throws up a smoke screen which blocks our awareness.

8) Congruence presupposes or excludes the communicating of external facts. Congruence means **communicating from the level of perception, feelings, and meaning from an internal frame of reference**.

9) One who communicates from a context of personal perception is not necessarily congruent, as this way of communicating may be used as a defense.

10) All of us tend to recognize whether another is being congruent or incongruent.

The Past Is Past And Tomorrow Never Comes

In order to prepare ourselves to become adept at discerning and interpreting our body-level responses and communicating from the level of our experience, we simply must reclaim the majority of our surface consciousness. Where is it? And what is it that we must reclaim it from? Until we clear our past, we will find most of our consciousness there, in the past—reliving and reprocessing the events of our personal history. This subsection of our psyche can be called Puzzling Pitfalls and Petrifying Paralyses of the Past. The rest of most of our consciousness we will find in a psychological category which can be called Fantastic Fantasies and Frightful Fears About the Future. Whatever little speck of consciousness is left over, we certainly need for brushing our teeth, going to the mall, handling those crises which keep on occurring, balancing our checkbook, and, oh, yes, doing our job!

Once we get serious about gathering all of our surface consciousness in one place—the present moment—we must resist the pull of the Puzzling and Petrifying Past and the Fantastic and Frightful Future by putting our consciousness to work noticing what is actually happening here in this moment...and this moment...and this moment.... Miracles begin to happen and we become amazed at the sheer number of things which are occurring now and now and now while we might have been *you know where.*

The practice of present-moment awareness seems more like work than practice in the initial stages, simply because the pull of the Pitfalls and Paralyses and the Fantasies and Fears is so strong. But taking notice of the leaves on the trees and even the spaces between the leaves; the branches on the trees and even the spaces between the branches; the blades of grass, the sun's shimmer on the water, the breeze that softly touches our cheek, the weight of our body on the stair, the sadness in the eyes of our friend, etc., the events of the past and the fictions about the future begin to lose their glamorous appeal to our long overworked mental machinery. What a surprise! We are really living in this moment...and this moment...and...this... "Look—a falling star!"

Once You Get The Hang Of It...

In formulating the model of Congruence as Context [Figure No. 18], I have represented each experience of being congruent as an **upward flow** of process—with a beginning, a continuing, and a completion—replicating a fundamental pattern within all of life, including all relational transactions. The model shows that being congruent is a process which includes three specific phases:

↑(3) choosing our communication and/or behavior.
↑(2) reading our inner responses;
↑(1) relating consciously with another person;

With an enhanced understanding of ourselves as human beings as the foundation upon which our process of congruent experience, awareness, and expression stand, we are equipped to respond spontaneously, thoughtfully, and confidently with emotional courage, self-discipline and gracefulness. Although there are clear distinctions drawn between the three aspects of the process in the model, it must be understood that our consciousness is naturally holding all three aspects at once. The model of congruence provides us with a reference by which to identify the area(s) in which we have been weak up to now and gives us a formula by which to contemplate and strengthen 1) our relational presence, 2) our inner discernment, and 3) our level of choice-making. And, though it is a subjective standard by which to judge our subjective human experiences, it accords us an effective methodology by which we may become more objective in our perceptions and in our verbal and behavioral responses based on those perceptions.

Being congruent eliminates inner conflict, neutralizes fear, generates self-trust, and puts you in charge of your life—with ease.

The model of congruence is something we can hold on to as we loosen our ego's tight grip on the bars of our prison cell. And as we apply the precepts and practices of *A Course In Congruence* over and over again in our daily life, our own deeper truth will begin to replace the pseudo-security of the prison bars, behind which we sadly cowered, with a now growing sense of self-confidence. As we discover and express ourselves from the well of wisdom, power and love which lies deep within us, our experience of personal empowerment will make unnecessary any use of what was before our standard operating strategy—approval-seeking behavior, fearful avoidance of conflict, and self-doubtful reprocessing of our relational transactions. Our growing confidence will undermine the ego's frightful arrogance and feeble sense of failure. Our need to win will be transformed into a desire to express ourselves from a high-minded perspective which will set us and others free from the endless round of predictable and stifling reactivity. We will become more energetic, more attentive, and more creative as our past begins to fade into the past where it belongs. And, we will become more available for the now, the new, and the next of our rich and potent lives. Such remarkable benefits!

As we see, the model depicting the context of congruence is a circle containing three elements or parts which, together, comprise a congruent transaction with another person. The context of congruence is actually the conscious intention to fully experience, correctly translate, and authentically communicate and/or behave so as to achieve self-discovery and Self-expression in a relational exchange. Within that conscious intention are the three stages or phases that we go through each time we participate in a meaningful exchange with another person. For purposes of presenting the three distinct elements—which require our awareness and interpretation, and which are the basis for our conscious choices as to what to say and what to do—the elements are separated. In reality, however, they are all three simultaneously present in our moment-to-moment awareness while we are actively engaged in any spontaneous, candid, and reciprocal dialogue which requires feeling-level responsiveness.

Having achieved congruence, when we complete the relational transaction and leave the person or hang up the phone, we will feel free and experience a sense of completion and personal satisfaction. We will not be processing and reprocessing the experience over and over again in an attempt to resolve conflict. We will not be conflicted. We will sleep peacefully and awake with a clear consciousness, at least as regards that particular interaction. Incredible!

The First Element: Consciousness in the Present Moment

FULLY CONSCIOUS PARTICIPATION WITH PRESENT-MOMENT EXPERIENCE

(Responsiveness)

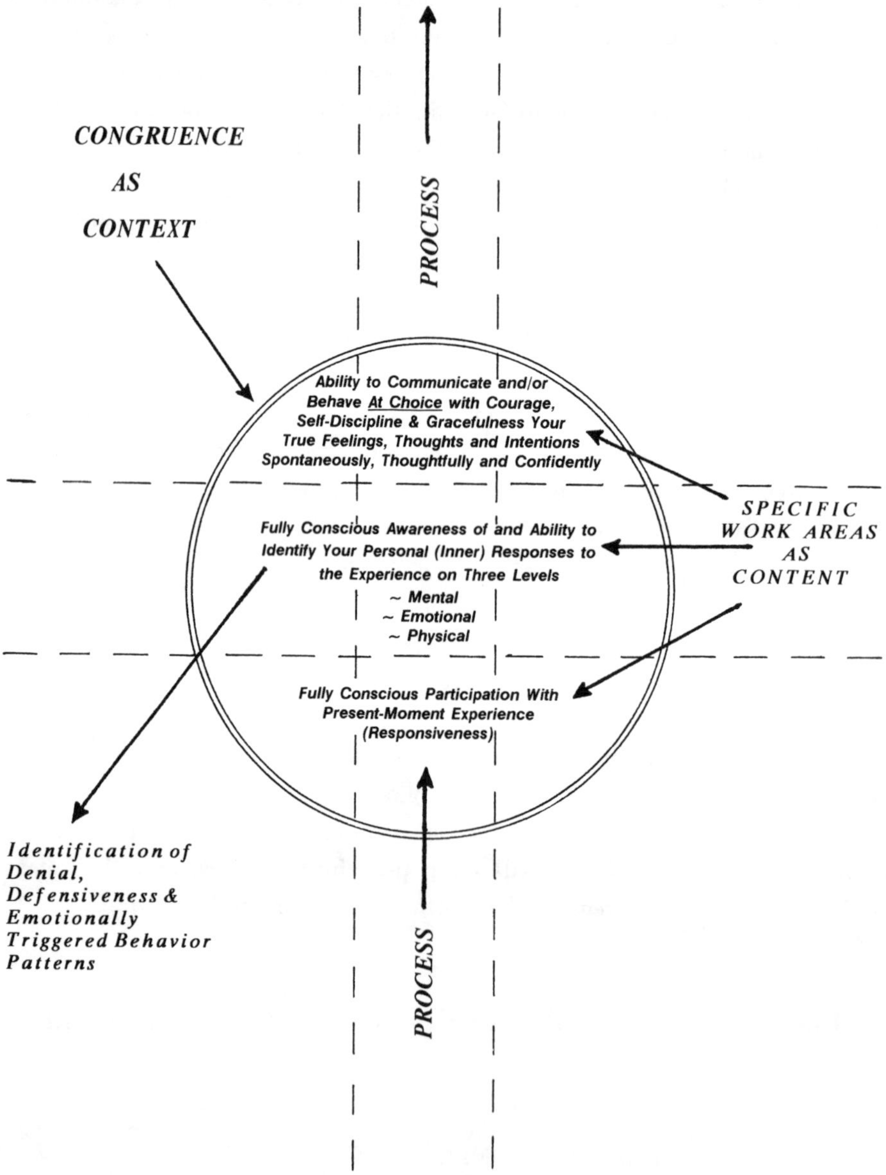
CONGRUENCE
AS
CONTEXT
PROCESS
Ability to Communicate and/or Behave At Choice with Courage, Self-Discipline & Gracefulness Your True Feelings, Thoughts and Intentions Spontaneously, Thoughtfully and Confidently
Fully Conscious Awareness of and Ability to Identify Your Personal (Inner) Responses to the Experience on Three Levels
~ Mental
~ Emotional
~ Physical
Fully Conscious Participation With Present-Moment Experience (Responsiveness)
SPECIFIC WORK AREAS AS CONTENT
Identification of Denial, Defensiveness & Emotionally Triggered Behavior Patterns
PROCESS

Figure No. 18

We are first of all participating with another human being with our full consciousness present.

We are in *full attendance*; that is, we have one-pointed attention in the present moment. We are attending to the other person, to ourselves, and to our environment.

Our attention is not drawn off into memories of the past or into concerns about the future. We are consciously focusing our attention on the events of these moments.

We are fully *present* and *responsive* in the moment.

(Remember: The only thing we have to give is our attention and our energy.)

The Second Element: Awareness of Inner Responses

Fully Conscious Awareness of and Ability to
Identify Our Personal (Inner) Responses to
the Experience on Three Levels
~Mental
~Emotional
~Physical

With our full attention present, and maintaining our relational connection with the other person, we have an impassive awareness of our inner experience.

With our Witness Self we notice the changes which occur in our body, and we are able to identify our inner *physical* response. For example, we may observe a quickening of our heartbeat; a rush of energy to our face and limbs; a concentration of energy in our gut area; a fluttering sensation (butterflies) in our heart and/or stomach region; a feeling that we are about to explode; a sinking feeling in our heart and/or mid-section.

With the Observer Self we notice the changes which simultaneously occur in our *emotional* experience, and we identify our inner emotional response. For example, we may observe an initial switch from a balance emotion to the confusion, pain and fear range of the inertia scale as our interaction with the other person becomes "cool." We may then become "hot" as we swing to the covert or overt levels of resentment in the activity scale. We may then observe a touch of sad/grieving as we experience "I didn't want it to be this way." And, we may note a return to balance at the level of unconditional positive regard as we realize the other person is sincerely communicating with us and we begin to hear what he is trying to say. When we complete the transaction we may feel loving and peaceful/content at having reached an accord within the relational exchange.

As the Impersonal Self we notice the changes which simultaneously occur in our mental experience, and we are able to identify our inner *mental* response to what is happening at the present time. For example, we may observe either a speeding up or a slowing down of our thought processes. We may become inundated with so many thoughts that we become mentally confused and unable to think straight. Or we may go blank and be unable to think at all. Or our mind may begin to jump wildly from one random thought to another, causing us to become mentally muddled. We may notice thoughts of the past flashing on our mental screen. As we bring our attention back to the present moment, again and again, and continue to participate within the context of the present transaction, our mind will begin to clear and to function more like a well-programmed computer which sorts and processes incoming information. Once that occurs, we will be able to quickly make the high-minded choices which are relevant to this interpersonal transaction.

The Third Element: Choice of Communication and Behavior

ABILITY TO COMMUNICATE AND/OR
BEHAVE AT CHOICE WITH COURAGE,
SELF-DISCIPLINE & GRACEFULNESS OUR
TRUE FEELINGS, THOUGHTS AND INTENTIONS
Spontaneously, Thoughtfully, and Confidently

With our attention fully present, and with a high degree of awareness and identification of our inner responses, we complete the process by making the high-minded choices as to what, if anything, we will communicate and how we will behave. In the beginning of our practice, our choice-making may be tentative, somewhat exclusive, insensitive to some of the factors involved and, to a degree, self-serving. With practice this choice-making will be done with a high level of inclusion and sensitive, on-the-spot processing of all the factors implicit in the transaction.

We **choose** our communication and/or behavior based on our feeling level truth. Having first identified our inner emotional responses we consciously go beyond them in order to experience and decipher our deeper feelings.

We **express** our feelings, thoughts, and intentions in clear and congruent communications which inform the other person of where we stand by expressing our perceptions, our emotional experience and/or our personal decision about the issue at hand.

We communicate to the other person with **emotional courage**. That is, we do not allow our fear of conflict, our fear of judgment and rejection, our fear of loss, or our fear of looking bad to dictate our responses. We honor our own inner experience and give it a voice by which to have its say.

> We communicate to the other person with emotional **self-discipline.** That is, we do not allow our emotions or our thoughts to override our deeper truth and our higher perspective on this matter. We notice our emotions and our thoughts, but restrain our tendency to act out their purely egoic level of reactivity. Instead, we honor ourselves and the other person by overriding such reactive conditioning and stating the clear and simple truth in this case.
>
> We communicate to the other person with **emotional gracefulness.** That is, we speak to the other person with a conscious awareness and an intuitive sensitivity as to their present psychological (physical, emotional, and mental) condition. Realizing that they, too, are experiencing their human response on all levels, we read their level of tolerance to us and our communications at the time. And, at their level of tolerance, we speak our truth. Their tolerance level should not prohibit us from expressing ourselves, and emotional gracefulness does not imply that they will not experience upset as a result of our communication. It only implies that they will be better able to receive and tolerate the communication. When two congruent people are communicating, the chances are much greater that the communications will be received and responded to immediately or within a short-term period after the transaction. When only one of the persons is practicing congruence, the burden for "response-able" communication and behavior falls squarely on that person.
>
> We communicate to the other person **spontaneously, thoughtfully and confidently.** That is, we speak candidly, naturally, with sincerity and self-trust from within the framework of the relationship. We avoid overstatement and understatement of our perceptions, feelings and intentions. We do not withhold ourselves nor do we attempt to force our views upon the other. We simply tell the truth.

As mentioned above, when we first begin to practice congruence, we realize which of the three phases of the process is weakest and most in need of strengthening and development. Due to the high levels of reactivity to which we have become accustomed, all areas will need some clear focus and steady practice.

As we see in the model, the middle stage of the process (the awareness and identification of our inner responses) is the stage which will disclose to us our conditioned denial of emotions, our defensiveness, and our emotionally-triggered behavior patterns.

By learning to consciously transcend the victimization of our higher sensibilities by our fluctuating emotional response and our careening mental functions, we will soon be able to notice what is going on within, maintain our sense of self, and, with a high degree of poise, we will speak and act out of the truth of ourselves in such a way that others can hear us. We will have exceeded the limitations of our previous level of neurotic dysfunction and will have become more fully human!

IT LOOKS GOOD ON PAPER, BUT...

Once you have studied the overall concepts, the presentations of the specific aspects which require understanding and practice, and have achieved a clear and strong intention to become congruent, you may still experience being somewhat at a loss: "So, how do I do it?"

First of all, it takes getting used to the idea. You cannot expect that tomorrow you are going to be a perfectly congruent person who is emotionally courageous, self-disciplined and graceful. Neither can you expect that you will be immediately capable of identifying and translating your emotional responses and correcting the reactive, judgmental thoughts which race through your mind. Likewise, it is unrealistic to assume that you will be able to make the highest choice in every case and express yourself spontaneously, thoughtfully and confidently all of the time. You will have to work up to what will become a natural state of congruence.

LET US GIVE THE ONLY THING WE HAVE TO GIVE—OUR TRUE SELVES—OUR AUTHENTIC, GENUINE, REAL, CONGRUENT SELVES.

But after a while, you will begin to remember that you *can* be the truth of yourself; and you will remember the model; and you will begin to do the best you can to be congruent. With the basic understandings you have achieved and with the strength of your intention pulsing within you, you will not be able to continue to live within the limitations of the way you have lived before. You will no longer be able to stand sadly and helplessly behind the bars of your prison cell and say, "It's all right. It's okay. I don't mind. Yea, that's fine."—and then go home angry and upset, having sentenced yourself to more time behind bars—the hateful bars of confusion, self-doubt, fear of conflict, approval-seeking behavior, mindbound, denial of emotions, lack of communication, lack of integrity, lack of awareness. Thank goodness, you will not be able to live it like that anymore.

Then, there comes a time—when you just do it!

AND YOU KNOW YOU DID IT;
AND YOU ARE SO EMPOWERED;
AND YOU KNOW THAT'S IT;
AND YOU KNOW HOW TO DO IT!
AND THEN YOU'VE GOTTEN THE HANG OF IT.

All of a sudden you are just doing it. You are doing it and doing it again and again. And pretty soon you are being congruent *naturally*.

Every once in a while you will fall back into your old, boring, conditioned responses: You will attack somebody and feel terrible about yourself afterwards. Or you will say "Yea, that's fine," and then you will go home and feel bad. But, the difference will be that you will clear it up. You will pick up the phone or you will go back to see the other person—and you will be congruent. You will say something like, "I want to talk about that again; I feel uncomfortable about what I said and the way I behaved. What I want to tell you is...", and then you will tell them the truth and clear yourself.

And, although you may expect to experience moments of being at a loss, being congruent is such a natural way of being that you will be amazed at how easily you will become adept at being the truth of yourself. You will soon be thinking to yourself, "I can hardly believe that for such a long time I did not express myself freely." One thing is certain: You will never be the same!

EXPECT THEM TO SQUIRM

When I am the truth of myself, I sometimes cause other people to have an upset—and that is okay with me. That is my freedom. I am willing to risk having another person get upset if I am the truth of myself. That is not a selfish arrogance nor a flippant, insensitive attitude; it is just that I know that if I **am** the truth of myself, some people are going to get upset. And, if I **am not** the truth of myself, some people are going to get upset. The abiding heartfelt intention which is implicit within my practice of being congruent translates as willingness to take the risks which are inherent to the process of becoming the truth of myself.

I learned the hard way that some of my relationships were not able to handle the truth of me. They could not accommodate the real me because they had been built on self-doubtful or self-aggrandizing lies or half-truths, and confusion about who I was and what I stood for. When I began to discover and express the truth of myself, I did not always get a standing ovation. Some people said (in one way or the other): "What happened to you? I don't like you like this. I want you to be the way you were before." And, although I suffered the loss of family and friends, I celebrated the gaining of a whole new circle, community, and network of like-minded others who appreciated and honored the always changing and *ever-new* me. An unexpected grace!

LOVE IS THE ANSWER

Being who you really are is the only way that you can really love another human being. All the other nonsense that we call love is not love at all—it is self-absorbed, self-projecting, self-protective, self-seeking, needy, approval-seeking neurosis. What we have come to call love is—instead of love—two imprisoned egos reacting to each other's attempts to meet their individual unfulfilled needs by trying to get whatever it is that they each want to get for themselves at the time. The less-than-love we have come to know has left us feeling empty and hurt and confused again and again and again. The less-than-love we have come to accept as the standard for interpersonal achievement has become a consolation prize which reeks with possessiveness and control issues straight out of the damaged ego's limited repertoire of mindsets and self-serving strategies. The less-than-love that we have participated in, because it has been devoid of self-acceptance and self-love, has caused us to seek that acceptance and that love from outside ourselves. Why do we inwardly weep behind the bars of our prison cell? Because we have not been able to find acceptance and love *out there*!

There is an amazing secret which lies within the consciousness of congruence: if we will discover who we are *now*, if we will be who we are *now*, we will heal our own damaged egos! We will, by expressing our truth in this moment, heal the wounds to our ego which were caused in our past when we did not know how to source and express ourselves. Amazing! No one else can heal our wounds for us—no therapist, no lover, no parent, no priest, no friend, no book, no seminar. We have been operating under an unconscious or subconscious false hope or false assumption that we could find or get real validation of ourselves—if we could only find that "right person" to get it from.

With an experience of yourself at the level of true Self, you begin to naturally express the truth and heal yourself. Only you are the authentic you and within that authenticity lies the source of your own healing! You can read a library full of books and you can attend an uncountable series of seminars and you seek the assistance of psychiatrists, psychologists and other caretakers, but nothing meaningful is going to happen until you begin to express the truth of yourself. Really! I mean really *express* it. When you begin to do that, your ego will begin to heal so fast that you will experience a most en**joy**able sense of future shock!

Beyond the limitation of the lower mind, the impossible becomes possible!

Ordinary Miracles

As a result of being congruent, we begin to integrate the different aspects of ourselves which we have, heretofore, experienced as and considered to be separate from each other. We notice and honor the at-one-ment of our body, our emotions and our mind. We stop ignoring, denying, or rejecting our physical sensations, our emotional energies, and our out-of-control mind activity in order to serve the ego's will to win, to be right, to look good and to survive.

Our level of integrity grows each time we are congruent. As Frances Vaughan states so eloquently: "What is expressed in the world must be aligned with what is genuinely believed and felt inside if healing and integration are valued."[6] Being aligned in outer expression with what we inwardly believe and feel produces a strong sense of personal satisfaction—a sense of wholeness—rather than generating personal conflict—a sense of fragmentation and disharmony.

- We begin to feel empowered and *in charge* of our lives.

- We quickly become more self-accepting, which allows us to relax and be more accepting of others.

- As we become more accepting of ourselves and others and continue to express ourselves truthfully, we begin to earn the respect of others, which is what we had wanted and had attempted to achieve all those years by utilizing approval-seeking behaviors.

- But, most important, we come to respect ourselves, and we no longer really *need* the respect of others. We become confident, highly-integrated, self-validating personalities, with a vast reservoir of inner strength, who are strong positive forces in the world.

- We expect conflict in our relationships, but learn by experience that conflict no longer translates as loss of valued relationships, loss of personal integrity, or loss of our feelings of self-worth.

- The bars of our prison cell no longer hold us captive. We are free to be who we truly are. The ego no longer controls our lives. We notice its reactivity but are not victimized by it.

- We feel our ego's hurts from the past (which it represents), and we heal those hurts in the present by telling the truth we were previously too frightened or too confused to speak.

- We recognize our own value, and we contribute that value by way of our own truthful Self-expression.

- Conflict is no longer a *win or lose* egoic competition, but an important part of healthy human relating which allows for discussion, negotiation and resolution.

- We discover what works for us and what does not work for us in each relationship, circumstance, and relational transaction.

- We discover what is all right with us and what is not all right with us, and we give ourselves permission to report that.

- We stop blaming others for what they feel and think, and we take responsibility for clarifying for ourselves and others our own thoughts and feelings.

- We notice our judgments, expectations, and demands of others and let go of them as they arise.

- We notice others' judgments, expectations, and demands of us, and we no longer allow them to dictate our lives.

- We keep our awareness centered squarely on ourselves; and, at the same time, we maintain a high level of sensitivity to what others are experiencing.

- We allow ourselves our emotional responses and others' theirs.

- We relate with others as equals rather than as superior or inferior to them.

- We notice our tendencies to behave combatively or as victims, but instead choose to get in touch with our truthful, Feeling Function responses and communicate those with natural dignity.

- We feel the ego's fearful resistance to change, and we make the high choices which are appropriate to our process of unfoldment.

- We give up our fearful attempts to control people and circumstances as we refocus our attention on taking charge of our own life.

- We maintain our clear commitment to serve our own highest good, and our experience of understanding, growth, and expansion begins to compound itself.
- We correct our thinking when it slips back into negative patterns of reactivity.

THE FILLING STATION STORY

A few years ago I had an unexpected experience of being congruent at a service station in Miami where I had been going for quite some time. The driver's side door of my BMW had begun to make a disturbing cracking sound when I opened it; it would go "ccrraaacckkk" and then snap open. It obviously needed some grease on the hinges. So I just drove over to my favorite old gas station, where I was always well taken care of, to get my car filled up with gas and to have some grease put on the door hinges.

On that sizzling **hot** summer day, I pulled into the full service lane. Now, at my filling station they had a rule that if you pulled into the full service lane you had to pull all the way up to the second pump, so that someone else could pull in behind you at the first pump. But it was very hot and very sunny, and the first pump was in the shade. Knowing that I was going to be there for some time, while they put grease on the door hinges, I pulled in and parked at the first pump.

The attendant who most often served me was standing in front of my car, out in the sun, by the second pump, and he was waving his arms for me to "Come on." He kept signaling for me to "Come forward." I waved and signaled back "No" and pointed to my door.

Wwweeeellll, his face became extremely red and very mean looking, and it was obvious that he was INCENSED because I did not pull up to the second pump. He came stomping back to my car with his face contorted and nearly purple with anger. I told him that I needed to have my car filled up and that I needed some grease on my door. **Well,** he was just "in his stuff." He was having a full-blown emotional upset, and he was acting awful to me.

He **stuck** that hose in that car and he **marched off** over there to that garage and he **marched back out** with a little spray can of WD-40. I said, "No, that is not going to work. I've already tried that. What it needs is that grease—you know, that white stuff that you put on door hinges." **Wwweeellll**, he just **stomped off** back over there into that garage, and he **yanked** that white stuff off that shelf, and he **stomped** back out to my car, and he **jerked** open that door—and it stuck! It stuck open!

Then he became even more upset; he lost even more of his composure to his reactivity. While he was working on the door, his rage continued to escalate.

I was just standing there, noticing all this, and feeling uncomfortable about what was going on. I had no judgments of him—I actually felt a bit sorry for him and also saw the humor in it all. I felt concerned about my car door, because, as usual, I had a very busy schedule and needed to be able to drive my car. But there was *something else* going on in me—at the Feeling Function level.

All of a sudden, as he stood with his back turned to me—obviously furious—struggling with my car door, which was still stuck open—I heard myself saying to him, "Wait just a minute!" And he turned around and looked at me for an instant. I looked into his eyes and said, "I don't want you to treat me this way." And he got it! He heard me! He understood! His face softened, his energy changed, the tension in his body relaxed—as his upset just fell away. He said nothing and I said nothing more. He went back to working on my door hinges and I went back to just waiting—in the shade of the canopy. But from that moment we became great buddies and stayed that way until I left Miami. He would always salute me when I came in for gas or service, and he would often give me a little service station gift from their promotional items. I felt my love for him—and I am pretty sure he loved me too.

CONGRUENCE=FREEDOM

How powerful. I said a few truthful words. I did not argue with him. I did not blame him or make him wrong in any way. I just said my simple truth: "I don't want you to treat me this way," and the whole experience changed—for him and for me. Being congruent can be that simple.

I did not say, "Don't treat me this way." I did not tell him what to do. He can do whatever he wants to do. All I told him was that I did not **want** him to treat me this way—and he had a choice to make. He chose to stop treating me that way.

When we really understand the concept of congruence, we clearly see that the simple truth is the most obvious thing that is missing in the world. All of the mental complexities and all of the emotional complications are generated by the enturbulations within the ego mind.

TAKING A STAND/STANDING ALONE

As our attention shifts from the self-protective and self-aggrandizing ways of relating and the absorptions of the lower self, we will soon become aware that a dramatic change must take place in our relationships with others. When our interest is captured by the fascinations of self-discovery and Self-expression, we no longer appreciate or have time for some of the people, places, and things which before stimulated our interest and consumed our time and energy.

The words "taking a stand" do not imply a militancy of attitude or behavior. The stand is actually a life-changing inner event which anchors our consciousness in the intention to evolve. As a result of this inner event, we become highly purposeful in our search for truth and most sincere in applying the principles and practices which support our intention. We thereafter "stand alone" in that we are deeply **dedicated to** and completely **responsible for** honoring *above all things* the silent vow we have taken within the privacy of our own hearts.

The strength of our conviction will be thoroughly tested by the expectations, judgments and demands placed upon us within our relationships with all *significant others*. Since all of our relationships have been forged from the combined egoity of ourselves and others, they will need to be brought into Lawfulness or renounced. That is not a rule. It is just the way we are once our attention is shifted from the lower to the higher nature. We are no longer capable of withstanding the manipulative control dramas of others, and we can no longer play by the unspoken rules of incongruent relational game playing. Having chafed against the restraints that have held us all of our life, we now must have the freedom to be and to become. The choices we must make are serious and difficult ones—and, yet, we make them with amazing ease, considering the losses we sometimes suffer. The vibrance of the divine impulse and the experience of rebirth which we enjoy compensate for the inner ache we feel from having to let go.

Toward Expansion and Self-Mastery

1. Practice bringing your full attention to the relational transaction you are a part of at any given time. Bring whatever attention is captured by thoughts of the past into the present moments. Bring whatever attention is captured by thoughts of the future into the present moments. Use all of your conscious attention to attend to what the other person is saying, to what you are feeling and thinking, and to what choices you need to make now. Give the present your full attention. You can remind yourself: "The power is in the present moment."

2. While you are watching an eventful movie, reading an interesting book, or speaking on the phone with a friend, practice monitoring your own inner responses to those outer stimuli. Extend your practice to include whatever you are doing at any particular time or place. Notice how your inner responses (emotions and feelings) change as you continue to participate either as a spectator or an active communicator. By way of this practice, become adept at taking accurate readings of your inner emotional and feeling level life.

3. Practice making conscious choices as to whether you will:

   - communicate fully at this time or not;
   - report your emotional experience or not;
   - act out the emotional energy in your body or not.

   This practice is more important than any specific communication or behavior in any one particular relational transaction. This practice is the touchstone for becoming capable of choosing the most intelligent and most appropriate response in each case.

5. Consistently practice accessing the feeling function level of your human response—the deeper feelings which lie beneath the emotions. Ask yourself: "How do I really feel about this?" and "What deeper feelings are the cause of my emotional reaction?" Process each transaction with

which you feel incomplete or about which you feel uncomfortable until you discover that deeper truth. It may take living in the question for a few days or a few weeks.

4. Debrief yourself after each relational transaction as to whether you were able to achieve all three stages of congruence. Notice where you are weak and where you are strong in the process.

   Were you able to be fully present and responsive to the moment-to-moment unfoldment of the transaction?

   Were you able to read your inner responses—physical, emotional, mental—as they were occurring?

   Were you able to consciously choose what communications you would make and how you would behave?

   Were you able to be spontaneous, thoughtful, and confident?

   Were you to able to exhibit emotional courage, self-discipline and gracefulness?

When you were not able to fulfill the parameters of one of the stages, do so carefully after the fact and recontact the person involved to communicate congruently.

Let us know that we are mystics
and "that the gleams which
flash across our minds
are not ours, but God's..."

CHAPTER ELEVEN

WHO'S GOT THE PROBLEM?

Deep down we must have real affection for each other, a clear realization or recognition of our shared human status. At the same time, we must openly accept all ideologies and systems as a means of solving humanity's problems. One country, one nation, one ideology, one system is not sufficient. It is helpful to have a variety of different approaches on the basis of a deep feeling of the basic sameness of humanity. We can then make a joint effort to solve the problems of the whole of humankind.

The real troublemakers are anger, jealousy, impatience, and hatred. With them, problems cannot be solved. Though we may have temporary success, ultimately our hatred or anger will create further difficulties. Anger makes for swift solutions. Yet, when we face problems with compassion, sincerity, and good motivation, our solutions may take longer, but ultimately they are better.

—*HIS HOLINESS THE DALAI LAMA*[1]

EQUALITY AND QUALITY OF EXPRESSION

A fundamental tenet of truthful relating is the presence of a clear space between the two people who are having a relational transaction. Because we are such responsive (and reactive) beings (remember the amoeba?), the clear space will fill up and have to be cleared, fill up and have to be cleared—again and again—as the present conversation continues and as the longer-term relationship unfolds. What will need to be cleared is any judgment either of us has which keeps us from being with each other fully. As we empty the space of the "stuff" of egoic judgment and emotional reactivity, we create a psychological space in which we both feel accepted. With an experience of being accepted rather than judged, we can be with each other fully in the present moment. We can speak to each other honestly and listen innocently to what each other has to say.

In a clear space we can relate with each other without the need to defend ourselves and without attempting to listen *over*, *around* or *through* what we have perceived as wrongness in each other.

In a clear space, we can approach each other with an attitude that says, "I want to be here fully present with you in this moment without anything that has happened in the past hanging around in our space. I want to transcend my ego's desire to be right in exchange for an experience of being heard by you and of hearing you. I want to communicate with you rather than to argue with you or to withhold myself from you."

We will be blocked from being able to achieve clear communication and true relationship to whatever degree the space is filled with hurtful or resentful thoughts and feelings. And to the degree our present-moment communication is obstructed, we will both be handicapped in our ability to hear. And to the degree that each of us is unable to hear the other, we risk misunderstanding and being misunderstood—causing more *hard* (hurt or resentful) feelings which will take up more of the space for communication.

1) In order to be successful at each conscious attempt to clear the space, we will need to be able to accurately discern **who's got the problem**. We will need to ask ourselves, "Is the 'stuff' I am feeling in the space my 'stuff' or is it the other person's 'stuff,' or do we both have something from the past that we have brought to the space of our present-moment conversation?" "Is this my problem or is it the other person's problem?"

   We must become adept at discerning whether our judgments of the other person are legitimate issues which must be dealt with in a "clearing" with that person or whether they derive from our desire to control others and have them think and behave the way we want them to think and behave.

2) In order to be successful at each of these conscious attempts to clear the space, we will need to be able to **separate our own emotional experience from the emotional experience of the other person** in order to...

   a) stay open to the other person;

   b) accurately read our own emotional responses;

c) listen to our own inner voice; and

d) remain fully at choice and fully relational with the other person.

We must become adept at separating our emotional experiences from the emotional experiences of others so as to free ourselves and to free those with whom we relate. We must learn to stand free as we *allow others to have their emotional experiences fully and freely* without being drawn into them. We must also learn to have our emotional experiences fully and freely without being overly sensitive to the tendency of others to be drawn into our experience. We must insist on a separation of emotional experiences with our relatives and close friends in order to bring our relationships into congruence and, thus, truth.

3) In order to be successful at each conscious attempt to clear the space, we will need to have our Observer Self present; we will need to have our experience fully; and we will need to a) continue to listen, b) express ourselves, and c) refrain from becoming reactive.

4) In order to be successful at each conscious attempt to clear the space, we will need to be aware of our own sense of well-being on all levels: physical, emotional, mental, and spiritual. Whether we are feeling strong or weak in any or all of those areas will have an effect on our ability to achieve and maintain clarity ourselves, and to cope with the moment-to-moment experiences of the clearing.

5) In order to be successful at each conscious attempt to clear the space, we will need to be aware of what is happening in our immediate surroundings which may be affecting our nervous system or otherwise influencing our level of tolerance.

With this high level of conscious awareness, we can then appropriately share our thoughts and emotional experiences and communicate authentically from the *feeling* level. We can then remain congruent throughout our communication and leave the encounter feeling gratified, genuine and with a strong sense of self—whether or not the conversation was difficult and uncomfortable or easy and pleasant.

Before becoming more explicit as to how to determine *who's got the problem* and how to *separate our emotional experience* from the emotional experience of others, I present here a model which illustrates the basic concepts with which we are working in order to achieve a methodology for healthy, effective, and congruent relating.

Full Spaces and Empty Expressions

The ten circles which make up this model [Figures No. 19 through 28] all represent an opening or a Space for Communication between two people—in this case, Bubba and Bonnie. This Space for Communication is actually a representation of the *commingled attention and energy* of the two people who are communicating with each other. In Circle A, we see that most of the space created by the combined attention of our hypothetical communicators is clear conscious space available for communication between them. This whole circle represents the space which they both intended and expected to have (whether they knew it or not) when they made their appointment to meet and talk about a business venture they have been wanting to start up.

As you will notice in reviewing the model, the Threshold of Understanding moves up↑ and down↓, depending on their individual ability to understand, accept, and have compassion for the other at any given time. The Threshold of Understanding fluctuates as a direct result of physical, emotional, and mental states as well as environmental influences.

Once we learn to clear the space and become accustomed to how it feels to have a clear space in which to relate, the slightest speck of "stuff" will be noticeable and uncomfortable.

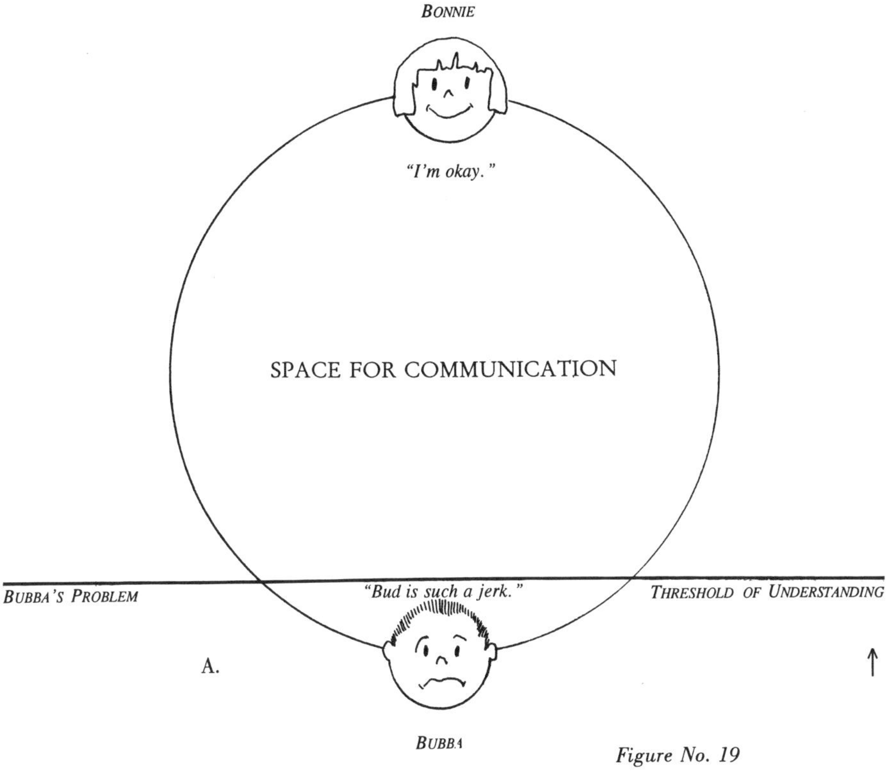

Figure No. 19

a) The Threshold of Understanding is very sensitive to the level of a person's *psychological well-being* (physical, emotional, mental).

b) At the same time, the Threshold of Understanding is very sensitive to the *behavior of the other person.*

c) And, also, the Threshold of Understanding is very sensitive to *what is happening in the environment.*

It is implied within the model that the circles contain three sections. The top section is designated as the space of one person's communication or problem. The bottom section is designated as the space of the other person's communication or problem. The middle section is the space which still remains clear and available for communication.

If one's emotions are significantly out of balance (low inertia or high activity), the Threshold may move way up and all but close the space so that there is little or no Space for Communication. For example, if one's attention is captured by thoughts which are generating anger energy in one's body, the Threshold of Understanding will temporarily close the space to the point that clear communication is significantly impaired. Or if one is not feeling well physically **and** is angry, the line may move way out into the other person's space. As a result, they may continue talking to each other, but there will be little real communication occurring. In fact, at that point they will just be talking "at" each other.

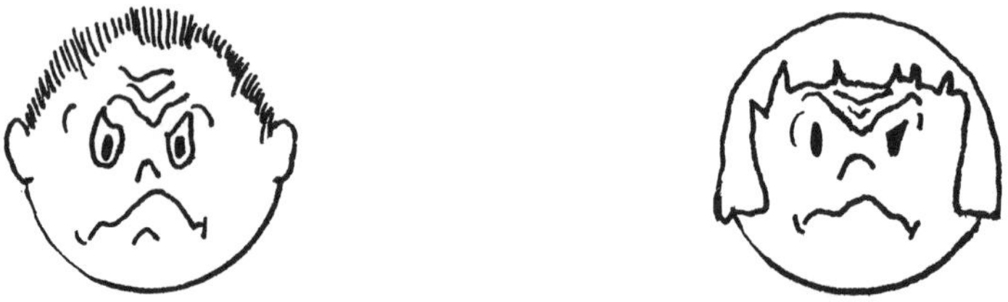
"YOU SHOULD HAVE TOLD ME THAT YOU HAVE INVITED JOE AND JOANNE TO STAY WITH US ALL SUMMER."
"I SHOULD HAVE KNOWN YOU WOULD BE VERY NEGATIVE ABOUT IT. WHY CAN'T YOU EVER JUST BE HAPPY FOR ME?"

Studying the scenarios depicted by Circles A through E, we see that in **Circle A** Bubba and Bonnie have come together and have begun a relational transaction. Some of Bubba's attention is captured by thoughts and emotions at the level of *covert resentment* which are left over from an argument he had with his boss, Bud, just before he left the office for this meeting. Since he did not clear himself from that previous transaction, his "stuff" about his boss is at a slow boil inside him. It says, "Bud is such a jerk."

Bonnie is "okay." Her overall sense of well-being is an indication that she is in emotional balance and that her physical body is comfortable. Her thoughts are not captured by other unresolved issues in her life. She is fully available for her meeting with Bubba. She may have noticed that Bubba is somewhat distracted when she first sat down, but that, too, is "okay" with her.

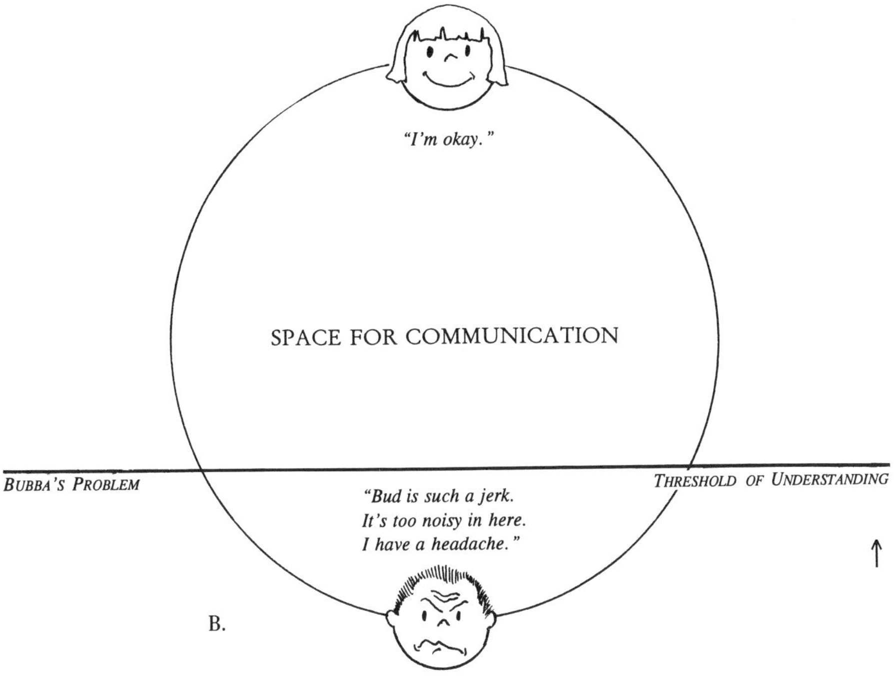
"I'm okay."
SPACE FOR COMMUNICATION
Bubba's Problem
Threshold of Understanding
"Bud is such a jerk.
It's too noisy in here.
I have a headache."
B.

Figure No. 20

In **Circle B** we can see that Bubba now has two other problems: the noise level in the restaurant where they have met and a headache which has resulted from the earlier upset and the noise in the restaurant. With his headache causing him distress, he now projects the increased anger energy in his body onto the noise. His mind races with angry thoughts about both the noise and his boss. With his Threshold of Understanding having moved way out into the Space for Communication, Bubba obviously has problems which are interfering with his ability to relate to Bonnie. But, attempting to act as though he is "fine," he says nothing about his headache, his argument with his boss, or the noise in the restaurant to Bonnie, even though he respects her to the point of wanting to start up a business with her soon. By now, Bonnie is sure to have noticed that Bubba is not his usual gracious and centered self. But she is still primarily just happy to see him.

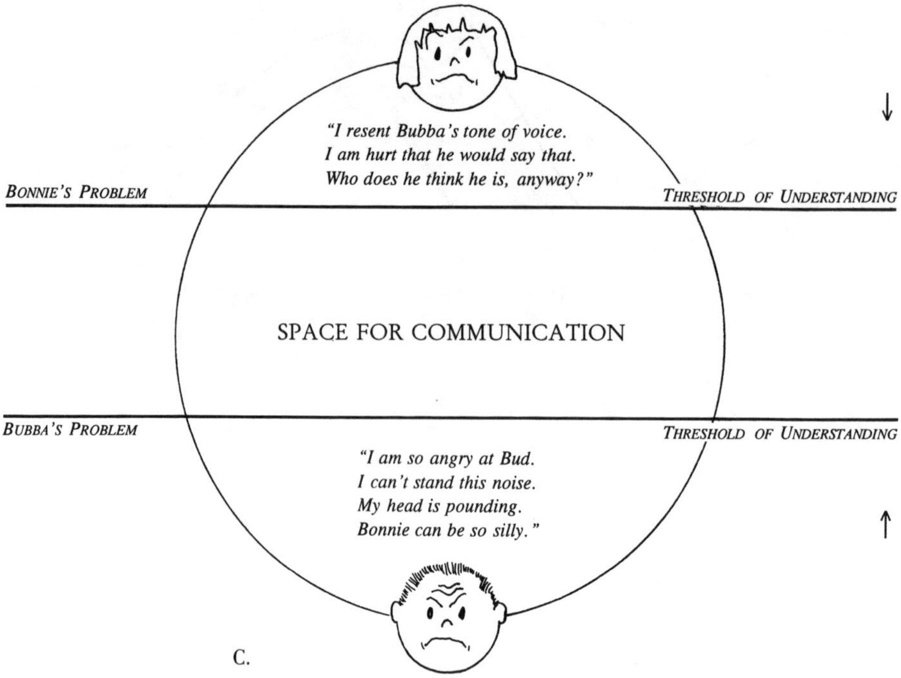
"I resent Bubba's tone of voice.
I am hurt that he would say that.
Who does he think he is, anyway?"
Bonnie's Problem
Threshold of Understanding
SPACE FOR COMMUNICATION
Bubba's Problem
Threshold of Understanding
"I am so angry at Bud.
I can't stand this noise.
My head is pounding.
Bonnie can be so silly."
C.

Figure No. 21

In **Circle C** we can see that Bubba's state of upset has caused him to begin to judge Bonnie harshly. As she begins to talk about her hopes and dreams and plans for their business, as she laughs and jokes with the waiter, and as she pokes fun at Bubba to try to evoke his good humor, he sits across from her being rather unresponsive. Then he says, "You'd better get your head out of the clouds. This is a serious business. Don't you think you are being a bit naïve about all this?" Uh oh! Shocked, Bonnie plunges into emotional pain, since her feelings are hurt by what Bubba has said. Her reactivity also includes covert resentment due to the tone of voice in which he said it. Her Threshold of Understanding moves out as soon as she begins to judge him—and now she has a problem which consumes some of the Space for Communication.

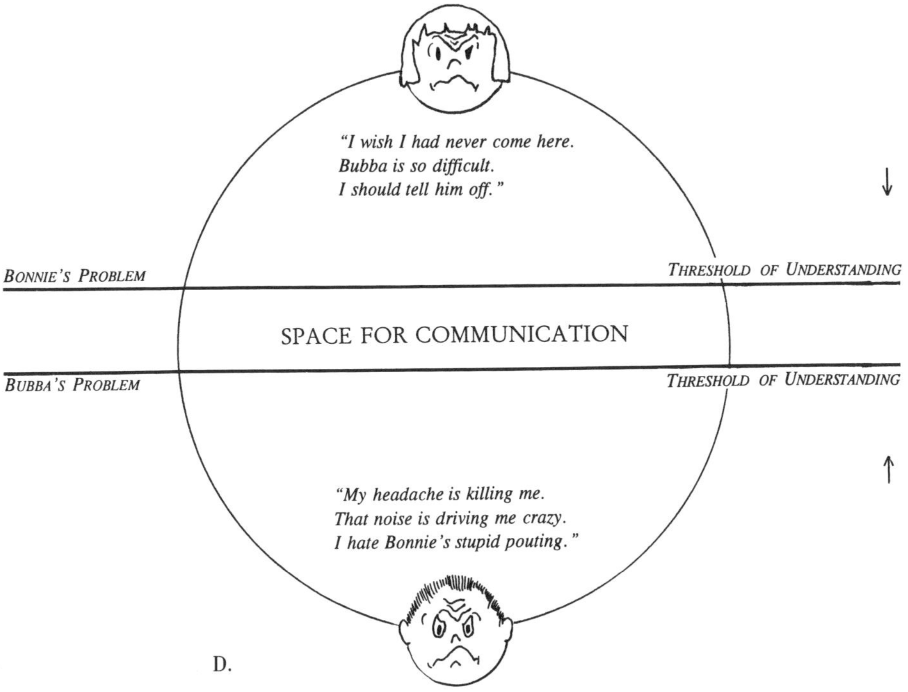
"I wish I had never come here.
Bubba is so difficult.
I should tell him off."
BONNIE'S PROBLEM
THRESHOLD OF UNDERSTANDING
SPACE FOR COMMUNICATION
BUBBA'S PROBLEM
THRESHOLD OF UNDERSTANDING
"My headache is killing me.
That noise is driving me crazy.
I hate Bonnie's stupid pouting."
D.

Figure No. 22

In **Circle** D we can see that the relational transaction between Bubba and Bonnie begins to deteriorate rapidly into personalized grievances against each other, and nearly all of the Space for Communication becomes used up by their individual problems. Bubba's resentment toward Bud, his headache, and his discomfort with the noise level are still problems. And now Bonnie's responses to his remarks and behavior are triggering even more judgments. His continued upset and negative attitudes are making Bonnie angrier and more judgmental.

In **Circle E** we can see that the escalation of each of their upsets has moved their Thresholds of Understanding to within inches of each other, as there is nearly no understanding at all between them. The attention and energy of both Bubba and Bonnie have become captured by their own negative thoughts and negative emotions. Both Bubba and Bonnie have become so stuck in their own judgments of each other that they both now only want to escape the uncomfortable situation and the upsetting interaction as quickly as possible. The *fight or flight response* is fully triggered and they are both now poised to flee. We can

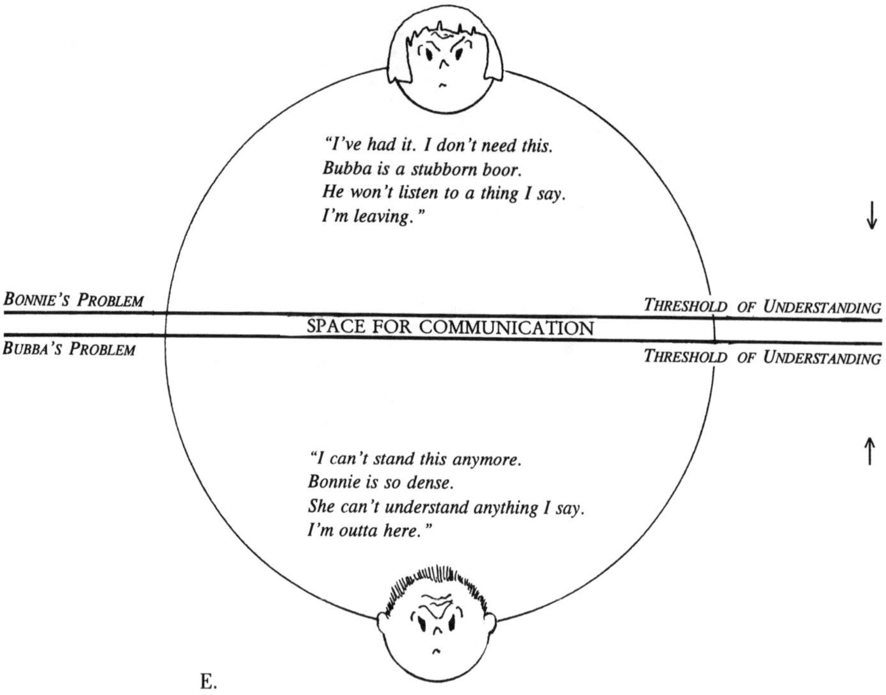

Figure No. 23

imagine that once they call off their meeting and say their stiff goodbyes, they will both still feel upset. And they will each carry the residual effects of their upset into the next relational transactions that they individually participate in that day. How awful!

EMPTY SPACES AND FULL EXPRESSIONS

Now let's go through it all over again and see how they might have handled the transaction in a way that true communication could occur.

In Circle A-2 we again have Bubba and Bonnie meeting each other at the restaurant. Bubba has some covert resentment towards his boss, Bud; Bonnie is "okay;" and most of the Space for Communication is available to them for their discussion of their mutually exciting business venture.

In Circle B-2, we see that Bubba's Threshold of Understanding has moved out some more because the noise in the restaurant is too loud, and because he now has a headache. Bonnie is happy to see Bubba, and her attention and energy are fully available for their discussion.

"I'm okay."
"Bud is such a jerk."
A-2

Figure No. 24

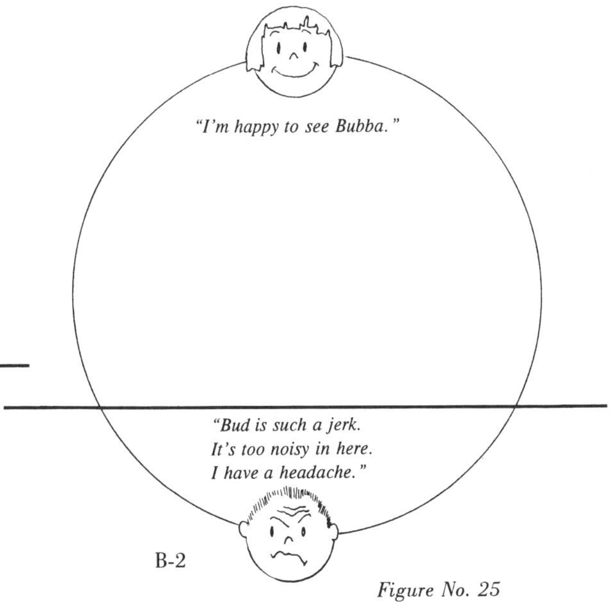
"I'm happy to see Bubba."
"Bud is such a jerk.
It's too noisy in here.
I have a headache."
B-2

Figure No. 25

In Circle C-2, where previously their individual problems began to seriously usurp the Space for Communication, we now see that something different has occurred which has kept Bonnie free and which has freed up some of the Space for Communication which Bubba's problem had before impinged upon. What has happened? Bubba has told Bonnie that he has a headache, that the noise in the restaurant is really disturbing to him, and that he had an argument with his boss earlier which he is still angry about. Bonnie listened innocently and responded compassionately to his messages; she then suggested that they leave and go to another restaurant just down the block where there is much less noise.

In Circle D-2, we see a dramatic difference in the amount of Space for Communication which is now available to Bubba and Bonnie compared to this point in their transaction before. Bubba's anger at his boss has dissipated as a result of communicating his experience of it to Bonnie and having her receive his communication without judgment. Surprisingly, Bubba's headache has even been relieved to the degree that it is no longer preoccupying his attention and draining his energy. The Space for Communication is now fully open between them, and they are now really able to have their intended meeting.

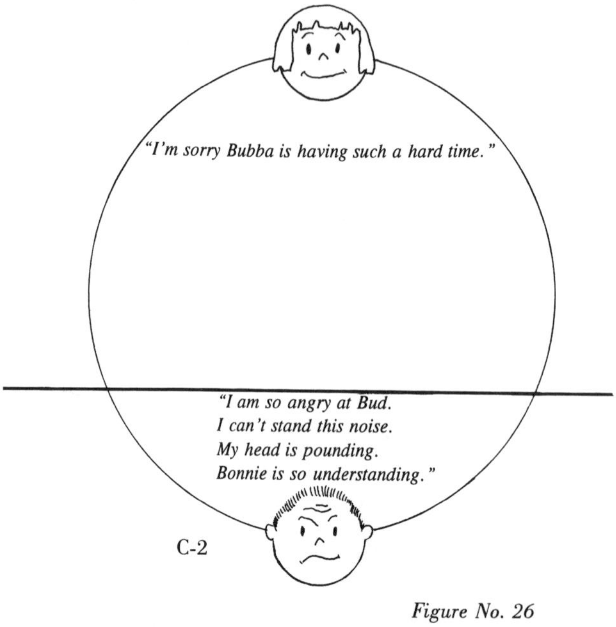

"I'm sorry Bubba is having such a hard time."
"I am so angry at Bud.
I can't stand this noise.
My head is pounding.
Bonnie is so understanding."
C-2

Figure No. 26

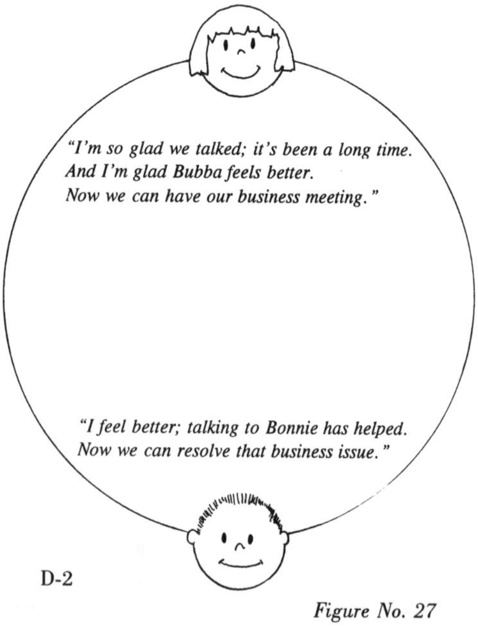

"I'm so glad we talked; it's been a long time.
And I'm glad Bubba feels better.
Now we can have our business meeting."
"I feel better; talking to Bonnie has helped.
Now we can resolve that business issue."
D-2

Figure No. 27

In Circle E-2, we notice that they have had their meeting, that they both feel very good about it, and that they both look forward to the next scheduled meeting to discuss their joint venture. How intelligent and satisfying!

The point is that we need to be consciously aware of the amount of Space for Communication which is available to us in relational transactions. We may or the other person may bring problems from other relational transactions to our present transaction which will fill some of the space and impede our ability to communicate with each other. With an intention to clear the space, we can identify and

"I feel so good about our meeting!
I look forward to the next one."
"That was a great meeting!
I'm really glad about our new partnership."

E-2 *Figure No. 28*

communicate our problems and support the other person to identify and communicate theirs in order to free up some of the space that has been swallowed up by those problems. And, even if the problems persist, we can both make allowances for them in our awareness and accommodate them in understanding to the point that our transaction will not be fouled by them. We do not need to be completely clear all the time in order to have a meaningful and productive relational transaction with another. But we do need to be aware of what is going on in our bodies, in our minds, in our emotions, and in our environment in order to discern how much Space for Communication is really available. We also need to realize that the person with whom we are attempting to communicate is likewise sensitive and vulnerable to all these relational influences. With this realization, our expectations of everyone else become much more realistic and our attitudes become, naturally, more compassionate.

Once we have internalized this model, it is amazing to watch people relating to each other through its eyes. So often we can see that the Space for Communication between people is so diminished that they are barely able to maintain a relational connection. And, in reflection, we will realize that thousands of times we have attempted to relate with another person who was not fully present, who had a problem which kept him or her from being able to be with us fully. And, in reflection, we will realize that thousands of times we have attempted to relate with another person when we were not fully present, when we had a problem which kept us from being able to be with the other person fully. The lack of the other person's attention to what we are saying can cause us real upset. And the lack of our attention to what the other person is saying can cause the other person real upset. That upset over the lack of attention, itself, can further fill the Space for Communication and usurp even more of our attention or the other person's attention. Thus, it becomes obvious that bringing lots of awareness to this whole subject of the Space for Communication is very important.

This model serves to support us in ascertaining *who's got the problem?* It champions our efforts to become more aware of what is really going on in our own experience, to drop denial of our own humanity, and to stop blaming others for all of the relational difficulties which are implicit in our relationships. The more we learn about ourselves (and, so, others) the more we understand the complex of commingled mental, emotional, and physical aspects which each transaction represents. We see that without a high degree of informed awareness, we are destined to fall into confusion again and again about who's got the problem and what to do about the problem.

So, who's got the problem?

It is often a bit trickier than it would seem to clarify just whose "stuff" is in the space. It is usually not difficult to discern that someone has a problem, simply because we can feel the tension in the space between us and the other person. And once we learn to clear the space and become accustomed to how it feels to have a clear space in which to relate, the slightest speck of "stuff" (judgment and withheld communication) will be noticeable and uncomfortable. Remember that to become masterful at discerning who's got the problem, you must be committed to becoming congruent and capable of becoming increasingly self-honest.

OUR "STUFF" (WHICH WE ARE ALSO CALLING A "PROBLEM" IN THIS MODEL) CONSISTS OF OUR UNHEALED EGO'S BAG OF GRIEVANCES BASED ON ITS PERCEPTIONS OF BEING UNFAIRLY TREATED IN THE PAST.

Our true problems with others are matters of principle which evoke a Feeling Function response from our True Nature.

To begin with, whenever we realize that a problem is taking up some of the space between us and someone with whom we are relating, we need to ask ourselves:

1) Do I have a problem? Or am I merely reacting emotionally from my wounded ego's perceptions?

2) If I do have a problem, what is my problem? Is it primarily physical? emotional? mental? Is my physical, emotional, or mental well-being disturbed to a degree that is overriding my genuine Self-expression?

3) Is my problem specifically with this person? Or did I bring some other problem to the interaction which is causing a problem in this transaction?

4) If I do have a problem, in what way is my well-being really being threatened by this person? In what way is my life being interfered with?

5) Is my reactivity merely a result of my expecting the other person to be and behave in ways that I want them to or expect them to?

6) What do I need to do in order to clear the space?

   Do I need to drop all judgments based on my expectations of the other person?

   Do I need to communicate my problem?

—And,

7) Does the other person have a problem? Or is he merely reacting emotionally from his wounded ego's perceptions?

8) If he does have a problem, what is the problem? Is it primarily physical? emotional? mental? Is his well-being disturbed to a degree that is overriding his genuine Self-expression?

9) Is his problem specifically with me? Or did he bring a problem to the interaction which is causing a problem in this transaction?

10) If he does have a problem, in what way is his well-being being threatened by or interfered with due to my actions?

11) Is his reactivity merely a result of him expecting me to behave in ways that he wants me to or expects me to behave?

12) What do we need to do in order to clear the space?

    Do we need to begin again, dropping all judgments based on our expectations of each other? Does he need to communicate his problem?

It is of great importance that we ask ourselves these questions with sincerity and that we answer these questions with a high degree of self-honesty. We must learn to ask and answer without twisting the questions and skewing the answers in such a way as to make ourselves right and the other person wrong. Our rationalizations have never and will never get us anywhere in our search for the truth of ourselves and for methods which produce healthy and enduring relationships.

We need to begin to see more clearly our egoic tendency to attempt to control others and the tremendous unhappiness that causes us and them. We must begin to identify our own expectations, judgments and demands of others whenever they surface—and surface they will, again and again and again. We need to identify and to *own* our expectations, judgments and demands of others. We need to acknowledge that those are *our very own* particular expectations, judgments and demands, and that they have no real legitimacy or value in our relationships. We really must free ourselves and others from the prison cell of these egoic *standards of behavior* which have been randomly manufactured and universally applied by us through the years. In fact, until we learn to discover the truth of ourselves, these highly prejudicial standards of behavior which are our reference points are little more than others' standards which we have internalized through the years.

As we judge others, we judge ourselves. As we become more fully human, we become more and more accepting and less and less prejudicial in our perceptions of ourselves and others. How hopeful!

OUR RATIONALIZATIONS HAVE NEVER AND WILL NEVER GET US ANYWHERE IN OUR SEARCH FOR THE TRUTH OF OURSELVES AND IN OUR SEARCH FOR METHODS WHICH PRODUCE HEALTHY AND ENDURING RELATIONSHIPS.

So, I've got the problem! Now what?

Hands Off. Once we identify the judgments, expectations and demands in the space of our relational transaction to be *our* "stuff," we have the necessary clarity to begin to clear the space in truth. Simply identifying the judgments, expectations, and demands that we are subconsciously and consciously projecting onto the other person changes the whole psychological complexion of our attitudes toward and our responses to that person. By giving up all attempts to control the other person and just entering freely into a relational transaction without the unspoken rigidity imposed by an expectation of how the other person should be, what the other person should say, and what the other person should do, we may have an entirely new experience of that person and come away with an entirely different perception of him than we have held before.

By taking a mental *hands off* approach to others, we actually provide space for them to be who and how they are in our company. We will be far less likely to take offense at their pomposity, their reactivity, their rudeness, their "poor me" attitude, their attempts to control us, or any other behaviors which previously have so easily set us off in a cycle of judgments and attempts to make them be and behave some other way. This *hands off* approach sets others free and it sets us free. We are no longer carrying the subconscious burden of responsibility for how that other person shows up. We are no longer holding ourselves accountable for making things turn out a certain way. We are no longer a psychological time bomb which is sure to go off when someone does something or says something which does not fit snugly into our preconceived notions of how they should be and behave. Instead, we are fully present as simply who we are—in touch with our own inner sense of self and sincerely committed to taking responsibility **only** for our own congruent behavior. What a relief!

"That does not work for me." Once we have identified our egoic reactions and have anchored ourselves in a *hands off* attitude, we are freed up to notice both the ego's reactions as they arise and to feelhear the Feeling Function messages which feelspeak to us as we relate with the other person. We are then able to communicate from that deeper part of ourselves wherein our authentic responses abide. And, if the other person expects or demands something which feels "not in alignment" with what we truly believe or know to be correct, high-minded, intelligent and just, we can respond (rather than react) by saying simply, "That does not work for me." By making that simple statement, we have taken a stand for what feels correct in this case, but without becoming reactive, making the other person wrong, and starting an argument. We can then undertake to explain what would work for us, including compromises that we would be willing to make in order to work it out.

It is very important that we not use this statement to disguise an egoic reaction. When it is used in that way, it merely puts the other person on notice that we are closing ourselves down on the discussion. The statement then becomes a wall between us and the other person, closing him out and demanding that we get our way if the wall is to come down. In that case the statement represents plain old egoic reactivity, making ourselves right and the other person wrong.

"That is not all right with me." Once again, as above—noticing both the ego's reactions as they arise and feelinghearing the Feeling Function messages which feelspeak to us as we relate with the other person—this statement may be used with great sincerity and honesty, emanating from the deeper truth of ourselves, when we are not yet clear as to what would "work" for us, but we can feel our inner response saying "no." By simply saying "*That is not all right with me.*" we communicate the truth without blaming the other person or making him wrong. By way of this simple statement we have continued to participate in the relational transaction, but have identified some point or area that will need to be worked out between us and the other person. If the other person becomes reactive and attempts to change our mind by lobbying for the point in question, arguing with us about the point, and making us wrong, we can simply reiterate our simple statement: "*That is not all right with me.*" We often may need some time to process ourselves to get to the further truth about this particular issue.

"Let me think it over and get back to you." When we are unable to reach a state of clarity in the moment (or during the duration of the conversation), we may simply say, "*Let me think it over and get back to you.*" This buys us much needed time to *live in the question* and to process ourselves about our deep feelings which are saying "*That does not work for me*" or "*That is not all right with me.*" Once again, in truth, we are continuing to communicate without being willing to argue and fight about something that we are not clear about yet. And once again, we are not making the other person wrong for his thoughts and feelings—we are merely expressing that we do not share those views.

While *living in the question* we can just go about our everyday life with awareness that there is something about that issue that is not all right and that somewhere in our inner consciousness the clarity abides. As we contemplate the issue, as we reflect on the discussion, and as we process ourselves by asking ourselves "*What is it that is not all right about that?,*" we will have unexpected moments of insight and direct knowing. We should make notes as these revelations present themselves and then review the notes from time to time. Sometimes it may take days or weeks before we are truly clear about what it was that was eating at us about a given issue. We should not allow others to attempt to influence us. For that reason, we should not discuss the issue with others; instead, we should keep our own counsel and allow the weight of the question to linger within us. We should not rush ourselves or let others rush us to try and get clear. If we **try** to achieve clarity, we will block access to the subtle Self. If we **try** to make clarity happen, we will most likely just *make something up*. If we **try** to get clear, we will be *thinking* about it rather than *feelinglistening* about it. When we **are** clear, we will feel a tremendous relief—and we will have discovered something about ourselves that had not been so clarified and so defined for us before. Such life-changing self-discovery!

A quick reference for clearing the Space of Communication between us and another person would include the following:

1) Identify which of the relational tension in the space is the result of our "stuff"—our egoic expectations, judgments and demands of the other person;

2) Consciously notice our ego's reactivity, but do no allow it to dictate what we say or how we behave;

3) Assume a *hands off* attitude toward the other person. That means that we will not attempt to impose our views upon him or attempt to *control* his reactions or responses. We will not attempt to make him over in our own image;

4) Become attentive to what goes on beneath our surface personality's reactions—at the Feeling Function level—as we participate in the relational transaction. Allow the responses from this deeper personality to determine what we say and how we behave;

5) If the other person suggests something that definitely elicits a "No" from our deeper Self, say simply, "*That does not work for me*" or "*That is not all right with me*;"

6) Continue to communicate openly with the other person and continue to listen *innocently* to his communications. Give him the benefit of the doubt when your ego begins to jump to conclusions and begins generating judgments of him. Allow him to have his experience fully, whatever it is. Notice when you feel that he is being reactive and when he is speaking and behaving from his deeper Self;

7) If you cannot achieve clarity on some issue that is of obvious importance in your relationship and/or the discussion, simply say, "*I'm not really sure how I feel about that. Let me think about it and get back to you.*" Then *live in the question* as long as you need to in order to get clear about that issue before communicating about it;

8) Continue to practice expanding your ability to accept others the way they are without attempting to change them; and

9) Continue to practice accessing, speaking, and behaving congruently —from your deeper Self.

Recreating relationships. Even though our relationships have nearly always been troublesome to us in one way or another, we have become somewhat accustomed to feeling the discomfort implicit in incongruent relating. We have been conditioned since childhood to endure the self-protective undercurrent of unspoken judgments, of withheld personal truths, and of unasked and unanswered questions. We have rarely felt completely at ease in our relationships with others; and when we have experienced such a natural and relaxed state, something has occurred to cause the relationship to go wrong. As we more fully discover and more fully source our deeper Self and as we become congruent expressions of our greaterness, the veil of misunderstanding will begin to lift from our heretofore enigmatic relationships. Having gained understanding about the workings of our lower mind and having transcended our own egoic reactivity, we will become naturally capable of *seeing through* the disguises, the pretenses, and the smoke screens of others. This new faculty of *seeing* will allow us to be naturally compassionate where we may have before been intimidated or contemptuous.

As we become more and more congruent, we will find it more and more difficult to spend time with those people who are still operating solely out of their egoic agendas and prioritizing their lives by way of their purely rational strategies. We will be able to accept and love them more than we were ever able to before, but we will not be able to tolerate significant relating with them simply because our expanded awareness and our fuller expression has become too large for the restrictive parameters of such relationships. We will need to allow some time for these relationships to be re-created as we begin and continue to express ourselves congruently with these significant others. Our more truthful expression will certainly get their attention as the undercurrent of relational tension dissipates and as our *hands off* approach frees both us and them from those hateful judgments, expectations and demands which we have generated so consistently over the years.

WE NEED TO BEGIN TO SEE MORE CLEARLY OUR EGOIC TENDENCY TO ATTEMPT TO CONTROL OTHERS AND THE UNHAPPINESS THAT CAUSES US AND THEM.

There may well be a period of discomfort of a different kind for awhile, until our *new* way of being and behaving becomes obviously a change for the better in most of our *old* relationships.

Completing relationships. As we become more and more congruent, we will find it more and more difficult to continue certain of our relationships—those which have been built on confusion and self-protective lies and which have been maintained solely for reasons having to do with ego gratification or for reasons having to do with uncertainty and self-doubt. These relationships, because they are not an expression of the truth of us, will become so offensive to us that we will need to complete them and let them go. In many cases this completion can be accomplished with emotional courage, self-discipline and gracefulness and in such a way that the other person is not left feeling embittered or abandoned. It will really always depend on the people involved and the circumstances surrounding their relationship. Even if the relationship cannot be completed gracefully and without hard feelings, it is, in most cases, to our highest good to complete such relationships—as always, in truth. It is of great importance that we clean up our lives and make room for relationships which will flourish in the light of our newfound greaterness—relationships which will offer us the space to *BE* and abundant opportunities to grow by leaps and bounds. Our heights still await us!

THAT'S YOUR PROBLEM, BUBBA!

On the receiving end. When we have no problem and the other person obviously has a problem which closes the Space for Communication between us, what do we do? The most important thing we can do is to remain centered and anchored in our own sense of self and follow the above guidelines for relating. The component that is added here is that we are the receiver of another person's judgments, expectations, and demands and his ego's reactivity which is implicit therein. We have grown accustomed to such behavior on the part of others over the years. It is nothing new. What is new now is the way we respond in the relationship.

By just being aware that the other person has a problem and *allowing* him to have his problem will change everything dramatically. Rather than falling into confusion, pain, and fear, or rather than becoming resentful and angry, we will be able to hold our own center, experience our own sense of self, separate our emotional experience from his emotional experience—and allow him to have his problem without getting all upset because he has a problem.

By not jumping in and trying to talk him out of his problem, and by not jumping in to argue with him about his thoughts or feelings, we can carefully listen to what he has to say with an objective and compassionate detachment. Sourcing our deeper Self, we can then respond congruently to whatever issue is being discussed, applying the same principles and practices outlined above for relational transactions.

By standing free from the upsets of others, we liberate ourselves from the insidious round of emotional upsets which have before been so easily triggered in us by the upsets of others.

Allowing others the space to just have their problems works minor miracles in getting to a clear space. The person with the upset will most often clear up quickly just by being able to be upset, by being able to *have his say*, and by being really listened to. We have all been made so wrong for having a problem or an upset, that we approach expressions of upset with a conditioned expectation that we will not be heard or understood. Acknowledging upsets as a normal, natural aspect of being human neutralizes much of the emotional energy bound up in the upset. We all really need to be able to *have our say* and we all really need to be heard. We do not necessarily have to agree with the other person about his thoughts or feelings; we just have to listen to his grievances. How easy!

Now Let Me Get This Straight—Is Conflict Good or Bad?

Relational conflict is a natural and an important aspect of being human. Conflict is very good when both parties to the conflict are well aware that it is natural and important—when the conflict itself is not made wrong by one or both of the parties and when the transaction does not consist of one or both parties simply blaming and castigating the other.

As is so evident in our society today, we have not been well enough educated to enter into conflict with each other for the purpose of clearing the space or resolving all kinds of differences. As a pre-millennial, high-tech, space age species of highly intelligent beings, we still behave like a primitive race in the area of relational conflict and its resolution. In becoming congruent, we become well-equipped to handle any type of conflict and to discover the truth of ourselves in the process.

Breaking The Cycle of Emotional Merging

It is essential to the process of self-discovery and Self-expression that we become highly capable of **separating our emotional experience from the emotional experience of every other human being.** Only by so doing will we be able to stand free as an integritous personality and interact with and support others out of the truth of ourselves. It does another person little or no good for us to collapse with them into the psychological posture of victimization, the mental cycle of worrisome self-doubt or hostile self-righteousness, or the emotional cycle of failure or anger. If we, instead, offer them our innocent and objective listening and then compassionately affirm them as worthy and capable beings who are equal to the circumstance, we provide them with value that far exceeds whatever empty consolation we would have dispensed as we wrung our hands and shook our head right along with them.

We must begin to identify our own expectations, judgments and demands of others whenever they surface—and surface they will, again and again and again.

In reflecting on our relationships, we will notice that we have so often been disappointed or upset because someone we knew reacted emotionally in a way that we did not expect or did not want them to react. We have actually said, "Don't think that," "Don't feel like that," "Don't say that," or "Don't be like that." How interesting! We have actually wanted to have the other person think, feel, speak, and be a certain way that they did not think, feel, speak, or behave. The amount of our attention and energy that has been tied up in concern for, control of, or reactivity to the emotional experiences of others has been an incredible investment of ourselves. We must *reclaim* that attention and energy and invest it in expanding *our own* awareness, in gaining insights about *our own* conditioned reactions, and in identifying *our own* very personal emotional responses. Our attitude must become one of self-acceptance and acceptance of others. Our attitude must originate in the bedrock principle of equality, by which we can, then, successfully live and relate with others. Its unspoken declaration of emancipation might be something like this:

> I am going to relate to you as an equal whether you are relating to me as an equal or not. And I am going to honor myself and honor you by that. You are a human being and I am a human being and you are having your experience and I am having my experience—and that is freedom.
>
> I am no longer going to get upset because you are upset; and if you get

> upset because I am upset, then that is your problem. I am sincerely open to talking to you about it and having us talk about it to clear the space. In fact, that is what I want. But I am no longer going to get sad because you are sad, and I am no longer going to get angry because you are angry. I am not going to have your emotional experience. I am going to have my own emotional experience over here—and, believe me, that is plenty for me.

We must become less threatened, less frightened and less influenced by the emotional experiences of others. The central focus of our awareness must be on our own inner experience. The central focus of our awareness must be utilized to discover how **I** am feeling, what **I** am thinking, what **I** choose to say or do. With our central focus being assigned to our own self-discovery and Self-expression, we will have plenty of awareness left over to attend to the communications of others and to be sensitive and responsive to others from the center or truth of ourselves. Without that central focus assigned to such specific and meaningful work, we lose our center or sense of self and become easily sucked into emotional merging patterns of experience and behavior.

Emotional merging is an awfulawful, horriblehorrible, viciousvicious form of relating which just keeps going on and on and on in the relationships of our society.

"I am upset because you are upset;" and
"You are upset because I am upset," and
"I am upset because you are upset that I am upset."

It is an insidious cycle that occurs millions of times every day.

IF I ALLOW YOU TO HAVE YOUR EMOTIONAL EXPERIENCE, AND YOU ALLOW ME TO HAVE MY EMOTIONAL EXPERIENCE, WE ARE BOTH FREE!

The implicit point of this model is that we MUST begin to separate our emotional experience from the emotional experience of others. It is the only way that we will ever be able to be free, and it is the only way that we will ever be able to have healthy, fully functional relationships.

One may initially misunderstand and feel that separating our emotional experience from the experience of others is pure selfishness. In fact, one of the primary reasons that we have allowed ourselves to merge with the emotional experiences of others is that we thought that by so doing we were demonstrating that we are decent, compassionate, understanding, loving and caring human beings. But when we see how emotional merging has drained us energetically, has blurred the lines of our own identification, and has blocked our awareness of our own thoughts and feelings, we realize that it is a trap into which we have fallen, and that it serves no real good. Rather than standing as an objective and sensitive other who can hold the highest thought for the person who is experiencing distress, we have instead become an amorphous blob of sympathetic same-saying which only compounds the already negative thought and behavior patterns of our friend, relative, acquaintance, or lover. Reclaiming our own sense of self and offering that to the relationship is the only way we will ever be able to discover and express the deeper Truth of ourselves. It is the only way we will ever achieve the next level of consciousness—from which we will be able to freely love and truly serve others at higher and deeper levels of compassion and understanding.

We must stop thinking and behaving within the same old conditioned patterns of reactivity, defending ourselves and blaming others in response to the same old triggers from the conditioned patterns of others. We must remember that the ego has a very limited repertoire of reactive thought patterns, speech patterns, and behavior patterns. It just does the same thing over and over again. We are and our world is very tired of the ego's less-than-intelligent and less-than-inspired patterns. We are ready to move beyond them now. When we leap beyond our littleness, when we become more than we have been yet, when we have a clearer idea of who we are and what we stand for in this world, we achieve a sense of personal freedom that is truly awe-inspiring.

ME, TOO!

I may have been one of the best examples of someone whose emotional experience was dramatically influenced by the emotional experience of others. I can recall that when I was involved in a mutually-exclusive loving relationship, I was extremely vulnerable to the emotional cycles of my lover. When he got angry, I got angry. When he was sad, my heart would break. When he felt wonderful, I felt wonderful. And on and on. Without informed awareness of what was constantly occurring to me, I just knew that it was "good" to keep him feeling "wonderful" so I, too, could too enjoy that "wonderful" feeling. I was not at all adept at transmuting his energy, or of offering the kind of sensitive, compassionate, and innocent listening which would have served to help him clear his physical, emotional, and mental experience. In fact, I most often did all of the wrong things in order to get through the uncomfortable periods as I waited expectantly for his mood to change. And, although I, of course, wanted him to feel good for himself, I, obviously, had a great personal investment in his state-of-being for purely selfish reasons, too. I realized later that I was living the emotional life of two people at once: my lover's and my own. What a burden!

In my relationship with my oldest daughter, we both were victimized by the influence we had on each other emotionally. She had a very difficult time learning to separate her emotional experience from my emotional experience. And because of the effect I had on her emotionally, her emotional experience would then have a strong effect on me. It would always happen like this: I would get upset and Michelle would plunge into failure. Once she was thus defeated, I would try to make her feel better. When she would stay stuck in failure, unable to return to balance, I would feel sad. My feeling sad would cause her to feel more failure. What a trip! And, even after I had set myself free, she still struggled with the conditioned tendency to merge emotionally with my upsets, feel responsible and terrible about it, and fall into the lower inertia emotions. The day she was able to maintain her emotional integrity when I was angry was a big day for both of us.

The breakthrough occurred early one morning when Michelle, on her way to work, stopped by my place in Miami to get my okay on an ad I had asked her to create for me. The deadline for submitting the ad was that day. She had put it off until the last minute and had stayed up most of the night working on it. I sat at my desk carefully scrutinizing the ad as Michelle stood next to me. I was well aware of her need to get out of there and get on the road; and I could feel the edge of her sense of urgency. I was well-rested physically, well-balanced emotionally, and clear mentally—my attention and energy were fully available for our relational transaction. Michelle was tired from staying up and working most of the night, she was precariously in emotional balance, and she was mentally concerned about getting to work on time. And, then, I saw a significant error in the ad. The date was wrong. Keenly aware that today was the last day the ad could be submitted, keenly aware that Michelle had to leave for work right away, and keenly aware that only she could make the correction, I became "downset" and "upset." My emotional energy changed from balance to frustration—a combination of "downsetting" disappointment (sad/grieving: "I didn't want it to be like this.") and "upsetting" hostility (overt resentment: "I resent having this problem thrust upon me."). I spoke about the dilemma that I now faced. I said something like "I don't know what to do. The date is wrong. Remember? I called and told you that I had changed the date." As soon as I began to speak, Michelle began to problem-solve the situation. She immediately said that she would call her office and let them know that she would be late. She said she had brought her art materials in the car, "just in case." She said that she would take the ad over to the clubhouse and work on it since I had a private client scheduled to arrive in just a few minutes. She said she would just open the door and leave the corrected ad on the dining room table as soon as she had it ready. I said, "Thank you, I appreciate this so much." She left; I continued getting ready for my day. I was in shock. Michelle hadn't plunged into failure. In fact, she had remained completely separate from my emotional experience, even though she was tired and hurried. What a miracle! She told me later that she felt like she floated and soared down Highway 1 on her way to work that morning. She said she had never felt so free. She said that she finally understood, by experience, what I had been teaching in *A Course In Congruence*.

We really must free ourselves and others from the prison cell of egoic standards of behavior which we have randomly manufactured and universally applied through the years.

There Is Another More Appropriate Response in This Case

One of the most dramatic examples of the transformative power inherent in the practice of clearing the space and continuing to communicate is what I call the mother-in-law story. This story was told during the fourth meeting of the first ten-week *A Course In Congruence* seminar. I will call the wife in this story Sybil, the husband, Sam, and the mother-in-law, Sophia.

Sybil and Sam were a couple who were in their early forties who had been married only three years. It was the first marriage for Sam and the second marriage for Sybil. They were very much in love and had a happy marriage, except for one thing: Sam's mother, Sophia. Because Sam had lived with his mother all of his adult life until he married Sybil, his mother was quite attached to him, quite dependent on him, and quite demanding of him whenever they were together. And although they now lived miles apart—Sophia in New Jersey and they in South Florida—she was a very real part of their lives and often a source of upset in their marriage. In fact, because they had had several highly emotional upsets as a result of Sophia's demands, they both feared anything that suggested another one.

We will take up Sybil and Sam's story on the night of their third anniversary with them driving in the car to a beautiful restaurant for what they intended to be a romantic dinner. After dinner they planned to attend a Broadway play that was appearing in Miami. And, after the play, they planned to meet their best friends at their favorite nightclub to share a special bottle of champagne. Sam had sent Sybil flowers that day, and Sybil had written Sam a love letter. They had also purchased special gifts for each other.

As they drove along Sam said, "There is something that I need to tell you. I hope you won't get upset. My mother called today and told me that she is arriving tomorrow to spend a month with us." Sybil froze. Sam's ensuing silence became weighted with dread. Sybil could feel herself plunging into confusion, pain, fear, and sad/grieving and, simultaneously, becoming incensed. Her disappointment and anger practically took her breath away. She felt like she might burst because of all the emotional energy and the mind activity which had been triggered in her. At the same time, she knew that her previous behaviors resulting from her mother-in-law "stuff" had caused Sam to close down completely. She was well aware that their anniversary celebration was dangerously teetering on the brink of destruction.

Since her mother-in-law problem had been the motivator for her registering for *A Course In Congruence*, Sybil began to try to remember what she had been studying. Aware that her emotions were fluctuating dramatically and that her mind was jumping from one thought to another, she first began to say to herself: "*There is another more appropriate response in this case*." To Sam she said, "Sam, I don't want us to get upset about this. I want us to have our beautiful evening and I want us to work it out about your mother's visit." The energy in the car changed immediately. Sam seemed to draw a silent sigh of relief from somewhere deep down inside himself. Sybil remembered also to *continue to communicate*. She said, "I am upset that your mother just made her own plans and called up and announced them to you. I don't understand why she wouldn't ask us if it would be convenient for us if she comes to stay for a month." As a result of speaking in this way, Sybil noticed that her emotional downset and upset began to dissipate. She also noticed that her mind stopped jumping from one thought to the other and began to settle down. She was still affected, but she was no longer totally at the effect of her emotions and her racing mind.

Then Sam began to talk, too. Instead of feeling as though he had to defend his mother, as he had done before, he told Sybil that he, too, was upset about Sophia's actions and that he knew he needed to speak with her about it when she got here. He also stated that he did not want to have to live the rest of their married life feeling caught between his mother and Sybil—and that he was now ready for them all to solve the problem to everyone's satisfaction. He said that he was so grateful that Sybil had not gone into an overwhelming upset and that they could still have their special evening together.

They continued their ride to the restaurant, whereas before they might have become so upset that they would have turned around and gone back home. They had a loving and romantic dinner, whereas before (if they had made it to the restaurant) they most probably would have sat at the table together in stony silence. They continued on to the theater and really enjoyed the play, whereas before (if they had made it to the theater) they most probably would have been too consumed by their upsets to be available for the richness of the production. They, then, met their friends and drank a champagne toast in honor of not only their anniversary, but also in honor of their remarkable new beginning. What a difference!

Thee and The Pea

In the fairy tale *The Princess and The Pea* we are amused and entertained by the test of authenticity which the princess is subjected to and which she passes: a test of her sensitivity. Without her knowing it, one small raw pea is placed under the bottom mattress of a pile of twelve mattresses on which she then sleeps. Her normally peaceful slumber is interfered with by the physical discomfort she experiences as a direct result of the presence of that tiny pea. And because she suffers such physical distress, those who tested her are convinced that she is the "real thing." The test for each of us is that same test:

- Are we sensitive enough to feel that pea of "truth" which lays hidden beneath the deep, dense layers of psychological "stuff" which we have accumulated through the years?

- Are we sensitive enough to feel the pea of "Yes" and "No" which is the silent inner guidance system which speaks to us all day long from our essential nature?

- Are we sensitive enough to feel the pea of our greater Self as it stands free of all of the influences of our ego's agendas, free all of the influences of our damaged ego's compulsions, and free of all of the influences of our ego mind's distortions?

- Are we sensitive enough to feel the pea of clarity and simplicity beneath the layers of confusion, complexity and complication by which our rational minds, our ordinary lives, and our struggling world have become overburdened?

- Are we sensitive enough to feel the pea of peaceful and innocent authenticity abiding beneath the layers of volatile and cynical role playing which has become our conditioned response to the unstable and skeptical masquerading of our contemporaries?

- Are we sensitive enough to feel the natural joy of our very existence which lies buried beneath the aggrieved depression which has become the standard psychological undercurrent of our species?

- Are we sensitive enough to feel the well of hopefulness that abides at the center of our being?

- Are we sensitive enough to feel the inherent strength and natural courage of our own hearts, which is our true nature?

- Are we sensitive enough to feel our heart-melting love for life, for each other, and for God which smiles within us?

The pea of *truthful discernment* which lies beneath the dense layers of our unresolved past experiences within our bulging psychological structures constitutes the source of our own on-going test. I identify this pea as the Feeling Function—using Carl Jung's term. I honor most highly the Feeling Function in all of us, for I have realized that therein resides our own essential truth—a clear truth so all-important to our unfoldment that our very lives depend on our accessing it continuously throughout our days.

Carl Jung's formulations on personality types include the four functions of Feeling, Intuition, Thinking and Sensation. These four functions work together to support our consistent participation with our divine unfoldment—and of these four functions, the Feeling Function is most critical, for on it the others depend.

The Feeling Function is the relational function; it is the source within ourselves that says "Yes" and "No" *in truth* as we relate to other people and with our world. It lets us know what is *correct* for us—who and what and where is *correct* for us in order to match us with our present level of growth and to prepare us for what is next. Unlike the ego, the Feeling Function (our true Self) is designed to always move us beyond our present level of consciousness and to keep us moving in the on-going process of transformation.

We can actually FEEL the signals from the Feeling Function in our bodies.

It FEELS like... "Yes" and "No."

It FEELS like... "There is something very wrong with this;" and
"This is pure, true, and exactly *correct* for me;" and
"There is something a bit off about this."

The Feeling Function is energetic, but in a different way than the emotional energies. Just as the mind and the body generate emotional energies, the Feeling Function does generate emotional energies, but because it lies deeper within us than our emotions, it demands more than a mere observing of its signals. Its signals need to be *listened for* and *listened to* with carefulness and quietude so that we may get its clear messages.

Whereas the ego must be undermined in its fearful and selfish attempts to get what it wants, the Feeling Function must be developed and strengthened and placed in the role of leadership in our lives. It is by way of moments of direct knowing and by constant internal signals via the Feeling Function that our higher Self leads us along our straight and narrow path. If we override these subtle internal signals, respond from our surface personality's (ego) reactivity or agenda, and go "off course," we feel the alarms and buzzers going off inside ourselves. If we are not responsive to these stronger signals, our higher Self is compelled to get our attention by way of someone or something or some circumstance in our manifest world. The more responsive we become to the silent signals of the Feeling Function, the fewer painful life crises we will experience and the more naturally flowing our process becomes. In fact, the more responsive we become to the silent signals, the more surrendered we have obviously become to the transformational process.

As we become more fully human, we become more and more accepting and less and less prejudicial in our perceptions of ourselves and others. How hopeful!

Deep Listening

With the awareness that there lies within us a "bindu" or speck of Ultimate Intelligence or Truth which knows the difference between *right* and *wrong*, we simply need to learn to listen for its signals. But this deep listening includes a dimension of *feeling* which results in a feelingseeing, feelinghearing, feelingthinking, feelingknowing, etc. This deep listening actually recaptures our vast higher Mind and reconnects it to our everyday experiences as an integral and primary component of every relational transaction. Our higher Self is no longer only an inspiring concept, it is a very real and very practical part of our everyday human lives.

With the awareness that we contain Ultimate Wisdom within our very Self, we can and must begin to sort out our reactions and responses thus:

a) Which of these strong emotions are being generated by my ego's experience of being somehow threatened?

b) Which of these strong emotions are being generated by my Feeling Function, which is obviously saying "No!" based on a basic principle which defines my own deeper Truth?

Let us apply the principle of the silent signals of the higher Self to the relational transaction between Bubba and Bonnie earlier in this chapter. There are a few junctures at which its signals could have caused Bubba and Bonnie to pause and look deeper than their surface emotions in order to more authentically relate with each other.

1) When Bubba's boss, Bud, said or did something which set Bubba into an emotional spin, Bubba most definitely could have begun to source his Feeling Function in order to offset the force of emotionality which overtook him. And even though he may not have gotten enough clarity to release himself completely from the emotional upset before meeting with Bonnie, at least he would have had the assurance of his Witness Self and his own ability to reference his inner response to the matter; and, as a result, he would not have been so blown away by his own anger and his harsh judgments of Bud.

2) When Bubba spoke in such a rude and insensitive manner to Bonnie, Bonnie could have a) felt the sting of the judgment in her ego; and b) remained open to Bubba as she listened to her own Feeling Function. Because of her very respectful relationship with Bubba, her Feeling Function may have only signalled a brief "That's not it." And along with that signal it may naturally have embraced his pain with unperturbed compassion. And, even if the sting of his remarks closed her down somewhat, the presence of her own Ob-

server Self and her Self-referencing would be a solid foundation on which she could stand rather than being dashed about by her own emotional experience.

3) When Bubba realized how vulnerable he was emotionally and how loud the noise was in the restaurant where he and Bonnie had met, he could have listened for those inner signals. Most probably he would have quickly experienced a feelingknowing that he needed to remove himself from what was a perfect setup for an aggravated emotional outburst. With just a little Self-referencing, he would feelknow that he was unable to withstand the erratic energy of his environment, struggle with his own emotional volatility, and give Bonnie the attention she deserved. In fact, if he got to the point of feelingknowing that he was not going to be able to attend to the meeting, he actually might have called off the meeting and rescheduled it for another day. This would have been an intelligent and responsible choice, if he were genuinely not able to attend to the business they had planned to address that day.

In the above discussion, it has become apparent that the presence of the Witness Self (or Observer Self or Impersonal Self) is the all-important component which releases us from the stranglehold of the ego's self-centered thoughtforms and emotional reactivity. This larger, impersonal, and, thus, neutral perspective frees us to view the relational transaction and our role in it in a dispassionate (and, thus, compassionate) manner. This dispassionate view allows us to see when we may have spoken or acted *primarily* from or *only* from the surface emotional experience of the ego—when we might, instead, have paused a moment to listen deeply to our inner Self.

The pea which generates discomfort from deep within us is a tremendous service to us in discovering the truth of ourselves. It will not allow us to sleep like a baby until the presence of its silent signal has been sensitively discovered beneath the thick mattresses of conditioned denial. On the subject of inner sensitivity there are some things which need to be said in the context of this discussion. The more mindbound we become, the more insensitive we become to the inner silent voice or signals of the deeper personality. Seeing how we, as a species, have become overly reasonable, rational, mental, and mindbound, it is easy to see **that** we have and **how** we have lost our natural sensitivity to our own inner dimensions—dimensions wherein abide the power, wisdom and love of our own essential God-given greatness. What used to be primitive (primary) and natural (of our nature) has now become an elusive, misunderstood, and *foreign* aspect of our being—an aspect which not only is little utilized, but often doubted, derided and, even denied significance by the sophisticated "talking heads" of our intellectual and grossly egoic era. "I think" has become the watchword of our times.

So how do we become masterful as this subtle art of deep listening? And how do we become adept at distinguishing between our ego's emotional reactivity and the emotional responses generated by our deeper personality?

First, we must **real**ize, or remember, or "make real," that subtle and silent language (what Fromm named the Forgotten Language) by the regular practice of becoming very quiet. It is really only in our personal quietude that we can become highly relational with the subtle dimension of ourselves to which we have become insensitive. We must undergo a process of *reconditioning* in which our focus is shifted from the outer world of gross speaking, gross listening, gross feeling, and gross movement, to the inner world of subtle speaking, subtle listening, subtle feeling, and subtle movement.

Practice quietness. You can do this by sitting in the silence alone with your eyes closed for thirty minutes every day, consciously practicing listening to the silence. Unless you have a completely silent place in which to do this practice, it is best to use earplugs to close out most of the noise of the outer world. Unless you have a very dark space, it is best to cover your eyes with a blindfold to close out the visual stimuli of the outer world.

Just sit quietly and bring your attention to your quietness. Become more and more quiet as the minutes go by. Allow your breath to breathe you freely and relax. Listen to your breath as it breathes in and out as a way to maintain a state of mental quietude. Do not expect any remarkable or breathtaking experiences. That is not what the practice is all about. In simple fact, the practice is just to quiet you, to recondition you to quietness, to allow you to become intimately relational with your inner sense of Self, to allow your subtle dimension to reappear in your inner experience naturally as you, over time, become more and more quiet.

Second, you must return to that *attitude of quietude* again and again throughout your day while you operate amidst the gross elements of the ordinary world. You can return to that attitude simply by remembering your simple practice of becoming quiet and of listening to the silence. You can affirm "yes" and "quiet" many times throughout the day to include the reconditioning process in your conscious awareness.

As we judge others, we judge ourselves.

Third, you must learn to listen to and translate the messages of your deeper personality which dwells, as real silence, beyond the levels of ordinary quietude. Quietude is the medium in which the silent messages appear and through which the silent messages pass to our conscious mind for moments of direct knowing or for brilliant translation. Its subtle negative *responses* to the ordinary elements of relational transactions will feel like a pea under the pile of mattresses. You will be able to override its signals, if you choose, but you will feel the "Something is wrong here" message as a nagging discomfort that will not let you slumber peacefully. Its subtle danger signals will feel more like a burr under a saddle; that is, you will not be able to override them without high levels of psychological numbness because they will be causing you so much psychological pain.

a) If you feel the subtle message "There is something very wrong with this," you may need to consciously process the relational transaction you are involved in over a period of days or weeks until you can attain a level of real clarity about what is wrong and what action you must take in order to act in accordance with the dictates of your own inner Self.

   Keep a notepad with you wherever you go. Make notes throughout the day whenever you have a clear thought or momentary insight into the relationship or relational transaction that you are attempting to clarify. As you live in the question "What is wrong with this?"—throughout your days and nights—you will become more and more objective about the whole thing and gain clear insights as to what has been happening that you have not been able to see before. (It will become apparent that your subconscious is also processing the transaction—sorting and re-sorting all of the information it has in order to find resolution.) Your insights will often be the result of the subconscious work that is constantly going on.

b) If you feel what seems to be a heart-leaping Inner message that says "Yes! This is it! This is *exactly* what I am to do now!," do not lose all sense of reason, immediately begin to turn your life upside down or straightaway jump the tracks of your life onto the tracks of what now seems to be *what you have been waiting for all of your life*. Stay on the tracks of your present life and continue to live within the parameters of your present life for some *reasonable* period of time, as you listen carefully for the inner messages and watch for the outer signs which will ultimately assure you that this is not a case of your ego "making something up." If this is truly what you have been waiting for, it will not go away. It will not lose energy when your ego mind gets a better idea. It will stay firmly planted in your space, it will call to you, and it will finally become so irresistible that you will gracefully complete your present life and begin anew—living in the new form your life is obviously to take. If you attempt to *make it happen*, the results will be sure to be less than remarkable—and surely less than you expected.

Fourth, you must learn to qualify some of your immediate emotional responses as "not the full truth," always remembering that there is more depth to you and more depth to your responses than the surface level egoic reactions which are easily triggered until your subconscious is cleared of its unresolved issues from the past. As you begin to discover and express the truth that lies deeper than your surface emotions, you will begin to heal your damaged ego and empty the reservoir of your subconscious of its distorted views of yourself and others. To serve that purpose, you must remember to caution yourself with "There is another way to look at this" and "There is another more appropriate response in this case," when your emotions spontaneously erupt into the activity scale or plunge into the inertia scale. The more authentic you become, the more conscious you become of your higher Self's responses in your ordinary experience of life.

Fifth, you must learn to live consciously with your Observer Self present. That Impersonal Self can be easily elicited by viewing the situation from the disinterested or neutral third-party position. Think about it, speak about it, and write it down as though you were reporting a story that you had seen happen to other people (instead of you and your mother or friend or lover. The Observer Self's perceptions add an intelligent and objective perspective to your very personal relational transactions—a viewpoint which allows you to see more clearly the bigger picture and which causes you to remember that your tiny ego with its self-serving agendas does not have the last word in such important and delicate matters.

Sixth, you must learn to be truly self-honest—neither too harsh and judgmental of yourself, nor too self-indulgent and easy on yourself. Becoming impersonal about your thoughts, actions, relationships, agendas, etc. is an all-important art which requires self-esteem and lack of self-importance at the same time. If your self-esteem is low—which it is until your ego is healed—this neutral view of yourself will soften your self-judgments. If your level of self-importance has risen as an overcompensation for your feelings of lack of self-worth—which it does until your ego is healed—this impartial study of your relational transactions will undermine such dishonest nonsense.

Seventh, you must honor the discomfiture you experience from somewhere inside you and allow it to speak to you from the level of Principle. Rather than attempting to override your discomfort with affirmations of how "fine" you are, feel the discomfort and listen to what it is silently saying. Rather than attempting to numb the pain of the discomfort with food, drugs, alcohol, sex, or shopping, feel the dull or sharp edge of that pain and listen for the Life Principle of which it is silently reminding you.

Within the consciousness of life itself, there exists a web or matrix of Universal Principles or Laws in which our very world and our very lives inhere. Whenever we act in ways which are unLawful or unPrincipled—in ways which are not in alignment with Life's Principles—we will feel the silent but powerful "No" messages from our deeper personality. Bringing our lower minds and our lives into alignment with these innate Laws is really what becoming congruent is all about. When we become conscious of the silent messages of our inner, deeper Self, we are able to easily stay in alignment with the Universal or Life Principles. When we are so aligned, we are easily moved by the flow of the Creative Process through an ongoing series of irreversible transformations which eventually result in our full Enlightenment. So, besides the resultant more agreeable nature of our relational transactions, the resultant more authentic and Self-expressive way of being, and the resultant more centered, stable, and confident sense of self, *hearingfeeling* and honoring the silent messages of the deeper personality will accelerate our process toward true Enlightenment. What a boon!

Toward Expansion and Self-Mastery

Who's got the problem? Ask yourself:

1) Does this behavior have any real, tangible, or concrete effect on me?

2) Am I feeling unaccepting because I am being interfered with, damaged, hurt, or impaired in some way? Or...

3) Am I feeling unaccepting simply because I would like the other person to act differently, not have a problem, feel the way I think he/she should?

Others are remarkably sensitive to the non-verbal messages we send. They read muscle tenseness, tightness around the mouth, facial expressions and body movements. If these "body messages" are in conflict with the verbal messages, others become confused—or they believe the non-verbal message and see the contrasting verbal messages as phony.[2]

1. Make a list of the people with whom you are most vulnerable to emotional merging. Beside each person's name, make a note of one example of your emotional experience merging with their emotional experience.

2. Practice feeling your own self of sense as distinctly separate from each of the people whose names appear on your list. Sit quietly, close your eyes, and visualize yourself and each of the others, one by one. As you breathe freely and fully, feel the lines of your emotional identity drawn with strong bold lines. Visualize the other person becoming very sad, grievous, bored or angry. As you watch them having their emotional response, visualize yourself standing free and maintaining your own emotional integrity. See yourself being compassionate or emotionally neutral as you continue to interact with them. Notice how you feel as a result of this practice.

3. Practice what you have done in visualization, above, when you are in actual face-to-face or phone-to-phone conversation with each of these people. Remember that strengthening your ability to maintain emotional integrity takes some conscious practice over a period of time.

4. Consistently practice noticing your physical, emotional, and mental conditions as a part of your relating with others. Also practice noticing the responses of your physical, emotional, and mental levels to the environment in which you find yourself and to the person with whom you are relating.

   "Is physical distress causing me to respond in a certain way right now?"

   "Is emotional inertia or activity influencing my responses right now?"

   "Is mental fatigue or stress producing the attitudes I bring to this relationship now?"

   "Is the environment too noisy, distracting, or otherwise incompatible with my condition and/or this discussion?"

Let us BE the thrilling news: "I am fresh"
as we stand new in the eternal present.

CHAPTER TWELVE

The Existential Choice

The egoic hero sets out to look for treasure and conquer the world.
The existential hero sets out to look for truth and conquer fear.

—*Frances Vaughan*[1]

Facing the Reality

The egoic hero can well be characterized as having a cloudy, narrow and myopic view of the world—a perspective which is typified by an intense desire to have things turn out a *certain* way—a way which will, of course, match his image of himself and his fantasy of how his life should be. He lives in a no man's land where his sentiments run something like this, over and over again:

> "This is not the way it **ought** to be."
> "This is not the way I **thought** it would be."
> "I **wish** it would be like that."
> "**If** only it could have been like that."

The egoic hero is not primarily interested in truth, and he will subvert the truth most any time he thinks it will not serve his self-serving purposes—although he will give lip service to his desire for truth and he will loudly protest when someone has been less than truthful with him. His search for treasure and his strategy for conquering the world do not include a direct confrontation with the reality of his very existence. In fact, in order to serve the agenda of his task, he will avoid the *big questions*. His attention and energy are invested in reprocessing the past and fantasizing and worrying about the future—all in the context of having things turn out a *certain* "special" way that he has imagined.

The existential hero can be characterized as having a clearer, more expanded view of the world—a perspective which is typified by an intense desire to face reality: to gain some degree of true understanding about life and about himself;

to give up imaginary pictures of how things should be; and to abandon his schemes to become rich, famous and utterly satisfied by the things of the world; and to come to terms with death. The existential hero is one who has become ready to face the shocking truth of his existence: he lives in a world, in a universe, and in a cosmos about which he knows so little. He does not know how his species came to be. He does not really know how to be fully human. He does not know what real significance his life represents. He does not know much about God—just what he has been taught at home and at church, which seems like pretty thin stuff to him, and what he has read, which often contradicts other things he has heard and read. In fact, he is not necessarily assured that there is a God. And, he certainly does not have an acceptable understanding about death. But, most of all, the existential hero is *inwardly resolute* about overcoming the ego's fear and finding satisfactory answers to some of the *big questions* which have been troubling him for some time: "Who am I?" "What is life all about?" "What is death all about?" "Is there a God?" "If there is a God, what or who is God and what is my relationship to That?" "How am I to live in order to evolve and to fulfill my potential?"

So, the transformational leap from the mental-egoic level to the existential level of consciousness is a leap from fearful, self-serving and pleasure-seeking agendas —which correspond to the ways of the ordinary world—to bold, courageous, Self-serving and Truth-seeking agendas which correspond to the ways of the higher Realms of Being. Where the ego treads, the high Self would find boring, indulgent, suppressive and silly. Where the high Self walks, the ego would find terrifying, austere, painful and irrelevant.

In the evolution of consciousness, existential angst (anxiety or dread) is generated by encountering (or becoming aware of) the two sides of the two major dualisms—the primary dualism of self vs. other and the secondary dualism of being vs. nothingness. Existentialism is thus "an attitude of squarely facing and dealing with these two major dualisms."[2] So whether he knows anything of existential philosophy or not, the journeyer will experience fear, dread or anguish as the self-protective illusions of the ego are discovered to be dreamy smoke screens which have hidden an entire higher reality. Having found the world and its egoic ways to be *not true*, the existential hero squarely faces and deals with the *big questions* inherent in the primary and secondary dualisms as he ventures beyond the world's reality for the truth he so earnestly seeks.

> *An existential path is one of reason and mind/body integration. Devotion to physical, emotional and intellectual honesty is coupled with a willingness to confront the absurdity of existence and being in the world as it is....*
>
> *Mastery on this level is evidenced in freedom and responsibility. The courage to be and the courage to create in spite of fear is what is valued.*
>
> *Perhaps this approach can only be considered a spiritual path when atheistic existentialism is transcended in choosing commitment to spirituality or God as the ultimate expression of freedom. But insofar as it is a genuine search for truth, existentialism can be characterized as a via negativa, a way of negation that attempts to strip away illusions that prevent us from facing truth.*[3]

FROM NEUROTIC TO AUTHENTIC IN ONE BOLD LEAP

As we have already seen, the existential level of consciousness is the fifth level of consciousness, and it is the level at which authentic expression begins to occur. This level is marked by its transcendence of the ego's automaticity; that is, it stands above and free from the conditioned reactivity of the third level of consciousness—the level at which the damaged ego reigns supreme and runs slipshod over the high thoughts and authentic responses of the higher Self. In the body it is located at the throat center (or in and as the throat chakra).

At the fifth level of consciousness authenticity is the natural state of being. At this level the lower nature—or first three levels of consciousness—have been transcended by a true *awakening* into the higher nature. This *awakened* state represents a healing of the *split* between the persona and shadow—which are now a "wholed" and healthy ego—and a healing of the split between the ego and the body—which are now experienced as the body/mind. Wilber's model of the Spectrum of Consciousness (Figure No. 14), shows that at this level we are returned to the state of *total organism*—or centaur. Wilber explains:

> *A centaur is a legendary animal, half human and half horse, and so it well represents a perfect union and harmony of mental and physical. A centaur is not a horse rider in control of his horse, but a rider who is one with his horse. Not a psyche divorced from and in control of a soma, but a self-controlling, self-governing, psychosomatic unity.*[4]

Having experienced ourselves primarily as a split or fragmented mind, separate from our bodies, this leap in consciousness is a healing for which we have long yearned and which brings us nearly indescribable relief. Using the metaphor of the centaur, it is as if the aspects of the human mind which are in opposition to each other (the persona and the shadow)—represented by the human portion of the centaur—were severed from their horse body and left incapable of doing more than lying, inert, in one place, and doing battle with each other. Without the body, the mind has been unable to propel itself out of its pitiful state of self-absorption.

This view of the third level of consciousness epitomizes the need for a transformational healing of the split between the persona and shadow aspects of the ego—resulting in a healthy ego—as well as a healing of the split between the mind and the body—resulting in a body/mind. Captured by and lost in our own thought processes—which at the third level, are dualistic and exclusionary—we experience ourselves, the world, all things, and life itself by way of our →*narrow*← view and our →*limiting*← personal preferences. It is the critical leap in consciousness from the third to the fifth level to which the awakening ones of our world are being called to attune themselves and for which they are being called to prepare themselves at this time. By way of intelligently participating with the great process which is obviously at work in our world and in our individual lives, we can and must make ourselves available for transformation, offering our sincere practice of congruence as our gesture of ↑*reaching*↑ for that next auspicious level of our potent humanity.

Figure No. 29 is a model of human consciousness from Frances Vaughan's book, *The Inward Arc*.[5] As we can see, 1) each level of consciousness is shown to be a closed circle, 2) the spectrum of consciousness is shown to be a series of five concentric circles, and 3) each higher-order level encompasses and contains all previous levels. Reconciling this model with the human chakra system (Figure No. 4), we see that the fourth level or heart chakra (the center in which transformation occurs) is not represented as a specific level of consciousness, and the sixth and seventh chakras combined are represented as the transpersonal Self.

THE EVOLUTION OF SELF CONCEPTS

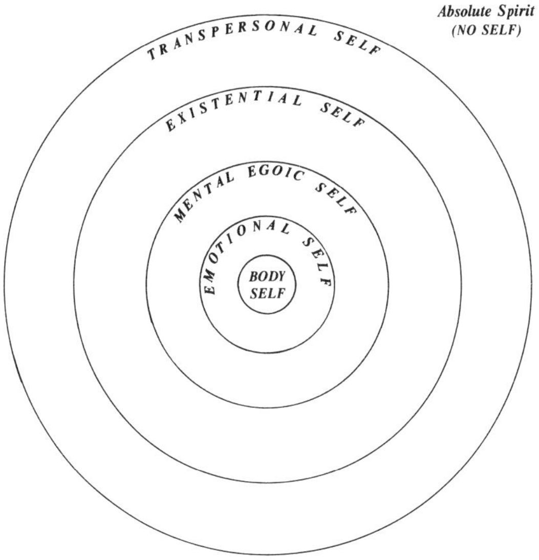

Figure No. 29

ACHIEVING INTEGRITY: REUNION OF BODY AND MIND

> *Indeed, my body seems to just dangle along under me. I no longer approach the world* **with** *my body but* **on** *my body. I'm up here, it's down there, and I'm basically uneasy about just what it is that* **is** *down there. My consciousness is almost* **exclusively** *head consciousness—I* **am** *my head, but I* **own** *my body. The body is reduced from self to property, something which is "mine" but not "me." The body, in short, becomes an object or a projection, in just the same way the shadow did. A boundary is erected upon the total organism so that the body is projected as not-self.*[6]

In the process of becoming congruent, and, thus, more fully human, at the level of ego, we heal the split in our ego—the separation between the persona and the shadow—by reclaiming the shadow aspects which we long ago rejected and disowned. At the existential level we heal the split between our mind and our body. To become intimately relational with our body, we need to bring conscious awareness to it and its voluntary and involuntary processes on a regular schedule. Deepak Chopra, in *Bliss and the Quantum Mechanical Body*, states:

Looking at the body from the quantum mechanical perspective, we find that the body is not a static thing, but a living process patterned in consciousness. Consciousness has its own physiology, whose primary value is wholeness. Any loss of wholeness, however small, is enough to cause a complete breakdown....

The cause of all disease is a breakdown in the self-referral process of consciousness. Therefore, the treatment of all diseases, at the level where they actually originate, is the same: reconnecting consciousness with consciousness....

Enlightenment represents the true state of health in any person; it is the condition where one is fully awake to the entire range of reality, perceiving that a single, self-contained flow of intelligence upholds one's individual life and the cosmos....

Carrying the quantum mechanical body from theory to practice is not difficult. It is the easiest thing to **be oneself**, *and yet the result is universal, because the same stream of evolution that keeps the stars and galaxies in perfect order along with every living thing automatically begins to nourish one's life with its infinite power. Unity is the simplest state of creation; it is bliss, in and of itself, recognizing no other reality.*[7] *[Emphasis added.]*

The following are some suggestions which will assist you to begin to attend to the life and responses of the body, and thus serve to support reuniting the body and the mind:

1) Observe the breath as you simply sit quietly with your eyes closed. Notice its rhythm. Notice its pauses. Notice its big breaths and its little breaths. Notice that you do not have to breathe—that instead you *are breathed*. Notice the effect the breath has on the body.

2) Observe the effect that eating a meal has on your body. Notice whether you feel more or less energetic after eating.

    Notice how you feel, energetically, when you are really hungry, and how that energetic experience changes when you have a glass of water, or a cup of tea, or a glass of juice, or a full meal.

Notice which foods cause your body to feel heavy and cause your energy level to plunge to a sluggish low, and which foods bring your energy level up quickly and leave you feeling light and full of pep.

3) Observe your body with keen awareness when you lie in bed at night before you go to sleep. Feel the energy flows in your body. Notice the places where your body feels exhausted or uncomfortable and the places where your body feels restful and comfortable. Allow your breath freedom to breathe fully as you consciously let go of the tension caused by the muscles of the body "holding" themselves in contraction.

4) Observe your body—its flexibility and energy level— before, during and after a yoga session, a run, a bike ride, a workout or a walk. Note how the physical exercise affects the physical, mental, and emotional condition of the body.

5) Discover what relational or environmental stimuli cause the body to contract or →close down← and become a hard shell. Discover what relational or environmental stimuli cause the body to expand or ←open→ and become soft and receptive.

6) Give your body a firm but gentle massage with a light oil daily, before or after your shower. Offer the massage as a tribute to the complex and magnificent system that the body/mind is—and which allows your earthly presence.

7) Become a student of some form of intelligent breath work in order to breathe through some (or all) of the blockages in the body/mind—residues from unintegrated past experiences.

8) Learn the language of your body and learn to hear its messages easily and consistently. Speak to your body frequently and allow it to speak to you.

FACING DEATH

At this level one becomes acutely aware of personal freedom and choice. The essential unity of mind and body as a total organism is recognized and attention is directed to fundamental concerns such as identity, authenticity, and the meaning of life. Well-being from an existential perspective means coming to terms with the finite nature of existence, accepting the inherent limitations of the ego, and being willing to face things as they are, without self-deception.[8]

That the leap in consciousness from the third level is major and significant is attested to in the richness of Vaughan's words. Within this stage of process, we actually face the fact of our own mortality—that scariest subject—from which the defense mechanisms of the frightened ego have protected us by strategies of avoidance and denial. Becoming authentic includes acceptance of the reality of our physical death and achievement of true humility, combined with an intense motivation to live a life of true meaning and authentic expression.

IN THE FACE OF DEATH, WE CHOOSE TO LIVE LIFE FULLY.

One of the chief reasons we have so much anguish and difficulty facing death is that we ignore the truth of impermanence. We so desperately want everything to continue as it is that we have to believe that things will always stay the same. But this is only make-believe. And as we so often discover, belief has little or nothing to do with reality. This make-believe, with its misinformation, ideas, and assumptions, is the rickety foundation on which we construct our lives. No matter how much the truth keeps interrupting, we prefer to go on trying, with hopeless bravado, to keep up our pretense.[9]

In the face of death, we choose to live life fully. It is this ability to face death squarely (without self-pity, despondency or paralyzing fear) which truly distinguishes the existential hero from the egoic hero. Uncomforted by religion's promises of *life after death* or "heaven," the existential hero sets about stripping away all of the illusory belief systems which have served to limit his view until he was ready for an honest looksee. With a growing awareness of his experience of "aloneness," the existential hero rises to the occasion with a natural use of his free will—which he has discovered is intrinsic to this fifth level of consciousness. Understanding and acceptance of his own death becomes an important process within the great process, of which he is a part.

In his book, *The Tibetan Book of Living and Dying*, Sogyal Rinpoche states:

> *Death is a vast mystery, but there are two things we can say about it:* ***It is absolutely certain that we will die, and it is uncertain when or how we will die.*** *The only surety we have, then, is this uncertainty about the hour of our death, which we seize on as the excuse to postpone facing death directly. We are like children who cover their eyes in a game of hide-and-seek and think that no one can see them.*
>
> *...Perhaps the deepest reason why we are afraid of death is because we do not know who we are. We believe in a personal, unique, and separate identity; but if we dare to examine it, we find that this identity depends entirely on an endless collection of things to prop it up: our name, our "biography," our partners, family, home, job, friends, credit cards.... It is on their fragile and transient support that we rely for our security. So when they are all taken away, will we have any idea of who we really are?*
>
> *...Without our familiar props, we are faced with just ourselves, a person we do not know, an unnerving stranger with whom we have been living all the time but we never really wanted to meet....*
>
> *And doesn't this point to something fundamentally tragic about our way of life? We live under an assumed identity, in a neurotic fairy tale world with no more reality than the Mock Turtle in Alice in Wonderland. Hypnotized by the thrill of building, we have raised the houses of our lives on sand. This world can seem marvelously convincing until death collapses the illusion and evicts us from our hiding place. What will happen to us then if we have no clue of any deeper reality?*[10]

Because our culture has not provided intelligent weight to the subject of death, we must learn to assume responsibility for providing that weight and for extending it to include the subject of honestly facing our own mortality. No matter how "modern" we may believe ourselves and our world to be, it is obvious that our so-called modernity does not epitomize truth—not even about our own fragile lives and our own mysterious and unpredictable deaths. We have been conditioned to expect to have a "normal" lifespan, and we have become a conspirator in the *conspiracy of silence* which—without a word—attempts to deny the reality of our human mortality by not looking it straight in the face. In our society, death is considered "a shame," "too bad," "awful," "untimely," "tragic," et cetera. When someone else dies, our personal loss is often more grievous to us than the reality of that person having lost his life. And when someone else dies, the veil of our own mechanisms of denial are rent, and our irrational fear of death and all of our unresolved mortality issues rise to the surface of our consciousness.

Because we have grown accustomed to living in denial in a "neurotic fairy tale" wherein others also disavow death, the subject of how to deal with the reality of death looms as a seemingly immense and overwhelming subject to us. However, reducing the bigness of the matter down to its central core element, we merely have the reality of death itself to deal with. And, it seems obvious that genuine contemplation of that reality will reorder our priorities, refocus our inner vision and reprioritize our conscious choices. In *Immortal Death and Human Civilization*, Georg Feuerstein states:

> *There are, in fact, no external circumstances that can alter the inevitability of death or modify its ultimate meaninglessness.*
>
> *Death is part of the chaos that forms conditioned existence. It has no meaning beyond its certain occurrence. Yet, mankind throughout its long history has given varied meanings to death as much as to life. Numerous complicated structures of belief and custom have been enacted around this fundamental phenomenon of existence.*
>
> *But death cannot be truly met with meaning or any of Man's symbol systems. Death defies meaning. It confronts Man with the ultimate meaninglessness of his existence and the futility of his desperate search for meaning. Death shatters all Man's plans, concerns, and philosophies, which, in the last analysis, are merely consolations in the face of universal anarchy.*[11]
>
> *...The ego is that phenomenon within the world-process which struggles to freeze the flux of events, to spellbind time, to delimit the Limitless, to define the Unqualifiable, to conventionalize the wholly Spontaneous. It is the ongoing activity of contracting away from Infinity.*[12]

BECOMING AUTHENTIC INCLUDES ACCEPTANCE OF THE REALITY OF OUR PHYSICAL DEATH AND ACHIEVEMENT OF TRUE HUMILITY.

Da Avabhasa authoritatively elaborates the process of death in *Easy Death*:

> *The "secret" or Law of the death process is the same that applies to existence during our born lifetime. The right relationship to the process is that of love-surrender, not recoil or withdrawal. The death process is simply another form of participation in the Mystery and Universal Unity of existence. Death is not self-suppression. It is not a process whereby the self is reduced to Zero*

> *or thrown into eternal Chaos. Such a passage, if it seems to arise, either during our lifetime or in the process of death, is an hallucination created by our own recoiling fear....*
>
> *The death process should not be engaged merely as a retreat from embodiment. It should not be used to retreat into the self. Rather, it should be engaged as self-surrender, or love-surrender of the total body-mind. As when going to sleep, we should simply relax and rest our hold on the states of body and mind. If we enter into the death process in God-Love, trusting the Radiant Being to the point of utter self-surrender, then the event will suffer no distortion, and we will emerge into a right, profound, and ultimately happy destiny—even as such surrender and trust relieve our life, and sleep, and dreams of distortion, fear, illusion, and doubt while we live in this world.*
>
> *And death is not a permanent event or effect. It is only a transition to further experience. It is a transforming event that prepares us for another birth, just as it stands before us, motivating us toward self-transcending surrender during our lifetime. Death and rebirth are the inevitable cycle of our existence, until we grow and evolve and surrender and serve beyond the limits of all the schools of Nature, and so Emerge permanently into the Eternally Radiant and Blissful Divine Domain, where we will exist in perfect Identification with the Divine Being as well as a perfectly evolved or elaborated Relationship with the Divine Being.*[13]

And so we arrive at a phase in our process at which we are ready to face the reality of death, although it is a difficult reality to accept. In order to achieve any meaningful level of maturity and in order to become deepened and expanded beyond the confines of the ego's surface limitations, we must face the fact that we are going to die—the reality that our ego has tried so hard to avoid.

> *We must look existence in the face if our aim is to arrive at a right solution whatever that solution may be. And to look existence in the face is to look God in the face; for the two cannot be separated.... This world of our battle and labor is a fierce dangerous destructive devouring world in which life exists precariously and the soul and body of man move among enormous perils, a world in which by every step forward, whether we will it or no, something is crushed and broken, in which every breath of life is a breath too of death.... We have to look courageously in the face of the reality and see that it is God and none else who has made this world in His being and that*

so He has made it. We have to see that Nature devouring her children, Time eating up the lives of creatures, Death universal and ineluctable and the violence of the Rudra forces in man and Nature are also the supreme God-head in one of his cosmic figures. We have to see that God the bountiful and prodigal creator, God the helpful, strong and benignant preserver is also God the devourer and destroyer. The torment of the couch of pain and evil on which we are racked is his touch as much as happiness and sweetness and pleasure. It is only when we see with the eye of the complete union and feel this truth in the depths of our being that we can entirely discover behind that mask too the calm and beautiful face of the all-blissful Godhead and in this touch that tests our imperfection the touch of the friend and builder of the spirit in man. The discords of the world are God's discords and it is only by accepting and proceeding through them that we can arrive at the greater concords of his supreme harmony, the summits and thrilled vastness of his transcendent and his cosmic Ananda.... For truth is the foundation of real spirituality and courage is its soul.[14]

EMERGENCE OF THE EXISTENTIAL HERO

So it is the existential hero who is the embodiment of and natural expression of congruence. That is any man, woman or child who at some unpredictable moment begins to serve the Principle of Truth above all other factors, and—in the face of all other influences and all other considerations—becomes a champion of authenticity and a journeyer into the realm of the higher Self. That *moment of truth* marks **the** pivotal point in a person's life and the stunning turn from the consensus reality. It represents the instant after which he or she will begin to be completely self-honest, meticulously Self-seeking, and truly Self-expressive. It is a never-to-be-forgotten moment.

My moment occurred one morning in March of 1983, while I stood in the kitchen of my Miami townhouse, speaking on the phone, as I looked out into my courtyard garden. I was having another one of *those* conversations with a person who had been my husband, who was the father of my children, and who had manipulated, humiliated, mistreated, threatened, tormented, and harassed me for twenty-five years. Once again, he was threatening me. He was saying that he would disallow me to visit my seventeen-year-old daughter who had just been hospitalized unless I left my life in Miami and moved to a small town in Indiana, where he and his third wife, their children and her parents lived. Once again my child was being used as a pawn in a high-stakes game of Life Chess, a game in which he seemed determined to achieve checkmate. Once again the consequences were serious if I did not do what he said I had to do. I tried to reason with him. I argued with him. Neither worked. Once again I felt terribly frustrated and completely helpless.

THE EXISTENTIAL CHOICE IS THE CLEAR CHOICE TO ACTUALIZE THE POTENTIAL FOR GREATNESS WHICH LIES DORMANT WITHIN US.

All of a sudden, my personal history flashed before my eyes. In what seemed to be no more than a minute, I saw simultaneously all the previous similar occurrences of just what was happening at that time. I saw people attempting to control me to serve their own agendas. I saw people attempting to force me to be a *certain way* that they thought I should be or attempting to force me to do *certain things* that they thought I should do. I heard their judgments, expectations, and demands of me. And I saw myself carefully and fearfully calculating what words to say, what actions to do, and what decisions to make based on their supposed power over me and the possibly awful consequences that might accrue to me if I did not yield to their demands. And in that minute, I WAS SET FREE! As I stood there hearing the same old judgments and expectations of me and a new version of the same old demands, I new that **I would suffer <u>any</u> consequences in order to be free**, to be the truth of myself, to stop the insanity of that relationship and all other dishonest relationships in my life.

The implications of that moment of truth and its effects on me were amazingly swift and powerful. I began to change without really realizing that I was changing so much so fast. I certainly experienced dramatic movement in my life quickly. Within a few months I had changed a codependent and enabling relationship with my older daughter to a relationship which served the highest good of both of us. I moved to a beautiful new apartment in a high rise on the bay, extricated myself from a job I abhorred (against the counsel of my big eight boss), took a new job which revitalized and stretched me, and finally ended a ten-year-long "love" relationship which had been a source of torment for the previous five years. Little did I know that that moment of truth was the requisite leap in awareness that set me up for a most radical transformation which mysteriously began nine months later. That moment of truth was to be the foundation on which I stood in really getting my life straight, becoming truly aligned with my deeper personality, and surrendering everything to That Greater Truth.

And, for the first time in my life, I began to feel that I was not standing **against** something, but that I was standing **for** something. I no longer felt as though I were at war with others or with myself. I felt instead that I was standing free, just being me. I now yielded not to *the demands* of others, but to *the consequences* of my own truthful words and actions. What a triumph! What a victory! What an honorable freedom!

Of course, that moment and the immediate changes which it caused in me were only the beginning. The path which opened ahead of me was a path which demanded rigorous self-honesty and consistent self-processing in order to get to the basic inner truth in each relational transaction and in each circumstance in which I found myself. But the sense of personal empowerment which accrued from each congruent choice and each authentic expression represented the inner growth which was taking place. I was still a tremulous and fearful person to some degree, but, in the pinch, my well-established dedication to the truth easily overrode any tendency to play it safe and sell out to the judgments, expectations, and demands of others. And my attempts to control others seemed to diminish in exact ratio to my choices not to be controlled. In setting myself free, I had also set everyone who knew me free.

At the effect of egoic fear and identified as only a fragment of ourselves—the persona—we have sold out again and again on the highest and best choice we could make. We chose instead to effect strategies which we figured were most likely to produce the results we desired: our egoic needs being met. To gain approval, we sold out. To be loved, we sold out. To achieve some sense of security, we sold out. To attain credibility, we sold out. To fit in, we sold out. Now we must bring truth to each of those decisions—turning each one of them into conscious choices to bring integrity to our lives.

In order to become congruent, we must 1) uncover and examine our basic attitudes; 2) discover the habituated thoughtforms, articulations and reactionary behaviors which are generated by those attitudes; and, then, 3) change our attitudes, our thinking, and our verbal and non-verbal expressions to match the level of sincerity and authenticity of our deeper personality. And, we must take an honest look at the reality we have created—our relationships, our work, our living situations, our use of personal time—in order to begin to transform these aspects of our lives from (unL)awful to Lawful expressions of our real Self.

> *Authenticity implies consistency between inner experience and outer expression and congruence between beliefs and behavior. When thoughts, feelings, words and actions are in harmony, when they do not contradict one another, one develops a sense of integrity and inner consistency that is essential to existential well-being. If, on the other hand, one thinks one thing and says another, or feels one way and acts in another, one creates internal conflict rather than coherence and experiences stress and disharmony or dis-ease.*[15]

As we begin the gratifying undertaking of bringing our selves into conscious existence, we may or may not be amazed to find that every single nook and cranny of our lives has been filled with incongruence—lies. As we make the existential choice to face the reality of our lives and change any untruth into truth, we will feel the integration begin to occur and we will experience the psychological (physical, emotional, and mental) relief of a growing sense of wholeness. Where before we have lied, we now just tell the truth. Where before we have told half-truths, we now just tell the truth. Where before we strategized and planned our approaches to relationships, we now just tell the truth and allow the relationship to create itself as we go along. Having come to accept ourselves, others, and things as they are, we no longer attempt to force ourselves or others to fit into some rigid mold which our ego minds have imagined to be highly desirable or required for one reason or another.

BECOMING EQUAL TO AND GREATER THAN THE CIRCUMSTANCE

The frightened, disillusioned, lonely Orphan of an egoic hero never really experiences being equal to the circumstances of his life. However, he may have such a high degree of denial of his sense of inadequacy, and such an overcompensation for those feelings, that he may identify with and present to the world an inflated self-image with various stylized posturings and attitudes, which are meant to convince everyone of his self-confidence and know-how. Any successes in the ordinary world are held as evidence that his arrogance and pride are justified. Standing on the thin ice of a self-made image, when the ego experiences a resounding defeat in life, that person either plunges into the deep and icy waters of self-doubt which the ego had, at best, covered with a fragile film of pretentiousness, or becomes so defensively self-righteous that he learns nothing from his experience and is, thus, destined to repeat it.

At the level of congruent awareness and expression, the existential hero proves time and time again to be equal to whatever circumstance he finds himself in. With a burgeoning confidence based on personal empowerment, which emanates from truthful living, the authentic hero realizes that he is truly greater than any circumstance. The once dreaded *consequences* no longer cause him to inwardly tremble and outwardly withhold or subvert the truth in order to avoid possible dangerous *repercussions* which might accrue as a result of his Self-expression.

With the simple truth as the solid and strong foundation on which he stands, the congruent person remains poised and at his ease in the face of the many surprises and challenges of life, ready to spontaneously respond from his inner Self to any eventuality, with assuredness emanating from that deep Center within himself with which he has connected and to which he continuously refers. Life is very big, full and fascinating, rather than being the overwhelming, frightening, and chaotic dilemma it used to be. Death, too, in its mystery and its bigness, looms not as something too frightening to contemplate and an event he does not feel *up to*; but, instead, death looms as a big circumstance which he feels equal to and, yes, Greater than. Really. Amazing!

WE REALIZE THAT WE ARE EQUAL TO AND GREATER THAN THE CIRCUMSTANCES OF OUR LIVES.

The existential hero's journey includes:

1) Achieving an existential perspective:
   - Looking at life honestly;
   - Coming to terms with the finite nature of existence;
   - Accepting the inherent limitations of the ego; and
   - Being willing to face things as they are, without self-deception.
2) Dealing with the reality of one's life:
   - Based not on how it *ought* to be;
   - Based not on how *we thought* it would be;
   - Based not on how *we wish* it would be; and
   - Based not on *romantic notions*.
3) Realizing one is *equal to* and *greater than* the circumstances of life and death.
4) Reuniting the body and the mind.
5) Becoming authentic.

FOLLOW YOUR BLISS

> *If you follow your bliss, you put yourself on a kind of track that has been there all the while, waiting for you, and the life that you ought to be living is the one you are living. Wherever you are—if you are following your bliss, you are enjoying that refreshment, that life within you, all the time.*[16]

The fairy tale transformation of Pinocchio from a wooden marionette to a flesh and blood human being is a brilliant tale of transformation from the mental-egoic level of consciousness to the existential level. Like Pinocchio, the ego is *a puppet on a string*—the strings being the unenlightened desires, addictions, and agendas of the physical, emotional and mental aspects of the lower self and the belief systems to which one has become conditioned. The string pullers are society-at-large and any particular persons whose judgments, expectations, and demands strongly influence one's choices or actions. Like Pinnochio, the motivations for untruthful actions are the same as the bars on the prison cell of our egoic hero: approval-seeking behavior, fear of conflict, self-doubt, et cetera.

FOLLOWING YOUR BLISS WILL INSURE THAT YOUR LIFE IS A PERFECT MATCH FOR WHO AND HOW YOU ARE.

It is at the existential (fifth) level of consciousness that Pinocchio becomes a real boy. Instead of lying, he begins to tell the truth, and his nose no longer grows out of proportion to his body. His long nose is a symbol of how obvious unauthentic behavior (lying) can be to the people we are attempting to mislead—it is often "as clear as the nose on your face." Pinocchio's true desire was to be **real**. And Jiminy Cricket, who acted as Pinocchio's guide or conscience—since Pinnochio was not in touch with his own higher Self—encouraged Pinnochio to *let his conscience be his guide*. Pinocchio actually had to prove himself a worthy candidate for transformation by beginning to tell the truth, and as a result of his truthfulness, Pinocchio's most fervent heartwish came true: he became real, authentic, genuine.

It is at the fifth level of consciousness that the Lion from *The Wizard of Oz* discovers his **courage**, that the Tin Man finds his **heart**, and the Scarecrow realizes his **intelligence**.

Just as our world heritage of myths have all pointed to transformation via truth and courage and Self-referencing, our world heritage of stories—found in books, comic books, movies, and on television—nearly all point to transformation via truth and courage and Self-referencing. This being the case, it is obvious that human beings are endowed with a code of ethics and a natural impulse to evolve by way of truth, courage, and Self-referencing. And even though humans really "know better," because previous generations have not risen to the occasion of discovering and expressing personal truth, succeeding generations have followed in the footsteps of the cultural consensus, producing billions of Pinocchios, fearful Lions, Tin Men with no hearts, and brainless Scarecrows. What a tragedy!

To *follow your bliss* means to follow the lead of the innate inner code of ethics and the inherent inner impulse to evolve which are the real Authorities to which you must look and listen. The code and the impulse are the guides which will show you the way through the labyrinth of your own life's journey to the truth of you, to the expression of that truth, and to fulfillment of the destiny with which your very life is intrinsically infused. They are the master designers who will weave a tapestry of richness and beauty from the *subtle stuff* of your life. They will insure that your life is a true transformational unfoldment, fascinating and rich with meaning.

AS AN EXISTENTIAL HERO, WE STAND FREE!

Your bliss calls you. Following your bliss will insure that your life is a perfect match for who and how you are. Following your bliss will set you free. Your bliss is the truth of you!

TURNING FROM THE CONSENSUS REALITY

> *Making the full sacrificial turn from the consensus reality is the High Heroic Expression of The Divine Impulse that lies deep within each of us. That Expression is the Ultimate Intelligent Causative Demonstration—the catalyst—that begins The Process of Unfoldment of our fullest human potential. The promise, of course, is a life of meaning, a life of significance, a life of Communion with The Divine Realm, a life of service to humanity.*[17]

What was once *unheard of* fifty-thousand years ago—the human ego—has now been *heard of* to the maximum that our planet and our species can bear. And, it is increasingly evident that more and more people are realizing that our societies and their institutions, which were built on egoic agendas and (unL)awful behaviors, are now dying, and that *something unheard of* is again going to happen in our human psyches—a transformation of consciousness. Some level of readiness for the next leap in consciousness is clearly in evidence as more and more of the world's present population of humans describe their sense of horror and their feelings of being fed up with the ego's narrow-minded views and self-serving strategies. Preparation for the leap in consciousness from the third to the fifth levels is, in fact, already happening quite gracefully and rapidly within the psyches of uncounted numbers of human beings around the world today. There are shifts and openings and changes occurring so fast now that even the hardcore naysayers are being softened and becoming a bit starry-eyed at the prospects.

The polarization between negative and positive is intensifying as the high-vibrational energy on the planet becomes more intense—and even the polarization is serving to accelerate the rate at which things are changing, rather than inhibiting and slowing change as it has done for so long.

The time is so ripe for congruent living, congruent expression, and congruent relating that it seems impossible already that we have not always lived, expressed and related congruently.

While still captured by the orphan ego, but *readyreadyready* to go beyond its pathetic limitations, we must make a clear choice to turn from the consensus reality of which we have been a part. We must stand free of the expectations, judgments and demands of our society insofar as they inhibit, repress, corrupt and/or destroy our authenticity—our realness. Without an ounce of adolescent reactivity and rebelliousness, we must choose to live sincerely, in constant accord with our own deeper personality, rather than to have our strings pulled by anyone who has been pulling them before we achieved our resolve. There has never been a better time to do so. There has never been a time when congruence was so supported not only by the Universe, but by aspects of our societies themselves.

The **existential choice** is the clear choice to realize or actualize the human potential for Greatness which lies dormant within us. The choice is then followed by learning to distinguish between our own frontal or surface personality and our deeper personality, and by allowing our surface personality to be *only* the mechanism of expression of that higher Truth. The surface personality's desires and agendas are undermined and given little or no weight, as we let go and allow the subtle unfoldment of our own greatness to occur **on its schedule** and by way of **its surprising modalities**. We operate with a peaceful acceptance that as surface personalities, we know nothing of real value about who we are or what we will do, or have, or be and become, no matter how strong our desires and opinions may be. And we rest assured that whatever our unfoldment is, it will produce in us a level of greatness to which the ego could perhaps aspire but which the ego could never manifest. We become innocent and childlike in our willingness and our ability to be taught the new ways of being and responding. We become clear, inspired and effective. And we realize that we are always *equal to* the circumstances and *greater than* the circumstances of our lives. As an existential hero, we stand free!

CONGRUENCE = THE TRUTH

AN ACCURATE MATCHING OF INNER EXPERIENCE & OUTER EXPRESSION

SELF EXPRESSION	*EMOTIONAL*	*EMOTIONAL*
...spontaneously	***...courage***	***...balance***
...thoughtfully	***...self-discipline***	***...activity***
...confidently	***...gracefulness***	***...inertia***

→ DROPPING "NICE GUY" AND "NOT NICE GUY" ROLES

→ CREATING CERTAINTY THROUGH SELF-TRUST & SELF DIRECTION

→ OWNING OUR OWN THOUGHTS & FEELINGS - DROPPING BLAME

→ SEPARATING OUR OWN EMOTIONAL EXPERIENCE FROM THE EMOTIONAL EXPERIENCE OF OTHERS

→ OVERCOMING THE FEAR OF CONFLICT

→ DEVELOPING THE ABILITY TO CONFRONT

Relating as "EQUALS"
Relating "AT RISK" with no fear
Living "AT CHOICE" with integrity

TAKING A STAND
STANDING ALONE
THE RIGHT USE OF WILL

Figure No. 30

Toward Expansion and Self-Mastery

1. Bring your attention often to the experience of separation which exists between your body and your mind. Notice that when you are mindbound you feel less connected with your whole body. Notice ways in which that separation shows up: cut fingers, broken toes, automobile accidents, etc.

2. Become keenly aware of the experience of union of the body and mind—namely that you feel very comfortable physically, as if you are wearing your body like a well-fitting glove.

3. Re-establish the union of the body and mind by doing simple practices which serve that purpose. For example:

    Sit quietly, close your eyes, and allow your breath to breathe you freely as you just notice your breath. Allow your breath to breathe in and out for fifteen to thirty minutes, as you simply keep your attention on the inhale and the exhale. Besides being very relaxing, this practice releases the ego mind's worrisome hold on your consciousness and allows you to experience the reconnection of your body/mind consciousness.

4. List the circumstances in your life to which you do not feel equal. Does your job seem to be overwhelming to you? Does your family situation seem burdensome and too big for you to handle? What other things in your life cause you to feel less than equal to the circumstances? Then, ask yourself:

    "What do I need to do in order to meet the challenges of this circumstance?"

    "In what way do I need to face the reality of the situation, make clear choices, and change myself and/or the circumstance in order to become equal to its demands?"

    "Can I bring more focus, more concentration, and more energy to my labor in order to achieve the results I desire?"

Let us acknowledge the Great Awakening
which has lain dormant and which now stirs
in the hearts and minds of humankind.

Let us joyously celebrate that Awakening.

CHAPTER THIRTEEN

BRINGING ORDER OUT OF THE CHAOS OF OUR LIVES

In the play of living we engage in three fundamental forms of action. We begin things, we continue to be engaged in things, and we bring things to an end. We are each obliged to be capable of fulfilling these three forms of action relative to every condition in our experience. To suffer disability to any of these three forms of action relative to any condition in our experience is to accumulate a tendency relative to that condition. Such is the way we develop our conventional "karmas." By virtue of such accumulations we are obliged to suffer repetitions of circumstances, in this life and from life to life, until we overcome the liability in our active relationship to each condition that binds us.

In the manifest process of existence, we and all other functions in the play are under the same lawful obligation to create, sustain, and destroy conditions or patterns that arise.

—*SRI DA AVABHASA*

THE THREE FORMS OF ACTION

It is very common today to hear reference made to the baggage which one carries from the past. We hear it mentioned in movies, read it in books, even hear it joked about in sitcoms and in stand-up comedy. It is good that we have awareness of our condition of *fullness* or *pollutedness* since we are, so lamentably, reflecting that condition in our poisoned rivers, streams, and oceans, as well as in the garbage-plagued and otherwise contaminated landscapes of our planet. We are also reflecting that condition in various types of disease which are ravaging the bodies of so many of us during these times. This *fullness* weighs heavily upon us, drags us down, and causes us continuous inner turmoil. The systems of our planet and of our bodies desperately need a purification—restoration to a state of fundamental cleanliness. That purification must begin with the emptying of our human psyches. With a restoration of our psychological structures to a state of clarity and wellness, we will mirror that condition in the relationships and lives we create and as the world we, together, exemplify.

Just as Ghandi's march to the sea clearly represented a conscious choice to break down the structures and patterns of the past in the form of British rule of India, our own personal march to the sea of congruence must just as clearly represent a conscious choice to break down the structures and patterns of our personal past.

As Da Avabhasa teaches us in the quoted material above, "We are each obliged to be capable of fulfilling these three forms of action relative to every condition in our experience;" namely, to begin things, to continue to be engaged in things, and to bring things to an end. In other words, we must learn to live our personal lives in accordance with the Laws of Life themselves. We must fulfill the cycles of beginning, continuing and ending in each relationship and each endeavor—the experiences of our lives. If we do not, our subconscious becomes a reservoir, full of the debris generated by uncompleted cycles of action.

Show me a person who is neurotic and I will show you a person who has not yet consciously completed a significant cycle or some significant cycles of his past experiences. The incompletion psychologically generates disturbances in the mind of the person for as long as the cycle remains incomplete. Those disturbances play havoc within the person's subconscious, generating confusion, self-doubt, and fear, creating a filter through which all ensuing experiences are interpreted, and strongly influencing every choice that he makes.

Because he has not *had his experience fully*, he has not passed all the way through the self-discovery phase of the relationship or circumstance, and has not come out on the other end of the cycle with his own sense of self intact and, even, strengthened. If he had fulfilled all three phases of the cycle—beginning, continuing, and ending—he would feel expressed, clear, satisfied, and at peace, no matter whether there had been a "happy ending" or an ending that was not so happy. The experience would then cause no chronic disturbances in the subconscious of the psyche. Instead, the entire experience would be used as a worthy self-reference for dealing with future experiences. The whole experience would have become a self-validating foundation on which to stand to do the further work of self-discovery, providing him a subconscious posture of being *equal to the circumstances* and *greater than the circumstances*—no matter what circumstances might arise. What a difference!

Unresolved issues which accumulate from uncompleted cycles of action not only fill the space of our consciousness, but they also require immeasurable amounts of energy to manage. These perplexing issues are suppressed to a degree that is sufficient to allow us to deny their importance enough to get by and to act as though we are "fine." **Suppression requires energy**. These unresolved issues are subconsciously and consciously processed and reprocessed hundreds of times over the course of years, in an attempt to reach a resolution, to release us from their unanswered questions, and to grant us clarity and peace of mind. **Processing takes energy**. The more crowded our subconscious becomes with unresolved issues from the past, the less psychic energy we have available for living our lives. We run mostly on nervous energy, which is generated by the psychological stress we are experiencing. As a result, we suffer from chronic exhaustion and all kinds of psychosomatic symptoms, which produce cycles of beginning and collapsing, beginning and collapsing. The *continuing* phase of the cycle is disabled, which means we consistently fall short of fulfilling the *completion* phase of our experiences, and our psyches become more and more filled up.

OUR OWN PERSONAL MARCH TO THE SEA OF CONGRUENCE MUST REPRESENT THE CONSCIOUS CHOICE TO BREAK DOWN THE STRUCTURE AND PATTERNS OF OUR PERSONAL PAST.

As Da Avabhasa tells us: "By virtue of such accumulations we are obliged to suffer repetitions of circumstances, in this life and from life to life, until we overcome the liability in our active relationship to each condition that binds us." These repetitions of circumstances are our obvious subconscious attempts to *work out* the unresolved issues which plague us and underlie our every waking and sleeping moment. We neurotically recreate the same type of destructive relationships over and over again unless we begin to discover other, more authentic, aspects of ourselves, after which we are able to consciously complete all destructive relationships from psychologically healthy choices which serve our highest good. For example, we may have subconsciously chosen to play the role of *needy doormat/dependent victim* in relationships out of feelings of unworthiness and self-doubt. That pitiful role will be quickly outgrown by anyone who begins to discover the truth of themselves and to experience the empowerment of Self-expression in all of their relationships. Or, we may have subconsciously chosen to play the role of *self-sufficient dictator/independent master* in relationships out of feelings of anger and inflated-ego arrogance, which are compensations for (guess what?) unworthiness and self-doubt. That pathetic role will be quickly outgrown by anyone who begins to discover the truth of themselves and to experience the empowerment of Self-expression in all of their relationships.

The "play of living" and the process of self-discovery, then, require living out all three phases of the cycles of action: beginning, continuing, and ending, "until we overcome the liability in our active relationship to each condition that binds us." Overcoming the liability translates as bringing consciousness and healthy high choice to our relationships and our circumstances, rather than muddling around in our relationships and circumstances out of the needy and self-defeating agendas of our damaged egos—which are suffering the effects of uncompleted cycles of action.

Da Avabhasa further teaches us the specific consequences of our failure to exercise our ability to **create**, to **sustain**, and to **become free** of conditions:

> **FAILURE TO BEGIN**: *The inhibition or suppression of the ability to create conditions (to realize that conditions are your creation and responsibility) is reflected as "tamas," or rigidity, inertia, indolence, and laziness.*[2]
>
> That is, if our ability to begin things is obstructed, we will perceive the world through our own rigid, inert, indolent and lazy perceptions, and we will express ourselves in a manner which epitomizes rigidity, inertia, indolence and laziness.
>
> **FAILURE TO CONTINUE**: *The inhibition or suppression of the ability to sustain (or to realize that the maintenance of conditions is your responsibility) is reflected as "rajas," or unsteadiness of life and attention, and negative and random excitation or emotion.*[3]
>
> That is, if our ability to continue things is impeded, we will perceive the world as inconsistent, and we will show up as unable to keep our lives together. Our attention will be scattered, and we will become emotionally unstable, stuck often in the inertia and/or the activity scale.
>
> **FAILURE TO END**: *The inhibition or suppression of the ability to destroy or become free of conditions (or to realize that the cessation of conditions is your responsibility) is reflected as artificial "sattwa," sentimentality, romance, sorrow, bondage to subjectivity, and no comprehension of the mystery of death.*[4]

> That is, if our ability to complete things is impaired, we will perceive the world and express ourselves as sentimentalists and romantics—prisoners of our own individual melancholy and personal predispositions—with no Witness Consciousness present and nothing but personal notions about death.

These clear distinctions of the three forms of action which are the very nature and content of the play of life emphatically instruct us about the fundamental necessity of activating and developing our native abilities to begin, to continue, and to end our experiences in order to become attuned to the basic flows and unfoldments of our lives—of which our experiences are all-important elements. Without living in accordance with these primary principles of the Universe, we can expect no more than to have our so-called lives consist of a series of random, uncompleted experiences which do not allow a flow toward wisdom nor support an unfoldment of our encoded potential, but, instead, fill our subconscious minds with tangles of confusing, unanswered questions about who we are and what our lives are all about.

Discovering the Deficit

In the context of the process of self-discovery, it is obvious now that we must take a good look at our own personal histories in a sincere attempt to see in which of the forms of action we are weak and in which we are strong. If for, example, our abilities are well developed in *beginning* and *completing* conditions and we are weak in *continuing* them (or sustaining or maintaining them), we will again and again pre-empt having our experiences fully simply by ending them too soon to accrue the full value of the experience.

If, for example, our abilities are well developed in *beginning* and *continuing* conditions and we are weak in *completing* them, we will again and again remain much too long in circumstances and/or relationships we have begun, but are seemingly incapable of ending. And, if the circumstance or relationship does end, we will still feel unresolved because we will not have completed the experience in the privacy of our own psyches.

And if, for example, our ability to *begin* or *create* relationships or circumstances is not developed, we will be stuck in a pervasive experience of disappointment wherein the world seems overwhelming in its bigness while our life seems shallow and empty of meaning. We will experience being *on the outside* of the life of the world, unable to penetrate its membrane. As disempowered outsiders, we will be vulnerable to being taken over by those persons who are strong at *beginning* relationships and circumstances. Since our ability to *begin* things is weak, we will tend to invest a great deal of energy in *continuing*, since we will have no confidence that if we complete the relationship or circumstance, we will be able to *begin* a relationship or circumstance of equal or greater value.

Being congruent means living our life with our past completed up to the present time.

By achieving awareness of our strengths and weaknesses in *beginning, continuing*, and *completing* conditions, we become capable of consciously correcting the unfulfilling ways we have lived our lives before; we become capable of undermining our uninformed tendencies to short-circuit our experiences in one or more of the phases of the cycle; we become capable of overriding the conditioned patterns of our approach to our experiences with clear, conscious choices which will allow for having our experiences fully; we become capable of bringing our lives into attunement with the principles of the play of life itself. By now, it is obvious that ascertaining in which of the forms of action we are weak and in which we are strong is crucial. Following is a list of questions to help us clarify this for ourselves:

1) Which relationships and circumstances have I consciously and effectively begun in the past year? Which relationships and circumstances do I know that I need to begin soon? Which of these am I avoiding? Why? What must I do in order to begin them?

2) Which relationships and circumstances have I consciously continued, serving them well with my energy and attention, in the past year? Which have I allowed to continue much too long? Which have I allowed myself to lose consciousness about? What do I need to do in order to serve the continuing stage of these particular relationships and circumstances? When will I do that?

3) Which relationships and circumstances have I consciously ended, bringing about real completion, in the past year? Which relationships and circumstances which have fulfilled their purpose still remain to be completed? Which of these completions am I avoiding? Why? What must I do in order to complete them? When will I do that?

THE PESKY PAST: CLEARING IT UP

You are where your attention takes you. In fact, you are your attention. If your attention is fragmented, you are fragmented. When your attention is in the past, you are in the past. When your attention is in the present moment, you are in the Presence of God and God is present in you. Let yourself die to all that does not really exist and discover what does. Let go of all you think you know. Be honest; all you know is the past. It does not exist in the eyes of God. In the eyes of God, your knowledge is but dust in the eye of a child, blinding you to the splendor of Creation.[5]

Being congruent means living life with our past completed up to the present time. In order to clear our past, there are three areas that we need to inquire into and of which we need to empty ourselves; they are what can be called incompletions, withholds, and attachments. We will discover that although we are able to separate these three areas and work to dispense with them as individual categories, they are, in many cases, intimately related, interwoven, or entangled with each other. By drawing clear distinctions between them, however, we are able to get a hold of them and to begin to take conscious actions which are relevant to one of the three forms of action, which represent particular phases of our relationships and circumstances—beginning, continuing, or ending.

Completing Incompletions. By completing our incompletions, we clear our subconsciousness of all the *continuing* relationships and circumstances which either long ago or recently should have been brought to a **conscious** conclusion. As we learned from the teaching above, we must complete the cycles of action in order to be aligned with, connected to, and in attunement with the basic flows and unfoldments of which our experiences are all-important elements. Whether we have been strong or weak in ending things, we can expect to have a list of completions to accomplish. We have left a trail of incompletions behind us because 1) we have not been aware of the cycles of action, their significance and importance to our life; 2) we have not had clarity about our specific responsibilities with regard to creating, sustaining, and destroying relationships and circumstances; 3) we have not been accustomed to making the high choice in every case; and 4) we have not had our priorities straight. But, sorry to say, those incompletions are not only trailing *behind us*; they are still alive and energized within our subconscious minds—part of the reservoir of unresolved issues of which we are full. Completing our incompletions now will serve to de-energize them and turn them into innocuous memories. That will clear the space they have been occupying within the reticular formation of our brain, which remembers all those promises we have made and keeps on reminding us of them.

INCOMPLETIONS ARE COMMITMENTS WE HAVE NOT KEPT THAT NEED EITHER TO BE KEPT OR THAT NEED TO BE CONSCIOUSLY UNCHOSEN. That is, if we now consciously choose not to do what we had previously said we were going to do, we need to communicate our new choice to whomever may still expect that we are going to fulfill the commitment. If we consciously choose not to keep the commitment but do not tell the person or persons whose life or lives are going to be affected one way or the other, then we will still suffer the drain on our energy by a nagging silent reminder from our own minds. When we make a commitment, some of our conscious attention and some of our subconscious attention becomes invested in that commitment. Until it is completed, or until it is consciously unchosen, we will be aware at all levels that we are committed to do that which we have not yet done. This being the case, we need to reflect on our past and clarify what commitments we made in the past that we did not complete. We must either complete them in order to empty ourselves, or we must consciously choose not to keep those commitments—and inform the other people who will be affected by our choice—in order to empty ourselves. Just as everything else is a process, remembering, clarifying and listing your incompletions will be a process. It may take a few days or weeks to remember all of the commitments which you have not completed, once you begin to allow yourself to *live in the question*.

WE NEED TO REFLECT ON OUR PAST AND CLARIFY WHAT COMMITMENTS WE MADE IN THE PAST THAT WE DID NOT COMPLETE.

If you recall an incompletion but the person who was to be directly affected by your fulfilled commitment is no longer available for you to speak to or write to, it is still important that you formalize your conscious choice not to fulfill the commitment by writing a letter or a note stating your present choice and stating also your apologies, if you have any need to apologize because of your unkept commitment. You can destroy the letter or note as a symbolic gesture of clearing that issue out of your psyche. Figure No. 31 may assist you in listing your incompletions.

Incompletions: [*Commitments I Have Not Kept That Need To Be Kept Or That Need To Be Consciously Unchosen*]

Commitment	*Keep Commitment*	*Unchoose Commitment*
______________________	__________	__________
______________________	__________	__________
______________________	__________	__________
______________________	__________	__________
______________________	__________	__________
______________________	__________	__________

Figure No. 31

It is important that we complete even the most mundane aspects of our life as we go about our daily living. For example, we complete our sleep cycle by making our bed, and we complete our eating cycle by washing the dishes and cleaning up the kitchen and/or dining room. We complete the items on our to do list or create a new list with the uncompleted items. We complete our work day by bringing order to the papers on our desk. If we have begun a project, we do something on a regular basis to engage with the project, and bring the project to completion within an appropriate period of time. If projects which we have begun previously have not been completed, we consciously involve ourselves again with the projects, fulfilling the *continuing* stage and, then, initiating and fulfilling the *ending* stage. The more we live our lives consciously, by assuming responsibility for the three forms of action, the quicker our lives will become true expressions of our higher nature. As we consciously practice *beginning*, *continuing*, and *ending* each thing we do, we will become accustomed to the gratifying experience of being complete, and we will notice the positive results which include feelings of being clear, of being equal to the circumstances of our lives, of being in charge of our lives, of being empowered and hopeful.

Communicating Withholds. In terms of the three forms of action, withholds primarily have to do with *continuing* and *completing*. Since they block the flow of true communication, they obstruct the *continuing* phase of the cycle and provoke a premature *destroying* of a relationship or circumstance without it having developed fully. Withholds can also block *creation* of possible relationships.

WITHHOLDS ARE WITHHELD COMMUNICATIONS WHICH KEEP US FROM BEING WITH ANOTHER PERSON FULLY. Withholds are 1) harsh judgments (or make-wrongs) we hold about another person, but which we have not spoken to that person; or 2) harsh judgments we have about another person and which we have stated to that person, but not in such a way that the judgment could be neutralized or cleared; we still harbor the resentment and hold onto the harsh judgment. In both cases the judgment acts as a barrier between us and that person. We withhold ourselves from truly open, honest relationship with that person as a result of the judgment we hold about that person. Because of our "secret," we develop a strong sense of separation between us and them, even though we may still see them often, communicate with them regularly, and even pretend to be "fine" with them. Usually, the more we withhold ourselves and judge them, the more our case against them will be strengthened. Unbeknownst to them, everything they say or do—most of which has little or no connection to our judgment of them—will, in our distorted perception, seem to validate our withheld judgment. It happens all the time.

It is of utmost importance for us to truly realize that our judgments are **our** judgments. They are projections of our own *shadow*—the thoughts and behaviors which our ego has refused to accept as part of its own humanity. Our judgments are generated by way of a configuration of personal beliefs which are products of our own personal history and the conditioning to which we have been subjected by the particular society in which we have been born and reared. We must realize that our judgments may well be products of a too-narrow view of another person—a view lacking in acceptance and compassion—and, we must release ourselves from the limited confines of our own *conditioned* egoic judgments.

Healthy relationships stand on a foundation of trust. Withholds are like cracks or fractures in the foundation. A relationship whose foundation is weakened by withholds will reflect that weakness. All of us have experienced feeling the separation between ourselves and someone with whom we have been very close. We have felt the barrier between us, and we have attempted to figure out what was wrong. Feeling as though we were thrashing about in the dark, we made vain attempts to re-establish our closely bonded relationship. But without knowing what was really going on in the other person, we were unable to make the relationship work. As long as a hostile communication is withheld, its negative energy hangs in the space of the relationship and generates mistrust and relational tension on the part of both people. Once the withhold is communicated to the person from whom it is being withheld, then the person who has been withholding is *free* and the person who was being judged understands what has been going on and has the opportunity to clarify the situation or to, with understanding, just let the other person *have his problem*.

From whom are you withholding a resentful, hostile, judgmental communication, which keeps you from being with that person fully? Who else? And who else? Take a moment now and write down at least one that just popped up when you read that question. If two or three names came to mind immediately, write their names down, and the during the next few days write down your specific withholds. Sit in the silence alone and get clear about the judgments that you are holding about those people and write them down. Confess them to yourself. Clarify them to yourself. That part of the process will clear you to a great degree. The following form for listing withholds may assist you [Model No. 32]. The next step will be to share your withholds with the people on your list.

COMPLETING OUR INCOMPLETIONS NOW WILL SERVE TO DE-ENERGIZE THEM AND TURN THEM INTO INNOCUOUS MEMORIES.

Person: | ***Withholds:*** *[Withheld Communications That Keep Me From Being With the Other Person Fully]*

________________	____
________________	____
________________	____
________________	____
________________	____
________________	____

Figure No. 32

Sharing Withholds. The sharing of withholds is done to clear the space between two individuals. It is primarily a service to the person who is *withholding* a judgment; but, of course, it serves both people since the relationship is undermined by that withhold.

1) Both the receiver and the sharer of the withholds should be seated across from each other and should be looking at each other, if it is at all possible.

2) It is, of course, best if both parties understand the psychological value which is intrinsic to the sharing of withholds. (In some cases, only one party will need to take full responsibility).

3) Both the receiver and the sharer of the withholds should understand that the process is highly honorable and that it serves the highest good of both parties, the highest good of their relationship, and the highest good of others with whom they interact together.

4) Both the receiver and the sharer of withholds should understand that the process may cause some short-term discomfort, but will ultimately serve to lessen tension between them.

5) The secret to clearing the space between two people by the sharing of withholds is the presence of *innocent listening* on the part of the receiver of the withholds. The person who has been withholding himself really needs to be heard in order to be free and to be able once again to relate openly with the other person.

6) The most effective formula for sharing withholds is that the person receiving the withhold say merely, "I see," "I understand," "Okay," "Thank you," or some other words which indicate that they have really heard and are willingly receiving the communication.

7) The receiver of the withhold should notice if his/her emotional reactivity is triggered, but should not defend or explain anything at the time of receiving withholds. It is to be expected that the ego will have an experience of being attacked and misunderstood; and that it will become reactive to some degree within us as we receive the withholds.

8) The sharer of withholds should notice if his/her emotional reactivity is triggered, but should maintain an objective attitude in "confessing" his/her judgment(s).

9) The sharer of withholds is to communicate with emotional courage, self-discipline, and gracefulness. (If only emotional courage is used, it may only hurt the other person and cause him/her to close down completely, making the relational tension worse than it was before the withholds were communicated.)

10) Both the receiver and the sharer of the withholds should thank each other when the sharing is complete.

11) Both the receiver and the sharer of the withholds should understand that shared withholds are not to be used in the future by the receiver to blame or malign the sharer.

The following is an example of Bubba and Bonnie sharing their withholds with each other:

Bubba: "Bonnie, I feel resentment about the fact that you just went out on your own and ordered furniture for our new office. I think that is something we should have done together. It seems to me to be very presumptuous and pushy on your part."

Bonnie: "Thank you."

Bonnie: "Bubba, I feel hurt that you rescheduled the Grand Opening party for the office without conferring with me about it."

Bubba: "I see."

Once all the withholds have been communicated, then the parties may talk about the judgments and the actions which provoked the judgments. Without defending themselves or blaming the other person, they can offer explanations that may help to shed some light on the motivations and choices which caused the other person an upset. The following is an example of Bubba and Bonnie offering each other explanations for their behavior:

Bubba: "I understand how you might be upset about the Grand Opening, but I had to make a decision on the spot and you were not available. Because the paving of the parking lot was rescheduled for the date we had originally chosen, and I had to tell the caterer for sure, one way or the other, by 5:00 p.m., I was forced to make the decision without conferring with you. I'm sorry it upset you."

Bonnie: "I understand now that you did the best you could and that you didn't mean to exclude me. Thank you for explaining it to me."

Bonnie: "I see now that I should have included you in ordering the furniture for the office. I actually went ahead and did it myself in order to relieve you from having to be involved with it—and I thought it would be a great surprise for you. I can see now that I should have at least asked you if you wanted to be a part of that process. I'm sorry it upset you."

Bubba: "I understand how you might have thought it would have been a relief to me not to be involved, since I was so impatient that day we went to look for furniture. But, I really would want you to ask me in the future about such things. And, by the way, I really like the new furniture!"

Withholds, which are so detrimental to relationships, are often not based on fact. One person may make an assumption about something which he thought the other person did or did not do, react to his own assumption with a harsh judgment, and withhold his communication about the assumption and the judgment. His *mind trip* will have the same effect on him as the action would have had if it had really transpired. The relationship is, of course, just as stressed as if the untrue assumption were true. As an example, I include here the story of something which happened to me some years ago.

When I returned to Miami in 1985 after having been on a spiritual journey for seven months, my townhouse was still occupied by friends who lived there while I was gone. So I needed a place to stay for awhile. I stayed for a few weeks with a person whom I had known casually, but whom I respected and who I knew respected me. We had always been very warm and open and accepting of each other. That continued to be the case, until after I had moved out of her place and once again set up housekeeping. Whenever I saw her after that I either received a very cool greeting, which was obviously full of her withholds, or she would completely snub me—which was also, of course, her withholding herself. I did ask her a couple of times if there was something wrong, and she told me icily that there was not. I thought perhaps she was just upset about my moving out and that she would soon soften.

HEALTHY RELATIONSHIPS STAND ON A FOUNDATION OF TRUST. WITHHOLDS ARE LIKE CRACKS OR FRACTURES IN THE FOUNDATION.

After several months of this kind of behavior, I called her up and told her that I could plainly see that she was either hurt or angry at me about something and asked her to please tell me what it was. I was very surprised when she said, "I think you stole my iron." Of all the things she might have said, this was the most unexpected, ridiculous, and even humorous allegation. I followed the protocol of receiving withholds and said, "I see," (or one of the other *receiving* responses). I asked her if there was any other thing that she was upset about or anything else she wanted to say about her suspicion of my stealing her iron. After she told me how the iron had disappeared at the same time I left, I told her simply that I did not take the iron. I reminded her that someone else in her apartment building had also been using the iron from time to time while I lived there, and suggested that maybe that person had forgotten to return it. Her attitude, her tone of voice, and her energy began to soften as soon as she had shared her withhold. She later told me that the visiting friend of her neighbor had borrowed the iron and had left it on the guest room closet shelf when she left a few months after I left. The neighbor had not opened the closet in that room since then. But whether she had found the iron or not, the point is that she had allowed her *assumption* the weight of authority and had judged me quite harshly for something I not only did not do, but for which I never could have guessed she was judging me. **Only** her communication of her withheld thought and feelings allowed me the opportunity to clear myself with her—and, in this case, to set us both free.

Clearing ourselves without sharing the withholds. Most of our pasts will include some people from whom we have withheld ourselves who are no longer available for us to share our withholds. Some may have relocated (without a trace), some may have died, some may be so closed down to us that we know that communication would not now be possible. In those cases, we must clear ourselves in another way. I suggest either writing a series of letters or having a close friend or loved one take the role of that other person for a face-to-face sharing. Both of these methods can prove to be highly therapeutic.

The procedure for clearing ourselves through the writing of letters is as follows:

1) Write a first draft of the letter, just allowing everything you have been withholding to fall out of you onto the paper. Pause and see if there is anything else you need to say. Write it down. Pause again. Write again, until you feel expressed. Then burn the letter without rereading it to symbolize your emptying yourself of its contents.

2) The next day, write a new letter restating everything you have already stated in the first draft. Pause. Write. Pause. Write. Burn the letter.

3) On the third day, write a new letter, but attempt to have this be the last letter you will write to clear yourself. You will notice that the energy of your communication has a different quality than the first time you wrote. By this time, your communication should be, naturally, not only courageous, but also self-disciplined and graceful. If you were to send the letter, your reader most probably would not have difficulty reading it without becoming reactive. When you have finished this letter, reread it and then symbolically burn it.

4) If you do not feel completely free from the discomfort you have felt for so long, write again the next day and the next, if necessary. The important purpose of this exercise is to clear up whatever amount of attention and energy has been being captured by those particular withheld communications. Even this type of expression can be very effective.

The procedure for communicating to someone who is taking the role of the person from whom you have been withholding communication will be exactly the same as the outlined above, except that the surrogate will only be allowed to listen innocently and respond with "Thank you." You may need to repeat this exercise a few times in order to feel fully expressed.

Letting Go of Attachments. ATTACHMENT IS MENTAL, EMOTIONAL AND/OR PHYSICAL HOLDING ONTO OR CLINGING TO PERSONS, PLACES, THINGS, OR CIRCUMSTANCES. In regard to the three forms of action which make up the play of life, attachment is an obsessive prolongation of the *continuing* phase of a relationship or circumstance, without the intention or will to take responsibility for the *ending* phase of the cycle. Interestingly, what is viewed and treated as addiction in the West is viewed and treated as attachment in the East. Jacquelyn Small equates addiction to attachment in her book, *Transformers*.

> ***Addiction = attachment.*** *When we are attached to something (or someone), we have forgotten who we are. We feel we cannot be whole without this something. We experience pain and suffering whenever our attachment threatens to leave us...like losing an arm or a leg. Attachment is the cause of suffering.* ***Addiction*** *is the cause of suffering. Non-attachment does not mean non-caring; it is non-***needing***...non-obsessing. It is removing emotional investment so that one can truly see clearly and therefore care appropriately for the* ***other's sake****. Paradoxically,* ***attachment*** *is non-loving.*[6]

Attachments are the ego's riveting desires which have become obsessive attempts to control relationships and circumstances in order to fulfill its agendas of winning, being right, looking good, and surviving. Driven by its own underlying fear-based thought patterns, tormented by countless perceived threats to its security, and burdened by its sense of having to "figure it all out" and "cause it all to happen," the ego strives to overpower all outside influences in order to make things turn out a certain way. Its obsessive behaviors become transparent once we realize that its controlling mentality shows up again and again as attachments—on which its pseudo-identity depends. It is not the nature of the ego to step back, to "chill out," to achieve a clear and broad perspective on things, and to let go. It is the ego's nature to worry and fret, to deny the realities of the situation, and to hold on tight to what it likes or loves.

In Nikkyo Niwano's book, *Buddhism for Today, A Modern Interpretation of the Threefold Lotus Sutra*, that principal sutra (teaching) of Buddhism identifies the stage of development at which the mind can discern things clearly through the five senses as the stage called "contact" and describes the characteristics of that stage, including attachment.

With such mental development, feelings of pain, pleasure, like, and dislike are produced. This is ***sensation****. When such feelings appear,* ***desire*** *for things arises spontaneously. The desire referred to here means attachment, whose meaning is little different from that of love as this word is commonly used. In other words, this is a state of mind that has preferences and that clings to what it likes. When we have desire for something, we try to hold onto it. Conversely, we try to avoid what we consider unpleasant, or undesirable. This state of mind is called* ***clinging****.*

Man's life develops in this way, so that the basic cause of a life of suffering is fundamental ignorance. Suffering occurs because man does not know the law applicable to all things and does not have a right view of the world and of life; even when he is aware of it, he disregards it. Only if man can rid himself of this ignorance and set his mind in the direction of the law will his deeds (practice) be correctly directed. When his mind is set on the right track, his sufferings in this world disappear, and eventually he will attain peace of mind.[7]

As has been stated in several different ways in this book, the ego function of the lower mind directly perceives all people, places, things and circumstances of the world as being comprised of a dual nature; it *accepts*, *approves of*, and *prefers* one aspect of that duality which it, then, relates to and identifies itself with—and it rejects and dis-identifies itself from the other aspect of the duality. The ego has as many preferences as there are things for it to judge, which is literally everything with which it comes into *contact*. The people, places, things and circumstances which the ego perceives as somehow capable of filling the hole of its considerable neediness, it *grabs hold of* and *holds on tight*. As Satprem tells us in *Sri Aurobindo or The Adventure of Consciousness*:

ATTACHMENTS ARE THE EGO'S RIVETING DESIRES WHICH HAVE BECOME OBSESSIVE ATTEMPTS TO CONTROL RELATIONSHIPS AND CIRCUMSTANCES...

...it is our nature, in the sense that we have grown accustomed to responding to certain vibrations rather than others, to being moved or pained by certain things rather than by others; and this set of habits has, apparently crystallized into a personality we call our "self." Yet, if we look more closely, we can hardly say that it is "we" who have acquired all these habits. Our environment, our education, our atavism, our traditions have made the choice for us. At every instant they choose what we want or desire, what we like or dislike. It is as if life took place without us.

> *...this small **frontal being** is surrounded, overhung, supported, pervaded by and set in motion by a whole hierarchy of "worlds" as ancient wisdom well knew.... **Yet we are conscious only of some bubbling on the surface.***[8]

As is also stated elsewhere in this book, it is the nature of the ego to fear and resist change and to strive to maintain the status quo—no matter how miserable or unfulfilling—unless it feels that a particular change is highly likely to or guaranteed to secure its future. With this intrinsic mandate, the ego will most certainly be inclined to get stuck in the *continuing* stage of the cycle of action, overidentifying itself with and clinging to the people, places, things, and circumstances of that particular stage. That being the case, we can see why it is of great importance that we learn to *let go*, so that we may be moved along with the natural flow of change—so that we may be *changed by* and *discover the deeper truth about ourselves* from the fascinating ebbs and flows of our life experiences.

In order to become changelings, heroic journeyers, Self-expressions, and great ones, we really must free ourselves from those persons, places, things, and circumstances to whom/which we are holding on. In order for our full humanity to be developed and for our destiny to be fulfilled, we really need to strip ourselves down and dis-identify ourselves from all that we have used to identify ourselves in the past. We must tear ourselves loose from those things which we have used as a statement of who we are. In order to become authentic, we must let go of our attachments to certain preferences which we have formed. In order for the always-changing process of life to unfold its secrets to us, we must let go. Jacquelyn Small calls the consciousness of the heart level Fourth Force, and she speaks eloquently about letting go:

> *Fourth Force is where we practice non-attachment, the art of "letting go and letting God." Letting go is an **active** force that **wills** our ego to release its perpetual judging and accept things exactly as they are. Both "the good" and "the bad" have become part of the **plan** for me....It feels like forgiveness... like being calm and centered....I am operating from my heart, but with intelligence, the beginnings of love....It is not a naive, mushy love that allows others to walk all over it. It has dignity and discrimination. It has understanding. It seeks, above all else, to harmonize the two natures I possess.*[9]

So take an honest look at your life. See as clearly as you can the persons, places, things, and circumstances to which you are attached. And even if you feel that you are not ready to detach yet, at least be honest with yourself about the fact that you are attached. Make a sincere commitment to begin to free yourself from those attachments. You are not them, and they are not really a representation of who you are. Why not write down at least one of your attachments now? The form I have created [Figure No. 33] may be of assistance in bringing clarity.

Attachments: *[Persons, Places, Things, or Circumstances That Do Not Serve My Highest Good That I Am Holding Onto]*

Persons	*Places*	*Things*	*Circumstances*
____________	____________	____________	____________
____________	____________	____________	____________
____________	____________	____________	____________
____________	____________	____________	____________
____________	____________	____________	____________

Figure No. 33

Getting Our Lives Straight

Becoming a congruent experience and expression of one's Self implies becoming clear on the inside and reflecting that clarity on the outside—as our manifest world. I have chosen this beautiful representation of Gautama Buddha's Fourth Noble Truth from Ram Dass' *Be Here Now* as the touchstone for the aspect of becoming congruent which I call Getting Our Lives Straight [Figure No. 34]. "Straight" in this case means "correct," "cleaned up," "brought into truth," or "made Lawful." As we can see from the model, Ram Dass' translation of the Buddha's Eightfold Path for getting rid of desire says:

FOURTH NOBLE TRUTH is:

THE EIGHTFOLD PATH
(for getting rid of desire)

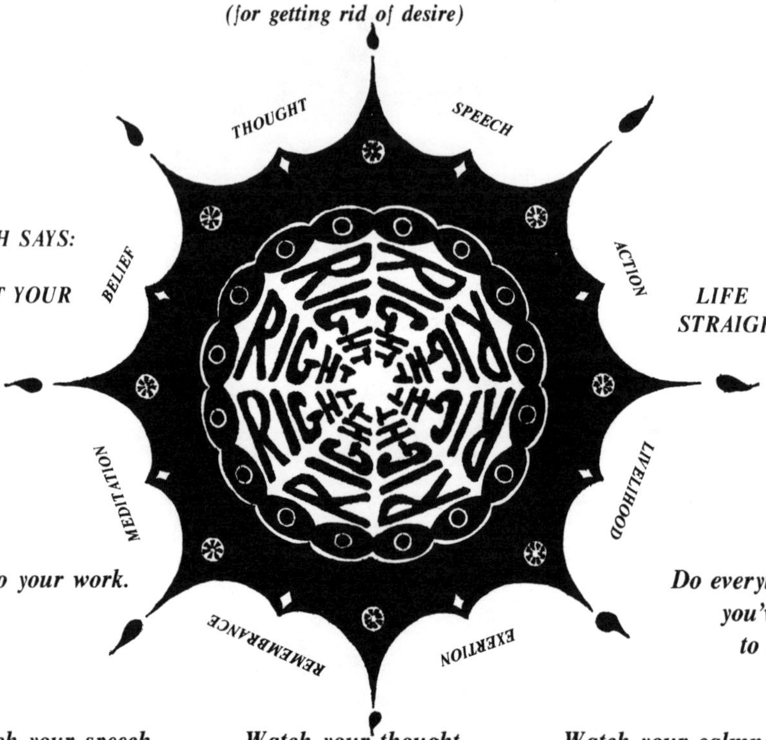

WHICH SAYS:

GET YOUR LIFE STRAIGHT

Do your work.

Do everything you've got to do.

Watch your speech. Watch your thought. Watch your calmness.

Get your calm center going. Live your life in such a way as to get yourself straight, to get free of attachment that just keeps sucking you in all the time.

Figure No. 34

Get Your Life Straight
Do Your Work
Do Everything You've Got To Do
Watch Your Speech
Watch Your Thought
Watch your Calmness
Get Your Calm Center Going

Live Your Life In Such A Way As To Get Yourself Straight—To Get Free Of Attachment That Just Keeps Sucking You In All The Time.[10]

"Desire" is the ego's preference for and attachment to particular people, particular places, particular things, and particular circumstances. As we know, the ego has strong desires that all of the elements of life be a *certain* way—a way that directly serves its personal purposes. In order to undermine and sublimate the ego's agenda and to consciously choose the thoughts and behaviors which will release our life from the ego's hold into the unfoldment which is its intrinsic nature, we must—*with the force of will*—pry the clutching fingers of the ego from all aspects of our life, as we *let go and let God* direct our life along its destiny path. We learn to relinquish responsibility for the *results* of our actions, but to take full responsibility for correcting our *thoughts*, for correcting our *speech*, and for correcting our *actions*. The teachings of the Eightfold Path of Gautama Buddha—as can all of the high teachings of all of our holy men and holy women—can certainly be supportive to all who take the hero's journey.

> *When a man clearly understands the Fourfold Noble Truth, then the Noble Eightfold Path will lead him away from greed; and if he is free from greed, he will not quarrel with the world, he will not kill, nor steal, nor commit adultery, nor cheat, nor abuse, nor flatter, nor envy, nor lose his temper, nor forget the transiency of life nor will he be unjust.*[11]

Nikkyo Niwano elaborates the Eightfold Path for us as follows:

> **Right Thinking**. *"Right thinking" means not to incline toward a self-centered attitude toward things but to think of things rightly, from a higher standpoint. This teaches us to abandon the **"three evils of the mind,"** covetousness, resent-*

ment, and evil-mindedness, and to think of things rightly...More precisely, these three evils are the greedy mind (covetousness) that thinks only of one's own gain; the angry mind (resentment) that does not like it when things do not turn out as one wishes; and the evil mind (evil-mindedness) that wants to have its own way in everything.

Right Speech. *"Right speech" teaches us to use right words in our daily lives and to avoid the **"four evils of the mouth"**: lying (false language), a double tongue, ill speaking (slander), and improper language (careless language).*

Right Action. *"Right action" means daily conduct in accordance with the precepts of the Buddha. For this purpose it is important to refrain from the **"three evils of the body"** that hinder right actions: needless killing, stealing, and committing adultery or other sexual misconduct.*

Right Livelihood. *"Right living" means to gain food, clothing, shelter, and the other necessities of life in a right way. This teaches us not to earn our livelihood through work that makes trouble for others or through a vocation useless to society but to live on a justifiable income that we can obtain through right work, a vocation useful to others.*

Right Exertion. *"Right endeavor" means to engage constantly in right conduct without being idle or deviating from the right way, avoiding such wrongs as the three evils of the mind, the four evils of the mouth, and the three evils of the body...*

Right Remembrance. *"Right memory" means to practice with a right mind as the Buddha did. It cannot be truly said that we have the same mind as the Buddha unless we have a right mind not only toward ourselves but also toward others, and still further, toward all things. If we hope that only we ourselves may be right, we will become stubborn and self-satisfied people who are alienated from the world. We cannot say we have the same mind as the Buddha unless we address ourselves to all things in the universe with a fair and right mind.*

Right Meditation. *"Right meditation" means always determine to believe in the teachings of the Buddha and not to be agitated by any change of circumstances.*

What we meditate on, we become. So, on what do we meditate? What must we meditate on? On the *greatness*, not the littleness. On the big thoughts, not the petty thoughts. On the big picture, not the narrow views of our ego's perception. If we meditate on the truth, we become the truth.

Right Belief. *"Right view" means to abandon a self-centered way of looking at things and to have a right view of the Buddha. In other words, it is to take refuge in the Buddha.*[12]

We have made life choices and have based many of our actions on bits and pieces of ideologies that have been given to us by other people since we were very young. We have taken on their belief systems. What we must begin to do now is *source our Self*. We source our Self through deep listening all day everyday—listening inside and listening to the signals and the messages from our outer world. And, along the way, we realize that a new belief system is emerging within us. It is **nurtured** by way of our own experiences and by way of our relationships with ourself, with our Self, with our fellow human beings, with all other creatures and life forms, and with God.

THE RESULT: A PEACEFUL MIND AND AN OPEN HEART

A much-needed experience of personal freedom results from reviewing our lives and taking specific actions in the context of the three forms of action, clearing our past and getting our lives straight. Each time we bring clarity where there was confusion, we feel relieved psychologically. Each time we consciously begin, continue, or complete a cycle of action, we feel better. Each time we empty ourselves of an unresolved issue from the past, we have an experience of being cleansed and healed. Each time we make a correction in any one of the eight areas outlined in Buddha's Fourth Noble Truth, we feel freer, more present, more at ease and peaceful. And, as we learn to keep our lives cleaned up and cleared and completed up the present, we will become accustomed to a sense of personal freedom with which we have not been familiar before. Although the process of bringing order out of the chaos of our lives does require some work on our part—and lots of self-honesty—the results are definitely well worth our efforts. Just do it!

TOWARD EXPANSION AND SELF-MASTERY

1. Reflect on your life regarding the three forms of action. Evaluate your strengths and weaknesses as to the beginning, continuing, and completing cycles of action. Are you strong or weak in beginning things? Are you strong or weak in continuing things? Are you strong or weak in completing things?

2. Begin to do each aspect of your life consciously in terms of the three forms of action. Break your practice down to smallest increments and be sure to complete each cycle: Begin the eating cycle by preparing the food; continue the eating cycle by serving and eating the food; complete the eating cycle by washing and drying the dishes; complete doing dishes by putting them away. Apply this kind of consciousness to each aspect of your living cycles. In this way, become more aware of your strengths and weaknesses as to the three forms of action.

3. Make list of the relationships with which you are presently involved. Identify which cycle of action you are presently experiencing in each relationship. Clarify whether it is time for the relationship to be taken to the next stage. For example:

BEGINNING	CONTINUING	COMPLETING
Joe	Joanna	Jean-Paul
John	Javier	Janice

Make similar lists for projects and other endeavors in which you are presently engaged. Also identify other relationships, projects, and endeavors that you want to or need to begin. Assess whether now is the time to begin them.

When the lists are complete, take whatever action is appropriate to serve your conscious participation with the cycles of action.

4. Use Buddha's Fourth Noble Truth as a guideline for clarifying which areas you need to concentrate on in terms of practice in order to support your own awakening and to get your life straight. If you realize that you need to concentrate first on "right thought" and "right livelihood," then begin to include the practice of correcting your thoughts on a daily basis and begin to take actions which will lead to a correction in how you make your living.

   When these practices are well-established as important parts of your conscious process, include another form of practice from the Eightfold Path.

5. Become more and more aware of when you create confusion or discord (chaos) in your life or the life of others and when you bring clarity and harmony (order) out of chaos. Whenever you have created chaos, process yourself to clarity and harmony and attempt to then bring order to the situation.

LET US ANNOUNCE THAT AWAKENING
TO THE WORLD SO AS TO THOROUGHLY
ACTIVATE OUR OWN REMEMBERING
AND TO HELP OTHERS REMEMBER.

Part Four

REACHING FOR THE STARS

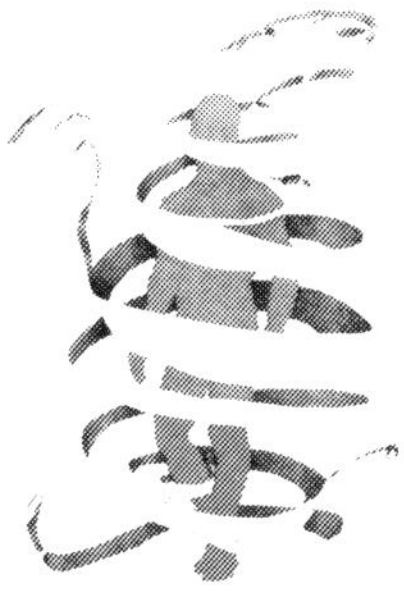

...It is possible to believe that all that the human mind has ever accomplished is but the dream before the awakening... Out of our...lineage, minds will spring, that will reach back to us in our littleness to know us better than we know ourselves. A day will come, one day in the unending succession of days, when beings, beings who are now latent in our thoughts and hidden in our loins, shall stand upon this earth as one stands upon a footstool, and shall laugh and reach out their hands amidst the stars.

—*H.G. Wells*
The Discovery of the Future[4]

Let us now be awestruck at the Vast, Complex, and Mysterious Cosmic Being in which we exist.

AFTERWORD

Although the basic elements of congruence are presented within the pages of *A Call To Greatness*, there is, of course, still much more than can be said and/or elaborated on this huge and important subject. However, if the sincere student will apply the precepts and practices as outlined here, he or she will begin to embody the intelligence of congruence and begin to be continually taught by the experiences of his or her own life. That is as it should be. The process of self-discovery and Self-expression is just that—a process of learning to learn from the substance of our very own lives. By learning to live consciously and congruently, our lives become fascinating personal explorations and adventures.

My heartfelt assertion is that many of us who are presently living on planet earth have somehow been awakened to the point that we now have the capacity to stretch ourselves enough to rise to the occasion of these enormously challenging times. I feel strongly that we are capable of living our lives more consciously and more selflessly than we have ever lived them before. And, although we are lavishly supported by the Intelligence of the evolutionary process itself, it is still a most difficult stretch. I often liken the challenge to pulling ourselves out of a pit of quicksand. The quicksand is the consciousness of the earlier stages of evolution which still exist within our body/minds and the mental-egoic stage itself, which has trapped our consciousness in constant rounds of mentalizing for a very long time.

Our ability to rise to the occasion of these complex and critical times is the amazing greater capacity which I point to, acknowledge and celebrate throughout *A Call To Greatness*. That capacity is the hope I see for all of us and for our world. Vive la capacité!

In the days of Gautama the Buddha and in the days after the death of Jesus the Christ, predictions abounded among the "enlightened" of things that were to come to pass at some future time—this time. The predictions included things which humans of those epochs could barely imagine, much less conceive of themselves. But, for those whose references were exclusively their own inner knowing and the God gleams which flashed across their minds, their capacity for receiving and communicating the prophecies proved both their faith and their understanding of the evolutionary nature of the spiritual unfoldment of humankind. As they looked upon their manifest world, these privileged few saw primitive conditions of mind and world which did not, of themselves, forecast the Age of Reason, the Industrial Age, the Space Age, the Information Age, or the Age of the New Paradigm.

Today, we need only to give a cursory glance at our manifest world to clearly see that a revolutionary Force/evolutionary Intelligence is at work within humankind and within our world. I was nearly forty-five years old before I fully accepted the fact that airplanes can fly. That fact was just too revolutionary for my mind to grasp, although planes were flying long before I was born. By that time humans had already logged many years of flying time, had orbited the earth wearing space suits and piloting spaceships, had traveled by spacecraft to the moon, and had "splashed down" back on earth, having forever changed our view of our world and our relationship to it.

By then our world had experienced another technological revolution which put computers first in our offices and then in our homes. By then the supersonic Concorde had begun to fly transoceanic routes in a fraction of the time it takes the impressive 747 jet aircraft. And since then, rather than a slowing down or a leveling off of technological breakthroughs, there has been an explosion of high-tech software and hardware which would cause the minds of Gautama the Buddha and Jesus the Christ to spin. Virtual reality has been breaking the barriers of the human mind and experience for a few years now, human fetuses have been grown in test tubes, and the science of genetic engineering is fast approaching the technology of changing the genetic structure of our biological systems and, perhaps, even cloning human beings. What a revolutionary/evolutionary time of changes in our manifest world which are a direct result of the leap in consciousness which is occurring within our human psyches. With only this perfunctory acknowledgement of a few of the amazing achievements which directly influence and reshape us in many obvious and many indecipherable ways, we are, at least, capable of *guessing* that the future of our species and of our world will include triumphs of technology which will be even more difficult to grasp (at least for me) than the fact that airplanes can fly.

In order to match in human thought and human behavior what is happening so fast in our human capacities to bring forth the unimagined, we must rise to the occasion of these truly promising times by stretching ourselves to become non-judgmental of, compassionate toward, and helpful to each other. As the yet-to-be-fulfilled prophesies of the revelationary future rush into our present, we must wrest ourselves free from the stranglehold of the self-centered ego which has had its glory day. The stuff of today and tomorrow is much too big to be contained within the narrow views and limited agendas of that now outdated level of consciousness which served us well for awhile and which has held us back for too long now.

The first step out of the prison of that egoic structure of mind occurs when we begin to access the higher Self which resides in all its brilliance just beyond the boundaries of that rigid, dreary, fearful littleness. The application of the principles and practices offered in the previous pages can serve both as battering rams (a throwback to medieval days) and as virtual reality shifts (a high-tech forward leap) in dealing with the walls of conditioned responses which have heretofore defined us. Once we can grasp the fact that planes can fly, that even our spacecraft are fast becoming obsolete, that realities are virtually the stuff of minds, that "all bets are off" and "the sky is the limit" in terms of breakthroughs on all levels of human life, we are able to redefine ourselves as the epochal changelings which we are. Once we can actually "see" the realness of what is occurring in ourselves and in our world, we are able to perceive ourselves within the vast context of human possibility and align ourselves with the call to greatness which the very air we breathe seems to represent to us now.

Having lost the ability to trust ourselves, we have lost the ability to trust each other. By realizing our Greatness-in-dormancy and recapturing the essential human faculty of Self-referencing, we become self-trusting, trustworthy and trusting of others. By becoming real (genuine, authentic, congruent), with all which that implies, we gain the condition of informed innocence which is the catalyst and the spongy attractor of innovation, revelation, and evolution.

With the urgent problems of our times impressing themselves upon our hearts and minds, the creative outpourings of new ideas, programs, and approaches have begun to remake our society. With our educational systems having run amuck, ingenious, original, and imaginative new programs are springing up throughout the land—programs which honor and celebrate the child's ability to learn about learning itself.

With our political bureaucracies having become bulging warehouses of unwieldy staffs, inefficient practices, and outdated procedures, we have full-scale investigations being led by the vice president and light shown on the musty and heretofore invulnerable secrets of a two-hundred-year-old system. As we peer through the dirty windows, we smell the dust and see the cobwebs in the government attic. We also sense that the freshness of these times holds within itself a promise not only of a housecleaning, but of a virtual reconstruction of the attic itself. We have wanted our politicians to change. But, instead, the times have changed. And in these big times, the mucky-duck politicians are being forced to change as the light through those dirty windows shines itself upon their littleness. Many are leaving office of their own accord as they, too, see more clearly what has been going on.

At the same time that major religious institutions were being exposed for being less than Holy, a spiritual renaissance began to show up across cultures and around the world. The freshness and bright new intelligence of the emergent spiritual culture captures within its consciousness the vibrance, the value, and the viability of the individual spiritual being. No longer are the unenlightened institutions able to hold us captive by our own desire for heaven and fear of hell. No longer does priest, or minister, or pastor necessarily mean holy person to us. We must see the evidence of true spiritual essence on the faces and in the lives of those we hold dear in this way.

While some of our senior citizens still focus primarily on their retirement, their pensions, and their social security, many others of our elders live lives of dedicated service which model for all of us the levels of wisdom that our maturity can denote. Some of these wise, compassionate, loving and giving seniors act as grandparents to children who need that kind of guidance. Others fulfill the role of classroom tutors, crossing guards, soup kitchen servers, group facilitators, builders of homes for the homeless, police aides, and more. Many now maintain their open-minded studentship, learning about themselves until their last day on earth.

By the very nature of the times in which we live, we have become more aware, which equates to more conscious and more intelligent. We now walk about in a heightened conditioned of awareness much as a fish swims about in a stream of life-giving water. We have begun to emerge from the period which proved that a little knowledge is a dangerous thing. We now have more informed awareness and we now know that we need more informed awareness in order to shine forth the potency of our own Greatness. Within that greatness abides the enlightened answers to all of the big questions—questions which act as evocateurs and catalysts for the changes which must and will now and next occur. As we learn better how to live in the world and not of the world, we will bring to each other the heartleaping surprises for which we all yearn and for which we are all responsible.

Although these are the days of the apocalypse, they can be the grandest of times—for each of us individually and for all of us collectively—as we awaken into the further reaches of our encoded potency. We can revel in these times in which age-old prophecies are being fulfilled. We can work and play and be together in the consciousness of awe and amazement and unprecedented change. We can now reach way beyond the point which we understood to be our limits, knowing that the limits have already been so extended that there is only spaciousness and possibility where before there were walls and ceilings of mind.

We are completely capable of "surprising the universe," as Brian Swimme suggests. And, as we surprise the universe we will surprise ourselves and each other by bringing forth a freshness and a greatness which will shine forth in human consciousness, human endeavor, and human relationship—we will love our God, our world, ourselves, our labor—and we will love each other. We will be the turning of the tide, the shift in paradigms, the promise fulfilled, the manifestation of what is now unseen and now unheard. We will be the universal human songs and the cosmic human dances which to now have remained unsung and unchoreographed in realms of being beyond the boundaries of our present awareness.

Our scientists have taught us that we are made of star-stuff. And when our human ears first heard such cosmic words, our starry hearts leapt beyond the confines of ordinary thoughtforms in a moment of remembering which shook us to our earthly depths and vibrated us to our cosmic heights. Just as Albert Einstein was "shattered" by his mystical moment of revelation which redefined all scientific thought in the field of quantum physics, we are "shattered" by the news of our inherent togetherness with all things. And, yet, it seems as though we have always known—that we had only forgotten. By always remembering that breathtaking news and allowing the awe of that truth to animate us, we can look into each other's eyes and see the Force of Creation and the ongoing Evolutionary Impulse which abide therein. By living in amazement about the mysterious beings we are, and living with a sense of wonder about the epoch in which we live, we can allow ourselves to "lighten up" as we shift our attention to things far fleeting tenure on this planet by taking the opportunity to utilize our lifetime to experience the only true human adventure—the quest for higher levels of Being. With our Divine Impulse pulsing powerfully within us, we can reach back to those starry skies from which we came, reconnecting with the beginning of Creation, wherein we will find revealed the secrets of our Source and the phantasms of our future. With the Alpha and the Omega as our touchstone, we are sure to become consummate star children once again.

LET US LEAP FROM THE HIGHEST PROMONTORIES
OF DOUBT AND FEAR AND FLING OURSELVES
INTO THE INVISIBLE ETHERS OF EVOLVING
CREATION WITH THE ULTIMACY OF TRUST
AND THE HUMILITY OF SURRENDER.

CHAPTER NOTES

Title Pages

1. Satprem, *Sri Aurobindo or The Adventure of Consciousness*, Mt. Vernon, WA: Institute for Evolutionary Research, 1993, p. 145.
2. Bhagwan Shree Rajneesh, *I Say Unto You*, Rajneeshpuram, OR: Rajneesh Foundation International, 1980, p. 7.
3. B. Roberts, *The Path To No-Self*, Boston: Shambhala, 1985, p. 121.
4. H. G. Wells, "The Discovery of the Future," *Nature*, Vol. 65, 1902, p. 326.

Introduction

1. Satprem, *Sri Aurobindo or The Adventure of Consciousness*, p. 3.
2. V. B. Tower, *The Process of Intuition*, Wheaton, IL: The Theosophical Publishing House, p. xiii.

Part One

Chapter One

1. S. Rinpoche, *The Tibetan Book of Living and Dying*, New York: HarperCollins, 1992, p. 20.
2. I. M. G. Dhyana, *MoreThanMe*, San Francisco: Dhyana Press, 1993, p. 180.
3. B. Swimme, *The Universe Is A Green Dragon: A Cosmic Creation Story*, Santa Fe, NM: Bear & Company, pp. 17-18.
4. *Webster's Third New International Dictionary*, Springfield, MA: G. & C. Merriam Company, Publishers, 1968, p. 1521.
5. Levi, *Aquarian Gospel of Jesus the Christ*, Marina del Rey, CA: DeVorss & Company, 1987, pp. 22-23.
6. T. Berry and B. Swimme, *The Universe Story: From the Primordial Flaring Forth to the Ecozoic Era—A Celebration of the Unfolding of the Cosmos*, New York: HarperCollins, 1992.
7. J. Campbell, *The Hero With a Thousand Faces*, Princeton, NJ: Princeton University Press, 1973, p. 58.

8. B. M. Hubbard, *The Evolutionary Journey: A Personal Guide to a Positive Future*, San Francisco: Evolutionary Press, 1982, p. 16.
9. J. Houston, *The Possible Human*, Los Angeles: J. P. Tarcher, 1976, p. 213.
10. R. Smothermon, *Transforming #1*, San Francisco: Context Publications, 1982, p. 34.
11. P. D. Ouspensky, *The Psychology of Man's Possible Evolution*, New York: Random House, 1974, p. 8.

Chapter Two

1. A. Einstein, cited in Stephen Mitchell (ed.), *The Enlightened Mind: An Anthology of Sacred Prose*, New York: HarperCollins, 1991, p. 191.
2. *Webster's Third New International Dictionary*, p. 1174.
3. P. D. Ouspensky, *The Psychology of Man's Possible Evolution*, pp. 12-13.
4. Ibid. p. 15.
5. C. Pearson, *The Hero Within: Six Archetypes We Live By*, San Francisco: Harper & Row, 1989, p. 141.
6. B. Swimme, *The Universe Is A Green Dragon*, p. 147.
7. V. B. Tower, *The Process of Intuition*, p. 68.
8. K. Wilber, *The Atman Project: A Transpersonal View of Human Development*, Wheaton, IL: Theosophical Publishing House, 1980, pp. 30-34.
9. K. Carey, *Starseed Transmissions*, Kansas City, MO: Uni-Sun, 1983, p. 52.

Chapter Three

1. Anonymous, *A Course in Miracles*, Tiburon, CA: Foundation for Inner Peace, 1975, vol. 3, p. 25.
2. I. M. G. Dhyana, *MoreThanMe*, pp. 181-185.
3. Anonymous, *A Course in Miracles*, vol. 1, p. 26.
4. P. Russell, *The White Hole in Time: Our Future Evolution and the Meaning of Now*, New York: HarperCollins, 1992, pp. 128-129.
5. P. Russell, *The Global Brain: Speculations on the Evolutionary Leap to Planetary Consciousness*, Los Angeles: J. P. Tarcher, 1983, p. 121.
6. Ibid. p. 131.

7. E. Haich, *Initiation*, Palo Alto, CA: Seed Center, 1974, pp. 175-176.
8. Anonymous, *A Course in Miracles*, vol. 1, pp. 88-89.
9. K. Wilber, *No Boundary*, Boulder: Shambhala, 1981, p. 88.
10. Anonymous, *A Course in Miracles*, vol. 3, p. 27.
11. K. Carey, *Terra Christa*, Kansas City, MO: Uni-Sun, 1985, p. 131-134.
12. Anonymous, *A Course in Miracles*, vol. 3, p. 78.

Chapter Four

1. J. Houston, *The Possible Human*, p. 212.
2. K. Wilber, *Up From Eden: A Transpersonal View of Human Evolution*, New York: Doubleday, 1982, p. 179.
3. T. Berry and B. Swimme, *The Universe Story*, p. 150.
4. Ibid. p. 11.
5. C. Hills, *Nuclear Evolution: Discovery of the Rainbow Body*, Boulder Creek, CA: University of the Trees Press, 1977, p. 662.
6. Russell, *The White Hole in Time*, p. 169.
7. T. Berry and B. Swimme, *The Universe Story*, p. 274.
8. Ibid. p. 154.
9. Ibid. p. 156.
10. P. Russell, *The White Hole in Time*, p. 169.
11. Ibid. p. 173.
12. T. Berry and B. Swimme, *The Universe Story*, p. 183.
13. K. Wilber, *Up From Eden*, p. 183.
14. Ibid. p. 24.
15. J. M. Jenkins, *Tzolkin: Visionary Perspectives and Calendar Studies*, Boulder, CO: Four Ahau Press, 1992, p. 154.
16. F. Vaughan, *The Inward Arc*, Boston: Shambhala, 1985, p. 46.
17. Ibid.
18. Ibid.
19. Ibid.
20. Ibid. p. 47.
21. Ibid. p. 39.
22. M. L. von Franz, "The Process of Individuation," cited in F. Vaughan, *The Inward Arc*, pp. 39-40.
23. B. Swimme, *The Universe Is a Green Dragon*, p. 130.

24. M. Fox, *The Coming of the Cosmic Christ*, San Francisco: Harper & Row, p. 133.
25. C. Pearson, *The Hero Within*, p. 25.
26. Ibid. p. 28.
27. K. Wilber, *No Boundary*, pp. 85-86.
28. J. Campbell, *The Hero With a Thousand Faces*, pp. 16-17.
29. C. Rogers, *On Becoming A Person*, Boston: Houghton Mifflin Company, 1980, p. 27.
30. K. Wilber, *The Atman Project*, pp.79-80.
31. C. Hills, *Rise of the Phoenix: Universal Government by Nature's Laws*, Boulder Creek, CA: Common Ownership Press, 1979, p. 352.
32. J. Small, *Transformers: Therapists of the Future*, Marina del Rey, CA: DeVorss & Company, 1982, p. 54.
33. Ibid. pp. 111, 159.
34. C. Hills, *Rise of the Phoenix*, p. 319.
35. Da Avabhasa, *The Holy Jumping-Off Place*, Clearlake, CA: The Dawn Horse Press, 1986, p. 85.

Chapter Five

1. Bhagwan Shree Rajneesh, *Mojud: The Man With The Inexplicable Life*, Portland, OR: Ansu Publishing, p. 49.
2. I. M. G. Dhyana, *MoreThanMe*, pp. 98-99.
3. J. Campbell, *The Hero With A Thousand Faces* , p. 58.
4. Ibid. p. 78.
5. Ibid. p. 65.
6. Ibid. p. 72.
7. S. K. Williams, *The Practice of Personal Transformation: A Jungian Approach*, Berkeley, CA: Journey Press, 1985, p. 40.
8. K. Wilber, *Up From Eden*, p. 81.
9. Ibid.
10. J. Campbell, *The Hero With A Thousand Faces*, p. 82.
11. C. Pearson, *The Hero Within*, p. 5.
12. Ibid. p. 12.
13. J. Campbell, *The Hero With A Thousand Faces*, p. 16.
14. Ibid.

15. C. Pearson, *The Hero Within*, p. 103.
16. J. Campbell, *The Hero With A Thousand Faces*, p. 25.
17. C. Pearson, *The Hero Within*, p. 5.
18. Ibid. p. 15.
19. J. Campbell, *The Hero With A Thousand Faces*, p. 167.
20. Ibid. p. 161.
21. P. Russell, *The White Hole in Time*, pp. 169-170.
22. K. Carey, *Terra Christa*, pp. 132-134.
23. K. Wilber, *Up From Eden*, p. 57.
24. P. Russell, *The White Hole in Time*, p. 172.
25. M. L. West, cited in John Powell, S.J., *Why Am I Afraid To Tell You Who I Am?*, Allen, TX: Argus Communications, 1969, p. 119.
26. J. Small, *Transformers*, p. 88.

Part Two

Chapter Six

1. Levi, *Aquarian Gospel of Jesus the Christ*, p. 82.
2. Mark 11:15, *Holy Bible: Student Bible, New International Version*, Grand Rapids, MI: Zondervan Bible Publishers, 1973, p. 887.
3. L. R. Hubbard, *Self Analysis*, Los Angeles: Bridge Publications, 1987, p. 122.
4. Ibid. p. 122.
5. *Webster's Third New International Dictionary*, p. 742.
6. S. K. Williams, *The Practice of Personal Transformation*, pp. 147-148.
7. C. G. Jung, *The Collected Works of C. G. Jung*, Volume 8, New York: Pantheon Books, 1960, pp. 108-109.
8. C. G. Jung, *The Basic Writings of C. G. Jung*, New York: Random House, 1959, p. 251.
9. H. Benson, *The Relaxation Response*, New York: Avon Books, 1976, pp. 23-25.
10. *Webster's Third New International Dictionary*, p. 1156.
11. B. Swimme, *The Universe Is a Green Dragon*, p. 17.
12. R. Young and L. Young, *Everything Is Energy*, Honolulu: Druk Enterprises, 1984, pp. 17-18.
13. B. Roberts, *The Path To No-Self*, pp. 52-53.
14. F. Vaughan, *The Inward Arc*, p. 41.

Chapter Seven

1. A. C. Clarke, cited in J. Thompson, *I Am Also A You: A Book of Thoughts and Photographs*, New York: Clarkson N. Potter, 1971.
2. J. Redfield, *The Celestine Prophecy: An Adventure*, Hoover, AL: Satori Publishing, 1993, p. 137.
3. Ibid. p. 130.
4. Ibid. p. 138.
5. V. Satir, *Peoplemaking*, Palo Alto, CA: Science and Behavior Books, 1972, pp. 63-70.
6. J. Redfield, *The Celestine Prophecy*, pp. 135-136.
7. S. K. Williams, *The Practice of Personal Transformation*, p. 113.
8. Ibid. p. 113.
9. J. Powell, *Why Am I Afraid To Tell You Who I Am?*, pp. 104-105.
10. Ibid. pp. 105-107.
11. Ibid. p. 108.
12. Ibid.
13. Ibid. p. 112.
14. Ibid. p. 112.
15. Ibid. 114-115.

Chapter Eight

1. F. Vaughan and R. Walsh (eds.), *Accept This Gift: Selections from A Course in Miracles*, Los Angeles: J. P. Tarcher, 1983, p. 46.
2. F. Vaughan, *The Inward Arc*, p. 46.
3. M. L. von Franz, "The Process of Individuation," cited in *C. G. Jung, Man and His Symbols*, p. 162.
4. K. Wilber, *Up From Eden*, p. 36.
5. C. Hills, *Rise of the Phoenix*, p. 371.
6. Meher Baba, cited in K. Wilber, *Eye To Eye*, New York: Doubleday, 1983, p. 213.
7. K. Carey, *Terra Christa*, pp. 132-134.
8. Da Avabhasa, *The Method of the Siddhas*, Clearlake, CA: The Dawn Horse Press, 1987, p. 74.

9. Ram Dass, *Journey of Awakening: A Meditator's Guidebook*, 1978, Hanuman Foundation and Bantam Books, New York, p. 6.
10. Ibid. pp. 8-9.
11. Ibid. p. 9.
12. H. Hurnard, *Hinds' Feet on High Places*, Wheaton, IL: Tyndale House, 1977, p. 76.
13. K. Wilber, *No Boundary*, p. 9.
14. I. M. G. Dhyana, *MoreThanMe*, pp. 109-110.

Chapter Nine

1. F. Vaughan and R. Walsh (eds.), *Accept This Gift*, pp. 28-29.
2. K. Carey, *Starseed Transmissions*, p. 43.
3. F. Vaughan and R. Walsh (eds.), *Accept This Gift*, p. 29.
4. Ibid. 28.
5. Ibid. 28.
6. F. Vaughan, *The Inward Arc*, pp. 15-16.
7. K. Wilber, *Up From Eden*, p. 6.
8. P. Russell, *The Global Brain*, p. 151.
9. F. Vaughan and R. Walsh (eds.), *Accept This Gift*, p. 29.
10. B. Roberts, *The Path To No-Self*, pp.155-156.
11. Ibid. p. 153.
12. Ibid. pp. 155-156.
13. Ibid. pp. 160-161.
14. Anonymous, *A Course In Miracles*, vol. 1, p. 415.
15. Ibid. p. 418.
16. S. K. Williams, *The Practice of Personal Transformation*, p. 111.
17. C. Pearson, *The Hero Within*, p. 28.
18. K. Wilber, *No Boundary*, p. 92.
19. H. Hurnard, *Hinds' Feet on High Places*, p. 67.
20. Ibid. p. 231-233.
21. F. Vaughan and R. Walsh (eds.), *Accept This Gift*, p. 48.
22. Ibid. p. 29.
23. Swami Muktananda, *The Mind*, South Fallsburg, N.Y.: Syda Foundation, 1981.
24. K. Gibran, *The Prophet*, New York: Alfred A. Knopf, 1988, p. 55.
25. J. Heider, *The Tao of Leadership*, Atlanta: Humanics Limited, 1985, p. 117.

Part Three

Chapter Ten

1. P. D. Ouspensky, *The Psychology of Man's Possible Evolution*, pp. 8-9.
2. C. Rogers, *On Becoming a Person*, p. 339.
3. Ibid. pp. 339-340.
4. Ibid. p. 342.
5. Ibid. pp. 341-342.

Chapter Eleven

1. His Holiness the Dalai Lama, "Love, Compassion, and Tolerance," cited in B. Shield and R. Carlson (eds.), *For the Love of God: New Writings By Spiritual and Psychological Leaders*, San Rafael, CA: New World Library, 1990, pp. 4-5.
2. T. Gordon, *Teacher Effectiveness Training*, New York: Peter H. Wyden, 1974.

Chapter Twelve

1. F. Vaughan, *The Inward Arc*, p. 28.
2. K. Wilber, *The Spectrum of Consciousness*, p. 257
3. F. Vaughan, *The Inward Arc*, p. 129.
4. K. Wilber, *No Boundary*, p. 80.
5. F. Vaughan, *The Inward Arc*, p. 22.
6. K. Wilber, *No Boundary*, p. 106.
7. D. Chopra, "Bliss and the Quantum Mechanical Body," *The Mind/Body Connection For Perfect Health & Enlightenment*, Issue No. 3, 1993, pp. 15-17.
8. F. Vaughan, *The Inward Arc*, p. 18.
9. S. Rinpoche, *The Tibetan Book of Living and Dying*, pp. 25.
10. Ibid. pp. 15-16.
11. G. Feuerstein, "Immortal Death and Human Civilization," in Da Avabhasa, *Easy Death,* Clearlake, CA: The Dawn Horse Press, 1983, pp. 1-3.
12. Da Avabhasa, *Easy Death*, pp. 47-48.

13. Satprem, *Aurobindo or The Adventure of Consciousness*, pp. 140-141.
14. F. Vaughan, *The Inward Arc*, p. 19.
15. J. Campbell, *The Power of the Myth*, New York: Doubleday, 1988, p. 91.
16. I. M. G. Dhyana, *Baby Steps and Quantum Leaps* (Manuscript).

Chapter Thirteen

1. Da Avabhasa, *The Eating Gorilla Comes In Peace*, Clearlake, CA: The Dawn Horse Press, 1987, p. 148.
2. Ibid.
3. Ibid.
4. Ibid.
5. K. Carey, *Starseed Transmissions*, p. 45.
6. J. Small, *Transformers*, p. 69.
7. N. Niwano, *Buddhism For Today, A Modern Interpretation of the Threefold Lotus Sutra*, New York & Tokyo: Weatherhill/Kosei, 1980, p. 108.
8. Satprem, *Aurobindo or The Adventure of Consciousness*, pp. 50-51.
9. J. Small, *Transformers*, p. 88.
10. Ram Dass, *Be Here Now*, San Cristobal, NM: Lama Foundation, 1971, p. 39.
11. B. D. Kyokai, *The Teaching of Buddha*, Tokyo: Kosaido Printing Co., 1966, p. 78.
12. N. Niwano, *Buddhism For Today*, pp. 33-35.

LET US NOW ALLOW THE COSMIC
SONG LINES TO SING US TO
OUR FULFILLMENT.

BIBLIOGRAPHY

Anonymous. *A Course in Miracles*. Tiburon, CA: Foundation for Inner Peace, 1975.

Bhagwan Shree Rajneesh. *I Say Unto You*. Rajneeshpuran, OR: Rajneesh Foundation International, 1980.

———. *Mojud: The Man With The Inexplicable Life*. Portland, OR: Ansu Publishing, 1988.

Benson, H. *The Relaxation Response*. New York: Avon Books, 1976.

Berry, T., and Swimme, B. *The Universe Story: From the Primordial Flaring Forth to the Ecozoic Era—A Celebration of the Unfolding of the Cosmos*. New York: HarperCollins, 1992.

Campbell, J. *The Hero With a Thousand Faces*. Princeton, NJ: Princeton University Press, 1973.

———. *The Power of the Myth*. New York: Doubleday, 1988.

Carey, K. *Starseed Transmissions*. Kansas City, MO: Uni-Sun, 1983.

———. *Terra Christa*. Kansas City, MO: Uni-Sun, 1985.

Chopra, D. "Bliss and the Quantum Mechanical Body." *The Mind/Body Connection For Perfect Health & Enlightenment*, Issue No. 3 (1993).

Da Avabhasa. *The Eating Gorilla Comes in Peace*. Clearlake, CA: The Dawn Horse Press, 1987.

———. *The Holy Jumping-Off Place*. Clearlake, CA: The Dawn Horse Press, 1986.

———. *The Method of the Siddhas*. Clearlake, CA: The Dawn Horse Press, 1987.

Dhyana, I. M. G. *MoreThanMe*. San Francisco: Dhyana Press, 1993.

Fox, M. *The Coming of the Cosmic Christ*. San Francisco: Harper & Row, 1988.

Gibran, K. *The Prophet*. New York: Alfred A. Knopf, 1988.

Gordon, T. *Teacher Effectiveness Training*. New York: Peter H. Wyden, 1974.

Haich, E. *Initiation*. Palo Alto, CA: Seed Center, 1974.

Heider, J. *The Tao of Leadership*. Atlanta, GA: Humanics Limited, 1985.

Hills, C. *Nuclear Evolution: Discovery of the Rainbow Body*. Boulder Creek, CA: University of the Trees Press, 1977.

———. *Rise of the Phoenix: Universal Government by Nature's Laws*. Boulder Creek, CA: Common Ownership Press, 1979.

Houston, J. *The Possible Human*. Los Angeles: J. P. Tarcher, 1976.

Hubbard, B. M. *The Evolutionary Journey: A Personal Guide to a Positive Future*. San Francisco: Evolutionary Press, 1982.

Hubbard, L. R. *Self Analysis*. Los Angeles: Bridge Publications, 1987.

Hurnard, H. *Hinds' Feet On High Places*. Wheaton, IL: Tyndale House, 1977.

Jenkins, J. M. *Tzolkin: Visionary Perspectives and Calendar Studies*. Boulder, CO: Four Ahau Press, 1992.

Jung, C. J. *The Basic Writings of C. G. Jung*. New York: Random House, 1959.

———. *The Collected Works of C. G. Jung, Volume 8*. New York: Pantheon Books, 1960.

Kyokai, B. D. *The Teaching of Buddha*. Tokyo: Kosaido Printing Company, 1966.

Levi. *Aquarian Gospel of Jesus the Christ*. Marina del Rey, CA: DeVorss & Co., 1987.

Mark 11:15. *Holy Bible: Student Bible, New International Version*, Grand Rapids, MI: Zondervan Bible Publishers, 1973.

Mitchell, S. *The Enlightened Mind: An Anthology of Sacred Prose*. New York: HarperCollins, 1991.

Muktananda (Swami). *The Mind*. South Fallsburg, NY: Syda Foundation, 1981.

Niwano, N. *Buddhism For Today, A Modern Interpretation of the Threefold Lotus Sutra*. New York & Tokyo: Weatherhill/Kosei, 1980.

Ouspensky, P. D. *The Psychology of Man's Possible Evolution*, N.Y.: Random House, 1974.

Pearson, C. *The Hero Within: Six Archetypes We Live By*. San Francisco: Harper & Row, 1989.

Powell, J. *Why Am I Afraid To Tell You Who I Am?* Allen, TX: Argus Communications, 1969.

Ram Dass. *Be Here Now*. San Cristobal, NM: Lama Foundation, 1971.

———. *Journey of Awakening: A Meditator's Guidebook*. New York: Bantam, 1978.

Redfield, J. *The Celestine Prophecy: An Adventure*. Hoover, AL: Satori, 1993.

Rinpoche, S. *The Tibetan Book of Living and Dying*. New York: HarperCollins, 1992.

Roberts, B. *The Path To No-Self*. Boston: Shambhala, 1985.

Rogers, C. *On Becoming A Person*. Boston: Houghton Mifflin Company, 1980.

Russell, P. *The Global Brain: Speculations on the Evolutionary Leap to Planetary Consciousness*. Los Angeles: J. P. Tarcher, 1983.

———. *The White Hole in Time: Our Future Evolution and the Meaning of Now*. New York: HarperCollins, 1992.

Satir, V. *Peoplemaking*. Palo Alto, CA: Science and Behavior Books, 1972.

Satprem. *Sri Aurobindo or The Adventure of Consciousness*, Mt. Vernon, WA: Institute for Evolutionary Research, 1993.

Shield, B., and Carlson, R., eds. *For the Love of God: New Writings By Spiritual and Psychological Leaders*. San Rafael, CA: New World Library, 1990.

Small, J. *Transformers: The Therapists of the Future*. Marina del Rey, CA: DeVorss & Company, 1982.

Smothermon, R. *Transforming #1*, San Francisco: Context Publications, 1982.

Swimme, B. *The Universe Is A Green Dragon: A Cosmic Creation Story*. Santa Fe, NM: Bear & Company, 1984.

Thompson, J. *I Am Also A You: A Book of Thoughts with Photographs*. New York: Clarkson N. Potter, 1971.

Tower, V. *The Process of Intuition.* Wheaton, IL: The Theosophical Publishing House, 1975.

Vaughan, F. *The Inward Arc.* Boston: Shambhala, 1985.

Vaughan, F., and Walsh, R., eds. *Accept This Gift: Selections from A Course in Miracles.* Los Angeles: J. P. Tarcher, 1983.

Webster's Third New International Dictionary. Springfield, MA: G. & C. Merriam Company, Publishers, 1968.

Wells, H. G. "The Discovery of the Future," *Nature*, Vol. 65 (1902).

Wilber, K., *The Atman Project: A Transpersonal View of Human Development.* Wheaton, IL: Theosophical Publishing House, 1980.

———. *Eye To Eye.* New York: Doubleday, 1983.

———. *No Boundary.* Boston: Shambala, 1981.

———. *Up From Eden: A Transpersonal View of Human Evolution.* New York: Doubleday, 1982.

Williams, S. K. *The Practice of Personal Transformation: A Jungian Approach.* Berkeley, CA: Journey Press, 1985.

Young, R., and Young, L. *Everything Is Energy.* Honolulu: Druk Enterprises, 1984.

SUBJECT INDEX

PERMISSIONS ACKNOWLEDGEMENTS

Grateful acknowledgement is made to the following for permission to use copyrighted material:

From TRANSFORMERS: THE ARTISTS OF SELF-CREATION, by Jacquelyn Small, Copyright © 1982 by Jacquelyn Small. Used by permission of Bantam Books, a division of Bantam Doubleday Dell Publishing Group, Inc.

From THE PSYCHOLOGY OF MAN'S POSSIBLE EVOLUTION, by P.D. Ouspensky, Copyright © 1950 by the Estate of P.D. Ouspensky. Reprinted by permission of Alfred A. Knopf, Inc.

From NO BOUNDARY, by Ken Wilber, Copyright © 1979 by Ken Wilber. Reprinted by arrangement with Shambhala Publications, Inc., 300 Massachusetts Avenue, Boston, MA 02115.

From THE INWARD ARC, by Frances Vaughan, Copyright © 1985 by Frances E. Vaughan. Reprinted by permission of Frances Vaughan.

From NUCLEAR EVOLUTION: DISCOVERY OF THE RAINBOW BODY, by Christopher Hills, Copyright © 1977 by Christopher Hills. Reprinted by permission of Christopher Hills.

From RISE OF THE PHOENIX: UNIVERSAL GOVERNMENT, by Christopher Hills, Copyright © 1979 by Christopher Hills. Reprinted by permission of Christopher Hills.

From BE HERE NOW, by Ram Dass, Copyright © 1978 by Hanuman Foundation. Reprinted by permission of the Hanuman Foundation.

Illustration of centaur on page 327. From THE GOLDEN TREASURY OF MYTHS AND LEGENDS, Adapted by Anne Terry White, Illustrated by Alice and Martin Provenser. Reprinted by permission of Golden Press.

ORDER FORM

✎

____ Please send me ____ copies of *A Call To Greatness*.

____ Please send me ____ copies of *MoreThanMe*.

____ Please send me ____ copies of the *Crystal Seas* audiotape.
(*Crystal Seas* contains thirteen songs, chants and prayers from *MoreThanMe*.)

____ Please send me information about IsanaMada's events.

Name: ____

Address: ____

____

Phone(s): Home: ________________ Workplace: ________________

A Call To Greatness — $19.95 *MoreThanMe* — $10.95
Crystal Seas — $10.00
(Sales Tax: Please add 8.5% for books shipped to California.)
Make checks payable to Dhyana Press

Shipping Information:

Book Rate: $2.00 for the first book / 75 cents for each additional book. (Allow three to four weeks.)

✈Air Mail: $3.50 per book / $2.00 per audiotape

☎**Telephone Orders**:
Call Toll Free: 800-549-0992

✉**Mail Orders**:
Dhyana Press, P.O. Box 470700-71, San Francisco, CA 94147

❤For further information, please call 415-749-7677 or 800-549-0992

The teachings of A CALL TO GREATNESS are offered as a weekend intensive in different locations throughout the world. For seminar information or to schedule an event in your area, please write:

Christian de la Huerta
Dhyana Press
P. O. Box 470700
San Francisco, CA 94147

Or call:
800-549-0992.